NO FRILLS

NO FRILLS

The truth behind the low-cost revolution in the skies

Simon Calder

This updated paperback edition first published
in Great Britain in 2006 by
Virgin Books Ltd
Thames Wharf Studios
Rainville Road
London
W6 9HA

First paperback edition published in Great Britain in 2003 by
Virgin Books Ltd.
First published in hardback in Great Britain in 2002 by Virgin
Books ltd.

A catalogue record for this book is available from the
British Library.

ISBN 0 7535 1044 8
ISBN 978 0 7535 1044 5

The paper used in this book is a natural, recyclable product
made from wood grown in sustainable forests. The
manufacturing process conforms to the regulations of the
country of origin.

Typeset by TW Typesetting, Plymouth, Devon

Printed and bound by CPI Antony Rowe, Eastbourne

For Charlotte, Daisy and Poppy,
for flying without frills but with enthusiasm

CONTENTS

PICTURE CREDITS

The author and publisher are grateful to the following sources for pictures reproduced in the illustrated section of this book.

Boeing	Boeing 737s, Edgar C. Turner, p. 5
easyJet	Stelios Haji-Ioannou, founder of easyJet, p. 1
	easyJet's protest against Go, p. 2
Go	Barbara Cassani, former chief executive of Go, p. 3
Ryanair	Michael O'Leary, chief executive of Ryanair, p. 1
	Ryanair's response to 11 September, p. 8
Sir Freddie Laker	Sir Freddie Laker, founder of Skytrain, p. 3
Southwest	Herb Kelleher of Southwest, p. 6
Virgin Blue	Sir Richard Branson christens the first Australian Virgin Blue 737, p. 4
Vladimir Raitz	Vladimir Raitz, inventor of the package holiday, p. 2

ACKNOWLEDGEMENTS

The research for the first edition of this book began at the start of September 2001, and – for the third edition – continued until the end of 2005. Throughout this time the airline industry has been in a state of upheaval. Thanks are due to the airline bosses, past and present, who gave generously of their time to be interviewed for this book: Bob Ayling, former chief executive of British Airways; Sir Richard Branson; Neil Burrows of Virgin Express; Barbara Cassani, former chief executive of Go; Tony Davis, former chief executive of bmibaby; Sir Rod Eddington, former chief executive of British Airways; Stelios Haji-Ioannou of easyJet; Joachim Hunold of Air Berlin; Sir Freddie Laker; Tim Jeans of Monarch; Franco Mancassola, founder of Debonair; Philip Meeson of Jet2; Michael O'Leary of Ryanair; Jim Parker of Southwest; John Patterson of GB Airways; Howard Putnam, former chief executive and president of Southwest; Peter Rothwell of TUI; and Ray Webster, former chief executive of easyJet.

Thanks are also due to Tony Anderson, former marketing director for easyJet; Gary Barone, formerly of AB Airlines; Jamie Bowden, airline consultant; Kenneth Clarke MP; John FitzGerald, formerly of Debonair; Vladimir Raitz, the inventor of the air package holiday; Eric Torbenson of the *Dallas Morning News* and dozens of other people in the aviation industry who agreed to be interviewed on their part in the story, some of them on condition of anonymity. Caroline Virr made a highly professional job of research and transcription.

For Virgin Books Stuart Slater developed the original idea. Finally, this book appears courtesy of the muggers who kindly took only my mobile phone, rather than the notes for this book, when they set upon me in the centre of Lisbon while I was attending the Association of British Travel Agents' annual convention.

FOREWORD

I love 'frills'. At the point in 1982 when the traditional airlines were conspiring to force my Laker Skytrain out of business, I was introducing 'Regency Class' on my transatlantic flights. It offered a superb business-class service for far less than my rivals – and gave my good friend Richard Branson some ideas for his unbeatable Upper Class service. But I also recognise that the ordinary man or woman is much more interested in getting where they want to go than in the free food and drink on board.

The whole point of Skytrain was to open up the skies to people who were prevented from flying by the airlines' fare-fixing. They had to keep fares deliberately high, to featherbed the expensive nests that they had comfortably constructed for themselves.

As I showed with Skytrain, and as Stelios and Michael O'Leary have demonstrated with easyJet and Ryanair, the traditional airline model keeps people out – but low-cost flying brings them in. Since the tragic events of 11 September 2001, the no-frills airlines have shown how public confidence in flying can be restored – enabling holidaymakers and business-people to travel at reasonable fares, providing the flights that can bring families together.

Simon Calder's book shows how the twentieth century largely belonged to the traditional, high-cost airlines (with a few snipers, like me, upsetting their cosy cartel). The twenty-first century is proving the preserve of the no-frills airlines, at least within Europe.

This book may even inspire you to start your own low-cost carrier. If you do, and you suspect that the existing airlines are trying to obstruct you, may I offer you the same advice that I gave to Richard Branson and Stelios? If the allegations are true, sue the bastards!

Sir Freddie Laker, Grand Bahama Island

1. THE FREEDOM OF THE SKIES

In 1976 I hitch-hiked from my home in Crawley, close to the runway at Gatwick airport, to Vienna. At the time the lowest return air fare to the Austrian capital was around £100, which represented two months' hard labour as a cleaner at the airport. The journey took three arduous days and nights.

I have just booked to fly from London to Vienna in 2006 (well, the actual airport is Bratislava, across the border in Slovakia – that's no-frills for you). The airline is SkyEurope, one of the new breed of agressive Eastern European airlines. At the start of October 2005 they launched a loss-leading promotion. The total return fare, including tax, is £10 – representing slightly less than two hours' work at Britain's national minimum wage. Yes, I was lucky to grab a seat on one of the rare occasions where airlines sell at a loss. But even the average fare on this route from Stansted is around £100. The same as thirty years ago in absolute terms – but one-quarter of the 1976 fare in real terms. Which could help to explain why you see so few people thumbing rides on the highways of Europe these days. No-frills flying has rendered hitch-hiking an uneconomic form of transport. If I opted to thumb in 2006, the one-way ferry ride alone would cost more than the return flight.

Since antiquity, man has yearned to take to the skies. In the fifteenth century, Leonardo da Vinci made sketches of how this could be achieved, getting impressively close to a blueprint for the modern helicopter. By the early eighteenth century, a Jesuit priest named Bartholomeu de Gusmão had proposed – and modelled – a hot-air balloon. In 1783, the first man had been lifted by the Montgolfier balloon. One hundred years ago, heavier-than-air flight became a reality when the Wright brothers took off at Kitty Hawk, North Carolina, on 17 December 1903. A century on, most of us are well past the amazement stage, and are simply concerned to get where we're going safely, cheaply and on time.

Rule 1 of air travel has applied almost since passenger flight began: the person in the next seat has always paid less than you for the same flight. But on 10 November 1995, any of the passengers on a British Airways (BA) jet on the apron at Glasgow who cared to look across at the funny orange Boeing arriving at the next gate would have seen an entire plane full of people who had paid less than them. Their attention would have been grabbed by the plane's exterior: instead of the usual safely conservative airline livery, someone had painted human-sized, bright orange digits along the fuselage of a 737. A wider perspective revealed a telephone number, 0582 445566. The dialling code indicated a number in Luton – the home of easyJet, an airline that owned no planes (it had borrowed a couple from a BA affiliate), and from where the plane had just arrived. The passengers had been obliged to dial this number in order to fly between Luton and Glasgow for £29 each way. Edinburgh flights – same price, same absence of free newspapers and snacks – began five days later.

A decade ago, people had barely heard of easyJet and Ryanair. One was a two-plane airline shuttling between Luton airport and Scotland, the other was a near-moribund second-string Irish airline. Now, these airlines are the giants of Europe, each carrying more passengers than British Airways and providing links from Spain to Italy and Germany to Poland. They are also extremely cash-rich. Their financial success has inspired dozens of others to try to emulate or improve upon the principles – with some spectacular failures along the way, as passengers booked on Duo or EUjet will testify.

'It's not rocket science,' says Stelios Haji-Ioannou, the founder of easyJet. No-frills airlines fly the same pieces of metal, burning the same expensive fuel, at the same rate as the traditional carriers. But they cut costs wherever they can, for example by plastering the reservations phone number (or, these days, the Internet website) on the side of planes to save on the marketing budget. When it comes to pricing, 'We look at the fare the customer can pay, not what the market can bear,' says Rob Brown, who speaks for the world's most successful airline, Southwest. This pioneering carrier began opening up the skies so long ago that Rod Stewart was a bright new hope whose first album was topping the charts on both sides of the Atlantic. The business plan (of Southwest, not Rod) has been emulated from Australia via Brazil to Canada. But the no-frills revolution is at its most fervent in the skies over the British Isles. A decade ago there were a dozen flights a day between London and Edinburgh on two carriers. Now there are almost sixty each day, each way, with five airlines competing.

The rebels with two causes – lower fares and higher profits – are slugging it out with the traditional airlines and, increasingly, with each other. The original, easyJet, is still in contention with Ryanair as Europe's largest low-cost carrier, but only because it bought out its arch-rival Go. This allowed it to catch up with the fast-growing Irish airline based in Dublin but with its main business concentrated at Stansted in Essex. Ryanair has undergone a remarkable conversion from failing full-service carrier to the most cost-conscious – and profitable – airline in Europe.

The 'legacy' airlines have indulged in plenty of if-you-can't-beat-them-better-join-them activity. Bmibaby has proved such a success that it has supplanted its mother company, BMI. But the failure of Buzz, which had a short, sad and extraordinarily costly life as the no-frills offshoot of KLM UK, possibly hastened the demise of its Dutch airline parent – now part of Air France. Buzz was ignominiously sold to Ryanair, whose chief executive, Michael O'Leary, describes the price paid as 'petty cash'. Others have been wounded but have survived, such as Virgin Express; this offshoot of the Branson empire was one minute the biggest airline in Belgium, yet the next had been kicked out of two of Europe's most important markets, Heathrow and Cologne-Bonn.

Charter airlines maintain that they were the original low-cost carriers. It took some time for them to wake up to the disconcerting reality that there are dozens of strange-looking Boeing 737s parked on sun- and ski-holiday runways from Alicante to Athens. Their business plan was for (too) many years based on the economics of package holidays, where people are flown in almost-full planes to stay in almost-full hotels for fixed durations of a week or two. Seat-only sales, which traditionally allowed charter operators to top up their planes to full capacity, have shifted to the low-cost scheduled airlines. When the independent traveller or villa owner could book a cheap scheduled flight from Cardiff to Faro, Liverpool to Palma or Nottingham to Malaga, the economics changed fundamentally for the worse for charter airlines.

Belatedly, they have moved into the no-frills scheduled market. Britannia Airways, the UK charter carrier for Europe's biggest holiday company, TUI, was erased at the end of October 2005. 'I'm sad for the passing of a great name,' said Peter Rothwell of TUI, 'but in the new world you need one name.' The airline has become Thomsonfly.com – those last three letters signifying the influence of the Internet. We are all travel agents now. Two other recent start-ups, Flyglobespan.com and Jet2.com, recognise the value of a name that is effectively a piece of computer code.

Like fundamentalist Christian sects, each no-frills carrier holds its particular version of the gospel of cheap air travel to be superior to the rest. One point of agreement is that the traditional airlines have done the traveller a grave disservice for most of the last hundred years.

A century after Orville and Wilbur Wright built the first successful aircraft, the world has shrunk. You can be virtually anywhere on the planet within 24 hours. One billion people annually take a flight somewhere in the world. Yet for the first half-century of its existence, aviation was the exclusive privilege of the rich. The first economy class was launched only in 1952 – on TWA, one of the many famous names eased into oblivion with some help from low-cost carriers.

The figures who have put air travel within reach of the people are not traditional airline bosses. Herb Kelleher, who has the greatest low-cost track record of all, once settled a dispute on behalf of his airline, Southwest, with an arm-wrestling contest. On this side of the Atlantic, from Sir Freddie Laker ('sue the bastards!') to Michael O'Leary ('the best thing you can do with some of these environmentalists is take them out and shoot them'), they are larger-than-life individuals with the guts to take on the establishment – and each other – plus the brains to win.

This book focuses on the men and women who stripped away the expensive frills and invited ordinary people on board. There is plenty of mutual admiration among the top tier in low-cost travel. Freddie loves Richard. Barbara admires Stelios. Michael kneels at the altar of Herb. But there is a vast amount of venom too. Put two or more of the airline bosses in the same room, and you have a combustible mix.

They all agree, though, that the no-frills business hinges upon nailing costs down – by flying planes for more hours each day, eradicating tickets and dispensing with travel agents' commission. Cut costs far enough, and you can afford – on occasion – to fly people around Europe at a loss. Germanwings, Ryanair and SkyEurope have run promotions where every seat they sell costs them money. I have been tracking European air fares for thirty years, during which time prices have gently declined in real terms. Now those complex calculations have ceased to have any meaning. When fares vanished, the calibration was rendered as obsolete as a ticket on AB Airlines (one of several no-frills failures). Yet the same airlines that are giving away seats can also report increased passenger numbers and earnings, even after the September 2001 attacks on America that dented confidence in air travel.

How do they do that, then? By squeezing every possible penny in earnings out of every possible seat, and using technology to fill as many seats as possible. 'What has put people on planes for next to nothing, more than any other technological invention, is the Internet,' says Stelios. 'The jet engine was an improvement on the propeller and previous technology but what really made it a mass market for everybody was the ability to fly someone for a pound. The ability to say "I will rationally and economically speaking let that seat go for £1" is quite a revolution. You can only do that with the Internet.'

Of course easyJet and its rivals thrive because the average fares paid are significantly above £1. Indeed, a common complaint is that the fares advertised so temptingly often seem mysteriously unavailable. But we travellers are learning that there is nothing so fluid as the price of a seat on a no-frills airline. The black art of yield management can mean that you are not only sitting next to someone who paid less than you, but that he or she is being subsidised by the airline.

Is this worrying evidence that the world of travel, which often appears to be a different planet from normal, rational life, has finally taken leave of its senses? No. Stop worrying and start travelling.

First, though, I have to clear a flight path through the fog of misapprehension and misinformation that hangs over no-frills flying. Partly, confusion arises because the airline world used to be simple to grasp. There was British Airways and its foreign counterparts: Air France, Alitalia, Lufthansa, and so on. The airlines agreed fares and frequencies between them, at levels to suit them – not travellers. They colluded on rules to make sure no one was giving the passenger too good a deal. 'We used to have meetings to discuss the permissible dimensions of a salt cellar in first class,' reminisces one airline executive, wistfully recalling the days when no carrier was able to demonstrate a competitive edge. None was necessary: on routes shared by airlines, revenues were often pooled, which meant there was no point in trying to outshine the competition. Fares were fixed; the only variable was the number of seats that were filled on each flight.

The message to the consumer was 'take it or leave it'. Mostly, they left it, because fares were way too high. In 1980, the cheapest return fare on what was then the world's busiest international air route, between London and Paris, was around £70. Today, any of four airlines will fly you between the British and French capitals for less than that, even though wages have trebled.

To allow such sweeping change to take place, much excess baggage has been jettisoned. Concepts that passengers had previously taken for granted, from paper tickets to in-flight meals, have been thrown out to help reduce costs to a level that could attract a whole new market of travellers. That sub-£70 London–Paris fare may be halved or doubled at any moment, as the airline juggles the price and the people it predicts can be tempted on board. Some passengers will pay much more, but the world has got used to the idea that if you book ahead and avoid the most in-demand departures you can travel cheaply. Eurostar, the company that runs trains between London and Paris, now mimics the pricing strategy of the low-cost airlines – as do the ferry companies on the English Channel, who have seen a slice of their market migrate to the airlines. And within Britain, rail and bus companies are doing exactly the same. Sir Richard Branson, a champion of no-frills flying in continental Europe and Australia, finds his Virgin Trains between England and Scotland in head-to-head competition with easyJet and Ryanair.

The journey to a low-cost revolution in the skies – and, now, on the seas and the surface – has been anything but smooth, encountering political turbulence and the adverse winds of protectionism. Vested interests still control a vast proportion of world aviation. Europe's skies, for example, have officially been open since 1997. But leading airports remain effectively closed to newcomers because of the shortage of available slots. Heathrow is the world's most desirable, and hence most difficult, place in which to land a plane. The present state of freedom of the skies can be roughly stated as 'you can fly anywhere you like within Europe, as long as it doesn't include Heathrow; Gatwick, Stansted, Frankfurt and Amsterdam are tricky, too.' There is simply not enough room in the skies or on the runways for all the flights that wish to be airborne at peak times. And in parts of Europe, obstructive governments act in collusion with 'flag-carriers' to constrict the freedom of the skies. Many countries regard an airline as an essential component of a nation's identity, in the same way that dud teams from dwarf countries get to play in European soccer tournaments, where they are customarily knocked out in the opening round.

With some ostrich-like exceptions, the no-frills revolution has forced the flag-carrier airlines to cut fares and, equally important-ly, restrictions. The rule that all cheap flights must involve a Saturday night stay, enabling traditional airlines to keep fare levels punishingly high for decades, has all but disappeared on routes where no-frills competition exists.

The no-frills airlines, and the Internet, have empowered many potential customers to organise their own tailor-made holidays – often at a lower price than in the holiday brochures – and, more crucially, to change their lifestyles. I bet you know at least two or three people who have bought property in France or Spain in the last few years, and who commute to and fro using a low-cost airline. Ryanair and easyJet have helped to revitalise waning communities abroad (though not all the locals see it like that). One of the most profound effects of the no-frills revolution has been to open up Europe, forcing the traditional airlines to slash prices and do away with mind-bogglingly complex fare rules. Thanks to low-cost airlines, second-home ownership abroad has rocketed. Lifestyles have been transformed, and long-distance relationships formed, thanks to a newly affordable Europe. Ryanair and easyJet have done more for European unity than any amount of EU propaganda.

'All we cut is the price,' promised British Midland in 1997, with a fare of £149 return from Heathrow to Frankfurt. At the same time, one of the earliest no-frills failures – Debonair – was offering Nice from Luton for £118. And British Airways took out an ad to boast that its best fare to Pisa was £159 return.

By 2006, the base fares to these destinations have been reduced by half or more. There is barely a big city within two hours' flying time of London that cannot be reached on a no-frills flight, routinely for fares of £80 or less. With revenue dwindling, no wonder British Airways and other full-service airlines are finding it so difficult to make money in Europe these days.

To make the most of the new freedoms, though, you have to be prepared to make compromises. If you fly from 'London' to 'Barcelona' on Ryanair, you will find yourself flying from a hard-to-reach corner of Essex to an airport on the outskirts of Gerona, a town an hour away from the Catalan capital. (And should anything delay the flight, whether by three hours or three days, you can expect the absolute legal minimum in compensation.) Even in America, which had a quarter-century head-start in the no-frills business, secondary airports are still the norm. If you want to go to Boston on Southwest, for example, the airline suggests you use Providence in Rhode Island or Manchester in New Hampshire – neither of which is even in the same state as Boston, the Massachusetts capital. But in the more realistic business climate that has prevailed since 2001, plenty of travellers have found that the benefits of cheap travel outweigh the cost in terms of inconvenience. And millions of people who would not otherwise have been able to fly have seen the world open up before them.

If you are an inveterate traveller, no-frills aviation allows you to see more of the world. If you are in business, you can afford to get out and about more. And if you are in love, cheap flights can bring you closer together – whether geographically (if you are hundreds of miles apart), or emotionally with a romantic getaway to Paris or Venice. Alternatively, anyone looking for Love need only fly on Southwest to its home base at the Dallas airport of that name.

Weekends away have become mystery tours for thousands of people thanks to some airlines' policy of flying to places you didn't know you wanted to go to. If you thought Bergerac was simply a dodgy 70s TV serial, imagined Klagenfurt was a type of sausage and had always assumed Vasteras to be an unpleasant urinary infection, you can find out how wrong you were by flying to these destinations from Stansted on the cheap. (Cabotage, incidentally, is not a quaint village in the Dordogne with the lovely church and friendly cafe, but the legal right for a UK airline to fly domestically in France from Paris to Nice.)

The geography of twenty-first century Europe has been transformed. I don't know which is the stranger phenomenon – that an ex-US Air Force base on a plateau above the Moselle Valley is now a leading European aviation hub, or that you can fly there any day you like from Prestwick, once a moribund airport but now Scotland's third busiest.

Until 1995, no one in Europe had heard of no-frills flying. Now, everyone knows about the concept, and has probably tried it too. Just like supermarkets, they have adopted distinct characteristics and appeal to different people: easyJet is Tesco, Bmibaby corresponds to Safeway, Jet2 is Somerfield, FlyBE is Marks & Spencer and Ryanair is Asda. (Go, before it went, was Waitrose.)

Staying with the supermarket analogy for a moment: imagine driving to your favourite store, only to be told to drive round and round the roundabout outside for ten minutes, because the car park and its access roads are full. When you are finally allowed in, you are instructed to park in a distant corner and told to wait for a bus to bring you to the main door. If you suffered this treatment week after week, without a word of apology, you might start looking for another supermarket. It might be a little further from home and take longer to reach, but if the overall journey time plus stress were reduced, and the new supermarket charged lower prices, you would soon get used to it. That is what some of the no-frills airlines count on. They believe that travellers can be persuaded to see the advantage of less popular airports. At a time when 'stacking' over south-east England is a necessity for planes heading for Heathrow, many passengers are beginning to agree.

Does cheap equal nasty? The number of people who think so is diminishing with every celebrity who chooses the no-frills option. Tony Blair and his family taking their holiday flights on Ryanair did the Irish airline as many favours as did its steward, Brian, winning the first *Big Brother*. Squads of Premier League footballers and television presenters on implausibly big salaries demonstrate a fondness for easyJet.

For some people, frills comprise half the fun of travelling. Under the Freedom of Information Act, I asked to see the aviation policies of the Foreign Office, which spends more on overseas travel than any other government department. None of the 'preferred' airlines is a no-frills carrier. Perhaps that is because beyond a certain grade, civil servants are entitled to travel in business class – not easy to find on the one-size-fits-all low-cost airlines. While some can still enjoy the benefits of a club class return fare of £400 for the half-hour flight between London and Paris, they should enjoy their frequent-flyer points while they last. As millions of employees of traditional airlines have found to their cost, the world is changing rapidly. Business travellers have always been part of the no-frills plan. The routes that have proved most successful are those with a mix of business and leisure travel, such as London to Edinburgh, Copenhagen and Barcelona.

Every week or so, another 737 destined for one of Europe's cut-price airlines comes off the production line at the Boeing factory in Seattle. To rent one of these shiny new specimens costs about $100,000 per month. To pay their way, they have to be kept aloft, and three-quarters full of people. And to do that, the carriers must flood the market with cut-price deals. This book aims to take you behind the scenes, where the decisions that change the way we travel are taken – and where scores are settled. You may conclude that the no-frills runway is more like a school playground; but to traditional airlines, and even some train operators, the no-frills carriers represent a potentially deadly threat. When asked to give advice to Willie Walsh, the new chief executive at British Airways, Stelios advised him to abandon European aviation and leave it to the no-frills airlines. 'By 2008, no one will be flying on traditional airlines in Europe,' says the easyJet founder.

Plenty of people disagree that flights with free meals and drinks are for the chop. But the map of Europe has changed for ever thanks to the swashbuckling figures whose planes and people work the hardest in the business. The roots of the routes from Luton and Liverpool, Stansted and Prestwick, Cardiff and Coventry are tangled. This book aims to unravel them, to help you make sense of an incredibly complicated industry, and to try to reverse Rule 1 – so that you always pay less than the person in the next seat.

'Low-fare carriers are here to stay; full-service carriers may not be here to stay,' says Steve Smith, who started up a Canadian no-frills airline. The old certainties, he says, have gone: 'The horse is out of the box, and it's running.' Some people in the traditional airline business have yet to grasp that what people are buying is not the dubious pleasure of sitting in an aluminium tube for a couple of hours, eating questionable food and sinking as much 'free' alcohol as possible in the time available. We are buying the sensation of warm sand and cool Mediterranean between our toes; the surge of adrenalin when a deal is done; the scent of a strange and beautiful Italian town; the euphoria of a goal at the Nou Camp stadium in Barcelona; or the smile on the face of your loved one who realises that the distance between the two of you has diminished.

With thrills like that, who needs frills?

2. A TOUCH OF CLASSLESSNESS

It began by a fluke, like everything else does
Vladimir Raitz, founder of the package holiday

Iberia – where only the plane gets more attention than you
Alitalia takes your fun very seriously
Advertisements in National Geographic

Nation states believed that to be a nation you needed a flag, a national anthem and an airline. The first two come cheap but the third is extremely expensive
Bob Ayling, former chief executive, British Airways

The great journeys of exploration by Marco Polo, Columbus and Livingstone share something in common with a short hop on Ryanair for a boozy weekend in Dublin or a Jet2 flight to Rome for a week of intensive art history. Ever since human beings formed themselves into communities that created a surplus of production, man has been a traveller. Thousands of years ago, the people of Mesopotamia journeyed through what is now Iraq to trade goods and ideas; later, similar trips were made up and down the Nile, across the Indian subcontinent and Asia. Mostly, the journeys were driven by desire for economic improvement or for military conquest – at the time, the two were inextricably entwined. The vast majority of human journeys to alien lands taken up to the end of the Second World War were undertaken for the purposes of conquest or colonisation, with a sprinkling of holy wars conducted in the name of religion.

Since Herodotus, there have been guidebook writers to prepare the ground for travellers, and since Thomas Cook there have been individuals determined to find solutions using the latest technology that allow people to travel decently for a fair price. Cook's concept of empowering new strata of society to travel parallels the development of low-cost flying.

Thomas Cook was not merely the pioneer of package holidays – he was also the first to encounter the massed ranks of vested interest blocking his path, and to find inventive ways to get around the obstruction. A statue outside Leicester railway station pays tribute to him. He had begun organised tourism in a small way in the city in 1841, running a temperance outing to the nearby town of Loughborough for one shilling and sixpence (7.5p). It wasn't no-frills, mind, because the price included tea. Anyone caring to visit the Leicestershire town nowadays would not be struck by its attractiveness as a holiday destination, and might even suggest that it would look better after several strong drinks. But exactly 160 years after Cook's first trip, Bmibaby announced no-frills flights from several Mediterranean destinations to Nottingham East Midlands airport – nearest town, Loughborough.

As is natural for travel entrepreneurs, Thomas Cook wanted to expand. The perfect opportunity was provided by the 1855 international exposition in Paris, the first to be held in the French capital, set in the dramatic surroundings of Baron Haussmann's newly redrawn city. The steadily rising incomes and increased aspirations of the middle classes brought about by the Industrial Revolution convinced Cook that there would be a market for trips from London to Paris. So he approached the leading shipping lines on the cross-Channel routes and asked for discounts on tickets in return for guaranteed group bookings. Thomas Cook recalled the event in an 1878 magazine article: 'I tried hard to induce the companies commanding the Channel traffic to give me facilities to work with and for them. But they could not or would not see it to be to their advantage to comply with my requests.'

He had assured them that this would open up a new market of people who would not otherwise travel. But the ferry firms turned him down, on the grounds that to sell below official rates would jeopardise their existing earnings. This same argument, between innovator and entrenched interests, has taken place repeatedly as the no-frills airlines seek to take to the skies.

Eventually, Cook was offered a deal on the Great Eastern route between Harwich and Antwerp. It is not ideal to start a journey from London to Paris by heading north-east to Harwich. Nor is the Belgian port of Antwerp, which lies almost on the Dutch border, especially convenient for the French capital; even Ryanair would be hard pressed to describe Antwerp as Paris. But Cook sought to turn the situation to his advantage. He constructed an itinerary that continued to Brussels and Cologne, meandered up the Rhine, branched off to Heidelberg and Baden-Baden, turned west to Strasbourg and onwards to Paris. The French side of the ferry operation was prepared to negotiate with Cook, so his parties completed their grand circular tour by returning to London across the Channel from Le Havre or Dieppe. 'Thus did I conduct a series of special parties, and inaugurate a system of tickets taking in all the points,' he wrote.

Foreign travel for pleasure, as opposed to trade or war, was still the preserve of the wealthy. Indeed, until the 1871 Bank Holidays Act, the working man or woman had no right even to take 25 December off. The new law assigned days off at Christmas, Easter, Whitsun and on the first Monday of August. The railway companies did well out of the change, taking millions of people in the Victorian equivalent of no-frills travel – third class – to resorts in Britain at bank holiday weekends. There was no prospect of the average worker ever venturing abroad for a holiday. Many people headed west to seek economic improvement in America, but the sailings were almost invariably one-way. When people waved loved ones off from quaysides at Liverpool, Southampton or Queenstown (now Cobh in southern Ireland), they knew it was extremely unlikely they would ever see them again.

The First World War took more British people abroad than ever before. A million of them died overseas, mostly slaughtered on the Western Front. The aftermath of the 'Great War' brought massive political shifts and social changes. And it also transformed travelling patterns in the aftermath of the war, as bereaved relatives demanded the opportunity to visit the fields of Flanders where a generation of young men had fallen.

During the war, many thousands of men had been trained to fly; enough of them survived to form the basis of the new industry of passenger air transport. It developed most rapidly in the United States. One reason was that the Americans were late entrants to the First World War and therefore had the opportunity to develop commercial flying sooner; more importantly, the sheer scale of the country and its thin rail links demanded another means of communication. The first civil purpose of aviation was to carry mail, not people. The pilots took risks but earned good money: it was a lucrative business working for national governments, and the cargo, unlike human freight, did not complain about the bumpy ride, the intense cold and the ever-present danger. Early in the twentieth century, people travelled on trains and ships, often in considerable comfort and at great speed. Only slowly did the mail planes start taking paying passengers, to supplement the earnings from postal contracts. 'Self-loading cargo' is one of the more pejorative terms for the people who ultimately pay the wages of workers in the travel industry, i.e. the passengers. If, at the end of a long, uncomfortable flight, that is what you feel like, then bear in mind the origins of civilian flight.

The first purpose-built international air terminal in the world was built beside the Purley Way, at the time well south of London. From the day the Air Minister's wife opened the new terminal in May 1928, until the final Lufthansa flight took off on the last day of August 1939, Croydon – or at least its airport – was the most glamorous place in Britain. The Aerodrome Hotel next door (another world first) could sell space on its roof at a penny per person as crowds gathered to welcome aviators like Charles Lindbergh and Amy Johnson, and film stars such as Douglas Fairbanks and Mary Pickford.

The 'Air Ministry Administration Building', now known simply as Airport House, became the model for the initial generation of airports. The main terminal hall has an art deco interior that seems to resound with the voices of the passengers who used to weigh in there. Yes, that's weigh in: then, as now, the standard baggage allowance was 20 kg (44 lb), though today it is less on Ryanair and some other no-frills airlines. But in the early days of civil aviation, each passenger was discreetly asked to step on to the scales, so that seats could be allocated in such a way as to maintain the trim of the aircraft.

In 1936, two significant events took place in England. Fifteen miles south of Croydon aerodrome, a circular building opened adjacent to the railway station. The first airport that allowed passengers to step straight from the train to the plane, without getting wet, was located at the small airfield adjacent to Gatwick racecourse. (The terminal, known as the Beehive, is now occupied by GB Airways, the with-frills competitor to many of the low-cost airlines, and the company that loaned easyJet's Stelios his first two planes.) The other notable development took place 120 miles

NO-FRILLS NAVIGATION

The first air traffic control system in Europe was introduced at Croydon aerodrome, south of London. Initially, it was a rudimentary affair: in poor weather, a man with acute hearing would venture out on to the walkway around the tower, and listen for aircraft. Once he heard one, he would report its direction to the controllers. A rotating transmitter would be wound around to point roughly towards the inbound aircraft. With luck, a Morse code conversation would ensue.

In the 30s, a new system was introduced that enabled pilots to fix their precise location, using the principle upon which the modern Global Positioning System is based. At an agreed instant, three radio stations in southern England took a bearing on the aircraft. A navigator at Croydon would collate the results to pinpoint the location, and tell the pilot where he or (very occasionally) she was. The aerodrome is now a museum, and in the faithfully recreated Radio Room, you can visualise ghostly figures crouching over dials, valves, maps, pencils and rulers.

Just as the X-ray revolutionised medicine by allowing doctors to 'see' through human flesh, so the invention of radar (RAdio Detection And Ranging) transformed aviation. No longer were pilots and air-traffic controllers constrained by what they could see; by bouncing high-frequency radio waves off objects in the sky, cloud and darkness ceased to be causes for concern (at least in theory). Radar is now used by everything from the ground controllers keeping the taxiways tidy at Luton to the 'air-prox' warning systems on board aircraft that warn of other nearby planes.

north of London. On Easter Monday, Billy Butlin opened his first holiday camp at Skegness. 'Our true intent is for your delight' was the main message, but the canny entrepreneur added an equation that wage-earners could understand: 'Holiday with pay … holiday with play … A week's holiday for a week's wage'. He lobbied vigorously for the passing of the Holidays with Pay Act. It became law two years later, and brought a dramatic change in entitlement to millions of families who could now look forward to a week away. Butlin chartered a special train to take every MP who had voted for it to his second camp, at Clacton. In 1939, eleven million workers earned a holiday – their last for six years because of the outbreak of war.

The Second World War, like its predecessor, changed the way that ordinary people looked at travel. Millions of young men were obliged to see much more of the world than they could have imagined. Peace, when it finally came in 1945, bestowed Britain with a different society than had existed before the war – one in which the concept of foreign travel for the masses was no longer alien. Servicemen who came home alive had acquired a taste for abroad that the prevailing travel industry could not satisfy.

On 1 January 1946, the first flight took off from the new Heath Row airport, west of London – destination Buenos Aires. It was a proving flight for British South American Airways, the airline for which the mother of one of the no-frills pioneers, Richard Branson, later worked. But air travel was still the preserve of rich people on official business; as a post-war austerity measure, the new Labour government actually banned leisure travel abroad for three years. It took an enterprising young man named Vladimir Raitz to get ordinary people travelling. Raitz had been born to a well-to-do family in Moscow in 1922, but when he was six the family fled to western Europe. He enjoyed a pedigree education, at the Goethe School in Berlin and the Lycée Français in Warsaw. Later, he read Economic History at the London School of Economics, which he calls 'a very dubious organisation'. (Stelios of easyJet went to the same college, as did Mick Jagger and Cherie Booth.) In 1949, Raitz was working as a journalist for Reuters in London. That August, he took his first overseas holiday; a Russian colleague invited him to Calvi, on the French island of Corsica.

At the age of eighty-four, he is still working in the travel industry, and is recognisable from a snapshot of that first Mediterranean sojourn. 'The property was called Club Olympique,' recalls Raitz, 'and was run by White Russian friends of mine.' The Soviet Union, which gave the world one of its most joyless airlines, Aeroflot, also provided it with the package holiday. The White Russians, themselves exiles from the 1917 October Revolution, had established a camp in Calvi before the war, where they would meet each summer. In 1949, they revived the idea, using ex-US Army tents that provided the accommodation for the first sun, sea and sex package holidays. 'I had a most excellent two weeks' holiday in the most spartan of surroundings,' says Raitz.

The holiday may have been excellent, but the journey was arduous: a train from London to Dover, a ferry to Calais, and another train the length of mainland France to Nice. The last stretch was an overnight crossing on the good ship *Ile de Beauté* to the port of Calvi. But it was worth it: at the end of the trip, he says, 'They asked me, "Why can't you send us some British clients?" I decided I could do this in addition to my day job at Reuters.' Raitz was not the only one to be inspired by the Club Olympique. A Frenchman named Gérard Blitz subsequently developed the concept in a different direction, and created the Club Méditerranée.

'It began by a fluke, like everything else does,' Vladimir Raitz now says. He had £3,000 in capital, bequeathed by his grandmother. That equates to about £60,000 today. He found premises in Fleet Street, London, above what was then D & S Radford's Snuffe Shoppe and is now a branch of Ryman the stationer. He recruited a secretary with the adventurous name of Connie Everest. And he chose a name: Horizon Holidays. All he needed now was to crack a problem that Blitz and his French clientele did not face: how to get people to Corsica without a 48-hour journey each way, which would take a large slice out of a fortnight's holiday.

The solution lay in the large number of ex-military transport aircraft that were in circulation (many of them owned and operated by an entrepreneur named Freddie Laker in Southend). Raitz called on an air broker, Instone Air Transport, to try to arrange suitable flights. But the company explained, as Raitz puts it, that 'British European Airways had the monopoly, and they didn't really want to tolerate any competition of any sort,' and the chances of persuading the Ministry of Transport to open up the market were remote.

'I had great difficulty in getting permission to start these series of flights,' says Raitz with some understatement. 'I faced the implacable opposition of the established airline.' British European Airways (BEA) was owned by the government and therefore enjoyed a monopoly on commercial flying. 'They trod on everyone's feet to maintain it,' says Raitz.

BEA would later become part of British Airways, which continued the obstructionist tradition by hampering Laker Airways and Virgin Atlantic in their attempts to open up the skies to North America. In 1950, Vladimir Raitz proved useful warm-up material. The state airline was happy for Raitz's clients to fly to their holiday destinations, but only on its scheduled services. 'Perhaps they saw what was coming,' says Raitz. Two problems: BEA did not fly to Corsica, and to the closest destination it served – Nice – the return fare was £70. Curiously, that is about what you might expect to pay for an off-peak return to Nice on easyJet or Bmibaby. But in real terms it equates to around £1,500 today.

After a series of 'fights with the Ministry of Transport' to get a licence to carry passengers on charter flights, Raitz was finally given permission to operate to Calvi shortly before Easter 1950. The licence was too late and too limited, he says: 'I was restricted to flying teachers and students only.' It had taken the government five months to permit Horizon to fly to Corsica – and only if the flights were restricted to the education profession. Travel to Corsica was deemed to be strictly of educational value, so only students, teachers and lecturers could apply. (Ever since, students, and people who pretend to be students, have enjoyed special fares.) To sign up for a week in Corsica, they had to be assiduous savers or enjoy a private income. Britain's first all-inclusive fortnight's holiday cost £32 10s 0d (£32.50, equivalent to £650 today). The price included the flight and two weeks' full board plus what Raitz promised to be 'as much food and wine as you could consume'; in austere 50s Britain, this was a seductive notion. But first, you had to get to Corsica.

'It really was absolutely no frills,' says Raitz about his first flight. The 32-seater DC-3, belonging to Air Transport Charter, took off from Gatwick on the third Saturday in March 1950; ever since, the Sussex airport has been Britain's leading charter airport.

The ex-military pistoned-engine plane had three big limitations. Its top speed was 170 mph; modern jets can fly three times as fast, and even high-speed trains travel 10 per cent quicker. The aircraft had no pressurisation, obliging it to fly at turbulent altitudes below three thousand feet. And the limited range allowed it to get only as far as Lyon in one hop. But the refuelling stop soon became a marketing advantage, because clients could enjoy a meal in the gastronomic heart of France – for many, their first taste of abroad – before the final two-hour hop. The total trip took eight hours; jet flights between Gatwick and Corsica now take around eighty minutes.

The first season was a great success with the public, but less so with the balance sheet; high start-up costs and poor margins comprise a common complaint – and frequent cause of failure – among airlines. Thanks to a friendly bank manager, Horizon was able to keep going for a second season, which saw a 9 per cent increase in price and a 40 per cent increase in bookings. Even better, from Raitz's point of view, the government changed. The incoming Conservative administration made aviation less restricted, and removed the teacher-and-student condition. Even so, Raitz was still obliged to battle for every licence: first before the Air Transport Advisory Council, then the Air Transport Licensing Board and finally the Civil Aviation Authority. At every hearing, BEA would oppose new, cheap flights. Yet there was no personal animosity: 'While we berated each other in front of the Air Transport Licensing Board, afterwards we all went for a drink,' says Raitz. 'It was all done in a very British way. We were all on the greatest of terms, and we all liked each other very much.' The traveller, meanwhile, had to endure for several years a rule designed to suffocate competition: on routes that BEA or another scheduled airline flew, the minimum price anyone was allowed to charge for a package holiday was the lowest prevailing fare set by the airlines' cartel, the International Air Transport Association. In other words, the total cost of a package that used a flight to Nice had to be at least £70. Consumers' champions were thin on the ground among the Establishment in the 50s.

Vladimir Raitz soon expanded into Spain. He began selling packages to Estartit on the Costa Brava, then moved to the island of Mallorca. 'When I went there, there was only one hotel on the island. There were no roads, you had to clamber down a mountainside to see a lovely little beach. That was what was so satisfying.'

What was less satisfying were the constant arguments over licences. BEA objected to flights to Mallorca's capital, Palma, on the grounds that they would cause 'material diversion of traffic'. The airline's argument was somewhat undermined by the fact that, at the time, it did not fly anywhere near the island and therefore had no traffic materially to divert. Raitz won. But BEA had one more trump card to produce – the concept of 'wasteful duplication' of resources. In a country still recovering from the ravages and privations of war, accusing a competitor of wanting to fly frivolously could prove a forceful argument.

Perhaps because of the endless tussles over licensing, competition was slow to arrive. 'For about four or five years we had the field to ourselves. Then other people started coming in,' says Raitz. At first, 'there was a certain spirit of camaraderie. And I didn't worry because the cake was getting very much larger anyway.'

THE TOURIST AGE AND JET AGE BEGIN

Just before Horizon's third summer season began, two events took place that were profoundly to affect later travellers. On 1 May 1952, the US airline, TWA, introduced a 'tourist' class. Before 1952, all scheduled air travel was one class – first class, with prices to match. TWA concluded that revenue would be higher if it cut fares and squeezed in more seats. The following day, the world's first passenger jet service took off. A de Havilland Comet in the colours of the British Overseas Airline Corporation (BOAC) took off from London Heathrow, heading for Rome. Like Concorde, it marked a turning point in aviation. It flew at twice the height and twice the speed of previous airliners. Comet was a thirsty brute: the Italian capital was just the first of a series of five refuelling stops that were needed between London and Johannesburg, the destination for that first flight. Today, five wide-bodied jets fly this route each day, non-stop. But the Comet, which built on the work of the jet-engine pioneer, Frank Whittle, halved the journey time. The aircraft's fatal flaw was that it kept crashing due to metal fatigue. Nevertheless, the pioneering jet proved that moving large numbers of people at close to the speed of sound could be done, and spurred American engineers into finding safe designs for passenger jets. The Boeing 707 and Douglas DC-8 quickly seized the market. Comet returned to the skies after much re-engineering, but became little more than a footnote in the history of no-frills flying: in the colours of Dan-Air and British Airtours, it was used for student charter flights to Greece and Spain.

One competitor was a company called the Travel Club of Upminster. Its proprietor, Harry Chandler, had a rival claim to have started the modern foreign package holiday, having organised inclusive rail groups to Schwangau in Bavaria as early as 1935. His son, Paul, who now runs the business with Harry's widow, Rene, says, 'I've always taken the family line that we invented the package holiday. But my father would never have called it a package holiday. He called it an inclusive tour.'

By now Vladimir Raitz had progressed from the war-surplus DC-3s to the high-tech Vickers Viscount. This superb British aircraft could fly at 300mph, and its pressurisation meant it could keep above the worst of the weather. The package holiday had come of age.

In 1950, three hundred Horizon clients pioneered the package holiday by air. Over the next half-century, the number of British travellers on packages increased to around eighteen million by 2000. Along the way, there were numerous crashes, both financial and fatal. Fiesta Tours collapsed in 1954, stranding two thousand holidaymakers. In June 1967, two British aircraft, both on Spanish charter flights, crashed within twelve hours of each other, killing more than 160 people; the following year, the charter airline British Eagle went bust. But the package holiday market was expanding inexorably in a climate of rapidly increasing disposable income.

In 1970, Raitz invented Club 18–30, a brand that quickly became a legend in its own Happy Hour. The company that specialises in holidays of sheer indulgence for young people has survived to middle age, and is presently owned by the Thomas Cook organisation – something that the original temperance campaigner might not have favoured (a BBC programme about Thomas Cook included half-a-dozen pundits who all proclaimed that the package holiday founder would be 'turning in his grave').

The year that haunts Vladimir Raitz, and many other veterans of the travel industry, is the tumultuous twelve months of 1974 – which began with a Miners' Strike and the Three-Day Week, and encompassed two General Elections.

'I loved what I was doing, I did it successfully for twenty-five years until the disastrous year of 1974.' In the 'Who Rules Britain?' election of February that year, Harold Wilson's Labour party won fewer votes than the incumbent prime minister, Edward Heath, but gained the most seats and took power. The enduring economic gloom, amplified by the Middle East oil crisis, finished off many travel companies that had hitherto prospered in a climate of expansion. One of them was Raitz's Horizon Holidays. Even though Raitz poured his personal assets into trying to shore up the company, the cash ran out. Horizon went into receivership, and its assets were taken over by the ever-expanding Court Line conglomerate.

Two months before the October 1974 election in which Wilson achieved a slim overall majority, Court Line collapsed and forty thousand holidaymakers were stranded abroad.

Strangely, Horizon survived. The Birmingham-based tour opera-

WHOSE FLIGHT IS IT ANYWAY?

'Nation states believed that to be a nation you needed a flag, a national anthem and an airline,' says Bob Ayling, the former boss of British Airways. 'The first two come cheap but the third is extremely expensive.'

When charter carriers started using modern aircraft, the scheduled airlines became unsettled – which helps explain some cheesy promotions during the 60s.

The Spanish carrier, Iberia, promised that 'only the plane gets more attention than you', while Alitalia announced it 'takes your fun very seriously'.

What alarmed the scheduled airlines even more was that some space was sold to independent travellers on 'seat-only' deals, at prices that drastically undercut the competition: the precursor of cheap no-frills flights today. The regulation that insisted on a minimum fare on scheduled routes had been lifted. Instead, arcane rules were drawn up that required accommodation to be an integral part of the holiday.

Even more tortuous solutions were found to evade them. The standard agreement issued by the travel agent who sold the ticket required the traveller to affirm that they owned property abroad and that they hereby granted rights over it to the agent who promptly rented what was invariably a notional property back to the traveller, for a pound.

The Greek authorities were particularly stern. Olympic Airways was well aware that using a cheap charter to go island-hopping was standard practice among independent travellers. Even today, passengers on charter flights may be denied the flight home from Greece if their passport contains evidence of their having left the country (e.g. on a side trip from Kos to Turkey) for one night or more.

tion had been spun off from the original company. It avoided receivership, and carried on trading under the name Horizon Midlands. Once the Court Line dust had settled, it floated as a public company and, after a decent interval, reverted to Horizon Holidays. The company even established a charter airline, Orion (to come up with the name, managers simply deleted the h, r and z from Horizon's name). Horizon was bought by the giant Thomson combine, and the name disappeared from brochures.

One short-lived low-cost experiment involved a bus from Aldgate in London to Southend airport, which at the time was a fairly busy place – way ahead of its rival, Stansted. A Viscount belonging to the late lamented British Island Airways hopped over to Ostend, where another bus was waiting (you hoped) for the drive into Brussels. On a good day you could cover the ground in six hours, for a fare of around £40 return, or less if you went only as far as Ostend, the starting point for many a hitch-hiking trip to Antwerp, Athens or Afghanistan.

Thomson later became part of the Prussian Mining, Iron and Steel Company, now known as TUI.

Before the German takeover, Raitz offered to buy the unused Horizon brand back, without success. 'I went to Paul [Brett, then in charge of Thomson] and I said, "Will you sell me the name and I'll start again?" And he said, "Vladimir, I'm not going to sell you the name, even for a million pounds, because I don't need any further competition." '

At precisely the time Horizon was folding, the backpack revolution was beginning. As the lights went off all over Britain, the first Lonely Planet book appeared. *Across Asia on the Cheap* appealed to a new generation of low-budget travellers. They might have started off on the Magic Bus, but when that involved too many hours plodding through Germany or risking the two-lane road through Yugoslavia, they demanded the means to fly without paying the outrageous fares charged by scheduled airlines.

By 1982, the quirky guidebook *Alternative London* was offering financial advice to impecunious British travellers: 'English 2p pieces work in most French Space Invaders machines; 5p pieces work as 1DM in German vending machines.' To test out this theory of improving exchange rates, thousands flew to Germany on the charter airline Dan-Air, which operated 'quasi-scheduled' flights from Gatwick to Berlin. Officially, these were charters. But every potential customer – mostly British servicemen stationed in the divided city, and budget-minded business travellers – knew they flew at the same time every day, offering a scheduled service in all but name. The fare in the 1980s was around £100, a bargain compared with the prevailing price on British Airways – the only scheduled airline allowed to fly the route.

THE BIGGEST NO-FRILLS AIRLINE OF THEM ALL?
Aviation in the Soviet Union was always a different activity
to that in the West. Indeed, for the USSR flying without frills
was the norm. The idea that the in-flight service should
consist of a starter of contempt, a main course of ignorance
and a dessert of blank incomprehension has been around
since 26 March 1932, when Aeroflot – which was to become
the largest airline of the twentieth century – got off the
ground. While the Soviet Union was still a going concern,
getting off the ground was just the first hurdle faced by
Aeroflot passengers. Once in flight, the catering comprised a
plastic cup of something that purported to be fruit juice but
had probably been manufactured by a petrochemical plant
in Omsk, and a 'cutlet' which involved a pulverised piece of
meat smothered in stale breadcrumbs some months previously in Tomsk. The meals were about as tasty and
nutritious as the fraying upholstery. The aircraft were
ear-splittingly loud; the jets that spluttered into existence
during the 50s were especially liable to bend the needle of
the noise meter. But, like the best no-frills flights, they were
reliably cheap. Aviation bound the fifteen diverse republics
of the USSR together much more than the Trans-Siberian
Railway. Air fares were kept low enough to enable the
ordinary comrade in the ulitsa (street) to travel widely. Even
as late as 1991, when the Soviet Union was in the final stages
of disintegration, it was possible to travel from Minsk in
Belarus to Kiev in Ukraine for less than £1.

Through the 1990s, the charter airlines continued to snap at the
heels of their scheduled rivals. Few would dispute the assertion
from Dr Keith Mason of Cranfield College of Aeronautics that
'charter carriers are able to achieve lower operating costs than
their no-frills, scheduled competitors' – because, with decades of
experience and load factors of over 90 per cent, they jolly well
should be. Yet apart from an abortive experiment by Britannia
Airways on the Luton-Belfast route, none tried no-frills scheduled
flying until MyTravelLite began in October 2002. Two years
later, the UK's biggest charter airline, Britannia, rebranded itself
as Thomsonfly, the first step in amalgamating charter operations
with low-cost scheduled flights.

Vladimir Raitz, now operating holidays to Mauritius, says the no-frills airlines are 'very welcome' – though he is not an entirely satisfied customer, because he never managed to find the promised low fares: 'I think some of their advertising is very misleading.'

Raitz has not made the money that some of his contemporaries achieved, but counts 'fathering three daughters and having a happy family life' as his greatest achievement. 'I certainly didn't think I was creating an industry. What I was doing was having a lot of fun, going to little villages, and what I had in mind was adding one resort after another. The idea of making a lot of money never entered into it at all.'

3. A LOUSY THIRTEEN BUCKS

If it's conventional, it's generally not wisdom. If it's wisdom, it's generally not conventional

Herb Kelleher, chairman, Southwest

How important's Herb Kelleher? Herb Kelleher's like God

Michael O'Leary, chief executive, Ryanair

It's statistically more difficult to get hired at Southwest Airlines than it is to be admitted to Harvard

Jim Parker, former chief executive, Southwest

SOUTHWEST FLIGHT 422: SEATTLE-KANSAS CITY

'Place the mask over that big old mouth and nose of yours –' clearly, this is no ordinary safety briefing '– and breathe like this: aaaaaah, ooooooh, uuuuuuh.' Duane Redmond, lead flight attendant aboard flight 422, is injecting novelty into the statutory safety briefing. When he has finished his heavy breathing, he adds, 'By the way, that wasn't me calling your house last night.'

I travelled with Duane when I was looking for Love: Love Field, Dallas, the First World War airfield named after a pioneering aviator, Lieutenant Moss Lee Love, who died in a crash in California in 1913. Eventually I reached it from my starting point in Seattle, by way of Kansas City and Oklahoma City.

You can tell you are finally in Texas when a joke waddles towards you on the ample belly of a T-shirted Texan: 'Why is it called Tourist Season,' the slogan on the convex garment asks, 'if we can't shoot them?' The anniversary of the assassination of President Kennedy in Dallas passed a few days ago. That date, 22 November 1963, is particularly poignant here at Love Field, the last airport where JFK touched down, alive, aboard Air Force One.

'Dwight is your dwiver,' jokes the sign at the front of the Southwest Airlines shuttle bus. 'Will you drop me off at the uniform department?' a flight attendant asks Dwight. 'No ma'am, but I'll slow down to thirty.' For the first mile of the ride to the headquarters of the world's most successful airline, Dwight's bus runs along the same road as John F. Kennedy travelled on his final, fatal journey. At about that time, a lawyer named Herbert D. Kelleher was working in San Antonio, 250 miles south-west of Dallas. He did not intend to change the way that people travelled; Kelleher had little interest in airlines. Forty years, and many legal tussles later, Kelleher is the man that the bosses of other no-frills airlines idolise.

'As far as low-cost travel is concerned, he was definitely the pioneer,' says Sir Richard Branson. Stelios, founder of easyJet, asserts, 'Southwest is really my role model.' And Michael O'Leary, chief executive of Ryanair, calls Kelleher 'the original genius, the Thomas Edison of low-fare air travel. This is the guy who created it, this is the guy who first dreamt of charging people $10 for two- and three-hour flights in the US, and he's the one who revolutionised the industry.' When Ryanair was floated, says O'Leary, his airline offered Kelleher 5 per cent of the equity and a seat on the board – for free. 'He didn't take it because he didn't want to be distracted. You've got to stay true to what you do.'

Herb Kelleher didn't stay true to his original training, as a lawyer, but has remained faithful to Southwest since his part in dreaming it up in 1966. Kelleher was born in a suburb of Philadelphia – Haddon Hills, New Jersey – in 1931. His first job was delivering the Philadelphia Bulletin for $2.50 a week. He studied law at New York University, then worked for a while for the New Jersey court system, before going into the legal business on his own account.

The sight of 'a Yankee in a one-way U-Haul' became a pet hate on the part of some Texans during the 60s, as thousands of northerners flooded south to the booming 'Sunbelt' economy. Fuelled by the huge federal investment first in NASA's space exploration and later by the military demands of the Vietnam War, Texas needed people, and people needed lawyers. Kelleher joined a legal practice in the fast-growing Texan city of San Antonio. It became Oppenheimer, Rosenberg, Kelleher & Wheatley. He recruited a young woman named Colleen Barrett as his legal secretary. She is now president of Southwest, while another former employee, Jim Parker, became the airline's chief executive officer for a time. 'It's like the development of humankind,' Parker says now about the early days. 'We were able to adapt to the environment that we were in, to prosper in that environment.'

Dwight's dwive to Southwest's HQ epitomises the choices that were open to Texan travellers when Kelleher moved to the state. The runway of Love Field is a wingspan from a railway line. By 1963, the heyday of the train had ended. The automobile was supreme. But Texas is so large that you could barely drive from one end of the state to the other in a day. Its strange shape, resembling a coyote splayed flat on Interstate 10, measures eight hundred miles from north to south and from east to west. Texas occupies more space than France, Belgium, Holland and Switzerland combined. The golden triangle plotted by the state's three largest cities – Dallas, Houston and San Antonio – is served by freeways, but the drive between any two of those cities takes four or five hours. In 1963 flying – which cut the journey to less than an hour – was the preserve of the rich and powerful.

The large, blanched building at 2702 Love Field Drive was built 35 years after President Kennedy touched down. It is a people's palace, a bright, comfortable and friendly headquarters building for America's most successful airline. Not the biggest carrier: that title rests with American Airlines, based a mere ten miles west of here. United and Delta also carry more passengers. But Southwest still manages to fly over eighty million people a year. Remarkably for an industry which haemorrhages cash, Southwest consistently makes money out of it. Southwest made its first profit in 1973 and has stayed in the black ever since. Its market capitalisation – the amount at which the stock market values it – is the highest of any airline in the world, and bigger than that of America's six largest traditional airlines combined.

During that time, none of Southwest's twelve million flights has crashed seriously enough to kill anyone. Within weeks of the terrorist attacks of 11 September 2001, which saw its rivals laying off a hundred thousand workers, a billboard appeared outside 2702 Love Field Drive reading 'Now hiring'. Southwest Airlines not only kept all its workers – it was soon advertising for more. But you had to be good to make the grade, says Parker. 'It's statistically more difficult to get hired at Southwest Airlines than it is to be admitted to Harvard.'

Almost everyone puts Southwest's success down to one man. Herb Kelleher is credited with reinventing aviation, by concentrating on providing what was necessary for safe, reliable and cheap air travel. As a lawyer, Herb Kelleher arrived at Southwest with none of the excess baggage that many people in aviation accrue. 'If it's conventional, it's generally not wisdom,' he likes to say. 'If it's wisdom, it's generally not conventional.' He did not hesitate to fly in the face of airline tradition, for example by ditching pre-assigned seating. 'Used to be we only had about four people on the whole plane,' he says, 'so the idea of assigned seats just made people laugh. Now the reason is you can turn the airplanes quicker at the gate.' Colleen Barrett, who succeeded Kelleher as president in 2000, says the alternative would involve spending over a billion dollars on new planes: 'If we had to extend our ground times by as little as ten minutes for assignments, we would have to buy 31 more 737s at a cost of $36 million each.'

The company line is that your seat on the plane is reserved, you just don't know which one. Instead, passengers checking in are given a boarding card, with a colour such as dark blue (which, for the colour-blind, is labelled Dark Blue Boarding Pass). This tells you how, or rather when, to get on board, and carries a large number.

'Hi,' says a message on boarding pass number 83. 'You're in the third boarding group and, once on board, you can choose whatever seat is available.' The assigned number depends on how early you check in: 'Hurry, better get a good number,' one Southwest employee at Phoenix urged me. A good number is in the range 1 to 30, meaning you have first choice of the 137 seats on one of the airline's brand new 737-700s. (On easyJet, which flies identical aircraft, an extra dozen passengers are packed in.) If you are in the 121-137 group, you can be pretty sure of getting a middle seat down the back. In any event, passengers get aboard quicker than when seating is assigned.

Inside the front door of Southwest HQ stands a scale model of Abraham Lincoln's memorial in Washington DC. The reception area is the size of a hangar for a Boeing 737. Talking of which, a fleet of ten miniature jets dangles from the glass and steel ceiling. Every few minutes, a real 737 streaks past the door on the Love Field runway on its way to another Texan city or a neighbouring state. The reception area is dotted with cases containing awards and tributes to Herb Kelleher, notably a ventriloquist's dummy of the man holding a trademark cigarette. Southwest's chairman is very fond of tobacco. 'I've had lunch with Kelleher on two occasions,' recalls Sir Richard Branson '– both occasions where I took up smoking again.'

'This will be a no-smoking, no-complaining and no-whining flight today. If you would like to smoke this afternoon, just step outside onto the wing. If you can light it, you can smoke it.' That's what flight attendant Duane Redmond tells passengers of this non-smoking airline.

As you wait for a hard-to-get appointment with Southwest's top brass, an impressively wide range of clothes wanders past the reception desk: women and men in polo shirts and shorts, or sweatshirts and chinos. And that's just the cabin crew. Most of the office staff wear jeans. The only people in ties are me and a pilot who awwived on Dwight's bus to seek a job. If he succeeds, he can expect to work twice as hard as pilots on other carriers. Southwest's flight staff, says Parker, perform 'more take offs and landings than any other airline in the world' – though some Ryanair flight crews shuttling between Stansted and Prestwick might dispute that.

Southwest has a simple proposition, which can be summarised as, 'Keep planes flying, because that is where they make money. And keep fares low enough to keep people travelling.' Each of Southwest's aircraft flies an average of eight missions a day, staying in the air for a total of twelve hours. The airline is consistently rated as one of the most punctual in America, despite the impression created by jokey cabin announcements like, 'Our flight time today is: when we get there, we get there.' The average passenger pays a fare of $88 (roughly £50) for a typical journey of 775 miles (about the distance from Luton to Barcelona or Stansted to Venice). This is around one-third less than the competition. Even on the longest Southwest flight, the 2,329-mile flight from Baltimore/Washington to Los Angeles, the maximum fare you will ever pay is $299.

It sounds a simple and devastatingly effective recipe. But before Southwest's first flight took off on 18 June 1971, the airline had to overcome powerful vested interests of the traditional airline industry. Fortunately, there was already an existing operation in California that proved a useful starting point. There are few completely original ideas in aviation, as in most areas of life.

Life in the 60s was tough for anyone with the temerity to want to start an airline. The commercial aviation network had been established primarily for the transport of the US Mail. Four decades on, the nation was neatly carved up among a few big airlines. Competition was minimal. As in the UK, the federal government frowned upon what was perceived as wasteful duplication of services. Washington could enforce this policy on a federal basis. Competition was permitted only within individual states, and only three were really big enough to make flying attractive. Alaska was far too thinly populated to sustain much competition, with an average of one person per square mile compared with seventy in the rest of the US. So if competition was to start, it would have to be in Texas or California.

Pacific Southwest Airlines (PSA) began life in 1949 during California's post-war boom, and pioneered many of the ideas that Southwest still employs. The founder, Kenny Friedkin, believed he could take passengers from road and rail if he offered fares much lower than the existing airlines such as Western (now part of Delta) and United. So he acquired some cut-price DC-3s and started to devise a network. The first PSA route was classic Southwest territory. It started at San Diego on the Mexican border; many PSA passengers were from the huge naval base at San Diego, which led to its nickname, 'Poor Sailors' Airline'. The first stop was Burbank, a low-cost airport serving Los Angeles, now a Southwest favourite. The flight continued to Oakland, then and now a cheap and efficient alternative to San Francisco. Operationally, PSA was rigorous, keeping the aircraft flying as much as possible, with short turns at airports between arrival and departure. To keep costs down, the pilots also helped out on the ground, and the cabin crew cleaned the interior. Friedkin valued what is nowadays termed 'corporate culture'. He started a company newsletter called *Skylines* (Southwest's is entitled *Luvlines*, WestJet has one called *Airlines*) and organised annual picnics. He used first names for everyone.

Civil aviation was expanding rapidly, and bigger, faster aircraft were appearing. When big airlines started buying state-of-the-art DC-6s, PSA's DC-3s looked antiquated. So Friedkin picked up some DC-4s; they were larger and more efficient than PSA's original fleet, and conveniently cheap as other airlines were offloading them. One problem: they lacked the distinctive rectangular windows of the DC-6. So Friedkin ordered rectangles be painted around the DC-4s' circular windows to make passengers think they were about to board one of the more modern planes.

Kenny Friedkin died suddenly in 1962. J. Floyd Andrews, known universally as Andy, took over. He ordered new Boeing

727 jets, and coined the slogan 'The world's friendliest airline'; to prove it, he painted smiles on the noses of his planes. By March 1966, when The Byrds released their homage to air travel, 'Eight Miles High', you no longer needed to be a rock star to afford to experience life at forty thousand feet – so long as you lived in California. But across the US as a whole, only one in six of the population had ever flown.

A San Antonio businessman, Rollin King, saw what Pacific Southwest Airlines was doing in California and decided it could work in the even larger state of Texas. But first, he needed a good attorney to cut through the bureaucracy. Late in 1966 he asked a local lawyer named Herbert D. Kelleher to meet him at the city's St Anthony Hotel – a fusty location for what was to be a revolutionary meeting. The original route map, linking Dallas with Houston and San Antonio, was sketched on the back of a napkin; a copy of it hangs in the boardroom at 2702 Love Field.

On 15 March 1967 Kelleher, whose first name had by now been abbreviated by all to 'Herb', filed the incorporation documents for a company called Air Southwest. He had already ploughed some of his savings into the paper airline. The name of the putative carrier later changed to Southwest Airlines; Air Southwest has lately been resurrected as a name by a niche airline flying from Newquay and Plymouth in south-west England.

Kelleher applied on 27 November to the Texas Aeronautics Commission (TAC) for permission for Southwest to fly between Dallas, Houston and San Antonio. Twelve weeks later, the TAC had approved the application. So why wasn't Southwest flying early in 1968? To find out, you need only climb to the upper floor of Love Field airport, and walk into the Frontiers of Flight Aviation Museum. It is an impressive collection that takes the traveller from classical legend to the first Apollo moon landing in July 1969. At the time that NASA mission control in Houston was directing lunar missions, Southwest could not even get off the ground. The relics of the opposition it faced are on show in the museum.

An airline named Braniff features prominently. This Dallas-based carrier painted its planes bright orange three decades before easyJet discovered the colour. It was a popular local company – one of the airport roads is named after its founder, Tom Braniff. In the late 60s, its bread-and-butter routes were within Texas. Its fares matched those on the main competitors, Continental and Trans-Texas. Not surprisingly, all three airlines objected to the prospect of a new arrival on their patch, upsetting their cosy arrangements. So they managed to get a restraining order banning the Texas Aeronautics Commission from issuing a certificate to fly. The grounds: that there was no need for a new airline. Kelleher appealed on behalf of Southwest, but the decision was upheld.

So far, Southwest had spent half a million dollars on legal fees yet had not carried a single passenger. Herb Kelleher had seen his own investment in Southwest consumed in the legal fight. He could have given up, but instead vowed he would continue the battle at his own expense. On the next stage up the legal ladder, there was a breakthrough: the Texas Supreme Court found for Southwest. The three existing rivals made a bid to take the case to the US Supreme Court in Washington DC, but this was disallowed. Southwest made preparations for take-off.

By now, Kelleher had carved a large stake in the airline intellectually, as well as financially. He had decided his future lay with the airline he was coaxing into existence. But while he had built up a great deal of experience in commercial law, neither he nor Rollin King knew much about commercial aviation. So they hired an industry veteran, Lamar Muse, as chief executive officer. 'Lamar Muse deserves the credit for the original fares of Southwest,' says Howard Putnam, who was Southwest's chief executive and president from August 1978 to September 1981. 'He was really the man that put together the operation, the team and a lot of the route strategy.' Rollin King, says Putnam, had the idea but lacked the skills to organise the operation, while Kelleher was focused on lawsuits and lobbying. Lamar milked his contacts for cash to replenish the empty coffers at Southwest, and recruited solid aviation professionals to run the operation. And he ordered three brand-new aircraft.

Boeing sold the airline a trio of 737s for $4m each, a 20 per cent discount on the prevailing list price. It turned out to be an excellent investment on the part of the manufacturer: Southwest now has close on 450 of the model, and the jet is established as standard equipment for no-frills airlines. The uniforms for the first cabin crew have not remained standard equipment. They comprised tight tops, hot pants and white leather boots. (The original chief hostess had previously worked for Hugh Hefner aboard the Playboy jet.) The initial advertising for recruits was far from politically correct: 'Attention Raquel Welch: you can have a job if you measure up.' Yet from day one, the flying was approached with utter seriousness, which has helped Southwest to achieve the best accident-free record of any airline.

Everything was set for the first flights between the Texas triangle – Dallas, Houston, and San Antonio – to begin on 18 June 1971. At the eleventh hour, Braniff and Texas International (which Trans-Texas had become) managed to obtain a restraining order preventing Southwest starting operations. The day before the first flight, Kelleher persuaded the Texas Supreme Court to throw out the injunction. When Lamar Muse wondered what might happen if the sheriff was still inclined to enforce the order, Kelleher replied 'You roll right over the son-of-a-bitch and leave our tire tracks on his uniform.'

When flights began the next day from Love Field, the sheriff stayed away. So too did many of the hoped-for passengers. There were twelve departures each day to and from Houston (nowadays there are thirty each way between the two biggest cities in Texas). The modest fleet could also manage six round trips between Dallas and San Antonio. On either route, passengers paid a flat $20 one way, saving 25 per cent on the rivals' lowest fares.

Loads were initially dismal, but improved when Southwest switched from Houston's new Intercontinental airport to Hobby: smaller, older and closer to the city centre. This enabled travellers to make the downtown-to-downtown journey between Dallas and Houston in as little as ninety minutes. Muse started employing a primitive form of yield management, the principle that now governs pricing for all low-cost airlines. Southwest charged higher fares – $26 each way – when the market could bear it on daytime services, but in the evenings and at weekends the fare was halved to $13.

Passenger numbers on the Dallas–San Antonio route remained poor, so in January 1973 Southwest started charging a flat $13 on every flight. Braniff reacted by introducing the same fare on the Dallas–Houston run, the one route where Southwest was making money. Lamar Muse trumped Braniff with a newspaper advertisement that read, 'Nobody's going to shoot Southwest Airlines out of the sky for a lousy $13.' It was a direct appeal to Texans' sense of fair play – and self-interest. For those who were travelling on business, Southwest offered the option of a $26 fare; this included a 'free' bottle of Scotch whisky or vodka for their personal use. (A similar trick was employed in 1996 by easyJet on the Luton–Aberdeen run.) That was not the only spirit at work, says Jim Parker: 'The pioneering spirit of the people of Texas made them side with the underdog, and want to fly this maverick airline that was doing things differently.'

Braniff threw in the towel on the fares war, and the route returned to profitable levels; 1973 saw Southwest turn a profit for the first time. It also saw Kelleher seek ways to fly more people and make more money. So he went to California. This is an event mourned on the website that records the history of PSA: iflypsa.com.

'In 1973, a Texan came out to San Diego. His name was Herb Kelleher, and he worked for Southwest. PSA showed him the entire operation, and told all their department heads to "open everything up for Herb". (Tom Irwin [a PSA executive] was sent to Dallas with manuals in hand. Southwest was so impressed that they took PSA's name off the manual, stuck their name on, and made it their manual.) In return, PSA got a lot of heartache in the 1980s.'

Why on earth would a successful low-cost airline open itself for a competitor? Because, in 1973, there was no prospect of Southwest competing with PSA. Each flew only within its own state. Just as Southwest has welcomed easyJet, Ryanair and other start-ups to look over the company and talk to senior executives, PSA saw no downside to helping Kelleher. (Southwest may be pleased to know that O'Leary has no plans, at present, to move in on its patch.)

Southwest was still fighting a battle for survival. The oil crisis that began late in 1973 put pressure on all airlines, as the price of aviation fuel tripled. Lamar Muse could do nothing about the international politics that had caused the jump in kerosene prices. But he could maximise the use of aircraft. The 'ten-minute turn' was introduced, bringing pit-stop principles to aviation. A Boeing 737 could arrive, offload, refuel, board passengers and depart within ten minutes, far quicker than the competition could achieve. It has not survived. 'Our ten-minute turn has stretched a little over the years – it's had to, due to more baggage, more customers and, frankly, regulations have caused us to spend more time on the ground,' says Greg Wells, vice-president of security for Southwest. But the airline still beats the competition on aircraft utilisation, with its jets spending half their lives in the air. Southwest's president, Colleen Barrett, says, 'Our employees and our customers participate in a ballet of motion each time we load and unload an aircraft.'

The staff certainly enjoy some ambitious choreography as they dance around the US. In the early days, the flight crews saw too much of three cities; these days, they see huge amounts of the country, often on a single shift. A Houston flight attendant might begin the day at Oklahoma City, having nightstopped from the previous day, and fly two hours west to Phoenix. There, the crew changes direction and goes three hours east to St Louis. Another flight takes them even further from home, to Columbus, Ohio. And while on board, they are delivering much more than droll announcements.

For an airline that has long been described as 'no frills', Southwest dishes out a lot of perks. You get free coffee and juice on board (and sometimes at the gate before the flight), free peanuts (each passenger gets through an average 1.2 packets) and, on flights of three hours or more, decent snacks. Many of the traditional airlines have eliminated meals on flights of under four hours, which means you are more likely to get fed on a low-cost Southwest flight than on a 'full-service' one. Southwest also offers one of the most generous frequent-flyer programmes in the business, with one free round-trip for every eight flights.

'Complimentary soft drinks are available. Beers, wine and cocktails are available for purchase.' Duane Redmond's in-flight announcement on Southwest flight 244 begins ordinarily enough. But then he adopts the demeanour of a temperance preacher. 'For those of you drinking so early in the afternoon – shame, shame, shame on you.' Southwest offers no in-flight entertainment in the accepted sense, but many of its flight attendants perform stand-up comedy for the ultimate captive audience: 'Those of you sitting on the left-hand side of the aircraft will get an excellent view of Mount Rainier. Those of you sitting on the right will get an excellent view of the backs of the heads of those looking at Mount Rainier.'

The cabin crew are following the example set by their wise-cracking founder. 'If you like what I have to say, I'm Herb Kelleher, president of Southwest Airlines. If you don't, I'm John Dasburg, president of Northwest Airlines.' That was how he accepted yet another business leadership prize, at the University of Michigan in 1997, adding 'It's great to be here to accept this award, but I'm a little bit anxious since I'm out of my normal environment. I'm sober.'

In the early days, Southwest gave away alcoholic drinks during the day, 'because we had almost all business travellers and they didn't drink anyway at that time of day,' says Howard Putnam. One of the legendary Southwest stories is that Herb Kelleher holds the record for the largest number of Jack Daniel's consumed in a single flight. This is how Putnam tells it:

'Herb and I were hosting lunch on Wall Street for some analysts in late 1978. I was asked, on a fifty-minute flight from Dallas to Houston, how many free drinks could one get? I replied: "The record is seven Jack Daniel's and water and it is held by our Chairman, Herb." Herb quickly responded, "Seven, Howard, I thought I had eight?" Got a big laugh.' The story, Putnam now confesses, was pure invention, though he stresses it was unrehearsed.

How Putnam happened to be at the Wall Street lunch reveals much about the early years of Southwest. Under the presidency of Lamar Muse, the airline expanded slowly. It took five years for the fleet to double to six aircraft; by the late 90s in Europe, the standard was a few months. Despite lobbying for greater commercial freedom the airline was still restricted to Texas. Muse is described by Howard Putnam as 'The finest airline entrepreneur of the last forty years'. Putnam adds: 'He controlled the authority and decision-making channels within the company. To put it bluntly, the man was a dictator.' Muse liked an extremely flat management structure, which meant the lines of control between Muse and any employee were very short. By 1978, the corporate profile began to impede the company's growth. Muse was also getting too autocratic for the board's liking, unilaterally taking decisions on new planes and bases. Muse told the story of his downfall to Howard Putnam over a game of golf in Dallas. According to Putnam, Muse said: 'I was always arguing with another member of the board and co-founder, Rollin King. We just couldn't agree on much in those days. Anyway, during one of the board meetings I called for a vote and said, "Either Rollin leaves the board or I quit as president." ' At that, the story goes, Lamar left the room while the board voted. Ten minutes later, they called him back to give him the results. 'Sorry Lamar, you lose.' Lamar said he was shocked, but 'at least I kept my sense of humour. When they broke the news, I just took my keys out of my pocket and threw them down on the table. Then I stared straight at them and said: "Damn, I'd have never called for a vote if I thought I wasn't going to win", and walked out of the room.'

Muse served out the two years of 'gardening leave' required by a 'non-compete' clause in his severance agreement, then started his own airline, Muse Air, with his son Mike – who had also been working for Southwest, and was fired at the same time as his

STAY SLIM

Southwest didn't get where it is today by overpaying its staff. Reservations sales agents must spend three weeks training, without pay, before earning $8.05 an hour for the first year; after that, it increases by 75 cents. Customer service agents, who handle passengers at the airports, earn $9.09 an hour in California and at Baltimore, but only $8.30 elsewhere; again, there is a modest increase after the first year. To get the job, they must be capable of lifting 70 lb (32 kg) 'repetitively'.

Flight attendants need lift only 50 lb (23 kg). They are paid entirely on a piece-rate basis; on a typical 250-mile flight, they earn $14.67. After six months, this increases by 23 cents; only after a year does it rise to $17.34. Hang on, you may be thinking, for a flight of less than one hour that's a fine rate of pay. But on a bad day the average shift of eight hours may include only four flights, meaning an hourly rate of just $8.67, even for experienced staff.

The fringe benefits, though, are considerable. A recruitment leaflet lists the following advantages: 'Casual dress; chili cook-offs; Hallowe'en celebrations; deck parties [these take place at the Dallas HQ each Friday from 3 p.m., with beer and wine for a dollar]; golf tournaments; spontaneous celebrations [possibly more fun than golf tournaments]; and parades.' Perhaps even more enticing is the prospect for free travel anywhere on the network for you and your family alike, subject to space being available and the payment of federal and airport fees.

'There are many opportunities to share your shining spirit with thousands of customers every day as a member of the Southwest Airlines Family.' But to get a job, you should be in shape. Don't apply for a job as a flight attendant or a customer service agent if you are overweight. The rules are phrased diplomatically: 'Weight must be of such proportion to height that a neat appearance is maintained and physical ability to perform all functions is not hindered. Only standard uniform sizes are available. Men's uniforms range in waist size from 27 to 42 inches. Women's uniforms range in size from 0 to 18. No tailor-made uniforms are permitted.' And don't think you can let go of your shape after you get the job. 'If hired, you must sustain compliance with the Appearance and Physical Performance Standards Policy throughout your employment.'

father. Its claim to fame was as the world's first totally non-smoking airline, but it did not last long.

Kelleher took charge of Southwest as chairman, chief executive and president. Some years later, he told *Forbes* magazine 'when Lamar left, a lot of people said Southwest Airlines is over, because Lamar Muse is Southwest Airlines. Well, Lamar left in 1978 and Southwest is still here.' Kelleher did not retain his trinity of titles for long. He stayed on as chairman but relinquished his other two positions to Howard Putnam, then group vice-president for marketing at United Airlines, who began work on his 41st birthday.

The second notable event of 1978 was that, three-quarters of a century after the Wright Brothers first flew, President Jimmy Carter stripped away the rules that had tangled aviation for decades. Jim Parker, now Southwest's chief executive, claims credit: 'Congress saw what was happening in Texas in a de-regulated environment and passed the airline deregulation act.' All the old laws that restricted routes and schedules and fixed high fares were shelved. Any airline that could satisfy the Federal Aviation Administration that it was safe was free to fly anywhere in America at a fare of its choosing.

With the brakes off, Southwest could have expanded dramatically, bought big planes and started flying them coast to coast. Certainly Howard Putnam, with his background with America's biggest airline, had the know-how. Instead, the new boss stayed focused on Southwest's original proposition. And he also wrote the Southwest Airlines vision statement in 1978. Putnam calls those 52 words 'the most important achievement of my tenure': 'The mission of Southwest Airlines is to provide safe and comfortable air transportation in commuter and short-haul markets, from close-in airports, at prices competitive with automobiles and buses, and to involve customers and employees in the product and the process, making the airline a fun, profitable, and quality experience for all.'

The airline slowly took advantage of the freedom to fly to other states. 'The first interstate route we picked was Dallas Love Field to New Orleans,' says Putnam. The company put a single aircraft on the route, with seven round trips a day. 'Immediate success,' recalls Putnam. So New Orleans was chosen as the destination of the next 'interstate', this time from Houston. The first three days of April 1980 saw three destinations – Oklahoma City, Tulsa and Albuquerque – join the Southwest network. Most crucially, this

Plenty of people still recall Braniff with affection: Tom Barry, who lives in Oklahoma City, reminisces about the days when 'the Big Orange' flew to Dallas. 'They used to put a clock out front, and if your flight was ten minutes late you got your money back.' But time was running out for the Big Orange. With deregulation, the airline expanded frantically, and even persuaded British Airways to operate Concorde between Dallas and Washington DC on Braniff's behalf.

By 1981, the plan had begun to unravel. Braniff poached Howard Putnam and Southwest's chief financial officer, Phil Guthrie, to try to rescue the business. Putnam now says he discovered some Enron-style creative accounting too late: 'We would have not gone to Braniff had they shown us the correct financials.' Accountants were, he says, 'cooking the books'. Once he and Guthrie unscrambled the numbers, they discovered the airline had only 'ten days of cash, $175 million less than the numbers we had been shown. That is where I learned crisis management.' Nevertheless, the pair kept Braniff afloat for seven months. They then placed it in 'Chapter 11 bankruptcy', known in corporate jargon as 'the car-wash'. It gives an airline protection from creditors, allowing it to keep flying while the financial fundamentals undergo surgery. 'We then had had enough "character building" and left the industry for other things.'

small airline was the first carrier to order the Boeing 737-300, which later became the biggest-selling aircraft ever.

'We did it with a total team of five people, part-time, doing the research and analysis,' says Putnam. 'A one-billion-dollar order was very big for a little airline.' The airline's first wholly owned Boeing was named Rollin W. King, after the man who dreamed up Southwest. Even so, Southwest was still a small regional airline operating in its home base of Texas and the southern states. It had a much lower profile than Braniff, the other Dallas-born airline, which had recently launched a flagship route from its home town to London Gatwick featuring a bright orange jumbo jet. Howard Putnam quit Southwest to move across town to Braniff in 1981.

Almost as soon as Herb Kelleher reacquired the titles of president and chief executive of Southwest, life became tougher for US airlines. America's air-traffic controllers went on strike.

They were promptly fired en masse by President Reagan, who replaced them with an assortment of military controllers, managers and retired staff. While new controllers were being trained, airlines were ordered to reduce their flights. Southwest's cautious expansion, and its conservative mission statement, meant it stayed in profit while others lost small fortunes. The following year, Southwest expanded to Los Angeles, San Diego, Las Vegas and Phoenix – cities that are now among the airline's most lucrative routes. It also started flying into San Francisco, but Jim Parker cut the Californian city from the Southwest network in 2001 because of congestion and unreliable weather. 'Our airplanes could spend four or five hours on the ramp there,' the chief executive says, 'when the fog comes in on the single runway. It was getting kinda embarrassing explaining to passengers at Albuquerque who were waiting four hours for a flight to Dallas that their aircraft was still in San Francisco.'

So far, Southwest was living up to its name – flying in the South, and the West, of the US. Some said the model could not work elsewhere in America, says Parker. 'We didn't understand that. We didn't think that people on the East Coast were from Mars. We thought that they would like the same things that people in Texas like, which is: low fares, good value, good service, and friendly, courteous people to help them.' Southwest moved east to Florida and north to the Midwest, both lucrative markets. As the airline's name and fame spread, local dignitaries were courting Southwest. Each year the airline is approached by more than a hundred cities asking if Southwest will start flying there. But in 2002 and the first half of 2003, no new cities were added to the network; opening a new destination costs money, and Jim Parker believed it was not a wise move when 'The revenue environment is just very weak, there are fewer people flying and those who are flying are looking for bargains.' There is growth, but it is 'joining the dots', linking city pairs that hitherto have had no non-stop connection.

Those 'friendly, courteous people' proved to be Parker's nemesis. Airlines are exceptionally susceptible to strikes. Being highly complex organisms, the failure of one part of the operation can quickly bring activity to a halt – as British Airways found when small groups of workers at Heathrow shut down flights in the summers of 2003, 2004 and 2005. Labour relations at Southwest had almost always been friendly and courteous, but as the fortunes of the industry improved in the couple of years after 11

September 2001, crews' demands increased. Jim Parker's negotiating style was deemed to be too confrontational, and Herb
Kelleher replaced him in the pay talks.

One highly significant development did take place under
Parker's reign: Southwest's first transcontinental, coast-to-coast
flights, linking Baltimore–Washington International on the East
Coast with Los Angeles and San José in California. When Howard
Putnam wrote the vision statement in 1978, it included the term
'short-haul'. Partly that was because the 737's range was strictly
limited – nowadays Boeing's biggest seller can cross the Atlantic
without refuelling. The next-but-one chief executive, Jim Parker,
believed coast-to-coast could work within the Southwest business
model. He drew the line, though, at international flights: 'We feel
like we know how to fly domestically, point to point, efficiently,
and better than anybody else.'

Southwest could take advantage of its relative health to expand
beyond the continental US; the new Boeings make Juneau and
Anchorage, the two most attractive cities in Alaska, accessible
from Southwest's Pacific coast cities. The airline's growing
strength in the north-eastern US puts it temptingly close to
Montreal, Toronto and Ottawa. And south of the border, the
booming Mexican economy makes a city like Monterrey an
obvious target for any Texas airline. Ryanair, easyJet and –
latterly – JetBlue have demonstrated that the Southwest concept
can work internationally. But the Southwest line is that there are
still so many unserved cities and routes in the US that it need not
deviate from its master plan.

Many dots on the network are still to be joined, and many more
cities clamour for Southwest services. 'When we go into a market,
fares go down and traffic goes up,' says marketing director Rob
Brown. He cites the example of the base that opened in Providence,
Rhode Island, in 1996. 'One year later, between Providence and
Baltimore, fares had decreased by 74 per cent, and traffic had gone
up by 790 per cent. That's the "Southwest Effect".' On the West
Coast, Southwest started a route from Burbank, north of Los
Angeles, to Oakland, serving the San Francisco Bay Area. Before it
opened the link, the route was not in the top 250 markets in the US.
It is now one of America's 25 busiest routes.

The travel industry is littered with case studies where a pioneering
company is upstaged by a rival firm that can emulate some of the
business model but learn from the first mover's mistakes. The UK

aircraft industry brought out the first civil jet, the Comet, but it was soon eclipsed by a bigger, safer aircraft, the Boeing 707. Laker Airways pioneered cheap fares across the Atlantic, but Virgin Atlantic succeeded where Laker's Skytrain failed.

Inevitably, Southwest has attracted imitators who believe they can emulate, or even improve upon, the original plan. United, US Airways and Continental all tried to set up low-cost subsidiaries, with 'Shuttle by United', 'Metrojet' and 'Continental Lite' respectively. But all failed. Delta launched its no-frills offshoot, Song, in 2003; Delta's then-president, Fred Reid, said he was confident costs could be contained. Within two years the Song concept had been abandoned, while Reid had left to head up Virgin America – which has yet to take to the skies. American Airlines, the biggest carrier in the world, has never tried the concept of a no-frills offshoot – for good reason, says Henry Joyner, the airline's senior vice-president for planning. 'There's not enough benefit to justify the difference that you make, treating one group of customers in a different way from others. Without significant cost-savings, you just cause brand confusion.' American Airlines and Southwest have one common interest: the former publishes the latter's in-flight magazine, *Spirit*, a relationship that makes money for both companies.

United has recently re-joined the fray, with its Ted subsidiary seeking to avoid the mistakes of Shuttle by United. Plenty of fresh start-ups have tried to mine the same rich seam as Southwest. 'There've been a lot of people who've said "we're going to be Southwest with improvements"', says Jim Parker, who lists a few: 'We're going to have first class seats, or we're going to have more seats in the aeroplane or we're going to have hot meals or we're going to charge for peanuts. We're flattered by the attention.' Sir Rod Eddington, former chief executive of British Airways, concurs: 'Herb wrote the book, literally, and I don't think it's any surprise that the most successful no-frills companies follow the game plan. And when they stop following it and start to diversify, they get into trouble.' Upstarts that have come and gone include Kiwi, Air South, Lone Star and Western Pacific.

One reason why attempts to emulate Southwest's achievements have rarely succeeded is the difficulty in mimicking the company's morale. When Southwest staff hear the word 'culture', they reach out for one another. There is no compelling need for gate C6 at Phoenix airport to have a collage of photographs showing the celebrations at the Southwest Airlines Christmas party – except that the airline considers its corporate culture to be as important as its planes. 'Our people transformed an idea into a legend,' wrote Colleen Barrett in the wake of 11 September. 'That legend will continue to grow only so long as it is nourished – by our people's indomitable spirit, boundless energy, immense goodwill, and burning desire to succeed. Our thanks – and our love – to the people of Southwest Airlines for creating a marvelous family and a wondrous airline.'

Besides all of the above, the wondrous airline's growth has also partly been achieved by acquisition. Southwest has at times bought up entire airlines. But its smartest expansion move took place in 1990: the great gate heist at Chicago's Midway airport. Midway used to be the busiest airport in the world, until the day when O'Hare opened on the far side of Chicago. Midway stayed open, and an airline called Midway Airlines began life there. In November 1990, rumours were circulating about the carrier's poor financial health. A Southwest team was despatched to Chicago. Because time was imperative, they had to fly non-stop from Dallas-Fort Worth, not Love Field – the extraordinary Wright Amendment then, as now, forbids direct flight from Love to Chicago. The airport management was desperate to avoid losing around half its passengers, and was prepared to hand over the airline's gates to a newcomer. Southwest thus negotiated an instant stronghold in America's third-largest city, giving it an instant, dominant position at Chicago's most convenient airport.

At the start of the 90s, business people from Europe started beating a path to Southwest's door – led by Ryanair's trouble-shooter, Michael O'Leary. The man who was trying to turn around a failing airline was amazed by Herb Kelleher's vision. 'What took real brains and real balls,' says O'Leary, 'was to say "We can charge $10 a seat and still make money."'

Stelios was not far behind. 'All you had to do was compare what people paid in the US relative to what people paid in the UK and Europe,' says Stelios. When the easyJet founder saw what Southwest had achieved and what European passengers were paying, he said to himself, 'There must be an opportunity here, someone must be able to do better than this – offer low fares and maybe make some money in the process.'

Virgin Blue and Virgin Express chairman Sir Richard Branson got to know Kelleher well, over some legendary lunchtimes: 'At about six o'clock in the evening, after a six-hour lunch, I remember thinking, "If anyone walks through this door and sees two airline

THE AIRLINE OF JESUS CHRIST OF LATTER-DAY SAINTS?

There are two reasons for one airline to buy up another. One is to achieve faster-than-organic growth; the second is to neutralise a rival. Most takeovers are a mixture of both.

In its history, Southwest has bought two airlines. In 1985, it acquired Transtar, which was what Lamar Muse's venture, Muse Air, had become. Then in 1993 it bought Morris Air, based in Salt Lake City – home of the Church of Jesus Christ of Latter-Day Saints, better known as the Mormons.

This operation had been started by a travel agent named Morris, who was appalled by the high fares that Delta and Western (now part of United) were charging to fly from Utah's largest city. The charters proved popular, so a young local businessman named David Neeleman was brought in to mastermind a scheduled operation.

Southwest was impressed by his success, concerned by the threat Morris Air posed to its expansion plans and attracted by the geographical cover that acquiring the airline could bring. So it made an offer Morris chose not to refuse.

'It gave them the Northwest, it gave them markets they wanted to be in,' Neeleman now says. 'One of the things they got that I'm not sure they appreciate: they also got the ticketless travel technology which has really helped them.' And Southwest also got Neeleman himself, though he lasted only six acrimonious months in Texas.

'There was a lot of people who thought I was there to take over Herb's job. It wasn't a pleasant time.' He left Dallas with a big pay-off but a five-year 'non-compete' clause that prevented him from working for, or starting up, another US airline.

There was nothing in the severance deal about developing software for airlines, so Neeleman called his former information technology specialist at Morris Air, and spent the next few years developing the 'Open Skies' software that most no-frills airlines now rely on. The computer giant Hewlett Packard bought Neeleman out ('It's one business I wish I hadn't sold') and he headed north across the 49th Parallel to work on the start-up of Canada's first no-frills airline, WestJet. 'His track record got their funding,' says a JetBlue insider.

When the 'non-compete' expired in 1998, Neeleman was free to start another US-based airline. So he turned to the same investors, many of them fellow Mormons, who had backed the rise of Morris Air. There was one additional face around the table: Richard Branson, chairman of Virgin Atlantic. But the rules that prevent a non-US citizen from owning an American carrier meant Branson could not own a controlling stake in the venture. 'Richard had the opportunity to do this and declined,' says Neeleman. 'I think he regrets it now. His people are all now our people.' He poached three key marketing executives from Virgin Atlantic. Branson's place was taken by the billionaire financier George Soros.

The trouble with starting up a low-cost airline in America is that Southwest dominates the market. But Neeleman planned to base 'New Air' – the airline's working title – in New York. Not only is this the biggest aviation market in the US, it is also one that Southwest has always studiously avoided on the grounds that congestion would defeat its low-cost model. Several airlines, such as Kiwi and Tower Air, had tried the no-frills route of flying old aircraft as relentlessly as possible, but none had succeeded.

The New York base that Neeleman chose was JFK, which many people regard – incorrectly – as America's leading airport. In fact, as Neeleman is fond of saying, 'You could go bowling most of the time on the runways at Kennedy': outside the peak hours for international flights, 3–8 p.m., there were no slot constraints on the airport.

Neeleman took decisions that went against the Southwest model. First, every passenger was to get at-seat live television. Next, those seats would be assigned at check-in, and leather-covered. And they would be on Airbus A320 aircraft: 'It's clearly a superior aircraft,' says Neeleman, 'for the pilots, the passengers and costs.' He calls the decision a 'poison pill' that meant Southwest would never bid for JetBlue.

The first flight was from JFK to Fort Lauderdale on 11 February 2000. The network rapidly expanded to four more Florida destinations, three cities in upstate New York, Oakland (the closest no-frills airlines get to San Francisco) and Salt Lake City. Crucially, JetBlue then opened a base in Long Beach, close to Los Angeles and in prime Southwest territory. Close, says Jim Parker, CEO of Southwest, but no cigar: 'We don't compete on an airport-to-airport basis anywhere with JetBlue at the present time, and I don't really envisage that changing in the near future. I think they have done a good job; I have got a lot of respect for the people at JetBlue. There's no reason why they should not be successful.' Not everyone agrees. Gordon Bethune, CEO of New York's 'home-town airline', Continental, disagrees. He said in 2002, 'The odds of JetBlue having long-term success are remote.' But Neeleman believes his Mormon faith will help JetBlue become an outstanding success. 'My faith helps me really appreciate people, and the true value of the human spirit. People tend to work harder for me.'

Neeleman is no slouch himself. Even though he has made more than enough money out of aviation to live comfortably for the rest of his life, he now sees JetBlue as a personal mission: 'We're in for a cause. I want to make this the best airline ever.'

owners puffing and drinking away, they'll suddenly be flying on someone else's airline." '

Not everyone joins the chorus of approval. Sir Freddie Laker believes Southwest is playing into the hands of its bigger rivals. 'These big boys love Southwest,' he says. 'Whenever someone says, "Your fares are too high" or "You're dominating the market", they just turn round and say "How can we be uncompetitive when Southwest are there?" '

'We know that, given half a chance, our competitors would combine together and try and destroy Southwest and everything we stand for,' counters Southwest's former chief executive, Jim Parker. 'All the old hub and spoke carriers combined have in common is the fact that they would love to see Southwest and the Southwest business model disappear. So we're constantly vigilant, and have our defences up at all times.'

As Southwest moves into middle age, its biggest rival, in every sense, is American Airlines – the world's largest carrier. Henry Joyner, American Airlines' senior vice president responsible for planning, says, 'We've got a longer history than anyone in competing with the biggest, most successful low-cost operator in the world.' Continental, based in Houston, and a competitor since Southwest's earliest days might disagree with that, but probably not Joyner's assertion that, 'While there is a price difference, there is also a product difference. People make trade-offs in terms of service and convenience to get that low fare.' But American Airlines has been finding the financial going very tough, while second-placed United Airlines was in Chapter 11 bankruptcy.

'We still are the underdog, make no mistake about it,' says Jim Parker. 'We still are small in relation to our competitors.' He sees an external threat, too, from high taxation: 'We are more taxed than the cigarette or liquor industry, and I don't think you ought to have to pay a sin-tax to fly an airline; it shouldn't be a sin to fly.'

From the executive offices on the top floor of Southwest's HQ, the view across the runway of Love Field invokes a sense of flying in the 50s: a clean, stylish and simple terminal. Where it diverges from the 50s is that planes don't crash like they used to.

'Along with peanut wrappers, snot rags and used diapers, you will find this safety information card in the pocket in front of you,' says flight attendant Duane Redmond. For almost the first thirty years of Southwest's history, the familiar plastic card was a superfluous document. But on 3 May 2001, Southwest passengers travelling from Las Vegas to Burbank went rather further than they were expecting. Flight 1455 overshot the runway. The Boeing 737 ploughed through the perimeter fence and ended up at a gas station on the adjacent highway. For the first time in its history Southwest 'totalled' an aircraft. Remarkably, none of the 142 people on board, nor anyone on the ground, was hurt; the two pilots were sacked six weeks later. As with Virgin Atlantic's most serious incident, when the undercarriage on an Airbus approaching Heathrow failed to open fully, Southwest demonstrated the art of crashing painlessly. But flight number 1455 was 'retired', a practice normally associated with fatal crashes, and the incident tainted the big party that had been scheduled for six weeks later.

On 18 June 2001, the airline – and Kelleher – celebrated thirty years of operation. The following day, Kelleher stepped down as president and CEO, passing on these titles to his ever-faithful right-hand woman, Colleen Barrett, and the former lawyer, Jim Parker, respectively. Kelleher remains as chairman and, according to Ryanair's Michael O'Leary, 'he'll still have a profound influence.'

MALICE IN DALLAS

Even in Texas, arm-wrestling is rarely employed to solve legal disputes. But in March 1992, Herb Kelleher used the sport to settle a trademark dispute. Kelleher turned a potentially bitter and expensive wrangle into a publicity stunt: the contest billed as 'Malice in Dallas'.

At issue was the right to use the phrase 'plane smart'. A small South Carolina facilities company, Stevens Aviation, had been using the slogan since the early 70s. It objected when Southwest started describing people who flew on the airline as 'just plane smart'. Scenting an opportunity, Kelleher and his counterpart, the younger and fitter Kurt Herwald of Stevens Aviation, decided to settle the issue by arm-wrestling. They hired the Sportatorium Arena in Dallas, packed it with staff from both companies and invited in the national TV networks.

In the manner of great heavyweight tussles, they monopolised the news in the days leading up to the event, with stories such as Kelleher's tough training regime of cigarettes and Wild Turkey whiskey.

The bout was over in less than a minute, with the younger man winning easily. But the pictures of 'Smokin' Herb' being carried out on a stretcher, saying, 'I don't care what you say about me, just remember my name,' were the ones that grabbed editors' attention. Afterwards, it transpired that both parties agreed they should share the 'plane smart' slogan anyway.

Kelleher's successors need all the help they can get. 'Wallet got jetlag?' enquires a billboard on Dwight's return journey from Southwest's headquarters to Love Field, before recommending a solution: 'Greyhound.com'. The Dallas-based bus company that transported generations of Americans is fighting back against the airline that pinched millions of its passengers.

Back at the airport, the evening rush is beginning, with flights shuttling to Houston and San Antonio every half hour. The souvenir shop does a nice line in T-shirts, including one reading, 'I'm drunk and I can't find my horse'.

I've touched not a drop of Jack Daniel's or Wild Turkey, and I can find my wallet. As an experiment, I feed a dollar into an

WRIGHT WAS WRONG

One obvious benefit that Southwest offers over its rivals, says marketing director Rob Brown, is access to small airports with 'Close proximity to downtown, to provide our customers with a quick and easy airport experience.' As everyone from the Kennedys to the Dixie Chicks have discovered, Love Field is handy for downtown Dallas; the airport is hemmed into a few square miles of suburbia, eight miles north-west of the city centre.

By 1964, it was clear that demand for air travel was outstripping what Love Field could provide. The city fathers were ordered by the Civil Aeronautics Board to team up with Fort Worth, thirty miles west, with which Dallas had always had an uneasy relationship. They were told to develop an entirely new airport midway between them. By the time it opened in 1974, Dallas-Fort Worth airport – abbreviated by everyone to DFW – was the biggest in the world in terms of area, occupying a patch of north Texas the size of Manhattan. Initially, travellers, meeters and greeters were confused by the two, as the gynaecologist-turned-Country-star Hank Wangford noted in his song 'I waited for you at DFW but you must have been in Love'.

The plan had been for all the airlines to vacate Love Field in favour of DFW, even though Love was much easier to reach from downtown Dallas. Southwest shifted its operations there, but concluded passengers were getting a worse service, and demanded to be able to return. In yet another legal battle, Kelleher managed to argue Southwest's case for being allowed to stay at its home base, but at what was to prove an extraordinary cost. A year after President Jimmy Carter deregulated aviation, a law was passed that prevented Southwest flying people from its home base to anywhere beyond Texas and the states that immediately adjoin it.

Every day, thousands of travellers are inconvenienced by the Dallas Love Field section of the International Air Transportation Competition Act of 1979. It is better known as the Wright Amendment, after the Fort Worth congressman who devised the rule.

Like many Fort Worth citizens, Jim Wright disliked and distrusted the bigger city to the east. He took the opportunity of his position as Speaker of the House of Representatives to push a law through Congress that comprises a shameless piece of protectionism for DFW. The Wright Amendment prohibits airlines with aircraft of 57 seats or more flying people between Dallas Love Field and any point beyond Texas, Louisiana, Arkansas, Oklahoma, and New Mexico. The law was weakened a little by the 1997 Shelby Amendment, which added three states to the list: Alabama, Kansas and Mississippi. But the rule is still like banning flights longer than ninety minutes from Luton.

Southwest cannot even hint at the possibility that a traveller could transfer at, say, Albuquerque or New Orleans to reach other destinations.

Today, it is my turn to be a victim of Congressman Wright's rule. For a simple journey from Kansas City to Dallas, I have to buy two separate tickets. (Despite its name, Kansas City is in the state of Missouri.) At the intervening stop, Oklahoma City, I have to collect my bag and line up again to check in. That is not because Southwest takes the easyJet and Ryanair view of connecting flights (bluntly stated, 'We don't offer them'). It is because, in the twenty-first century, an absurd piece of federal legislation still interferes with free consumer choice, making air travel tougher and more expensive than it needs to be. One consequence is to reduce the number of tourists to North Texas – which may not have been what Jim Wright intended.

automatic change machine. It regurgitates a nickel, two dimes and three quarters – $1-worth of change. But for a time in 1974, I would have received $1.05 in change. Kelleher discovered that the machines at the newly opened Dallas-Fort Worth airport delivered only 95 cents. He ordered the Love Field machines to be programmed to pay out $1.05, and made sure the media knew all about it. Some passengers took advantage (you could tell which ones they were when they tried to walk through the metal detector), but the exercise was much cheaper than advertising.

Turning $1 into $1.05, for the benefit of the public – and his staff, and himself – is pure Kelleher. Barbara Cassani, who created Go on the Southwest model, believes Kelleher's greatest achievement is in creating strong bonds with staff and customers. 'A good relationship with your people and making a lot of money go together. I think good relationships with your people and good relationships with your customers go together. It is a very virtuous relationship.'

Jim Parker, who steered the airline through what he called 'the most challenging time we have seen in the entire history of the airline industry,' says Southwest is about far more than cheap tricks: 'Success does not arise from one single thing you do. It is built as a result of things day by day throughout the history of a company. Certainly failure can be caused by one cataclysmic mistake, but success is the result of consistently doing the basic things; in this business, if you can do the basic things well – flying on time, safely, delivering people's bags, where they're going, when they get there, treating them with courtesy and respect – you have outdone the competition. We don't have hot meals, we don't have lounges in the airports, first-class service, seat assignments, boarding passes that you get weeks in advance, so we have to make up for that by just focusing on basic simple, human things. That's where Southwest has its competitive advantage: we do the basic, simple things better than anybody else.'

And his company also does songs better, too, as the passengers aboard flight 422 are about to discover, as Duane Redmond welcomes them to Kansas City and thanks them for flying Southwest.

We love you and you love us,
We're so much faster than the bus,
So come back soon for our hospitality,
If you'd married one of us you could have flown for free.

4. SKYTRAIN: POWER TO THE PEOPLE

It never occurred to them that there was a fourth class out there called the human race who just want to fly at the lowest fare

Sir Freddie Laker

Even twenty years after the fall of his airline he still remains bitter. Really, I can't blame him

Stephen Bath, managing director of Bath Travel
and Former President of ABTA

LAKER AIRWAYS FLIGHT 1: FORT LAUDERDALE, FLORIDA–FREEPORT, GRAND BAHAMA

Tens of millions of people have flown on aircraft bearing the name Laker Airways. Few of them realise that Freddie Laker's first flights were shuttles between the British-controlled fragments of post-war Germany. The man who was to bring no-frills flying to the North Atlantic cut his teeth carrying coals and clothes across East Germany as part of the Berlin Airlift.

At the end of the Second World War, after Hitler killed himself amid the ruins of Berlin, the remains of the Third Reich were carved up by the Allied powers. Britain, France, the US and the Soviet Union each received a tranche of German territory. The first three were later amalgamated to form the Federal Republic, better known as West Germany, while the USSR's chunk became the German Democratic Republic, at least in name. Berlin was a special case because of its political and propaganda significance.

The former capital lay far to the east, in the middle of the Soviet sector. At the Yalta talks in 1945 that decided the way that post-Nazi Europe should be divided, the Allies insisted that the victorious powers should all have a share of Berlin. So the British, the French, the Americans and the Soviet Union were each awarded a chunk of the capital. Checkpoint Charlie was established as the crossing point between the American and Soviet zones.

One problem: how to keep the military and civilian populations of the isolated Allied sectors supplied? The Potsdam conference, where the precise boundaries were drawn, specified rail, road and air corridors that cut through Soviet East Germany. West Berliners, and anyone who wanted to supply their needs, could travel between the Allied zone and Berlin only along these narrow passages. In 1948, as Cold War tension mounted, Moscow unilaterally blockaded the surface corridors. West Berlin became a city under siege. Blockading the autobahnen and railways was one thing, but short of shooting down Western aircraft, possibly triggering a Third World War, the USSR could do nothing to seal the air corridors. So for the next year, a constant shuttle of flights kept the supply lines open. Many wartime aircraft were pressed into service to fly thousands of missions of mercy – and money making.

A large number of the planes were owned and operated by a young Freddie Laker. Vladimir Raitz calls Laker a 'freebooter'. 'Everything that could fly was used,' he recalls. At the time, Raitz was a journalist for Reuters. Later he became a customer, and sometimes competitor, of Laker.

The Berlin Airlift provided Laker with a great deal of experience and money. He would need plenty of both when trying to establish the right to offer low-cost flying between the UK and US. He succeeded, for a while. Which is why, 53 years after the missions began, I found myself waiting in room 107 of the Clay Hotel.

A cloud the same fierce grey as the underside of the British Airways jet that brought me here hovered low over Miami Beach, occasionally dousing the few tourists foolish enough to step out on to Washington Avenue. The rain made the pastel pinks and yellows, greens and blues of the art deco district of South Beach look forlorn. South Beach, like the world of aviation, was very different when I first flew to Florida's largest city in 1981. Like millions of transatlantic travellers, I arrived on the Laker Skytrain, a no-frills service that transformed travel across the North Atlantic.

'All the people that I said would turn up, when I formulated the plan in 1971, are here,' Laker said on the day Skytrain first took off from Gatwick. 'Students, old age pensioners, people from all over Europe, Americans wanting to go home, all the low-income earners who need to travel instantly and for an undetermined amount of time.' His words presage those of today's no-frills entrepreneurs: 'There will be a seat for everyone, all through the winter,' he insisted. 'This is geared, and built, for the instant traveller. We've got 345 empty seats every day.' The seats were just like those of the other airlines, and were located aboard a big, safe plane. The flights took the same time as those of his more familiar rivals: British Airways, Pan Am and TWA. They, too, offered some low fares. But the difference with Skytrain was that Laker's lowest fares were also his highest fares. 'Look: I've got to give you a better deal,' Laker said in one advertisement. 'I've got my name on every plane.' He reinvented air travel – cutting frills, slashing costs and passing on the savings – in a way that still benefits a generation of travellers who never knew Skytrain, through lower fares between the UK and US. At the Clay Hotel, a few British backpackers were staying; they reached Florida for around £200 return. So low a fare was achievable only because, a quarter-century earlier, Freddie Laker had created true competition across the Atlantic.

The hotel's exterior projects a fine example of Mediterranean Revival in the self-styled Spanish Village; inside, it is a no-frills sort of place. Room 107 has a 'semi-private bath', which means not very private at all. A connecting door with a bolt on either side leads to a bathroom that I shared with the occupants of Room 109 (who, to judge by their enthusiastic performance the previous night, were a lively couple). The bolts have to be opened and closed in the right combination to avoid scenes worthy of a French farce. But I felt less a character in *Whoops! There go my trousers*, and more like something miserable by Beckett or Kafka about the futility of life, and the fatuity of communication. I had pressed every possible combination of numbers on the telephone keypad, but I still could not get beyond the automated exchange for Laker Airways and speak to a human being.

The airline serves the needs of gamblers heading for the island of Grand Bahama. Its headquarters are in Fort Lauderdale, thirty miles north along Highway 1 from the noisily romantic couple in

Room 109 of the Clay Hotel. For around $300, the company flies weekenders from Fort Lauderdale to the island on a Saturday morning. They get a night in a ritzy resort, and are flown back to Florida on Sunday afternoon, older, wiser and usually poorer than they were when they arrived. To fly on Laker Airways these days, you have to start from Fort Lauderdale or Grand Bahama, which is where Sir Freddie respectively works and lives these days. He is a man I had to meet.

When I arrived at Miami airport a few days earlier, I called Sir Freddie Laker's assistant, Irma, from the terminal. 'I'm away from my desk right now . . .' I let her voicemail know where I would be staying.

At an Internet cafe on the corner of Washington and 15th Street, I prepared and faxed a reasonably smart-looking document asking respectfully for an interview. That was twenty hours, five inches of rain and many phone calls ago – all of them outgoing.

Outside, it has stopped raining; inside, it has never started ringing. I call Irma again, but she is still away from her desk right now. I leave a message of the kind that implores any kind of news, good or bad. Maybe Irma has responded to the fax I sent with a fax of her own? I plod down to the Internet cafe to be met with shrugs.

Friday afternoon is nearly over, and things are going unhelpfully badly. Tomorrow, I will have to fly to Freeport, Grand Bahama, on Sir Freddie's own airline, to see if I can track him down. By now I know one of the automated options offered when you call his airline's flight reservations. It refers callers to a toll-free number. I dial 1 800 432 2294, carefully. 'Thank you for calling Grand Bahama Vacations.' I wait for an operator, the first real person to whom I have spoken by telephone all day. I explain I want to fly next morning to Grand Bahama. Given the uncertainty of my mission, I am a little reluctant to pump another few hundred dollars into this venture for the half-hour hop to the island and a night in a hotel. So early on I ask about costs.

'Are you a regular player, Mr Simon?' she asks after taking my name. When someone asks a question like that, you do not want to be thought an amateur. 'Er, yes, but I've never played in Grand Bahama before,' then add as an afterthought, 'Vegas, mostly.' I had once lost some cash while filming in the city.

'Mr Simon, I'm going to transfer you to Sal, the Director of Players.'

As Sal comes on the line, I realise that an impromptu interview is about to begin.

'Are you a serious player?'

'Pretty serious,' I fibbed.

'That's good, because we're going through renovations and we need a lot of cash,' he laughs. 'What do you play?'

'Blackjack.' I know enough about the uncharitable probabilities of gambling to be aware that blackjack is a favourite of proper gamblers. Amateurs believe the aim is to get cards totalling 21; professionals know that the sole purpose is to beat the dealer, who is constrained by some rules that mean the odds are only slightly stacked against an expert player with a steady nerve who adheres to a memorisable set of mathematical rules. In the long term, that means you lose money more slowly than at roulette or on the slot machines (or, indeed, the airline business). In the short term, there is a fair chance of getting ahead quite quickly. Casinos are happy for a player to make modest gains, in the expectation that he or she will blow it all in the end. So blackjack marks out a serious player and a reasonable prospect as a new customer.

'How much do you bet?'

'Twenty-five.' Another fib. But I recall that in Las Vegas the lowest stake for each hand is usually $5, and inflate that to come up with something that sounds respectable but not boastful.

'OK, the flights are free and the room is $85 double. Too bad there's only one of you. How much are you going to bring?' About $2,000, I lie. 'That's good,' he says, implying I had supplied the right sort of answers. 'Make sure everyone rates you properly,' he urges. 'On the tables, in the restaurant, anything you charge to your room.' The technique of 'rating' enables the casino to keep tabs on your spending, to find out who the high rollers are. They can then make sure that guests who are betting seriously are rewarded with 'comps' (free drinks, dinners, flights etc.) and are betting generously.

The last time I called a Laker airline to book a flight, I explained I wanted to fly to Miami. I was given the price, quoted my credit card number and was told to pick up the ticket from the desk at Gatwick. The only similarity with this transaction was the last bit, about picking it up at the airport. 'The flights are free.' Sal's words echo around the empty walls of room 107. Is this no-frills heaven? No. Sal has 'comped' me and expects a substantial pay-off to help with those builders' bills. While he transfers me to an assistant to make the booking, I wonder how big he and his friends are.

'I've got you booked at 9 a.m. tomorrow. Turn up at Fort Lauderdale airport, Terminal 4, two hours ahead, don't bring knives or scissors, you'll pay taxes of $43 going, $18 return.'

How, I wonder, do I get to the casino from the airport at Grand Bahama?

'They'll pick you up at the airport.'

The thought that Sal and his pals might be waiting in a stretched limousine to see the size of my wad haunts me for the rest of the day. I stare out of the window at the rain that is now bucketing down. A banner over the art deco Cameo cinema announces AMERICA WE STAND TOGETHER & UNITED. The *Miami Herald* tells the travelling public that, 'Troops in airports, stun guns for pilots are likely measures'.

Ten minutes before close of business for the weekend, I make one last call to Sir Freddie's office. When Irma herself answers I am so startled that I can barely speak. 'Didn't you get my messages?' she asks. 'I called a few times but there seems to be something wrong with the hotel switchboard. Sir Freddie will see you tomorrow morning in Grand Bahama.'

'Ft Lauderdale-Hollywood Int'l Airport wishes to express its deepest sympathy to families and friends of the victims of the attack on America'. The message flickers on and off opposite the sign announcing that Spirit Airlines' flight to New York has been cancelled. A Mike Peters cartoon in the *South Florida Sun-Sentinel* shows a smiling check-in woman asking 'Thank you for flying today. Do you have reservations?' and a fearful passenger answering, 'Yes, but I'm still going.'

Shortly before 7 a.m., with a tropical storm brewing outside, I approach the counter with the familiar red and black logo spelling out the name of Laker Airways.

'We don't have anyone of that name, sir. When did you make the reservation?' Eventually we find me under Mr Calder Simon, with my date of birth shown as 11:11:11. Not even Sir Freddie is that old.

Frederick Alfred Laker was born in Canterbury on 6 August 1922. He enjoyed a chequered career in aviation before launching the innovation he will be remembered for: the no-frills Skytrain service across the Atlantic that began in 1977. 'If you fly round trip to London on one of the high-priced airlines,' he told the US public, 'it can cost you a bundle. But if you take a Laker to London round trip you can save from 10 to 50 per cent off regular economy fares.' Skytrain got off the ground when Laker was a relatively young 55. Five years later the no-frills airline went bust, leaving hundreds of staff out of work and thousands of passengers stranded on both sides of the Atlantic.

Undeterred, in the 90s Laker – then aged 75 – started up another link between Fort Lauderdale airport and Gatwick, offering a luxury economy class across the Atlantic. 'He tried again,' says Sir Richard Branson, 'but he didn't get it right second time round.'

But the spirited Sir Freddie, now an octogenarian, still flies, frequently, on his own airline between Fort Lauderdale and Grand Bahama. Before I can follow, a complicated transaction is required where I hand over $43 for the taxes and sign a form headed 'Rated Player Transfer and Receipt Coupon'. A proper gambler would be delighted to be thus recognised; I find it menacing. A 'goody pack' provided with the ticket informs me I have missed Harold Melvin's Blue Notes by several weeks, but that I am in for a 2-for-1 Sports Day drinks special this evening. I feel slightly nauseous at the prospect, because it reminds me of my pact with Sal.

'Flight 1, Gate 1. Have a nice trip.'

The lounge is thinly populated. At 7.47 a.m., a Boeing 727 draws up at the gate. Twenty years after I first stepped aboard one of Freddie Laker's aircraft as a passenger on Skytrain, I look eagerly for the brash Laker Airways livery, the symbol of a great aviation survivor. Oh dear. This plane has Transmeridian Airlines written all over it. Does that mean the Laker magic has deserted Sir Freddie once again?

'Good morning, we're about to begin boarding Laker flight zero-one to Grand Bahama. Boarding all rows.' About forty people, around one third of the capacity of the jet, wander towards the gate. Five minutes early, the plane is pushed back, and flies through thick cloud to a wet, stormy and uninviting Grand Bahama island. Had this been a normal charter flight carrying sunseekers in search of an idyllic beach, we would have been disappointed. But gamblers, and interviewers, have different ambitions. As did the tall, tanned and smiling man waiting for me in the corner of the customs hall.

Freddie Laker is to aviation what Paul McCartney is to music. Sir Freddie, I say with sincerity, it is a pleasure to meet you.

'I left school when I was sixteen, because I wasn't very bright.'
East Kent in the 30s was not the most promising place or time in
which to grow up, but two events made Laker determined to fly.
'I had a flight in an aeroplane with Alan Cobham and his Flying
Circus – a five-bob flight around the airport. It was one of the
reasons I wanted to get into aviation.' The other was seeing a
Hindenburg balloon and a Handley Page biplane flying over his
home city of Canterbury. A painting of the scene is given pride of
place in his home on Grand Bahama's millionaires' row, Princess
Isle.

'I got a job at Short Brothers at Rochester.' This aircraft
manufacturer, which still makes parts of planes in Belfast, was
Britain's fraternal answer to Orville and Wilbur Wright. 'I had
two jobs in the first hour,' says Laker. 'One was sweeping the
floor, the other was getting the tea.' We are drinking coffee and
watching the rain from the terrace at the Casino Towers at
Bahamia, the resort that has a room booked in my name – and a
Director of Players named Sal. I keep this information quiet and
listen to a man who changed the world.

Laker was barely seventeen when the Second World War broke
out. His early attempts to serve were thwarted because he was
working for an aircraft manufacturer. 'I wanted to get into the
war, hopefully to fly, but every time I went along they said, "No,
we can't take you, you're in a reserved occupation." The
recruiting officer explained to me that it wasn't pilots they
wanted, it was aeroplanes. What point were the pilots without the
aeroplanes?'

The teenager saw a newspaper advertisement from the Air
Transport Auxiliary, which ferried aircraft around Britain, for
engineers. 'I went along and they were reasonably interested in
me, and asked me what I did now. "I'm working on the Stirling
bomber for Short Brothers." I wasn't the world's greatest aviator
with my one Flying Circus flight, but to cut a long story short, I
got in.'

When the Second World War ended in 1945, Freddie Laker was
23, a qualified pilot – and a survivor. His wartime experience
earned him a job at British European Airways (BEA), an airline
newly created by the incoming Labour government at the end of
the war: 'Mr Attlee got into power and nationalised all air
transport,' says Laker. BEA was based at Northolt airport in
Middlesex; anyone who has driven to or from London along the
A40 will have noticed this now-military airfield, whose runway

almost strays on to the road. BEA soon moved to the new airport at Heathrow, and 27 years later merged with BOAC to form British Airways. But Laker had left very much earlier.

'I stayed with them for three months, and said, "Well, I can't do this. It's impossible." Everything had been nationalised, and of course with a Conservative mother that didn't work very well.'

What about your father, I ask.

'My father was a disaster, a total disaster. He locked me in the coal cupboard, under the stairs, when I was five years old. He was so incompetent he couldn't even drive a truck; he had to be the lorry driver's mate. He ran off and left my mother. I only saw him once after that, during the war. I was in uniform at the time, and I was in a pub, and a person came up behind me, tapped me on the shoulder and said, "Aren't you going to buy me a beer, then?" I looked him straight in the face and said, "No." I didn't see him again. He died a long time ago. He's not part of my life.

'My mother was a different thing altogether. She was absolutely out of this world. A wonderful lady. She fell in love with a fellow. His name was William James Allin, and he was such a wonderful fellow that he changed his name to Laker. Now that's a man and a half. That was a real father.'

Laker is a father figure to many of the Bahamians we encounter. Our conversation is repeatedly interrupted. Every one of the passing staff greets 'Mr Laker' ('Sir Freddie' is the correct form, but in the Bahamas that seems to carry familiarity too far). A holidaying Londoner wanders over and introduces himself as a happy Skytrain customer. The Laker legend is alive and well, as is the man – despite a prostate cancer scare fifteen years ago – and his mind.

After treating each person he encounters with grace and meticulous good manners, Laker returns to talk animatedly about the subject he knows best: his life in aviation.

In the post-war years, Britain's aviation industry was hurriedly changing gauge from a military to a civil footing. There was plenty of scope for an entrepreneur with fast footwork and good contacts to oil the wheels – and line his pockets in the process. 'I hold the record of buying three aeroplanes from BEA [owned by the government and run by the Air Ministry] and selling them to BOAC [ditto].' Freddie Laker bought almost any aviation surplus that the Ministry of Supply was offloading, selling scrap aluminium to saucepan makers and buying obsolete aircraft engines solely for the value contained in the platinum points on the spark plugs. But the making of Laker was the Berlin Airlift across the Cold War frontline.

When the Kremlin decided to seal the land corridors to the city in June 1948, closing Checkpoints Alpha and Bravo in the process, the West had three options. Of these, the unthinkable one was to do what the USSR hoped for, and abandon the city. Equally unpalatable, the Allies could launch a military strike, precipitating a conflict that could quickly escalate to atomic weapons and cause even more carnage than the Second World War. The third possibility was that Western aircraft could attempt to ferry in fuel, food and every other essential by air. It was a huge logistical and financial challenge, yet the only feasible course.

To sustain West Berlin, aircraft were needed to arrive in the city at the rate of one every two minutes. Initially, military transports were used, but quickly private operators had to be drafted in. Freddie Laker realised the Western Allies were prepared to spend heavily to protect their easternmost enclave. He leaned upon his trading skills to earn his share of the Cold War cake. 'I was buying brand new bombers, with two hours flying time on them, for £100 apiece. We painted them silver and put them on the Berlin Airlift.' Aviation Traders Limited, his first proper company, was based in Southend, but most of its aircraft shuttled between British bases in western Germany and Tegel airport in the British sector of Berlin. As the propaganda battle intensified, with the West outfoxing the USSR, Laker got rich. 'By any normal standards I was making an awful lot of money. But I didn't go off having a party. I started buying aircraft parts.'

Laker recognised that the bonanza could not last for ever. In the end, the Berlin Airlift continued for nearly a year before the Soviet Union relented and reopened the land corridors. Laker had planned for a soft landing once the earnings dried up. He continued to wheel and deal in a fertile environment in which civil aviation was increasing rapidly yet the UK government was still selling off valuable equipment at bargain prices. And then he went into the car ferry business.

At the time, taking a vehicle on the ferry between Dover and Calais was long and precarious. Each car was hoisted by crane into the hold of the ship. 'All these cars were getting damaged because they were swinging them over on chains,' says Laker. Besides denting vehicles that were, at the time, luxury goods, the journey took all day because of the painful slowness of winching each car on and off.

'I thought to myself that with a Bristol Freighter, updated, I could run a car ferry operation by air.' Laker bought what he calls a 'Bristol Frightener' from the Second World War hero Douglas Bader, then managing director of Shell Aviation. He adapted the aircraft to carry two cars and their occupants. The first passengers that a Laker airline flew were motorists, along with their vehicles, from Southend. Initially the air ferry served Calais and Ostend. Laker later added Rotterdam to the network, and converted a much larger DC-4 into the Carvair (short for 'Car-via-air'). 'We cut the nose off the DC-4 and put it up above the fuselage like a 747, and we could carry five cars and 22 passengers.' While loading, the aircraft looked faintly ridiculous, with a gaping hole where the nose cone and flight deck should be. Yet the idea of front-loaded freight was ahead of its time – the same concept led to the development of the Boeing 747. And it also enticed the travel-hungry middle classes to the Continent. Before giant roll-on, roll-off superferries every half-hour from Dover, and the Channel Tunnel, the smart route for anyone who wanted to take a motor car abroad was on an air ferry.

In the 50s, few British citizens could realistically expect to own a car, let alone fly it abroad. But many could dream of foreign travel. In 1958, the Queen opened the new terminal at Gatwick. The Sussex airport soon became the low-cost alternative to Heathrow. By then, many of the fragmented private enterprises of UK aviation – including a couple of Laker's companies – had consolidated, with Freddie at the helm. The resulting combine was the biggest independent rival to BEA and BOAC. The chosen name was British United Airways (BUA), which Laker says led to a 'terrible row' because of its inclusion of the word 'British'.

BUA built up a strong scheduled operation, including lucrative flights to the Libyan cities of Benghazi and Tripoli, as well as carrying charter passengers on behalf of tour operators like Vladimir Raitz's Horizon. Initially BUA operated only propeller aircraft, but Laker's airline became the launch customer for the 1-11. This was the new twin-jet being built by the British Aircraft Corporation as a late bid to rival the French Caravelle and the American DC-9. Being a launch customer means you can drive a better deal, but it also carries large risks from untried technology – as BOAC found with the accident-prone Comet. For a British jet aircraft, the 1-11 turned out to be quite a success; indeed, it would later underpin Ryanair's development as a no-frills operation.

Laker's career at BUA ended – and his own airline began – in tragic circumstances. The shine disappears from his eyes as he tells the story. By 1965, Laker was on an annual salary of £3,500 as managing director of BUA. This translates to £40,000 today – not a fortune for an airline boss, but enough for him to run a yacht, which he kept moored in Italy. By his first marriage, Laker had a son named Kevin. (He went to Wellingborough School with Philip Meeson, now chief executive of Jet2.) It would have been natural for Kevin to work for what had become the family firm. But he did not want to work for his father in BUA, saying, according to Freddie, 'I will always be in your shadow.' So Laker Senior proposed a joint venture into the rapidly expanding package holiday market. The plan was to buy some hotels, and to charter BUA to fly the passengers. But one day Freddie was aboard his yacht in Italy when he received a telephone call from Britain saying that Kevin had been involved in a road accident and was gravely ill in hospital.

'I got back, and went to see him, and I said, "Who is this?" and he said, "Oh, you're my Daddy". That's the last I heard from him. Then he died.'

The personal tragedy had immediate professional repercussions. 'Of course now there's no reason for me to leave BUA,' says Laker. But by now rumours were rife that his relations with the airline's chairman, Miles Wyatt, were strained, and that Laker was planning to set up his own operation. On the day Kevin was to be buried, he was called by Wyatt. 'He knew it was the funeral of my son, and he said, "Are you going, or are you staying?" And I said, "Miles, my kid's outside in a box. Please don't ask me that today. Let's talk about it tomorrow or the next day or something." He said, "I want to know now." I said, "Miles, if you want to know now, the answer is I'm going." And that was that. I'm out of BUA, and I thought, "I'm going to keep going." So I formed Laker.'

The company was not the package holiday operation he had originally envisaged for Kevin Laker. Instead, he established an airline that would prove to be a thorn in the side of BUA. Laker Airways began with a couple of leased Britannia propeller planes, but soon had the distinction of possessing Britain's first all-jet fleet, comprising three BAC 1-11s. The airline grew rapidly on the rising tide of holidaymakers keen to follow the path that Vladimir Raitz had pioneered to the Med. In an early move towards vertical integration – where the airline and tour operation are under common ownership – Laker picked up a couple of tour operators, Arrowsmith and Lord Brothers, which would later become Laker Holidays. But the most crucial move was to acquire a Boeing 707 and move into so-called 'affinity charters' across the Atlantic. These flights were the convoluted means by which, prior to 1977, ordinary people could fly the Atlantic without first robbing a bank.

The arcane rules of the International Air Transport Association (IATA) forbade any kind of discounting by scheduled or charter airlines. They did, though, permit cheap fares for bona fide groups of passengers on 'affinity charters'. And what comprised a bona fide group? 'Members of a club, which has been formed for a purpose other than air travel, who attended regular meetings.' There was one further condition: the booking must be made three months in advance. But like the other rules it was widely flouted. In practice, word-of-mouth recommendations and handwritten cards in newsagents' windows led prospective passengers to Gatwick. Early on the morning of the flight, they handed over cash in shady corners of the airport in return for a ticket which showed a date of issue three months earlier, and a membership card for some spurious society. This latter document was to be presented if IATA inspectors should show up and demand evidence of membership of a bona fide group. Inspections were by no means unknown. So to add to the illusion that everyone was a paid-up member, sometimes a lawyer with a Bible was on hand as part of the check-in procedure; the passenger had to swear their loyalty to the affinity group, and hope that God would overlook the mild exaggeration. Perhaps the concept of club membership inspired British Airways to call its premium business service 'Club World' a decade later.

One day in 1970, Freddie Laker received an urgent call from the duty office asking him to get to Gatwick immediately. Instead of the normal bustle that preceded the departure of an affinity charter, he was greeted by grief.

'The Civil Aviation Authority are interrogating every passenger and chucking old women off the aeroplanes,' he recalls with eyes ablaze – as though the event was yesterday, not half a lifetime ago.

When asked, 'Why are you going to New York?' one elderly woman answered, 'To see my son.' That confirmed to the officials that the affinity group rules were being flouted. About 25 people were unable to convince the inspectors that they were regular attendees at club meetings and were left behind. Besides the distress of each of the stranded passengers, the inspectors' haul spelled a large fine for Laker – and led directly to the creation of Skytrain. Freddie climbed on to a box in the terminal and started shouting, 'They will never do this to me again, no one's ever going to be chucked off my planes again, I'm going to fight.'

By now, the press had been tipped off that a story was developing at Gatwick. 'I got the best write-up ever known to man,' says Laker. After the Boeing had departed, with a couple of dozen empty seats, he went back to the office and hatched a new plan: 'Right. We are going to start a new system altogether. We are going to have a thing where people can get on and off aeroplanes when they like, how they like. They can eat the food or not eat the food, they can buy the ticket at the door and get on the aeroplane, just like when you want to go to Glasgow. The only thing you can't do is hand-strap. Just like a train – skytrain.'

Easier said than done. The seven years of legal battles on both sides of the Atlantic might have exhausted a less determined man. But Freddie Laker is endowed with profound self-belief.

'If he didn't have such an enormous ego he wouldn't have built the business that he did,' says Stephen Bath, managing director of Bath Travel and former president of the Association of British Travel Agents. 'So good luck to him.' Those seven years were spent finding a way through a bureaucratic jungle that had been judged impenetrable by everyone else. Airlines were emblems of national prestige, which governments felt they needed to protect by every means possible – starting with the stifling of competition. In both the UK and the US, Laker fought a series of legal battles to win the right to fly people cheaply across the Atlantic.

The media loved the no-frills chase, and the Skytrain struggle gripped Britain through most of the 70s. To illustrate that truth, Laker drives me through the downpour to his oceanfront house, where a collection of cartoons from national newspapers decorates the garage walls. The single-storey structure has touches of Mediterranean Revival about it. It is a beautiful new construction, set in ample grounds that yield only to the Atlantic Ocean. The motif that begins at the gates and continues through the ensemble is the heron, an elegant bird whose name was bestowed on a De Havilland aircraft. I am too polite to ask what the house cost, but according to the real-estate listings, the smallest lot on this exclusive peninsula starts at £500,000 – mansion not included.

One cartoon shows airline passengers shovelling coal. The caption reads 'What do you expect for £32?' This was the price originally quoted by Laker, but in the high-inflation 70s it increased quickly – as did Laker's legal bills. 'I fought, kicked, shouted at them day after day,' he recalls.

Initially, the Tory government saw BOAC and BEA as national treasures that could not be put at risk. The two jewels merged in 1972, a move that some long-serving staff still regard as a mistake. The Bermuda agreement prevailing at the time governed flights between the US and the UK. Pan Am and TWA (both now extinct) were allowed to fly the Atlantic, as was British Airways – which left room for another UK airline. In 1973, the Laker Skytrain was designated as a transatlantic carrier by the outgoing Conservative administration.

The Heath government lost the February 1974 election to Harold Wilson, who led a Labour party that was still a quarter-century away from embracing freedom of the skies. Laker found his entrepreneurial drive left him on the wrong side of the ideological fence. His adversary in the Department of Trade, Peter Shore, was implacably opposed to Skytrain. In 1975 Shore retracted Laker's authority to start transatlantic flights. Laker 'wriggled' an appointment to see the Secretary of State. 'He's got a couple of his minions there. And one of them was Bob Ayling.'

The man who was later to lead British Airways was, at the time, a government lawyer. Laker told Shore 'What you're doing is morally wrong. But that's a question for your conscience – I can't do anything about that. What I can tell you is that what you're doing is illegal. That is a different thing.' Laker says that Shore asked his advisers to comment. 'They both looked at him, and refused to look at me, and said "It's pure rubbish, Minister". So off we go, Peter Shore does his stuff, and there's a new appeal.'

Bob Ayling disputes this version of events. 'Freddie Laker is a great pioneer and it would be a nice story, but he's got the wrong man. I was advising on European Community law then. Aviation law came later for me.' Ayling says that, 'in all probability' he would have given the same advice. 'The issue was whether or not Peter Shore could de-designate Skytrain. He decided to do so. Freddie challenged the minister's decision. The ruling was upheld in the High Court. The Court of Appeal overruled the High Court and held that the Secretary of State had acted in excess of his power.'

Eventually, Peter Shore was moved to the Department of the Environment. His replacement at Transport was Edmund Dell. One of the new minister's first tasks, says Laker, was to call with his support: 'We're behind you 100 per cent.' There remained the problem of getting permission from the US. Pan Am and TWA fiercely opposed opening the market to further competition. Laker Airways was still flying tens of thousands of people across the Atlantic on affinity charters, but running the risk of the wrath of inspectors – particularly in the US. Like a serial poacher, Laker got to know the aviation gamekeepers well. 'They had this number one enforcement officer who called me and said, "Freddie, I'm going to fine you more than any airline has ever been fined – $102,000." I asked why $102,000, and he said that there had already been a fine of $100,000 and he was going to top it. So I said that I'd pay the fine on condition that I got a hearing for Skytrain.'

Laker maintains that he did not pay a fine of $102,000 – he bought a Skytrain hearing for $102,000. 'We got the hearing, and won.' In June 1978, President Carter gave permission for him to start flying.

As Herb Kelleher had found at Southwest, even when adversaries have no further legal recourse they can go to court to try to make life as uncomfortable as possible for the new competitor. One restriction they successfully demanded prevented passengers checking in at the airport. 'They said you can't check in the passengers at Kennedy. You've got to have a check-in facility that's at least five miles away. It actually turned out to be an asset.' Anyone who has ever visited New York's most prominent airport will appreciate the benefit of checking in away from the kerfuffle of Kennedy. Laker rented a large hall in the borough of Queens, and bussed passengers direct from the hall to the aircraft steps. On the British side, passengers were on the brink of having to check in on Hackney Marshes and fly from Stansted airport in Essex. But the government made an eleventh-hour climbdown and allowed Skytrain to fly from the Laker base at Gatwick – again, with the insistence that passengers were checked in away from the airport.

While at BUA, Laker had made lasting friends with executives in British Rail. They had come up with a prototype version of the Gatwick Express about twenty years before fast rail links to airports became fashionable. Thanks to his connections, Laker knew of a disused building at Victoria station in central London, and turned it into the Skytrain check-in. The concept worked better than he could have hoped. In the days before the first flight, queues began to form composed of anxious Americans wanting to get home on the cheap, and adventurous Brits seeking the chance to start seeing the world. The line around the block became a regular fixture on news broadcasts. The 'turn up and go' concept was, initially, more like 'turn up and don't go anywhere'. But the impression the images created – of unstoppable demand for a new, democratic form of travel – was better publicity than a million-pound advertising campaign.

'They were absolutely dedicated to kill me,' says Sir Freddie, who is in full flow on his favourite subject. 'But everything they did, thinking they were frustrating me, actually turned out to be the right way to do it.'

When I ask about the first Skytrain flight, on 26 September 1977, a tear forms in Laker's eye. 'I still get emotional about it. All of us, all the crew, the passengers, were in tears.' Sir Freddie was on hand before the flight to milk the publicity, then joined the pilots in the cockpit for departure. He gave the passengers a commentary during the take-off roll; the cheer when the wheels lifted off the ground was audible even over the roar of the engines at full throttle. With almost a decade of free publicity to support the operation, it quickly became a success – at the expense, initially, of the affinity charters that had been the previous low-cost option. In his advertisements, Laker made the point that, 'You don't have to join a club to take off in one of my beautiful DC-10 aeroplanes.'

Within nine months, Freddie Laker's status as national hero was confirmed. He received a knighthood in the Queen's Birthday Honours in June 1978. Was he, I wonder, surprised when he got the call from Buckingham Palace? 'Christ, with what I'd done to the government? Execution by hanging, yes. Knighthood, never.' He keeps the awards that he was given by the trade paper, *Travel News*, as Travel Personality of the Year for five straight years from 1977. Laker was on top of the world, and to prove it he expanded Skytrain, adding Los Angeles and Miami to the network.

Executives of US airlines, such as Franco Mancassola, then at Continental, were impressed. 'When Freddie Laker came into the market, I did nothing but applaud him. I admire people that have the guts to stand up for what they believe. I don't have much time for chief executives of big state airlines. They risk nothing of their own money. They blame fuel, they blame wars, they blame anything there is to blame, they ride for a few years and then they move along with big bonuses. But Freddie Laker was a man who had courage and vision. He was brave.'

Laker needed courage. Within a year of the knighthood, things began to go badly wrong. As the second winter season approached, rival airlines cut their fares to match Laker's – with the added bonus of more frequent flights, and providing meals on board free of charge. Soon, British Airways and Pan Am had queues of their own stretching from their ticket offices in Victoria. On 29 May 1979, all DC-10s were grounded worldwide after a series of fatal crashes involving other airlines. Two Laker Skytrain flights in mid-Atlantic were ordered to return to Gatwick. It was a catastrophic start to the peak summer season, when transatlantic airlines make the bulk of their money. By the time the ban on DC-10s was lifted, one month later, Laker had lost millions of pounds in revenue.

Worse was to come. After a fatal Turkish Airlines crash at Paris, in which more than a hundred British travellers died, many passengers now regarded the DC-10 as a dangerous aircraft and opted to travel on the Boeing 747s of British Airways, Pan Am or TWA.

Nevertheless, expansion plans continued. Sir Freddie had filed for permission to start a Skytrain Europe service. It would have comprised a network to match the most successful of today's no-frills airlines, but the plans did not come to fruition. Neither did a promised new route from Prestwick in south-west Scotland to Tampa in Florida. Laker did introduce a cabin aimed at the business class to his previously egalitarian Skytrain service. 'Regency Class' was, by all accounts, very comfortable – and a reaction against Laker's transatlantic rivals: 'If you attack from the back of the aeroplane, operating below cost, then I'm going to attack from the front.' But the Regency cabin looked very empty, as did the rest of the plane. Transatlantic flights were being cancelled or consolidated (two departures combined into one) on the say-so of the commercial department. These measures helped to fuel rumours that the airline was ailing. But whatever mistakes were made towards the end of his airline's life, Sir Freddie remains convinced that collusion between rival airlines was responsible for his corporate demise. 'What I was doing was revolutionary. They had to kill Freddie Laker.'

Death, when it finally came, was precipitated by the banks' refusal to extend the airline's overdraft to help Laker Airways through to a profitable summer season. As the news emerged, the scenes at Gatwick were just as powerful as the images that surrounded the launch of Skytrain. Staff who had complete faith

TREATING CATTLE LIKE PASSENGERS

When Laker set up his car ferry operation in the 50s, there was a strong American military presence in Europe. The quartermasters for US bases on the Continent were concerned about the quality of British abattoirs, and refused to buy meat from the UK for their soldiers.

'They would if it was killed in Rotterdam,' says Laker, 'because they thought the Rotterdam abattoirs were cleaner. If we had a space on the aeroplane, we would put a cow in it. We put a tarpaulin on the floor of the Bristol Freighter, and partitioned it off from the passengers. We carried dry cows that won't give milk any more, they're only fit for meat (and not very high-quality meat either, because they were old as well).

'We had a fair supply of deodorant, of course. At Southend we had a hay rack. I had a fellow that used to go round the markets in the county buying dry cows. I paid him ten bob (50p) for each cow. We'd keep them in the lairage, and every time we had a space we'd pop one in. And within two hours of popping them in the aeroplane they were dead and hanging up in the abattoir in Rotterdam.'

in their boss to ride out another storm were in tears. Passengers whose savings were tied up in now-worthless air tickets were distraught (though other airlines agreed to carry them for nominal payments). And public sympathy was immense. Pensioners sent cash to the liquidator in the vain hope that the money might save Laker – but not in the millions that Sir Freddie needed.

The deserts of the south-western US are littered with the evidence of airlines that expanded at an unsustainable rate. Laker believes it was not his blind ambition, but his rivals' blind panic, that killed his airline. He says his earnings were crippled by the other airlines cutting their fares to below cost in a concerted effort to force Laker Airways out of business, and to prevent him establishing the sort of network in Europe that twenty-first century no-frills carriers have.

'The real reason they went for me at the jugular was because of our application for Europe. With the Economic Union and everything else, we were going to get freedom of the skies in Europe. Even Norman Tebbit was on my side. Imagine having

Laker in Europe twenty-two years ago. How much is that worth? Billions. Billions.' Another legal fight began: a lengthy and complicated legal battle about alleged connivance to force Laker out of business and then raise fares. It took half as long as the interminable first battle, before ending to Sir Freddie's partial satisfaction. 'It's all documented out there what the bastards tried to do.'

Margaret Thatcher – the prime minister who had presided over Laker's downfall – was keen to privatise British Airways. Before a single share could be sold, though, the Laker dispute had to reach closure, to avoid saddling the new company with uncertain liabilities. 'We sat down until three o'clock in the morning with Colin Marshall [then chief executive of BA]. John King [then chairman of BA] was in a room above, because John King didn't have the guts to talk to me personally. So I said, "You can solve the problem easily. I want all the creditors paid." He said, "Done." 'I said, "I want every member of the staff paid, and every member of staff's pension to be paid in full."' There remained the question of what Sir Freddie himself would recover from the experience, which he now reveals to be 'Eight million dollars. And change.'

Six competing airlines agreed to compensate transatlantic travellers. Any passenger who could prove they had taken a transatlantic flight since Laker Airways' demise was entitled to a voucher worth £30, which was taken as an admission that other airlines' fares had been held artificially low and then inflated after the rival disappeared.

'I won. I had them. Remember we're three and a half years down the road, and you know something about three and a half years down the road? You can't put Humpty Dumpty together again. I'm a winner, but I can't get my licences back, so I lost from that point of view.' Still, Sir Freddie earned enough to set him up with a property in the Florida resort of Boca Raton, besides this one in Grand Bahama, and says, 'At the end of the day it's probably put ten years on my life.'

That life has been shared with four wives, the youngest of whom is the current Lady Jacqueline Laker. She is a former Eastern Airlines flight attendant whom Sir Freddie met on an overnight transatlantic flight from Miami to Gatwick on Air Florida in the early 80s, though they did not meet again for two more years. They married on 6 August 1985, Sir Freddie's sixty-third birthday. Back in the Bahamas Sir Freddie and his wife move in the upper echelons of Bahamian society, and he has become an unofficial ambassador for his island. 'All I am interested in is, can we get tourists to Grand Bahama. Why do I want to do it? Because they've been kinder to Freddie Laker. Skytrain produced affordable fares to the masses and competition in world air transport. It is laughable that Laker Airways Bahamas is one of the few solvent airlines in the world. In the Bahamas we do not get any government subsidies.' The bitterness that he still feels against the British establishment surfaced a month before my visit, at a dinner where Lady Thatcher was guest of honour. 'They sat her next to me. And she said, "Freddie, the press didn't treat you very well, did they?" And I said, "And neither did you, Margaret."'

'Your interview is over.' And so it is. With no pressing reason to remain in Grand Bahama, and specifically no wish to meet Sal and his pals, I ask Sir Freddie if his airline would be flying back to Fort Lauderdale that day.

When you are travelling with a ticket that is 'non-endorsable, non-transferable, non-refundable and valid only on the designated flight and date', and you want to change your plans, it helps if you turn up at the airport with the boss of the airline. Sir Freddie gets me a boarding pass, and accompanies me through to the departure lounge – to give the waiting passengers the surprise of their trip. Grabbing a microphone, he says, 'Ladies and gentlemen. This is Freddie Laker speaking. We want tourists to come and we'll do everything we can to make you safe. Please remember that Grand Bahama is the best place in the world. I know, because I live here. Thank you very much for supporting us.'

As the applause dies away, we adjourn to the bar, where this well-mannered, straightforward man allows one last sliver of bitterness to surface. 'It never occurred to them that there was a fourth class out there called the human race who just want to fly at the lowest fare.' I didn't tell him about Sal and my deception, but I think he might admire my desire to fly at the lowest fare.

The Skytrain story did not end in 1982. The following year, PEOPLExpress attempted to emulate Laker, without success. In 1998, those familiar DC-10s in Laker colours appeared once more on the runway at Gatwick. Laker Airways mark two flew from the Sussex airport to Fort Lauderdale, offering leather seats, high-class catering and seatback videos for a price matching that of Virgin Atlantic. Richard Branson was taken aback to see Sir Freddie reappear as a competitor, but the challenge did not last for long. 'He didn't have the right equipment, he had a lot of technical problems, and in a sense there wasn't the opening in the marketplace,' says Branson.

Laker Airways is still going, however. The Transmeridian aircraft that is waiting to take me back to Florida is a temporary aberration, chartered in while Sir Freddie 'changes gauge' with his airline operation and awaits replacement aircraft. Not many people in their 80s would decide to order some new planes. But Laker, the man who fought the battle of the North Atlantic, wants to fly his small corner of the Atlantic just right.

5. VIRGIN TERRITORY

During the 70s, what was offered in the air was an absolutely miserable experience – which was why we decided to get into the airline business and try to change things
Sir Richard Branson, chairman of Virgin Atlantic, Virgin Express and Virgin Blue (and of Virgin Books)

I love Richard. It's as simple as that
Sir Freddie Laker

Virgin Express has been an embarrassment to the Virgin Group
Barbara Cassani, former chief executive, Go

VIRGIN ATLANTIC FLIGHT 200: MAASTRICHT–GATWICK

Airline award ceremonies began to get dull during the 90s. The winners were almost invariably some combination of Singapore Airlines, Emirates and Virgin Atlantic. They win prizes by piling on the frills, from seatback TV to in-flight massage. Yet Virgin Atlantic was also the airline that pioneered no-frills flying within Europe. The venture was abandoned after five years, a decision that the founder now regrets. Today, flight 200 no longer hops from an obscure Dutch city to Gatwick; the number has been transferred to Virgin's prestigious Hong Kong–Heathrow service. But the record industry tycoon who started the airline now runs not one, but three low-cost airlines, with the promise of more to come.

To understand this strange state of affairs, a flashback to the 70s is in order. The decade was barely three weeks old when the

first Boeing 747 in commercial service took off from New York
JFK, destination London Heathrow. (Pan Am flight 2 arrived
three hours late.) Subsequently, the jumbo would later become the
airborne target of choice for a generation of terrorists. Nonethe-
less, the 747 precipitated the greatest transformation of our
travelling habits that the world has ever seen. The main long-haul
jets were the Boeing 707, DC-8 and VC-10, typically carrying
fewer than two hundred passengers. The 747 holds over four
hundred. With more than twice as many seats to fill as the existing
aircraft, airlines were obliged to cut prices. BBC Radio 1's
then-megastar, Tony Blackburn, was wheeled in by BOAC – now
part of British Airways – to advertise flights from Heathrow to
New York for £103 return (now £900) in the pages of *Melody
Maker*. But most of the music weekly's readers were more
interested in an ad from a new and unfamiliar company called
Virgin Records.

Britain's music industry had just undergone the equivalent of
airline deregulation. Resale Price Maintenance, the rule that kept
the cost of discs artificially high by banning discounts, had been
abolished. Henceforth albums by Yes, Led Zeppelin and, if you
insisted, Deep Purple, could be sold at any price the shop liked. The
big retailers at the time were such celebrated music heavyweights
as W. H. Smith, Woolworth and Boots. They appeared not to have
noticed the change in the law, and continued to charge £2 (now
£18) or more for an album. Since the public seemed prepared to
pay inflated prices even for *Deep Purple in Rock*, and no one had
stepped in with an alternative, they had no incentive to discount.

Soon, an alternative was provided by Richard Branson. When
most sixteen-year-olds were getting into sex and/or drugs, Branson was getting into the rock'n'roll business. He began his first
venture while between detentions at Stowe School. *Student*
magazine was an ambitious attempt to harness the ideals of the
60s. By the time Branson was a precocious twenty-year-old, he
had decided on the first of many business diversifications and
moved into music. Branson identified a truth that had eluded
many in both the music and airline businesses: with lower prices,
markets expand, and profits rise despite slimmer margins. There
was plenty of business to be seized while the slow, sclerotic giants
figured out what to do next.

Virgin Records promised cheap music – and innovative service.
For the record buyer, the first few retail branches comprised an
early prototype of Upper Class relaxation: you could flop across

giant cushions within tripping distance of Brighton's Clock Tower, inhaling joss sticks and other vapours that prevented you realising just how awful Deep Purple could be. The present-day Virgin Megastores are disappointingly mundane by comparison. Around the corner from the record store in Brighton stood a club called the Big Apple – venue for bands such as the Rolling Stones, and the closest that most people in the audience imagined they could get to New York.

Virgin Records, being run on a pre-decimalisation shoestring by Branson and some pals, was a no-frills sort of operation. The ads in the music press were nothing to write home about. They were, though, something to write to South Wharf Road, London W2 about. This was the address of the warehouse around the back of Paddington railway station whence the orders were despatched. Virgin Records could sell Neil Young's *After the Goldrush* for 30 shillings and 8 pence (£1.53, now worth £13.50), including postage, when every other retailer wanted 10 shillings (50p) more. But in the same way that twenty-first century passengers express mild mystification about some of the fares offered by no-frills airlines, most buyers could not care tuppence (1p).

Branson soon did the paper napkin thing. This restaurant ritual is evidently an essential part of no-frills start-ups; a napkin was also the vehicle for the original Southwest route map, and the medium on which easyJet's choice of name was first scrawled. In Branson's case, it was the company logo – born in return for a £200 fee for the designer, Trevor Key.

The logo adorned the expanding chain of record shops, and was soon applied to the new elements of the 'vertically integrated' Virgin group, which included the Manor recording studio in Oxfordshire and the record label. It would be another decade before the familiar Virgin scribble was applied to the tail of a Boeing 747.

Meanwhile, there was much business to be done. Richard Branson was the first to realise just how profitable the multi-instrumentalist and composer Mike Oldfield could be. In retrospect, Oldfield was the first one-hit-album wonder. But by catching the concept music wave of the early 70s, his *Tubular Bells* surfed to the front of many a music collection. The Virgin label was made. By the time the dismal follow-up *Hergest Ridge* was released, most of us had realised that the quasi-electronic symphony of special effects had all the staying power of Little Jimmy Osmond. We waited for punk to arrive. But with everyone from the Human League to Genesis on his books, Branson knew how to pick a winner.

One downside of the music business was that it involved a great deal of flying. 'We certainly ended up travelling a lot more during the 70s, but the quality of travel was absolutely dire,' says Branson today. 'What was offered in the air was an absolutely miserable experience – which was why, in the early 80s, we decided to get into the airline business and try to change things.'

Sir Freddie Laker had demonstrated that the demand for transatlantic travel is as 'elastic' as it is for music – in other words, dropping the price by 10 per cent causes an increase in demand of more than 10 per cent. Laker had also gone bust, despite the custom of people like Richard Branson, who flew Skytrain 'on a point of principle'. But it was two years before the vacuum left by the failure of Laker Airways was filled by Branson's airline. In the meantime, the need for cheap, fun transatlantic travel was initially filled by an interesting American operation called PEOPLExpress.

Like many enterprises that catch the public mood, this company – or commune – was phenomenally successful for a short time. PEOPLExpress began life in Newark, New Jersey in 1981, one of many start-ups to arise from President Carter's policy of airline deregulation. Organisationally, it was a partnership, rather on the lines of the British retailer, John Lewis. It flew mainly in the north-eastern US. Karl Marx would have been proud of its egalitarian principles, whereby pilots took a turn at check-in and loading baggage.

The PEOPLExpress partnership philosophy, and the low fares that it generated, caught the early 80s mood. The airline was so keen to cut costs that it aimed to do away with baggage handlers. Passengers were encouraged to carry all their luggage into the cabin, where extra storage was laid on. Indeed, a financial penalty of several dollars applied to anyone who insisted on checking baggage into the hold. (Plenty of frequent travellers wish the same philosophy applied today, and indeed Michael O'Leary of Ryanair has advocated such a system.) Within two years, PEOP-LExpress had become America's fifth-largest airline. The company paid for the vast Terminal C at Newark airport, New York's busiest gateway. It then established a flagship route from Newark to Gatwick airport that attracted passengers who had previously flown with Laker.

By now, British Caledonian had joined British Airways on transatlantic routes. But even under the terms of the highly restrictive agreement that governs flights across the North Atlantic, there was space for another UK competitor.

Early in 1984, a young American lawyer named Randolph Fields had touted around the idea of an all-business class airline called British Atlantic. (This business plan kept appearing, but it took 21 years before it finally took off – late in 2005, not one but two airlines, Eos and MAXjet, launched services between Stansted airport and New York JFK.) As an innovative entrepreneur with cash to spare, Branson was an obvious target. Fields approached the Virgin boss, who decided the risk was too great for a business-class only operation. But the music tycoon had been bitten by the idea of owning an airline. He modified Fields' concept to a two-class operation: the economy-class cabin would introduce a degree of fun into transatlantic flying, while the business-class product would be far superior to the standards prevalent on traditional airlines. Sir Freddie Laker gave the business model his blessing, reports Branson: 'Freddie said that if you're economy-only then you're vulnerable, because [competitors] can always cross-subsidise their economy fares with business passengers.'

Branson's mind was made up when he tried to phone the PEOPLExpress reservations line from his Oxford home, and found the line permanently busy. Either the Gatwick–Newark route was incredibly popular, he deduced, or the airline was incredibly badly run; either way, Branson believed, there was clearly room for a new player doing something different from the existing competition.

PEOPLExpress was doing something different, but the product was not distinctive enough. And as with many communes, internal squabbles soon intensified. The airline hit financial turbulence and was taken over by the giant Texas Air combine, which owned Continental Airlines – one of Southwest's biggest rivals. The 'workers' co-operative' model does not appear to work well in aviation.

Branson was employee-friendly to the extent that he loaned his staff enough cash to buy British Telecom shares in Margaret Thatcher's first privatisation giveaway, enabling them to make an instant profit. But the record-company-boss-turned-airline-chief drew the line at collective decision-making. Instead, he recruited staff from Laker Airways to run the company. It was to be called Virgin Atlantic, partly because Branson was determined to see his £200 logo on an aircraft tail, and partly because British Atlantic was deemed unsuitable: one BA was quite enough.

Fields had some radical ideas, such as cutting out the travel agent – a move which would have to wait another eleven years for easyJet to introduce. But the lawyer's eccentricities soon began to grate on senior executives. Relations deteriorated to the point where Branson sacked Fields; the New York lawyer almost grounded the maiden flight because he felt his £1m pay-off was insufficient.

One million pounds is not the sort of cash a fledgling airline can easily afford to part with, especially when Virgin Atlantic was faced with the huge marketing spend of its established, much larger rivals. So Branson took on board Laker's exhortation to sell himself in order to shift some seats.

'I'd always taken my mum and dad's advice about keeping a low profile and keeping separate from the business,' says Branson. 'But when I had lunch with Freddie Laker and said that I was thinking of going into the airline business, he said, "You're up against Pan Am and TWA and British Caledonian and British Airways, and they've all got more money than you. So you've got to use your personality to promote your company, and milk it for all it's worth." And I've been doing that ever since. If you're a relatively small independent airline, advertising is extremely expensive, and you have to try to make yourself heard.'

Life is never easy for an infant airline. Branson, like his Virgin organisation, was unfamiliar to many of the airline's prospective customers. So too was Newark, the New York airport to which the new airline would fly. Newark is no further from Manhattan than JFK, and from a traveller's point of view a less depressing proposition, but it is the 'wrong' side of the Hudson River and in a state – New Jersey – that many people regarded as a joke. Freddie Laker had managed to get access to the premier New York gateway of JFK. But the presence of British Caledonian on the Gatwick–JFK route meant that Virgin had to make do with an airport with which few UK travellers were familiar. The London end of the operation was not perfect either: Gatwick is 28 miles from the capital, with diabolical road links. Virgin Atlantic also faced big problems carving out a market between the UK and US. The new airline was not allowed to advertise flights in America until it had a licence, which came through only the day before the maiden flight.

Branson was keen to cash in on the summer traffic across the Atlantic, when economy fares are highest. This meant a very fast build-up to the launch, which helped to generate vast amounts of media coverage. No record company had set up an airline before, and speculation was rife about the rock stars passengers might find themselves sitting next to. Some gimmicks – including the in-flight live entertainers, and a free economy ticket for every business-class passenger – proved highly newsworthy, but have not stayed the course. The notion that has succeeded most visibly is the Upper Class cabin. Initially, this comprised just eight luxurious seats in the 'bubble', the upper deck of the Boeing 747. It caught the imagination both of the media and the passengers down below in economy class, which Branson had to be dissuaded from calling 'riff-raff'.

The self-publicity worked. On 22 June 1984, the first Virgin Atlantic flight took off from Gatwick to Newark, with a full payload and a huge amount of attention. The maiden voyage ran out of champagne somewhere over Newfoundland. It set a style of fun that has endured ever since (though with better-stocked drinks trolleys). 'We all have name badges on,' begins a typical on-board welcome message, of the sort that you rarely hear on traditional airlines. 'Please call us by our first names. We prefer that to "Honey", "Love", or a slap on the bottom. You have been warned.'

The Virgin boss found himself in the unexpected role of Britain's favourite entrepreneur, the post recently vacated by Laker. Sir Freddie felt Branson was a worthy successor: 'I love Richard. It's as simple as that.' Public affection for the entrepreneur's transportational innovation continued for a decade, until Branson became involved in the railway business in the 90s.

Buoyed up by fresh thinking and positive media coverage, the airline started making money almost at once. Branson says now, 'Virgin Atlantic only cost us a million and a half pounds because we used some of the cash flow to get it going, and second-hand planes.' Indeed, it would be tough for any airline to lose cash across the Atlantic in summer. The tricky bit starts when the June–September high season ends and load factors dwindle, which is why Branson diversified into no-frills flying.

Shortly after launching the Newark service, Branson devised a route from Gatwick to the Dutch city of Maastricht. This was a classic no-frills operation that predated Ryanair, easyJet and Go by a decade. Interestingly, this chapter of the infant Virgin Atlantic fails to make it into both Branson's compendious autobiography, *Losing My Virginity*, and the airline's official history.

The origins of this low-cost foray has its roots in the problems Virgin Atlantic faced in carving out a year-round market between the UK and US. There were already eight different airlines flying between London and New York, once the 'fifth-freedom' carriers – Air India, El Al and Kuwait Airways – were counted. These airlines are allowed to fly on the world's premier intercontinental air route as part of complex agreements to give US and UK airlines access to their markets. In summer, there was plenty of transatlantic traffic to go around. In winter, every carrier was desperate for London–New York customers. Yet travellers in continental Europe had little access to cheap transatlantic flights. So the Maastricht connection was hatched to help fill the plane at the end of the summer season.

Virgin Atlantic flight 200 connected with the Gatwick–New York service, to feed the route with traffic to and from the Continent. Maastricht was still years away from the treaty that put it on the map, but ideally located at the south-east corner of Holland for travellers from Belgium and West Germany. The idea was that, on quiet days, the flight would be operated by the Vickers Viscount, a small turbo-prop aircraft owned by British Air Ferries (BAF). The technical arrangement was that this was a 'damp lease'. The pilots were from BAF, while the stewardesses were Virgin's (a state of affairs that caused mirth at BBC Radio 4's *Going Places*, which broadcast a feature based on the staffing arrangements).

Branson initially had grand ambitions for the Maastricht link. There was enough leeway built into the 747 schedule to allow, if demand was sufficient, for the Jumbo inbound from New York to continue on from Gatwick to Maastricht. It never did, perhaps because the potential of the Continental connection was never marketed to the British as it might have been.

Crucially, the Gatwick–Maastricht hop was not restricted to transatlantic passengers. For the first time, British travellers had a low-cost option to fly to a part of Europe that was difficult to reach by train and ferry. The Maastricht connection was the original no-frills flight to the Continent, available for a flat £19 each way; this was far lower than the prevailing fares to Holland, which were around twice as high. It could have precipitated a low-cost revolution in the skies – yet after five years of poor marketing and underperformance, by which time the transatlantic operation had started picking up awards by the shelf load, the Maastricht link was quietly dropped.

BRAND AWARENESS
The idea of a record company running an airline struck many as absurd – but it helped build both sides of the Virgin empire. To have the logo of a record company on the tail made it comfortably familiar to the market of young travellers that Branson was keen to cultivate. And to be a record company that owned an airline did great things for the brand. 'An airline is a wonderful flagship for a company,' says Branson. 'The airline has put the Virgin name on the map.' In 1984, when Virgin was mostly music, no other record label could boast that its logo flew each day between the two world capitals of music, London and New York.

Why did Branson abandon no-frills flying in Europe when he was so far ahead of the competition? Largely, he says, to avoid tainting the main Virgin Atlantic product: 'There was concern that a low-cost, no-frills airline was detracting from the Virgin brand in the market place.' With so much favourable publicity being generated over the transatlantic route, Branson decided it would be counterproductive to muddle the message by promoting the European add-on. In retrospect, he says, that was a mistake: 'We certainly missed an opportunity. It would have been fine for us to have both brands.'

No one much noticed the disappearance of the small once-a-day flight. Maastricht had to wait until 2003 to get back on the no-frills map, with a Ryanair flight from Stansted. (It barely lasted for one season.) Branson had other concerns; 1984 nearly became a nightmare for the Virgin Group, because a film of that title based on George Orwell's novel was as over-budget as it was overdue. But 1984 was also a nightmare year for British Airways because Virgin Atlantic got started. Over the next few years, Branson methodically cherry-picked the most profitable US routes from London: Boston, Miami, Los Angeles, San Francisco, Washington DC. Virgin also gained access to Heathrow, which had two great advantages. The first is that the recognition and familiarity of Heathrow was far higher among travellers than for Gatwick; the second, that the average fares paid from Heathrow were significantly higher. Branson secured rights for the other glittering prizes in aviation: routes to Hong Kong, Johannesburg and Tokyo. In an industry that is notorious for helping people lose fortunes, owning an airline helped make Branson famously rich.

British Airways was furious. Unlike its big European rivals, Air France and Lufthansa of Germany, the giant airline had a high-quality competitor on its home turf. BA's management tried every trick in the book, and many that are not, to put Branson's airline out of business. The most notorious episode was the so-called 'dirty tricks' campaign. BA's computer network hosted the Virgin Atlantic reservations system; it is common for competing airlines to reach commercial arrangements for some elements of their operations. But BA staff were instructed to delve into the Virgin reservations system and identify 'premium' passengers. The details held on computer included contact numbers. Staff called passengers booked on Branson's airline and pretended to be from Virgin. They made up tales of cancelled or overbooked flights, and offered alternative flights on BA. This made Virgin look incompetent, and also earned money for BA; full-fare premium tickets are interchangeable between airlines.

When the subterfuge came to light, Branson recalled Sir Freddie Laker's admonition to 'sue the bastards' and spent many years in litigation. Despite BA's best efforts, Virgin Atlantic survived. Indeed, of the original competitors that Virgin Atlantic faced, only BA is still in business; BA swallowed up British Caledonian in 1987; Pan Am went bust three years after the 1988 Lockerbie disaster, giving its London slots to now-bankrupt United Airlines, and American Airlines bought the failing TWA and erased the brand in 2001.

Fifteen years after the original flight, Branson sold a 49 per cent stake in Virgin Atlantic to Singapore Airlines for £500m. Part of the cash was sent to Brussels to shore up Branson's second venture into aviation: Virgin Express.

On St George's Day 1996, Richard Branson bought a majority stake in EuroBelgian Airlines. He had witnessed the birth and rapid rise of easyJet six months earlier, and decided it was time to re-enter the European no-frills business that he had abandoned seven years earlier. The ailing charter airline Branson bought became Virgin Express, and soon started losing him money – and reputation.

The plan was simple enough: to establish a low-cost, hub-and-spoke network based in Brussels, serving primary airports. The Belgian capital had a large airport with plenty of capacity. The resident airline, Sabena, was a standing joke in aviation: not so much for the suggestion that its initials stand for 'Same awful

bloody experience, never again', but because it was chronically
unable to make any money. In its eighty years of existence, it had
failed ever to turn a profit.

In most industries, having a hopelessly inefficient competitor
would be seen as an advantage; but in aviation it can prove a real
drawback. Sabena could slash its prices to match Virgin Express,
safe in the knowledge that the Belgian government would make
up the resultant losses. 'We were competing with a company that
had no interest in profit,' says Branson. Yet initially relations were
warm. Sabena handed over its routes linking Brussels to Heathrow, Barcelona and Rome in return for a guaranteed allocation of
seats on these flights; Sabena passengers at Heathrow soon found
themselves boarding a Virgin plane.

Virgin Express's intention was to offer a low-fare, high-
frequency service that would appeal to both the business and
leisure traveller. Unfortunately, it lacked the necessary management, operational expertise and planes. When I first tried Virgin
Express, it was a low-fare, no-frequency service. One day in
October 1998, I turned up at Heathrow for the dawn flight to
Brussels, only to be offered an afternoon train from Waterloo to
the Belgian capital. I tried again the next morning. There was an
aircraft, and I was able to check in for it, but after a few more
hours in the departure gate – a wait made more entertaining by
the arrival of a British Airways crew and passengers expecting to
use the same gate for a flight to Berlin – I abandoned the mission.
The VEX code that Virgin Express uses as a prefix for its flights
seemed appropriate.

'Virgin Express was an example of what not to do. It was a
mistake,' says Branson. 'We should have actually set it up in the
UK. Instead, we bought a small company in Brussels with all the
adherent problems, and the cost base was far higher than most
low-cost carriers.' Branson could have cut his losses and closed
down Virgin Express. But instead he found a military solution.

Neil Burrows is an RAF man. He studied at Cranwell, the
world's oldest aeronautical college, and spent eleven years in the
air force before moving into civil aviation. Burrows rapidly scaled
the flight deck career ladder from co-pilot to senior training
captain, and worked as an inspector for the Civil Aviation
Authority. He flew for the ruler of Abu Dhabi for eighteen
months, and then helped start up the charter carrier Air 2000
(now First Choice Airways). In 2000 (the year, not the airline), he
joined Virgin Express as operations director.

'We had a really terrible year,' he says, 'with the tripling of fuel prices, the 30 per cent fall of the euro against the dollar, and overcapacity. This company lost a lot of money.' That loss worked out at £10 for every passenger on its scheduled flights. One cause was Virgin Express's code-sharing agreement with Sabena, which meant it was obliged to offer a two-class service with more legroom (and fewer seats). No low-cost start-up would countenance such an arrangement.

To add to the problems, Swissair had taken a half-share in Sabena, and was in the process of doubling capacity at Brussels – 'hammering the market', as Burrows puts it. In 1998 Virgin Express had made an excursion into traditional no-frills territory at Stansted but, Burrows says, 'The airline went in too late, when other low-cost airlines had got a toehold in there. To have all these low-cost airlines fighting for the same patch meant that you were going to have to stay in there losing quite a lot of money to develop. We didn't have that sort of money to throw at that sort of battle so we beat a retreat.'

Burrows' predecessor as managing director beat a retreat from Virgin Express; he got a job at Ryanair, which was establishing a hub in Charleroi, south of Brussels. (To try to spoil the new operation, Virgin Express offered any Irish citizen whose last name was Ryan a free flight to Gatwick.) Burrows took over in November 2000, and started wielding the hatchet – assisted by a £20m injection of cash by Branson. To staunch further losses, Virgin Express spent another £13m getting rid of half the aircraft, closing its Irish affiliate and shutting down bases at Shannon, Gatwick and Berlin to concentrate on Brussels.

Less than a year later, it appeared that this policy had paid off. In the aftermath of the attacks on America on 11 September 2001, Sabena went spectacularly bankrupt, along with its part-owner, Swissair. Overnight, Virgin Express found it had, by default, become the national carrier for Belgium.

'Sabena were bust and Virgin was poised in a fantastic position in Brussels to take over,' says Branson. 'But the Belgian prime minister decided that they just had to have a state airline. They got the King to go and twist the arm of a hundred businesses to put in a million pounds each, including one of our non-executive directors of Virgin Express, who said if he didn't do it he would be ostracised in Belgium.' The result: SN Brussels ('SN' was the old Sabena flight prefix). To make matters worse, SN Brussels laid claim to the Virgin Express slots at Heathrow, which had originally belonged to Sabena, and promptly sold them to British Airways. Virgin Express's Heathrow connection was severed on 27 October 2002, though the airline resurfaced at London City in 2003, on a code-share arrangement with VLM.

Neil Burrows' master plan was to shift the airline's focus eastwards. He announced a new Virgin Express base at Cologne-Bonn, at the heart of a large and wealthy catchment area that was unserved by low-cost airlines. A few weeks later, the plan was abandoned when two new carriers, Germanwings and Hapag Lloyd Express, said they would be establishing their own no-frills hubs at the same airport.

Tim Jeans, managing director of Monarch Scheduled and a man with many years of experience with no-frills airlines, believes Virgin Express was burdened with fundamental flaws: 'A vastly high-cost hub in Brussels, a very expensive operation and leased aircraft.' Branson disagrees: 'Virgin Express should have been a very, very profitable airline. We are obviously profitable but it is much more marginal as a result of what happened.'

Neil Burrows believes Virgin Express's greatest strength is the Branson marque. 'It's one of the most valuable assets, to have the Virgin brand on the aircraft. We try to live up to it.' Not everyone in aviation believes the airline has. Barbara Cassani, who founded Go, contends that Virgin Express 'has been an embarrassment to the Virgin Group', while Michael O'Leary says that Branson has 'a long history of very poor business models', though he concedes that the Virgin boss has had 'one or two fantastic successes: the record company and the transatlantic airline'.

In 2003, Virgin Express announced that it had become the leading carrier at Brussels – which was the first major airport in Europe whose market leader is a low-fare carrier. Some vindication for Branson – but he agrees that it could all have been very different: 'I suppose I just have to accept that you can't have everything in life, you have to let others get in there and show you how it's done. At least, we learnt our lesson, and moved quickly in Australia.' The result: an Australian domestic airline known as Virgin Blue, whose slogan is 'You're just buying the flying'.

Australia, unlike Belgium, is 'An enormous country, where everyone has to fly,' says Branson. Late in 1999 he flew to Australia to launch a new no-frills airline – starting with a competition to name the carrier. At the time, the incumbents were Qantas and Ansett, which had been enjoying a comfortable duopoly for decades. Occasionally a new low-cost airline, such as

East-West, would stir things up for a while before going bust or being swallowed up.

The familiar red logo of Virgin combined with the Australian sense of humour made it inevitable that the airline would be called Virgin Blue. Plenty in the Australian aviation industry did not rate Virgin Blue's chances – especially since the new airline had an uncomfortable birth, with the aircraft sitting on the tarmac at Brisbane airport for several weeks while licensing wrangles were straightened out. This allowed another airline, the former charter and freight operator, Impulse, to get in ahead and establish itself as Australia's third airline. Gerry McGowan, the executive chairman of Impulse, promised his airline would 'not allow anyone to interfere with the mission to become the domestic airline price leader and price innovator.'

Cynics also observed that the majority of Australia's population resides in Sydney, Melbourne and the region between them, yet Virgin Blue was based in Brisbane, the sleepy state capital of Queensland. Wasn't this, I suggested to Branson, like opening an airline in the UK and basing it in Newcastle?

'Australia has this wonderful situation where you can play states off against each other for grants.' Queensland came up with a better offer than either Victoria or New South Wales. 'In fact, the grant that they came up with meant we launched Virgin Blue with almost no investment at all. Queensland didn't have an airline as such. It's a fast-growing area and they've adopted us as their airline. It's a very pleasant place to have a head office. You're one hour away from some of the most beautiful beaches.'

Once Virgin Blue was allowed to take off, Branson was sniffily dismissed by the Qantas boss, Geoff Dixon, as 'Richard some-body-or-other' on ABC television. But the public loved the sudden outbreak of competition that Virgin Blue and Impulse brought. Fares fell as low as A$39 (about £15) on routes that had previously cost a minimum of five times as much. But in May 2001, Impulse was taken over by Qantas. And by the end of that year, Australian travellers found their choice reduced once again to two carriers. Ansett, Australia's second airline, went bust within a few days of the attack on the World Trade Center on 11 September. Several vain attempts were made to resuscitate Ansett, but eventually the airline was allowed to die. Eight of its 737s were bought by Philip Meeson, enabling him to start Jet2, based at Leeds-Bradford in Yorkshire. Meanwhile Virgin Blue suddenly found itself as the new number two Australian airline – 'keeping

Qantas honest,' says Branson, and perfectly poised to expand: 'The price of new planes collapsed and Virgin Blue actually benefited from the problems that other airlines were suffering around the world.' Partly because of the favourable prices, says Branson, 'We've got the airline with the lowest cost base in the world.'

One of Australia's most frequent travellers, Tony Wheeler, founder of the guidebook publisher, Lonely Planet, believes Virgin Blue has a natural advantage: 'They're making new employment agreements which are always better (from the airline viewpoint) than old ones.' These, he says, date back to the days 'when airline pilots were gods (not glorified bus drivers) and flight attendants goddesses (not fast-food servers).'

Branson calls Virgin Blue 'the best investment ever, a startlingly magnificent brand,' and believes that 'if you talk to any granny or student in Australia they will be forever grateful to have Virgin Blue there because otherwise they would not be able to afford to travel as often as they do.'

Once the key routes within Australia had been established, the airline's management looked across the Tasman Sea for more opportunities: New Zealand has a similar profile to Australia, of a thinly populated nation with a high propensity to fly. But Branson's sale of 49 per cent of Virgin Atlantic to Singapore Airlines had involved limitations on the future extent of carriers using 'Virgin' as part of their names. So outside Australia, Virgin Blue mutates to Pacific Blue. Same aircraft, same crews, same style but a different name. The Pacific Blue operation now extends deep into the South Pacific, with routes reaching as far as Fiji. Soon it may be possible for travellers to cross the world's biggest ocean entirely on no-frills airlines. And when they reach the US, they may be able to fly on Virgin America.

The US is by far the biggest aviation market in the world. It also has a substantial oversupply of existing airlines, and rules that heavily restrict foreign investment. But Branson believes a Virgin-branded airline should thrive in the US, and has teamed up with American investors to begin such a venture. Virgin America has a base – San Francisco – and a chief executive: Fred Reid, formerly president of Delta. What it does not have, at least at the start of 2006, is any flights. The airline business is simply too crowded. Half the giant US carriers – United, Delta and Northwest – are in Chapter 11 bankruptcy, trying to stave off financial failure. Until one or more airlines closes down, reducing the competition that

ONLY JOKING
'Last time I went down to Australia, we were under enormous pressure to sell out Virgin Blue to Air New Zealand [owner of Ansett, and keen to dampen domestic competition]. Twelve months in, they sent me over a cheque for A$250m [£100m]. Virgin's always spending before we've actually got money so it's always tempting to take it. So we called a press conference for 12 o'clock, in front of one of our planes, and we got up in front of cameras and the press and I said, "It's a sad day for the Australian aviation industry but we've decided to sell. We have saved people all this money and it's been a great year, a great start." And there was this deafening hush and I hadn't realised that some of the staff were standing just behind bursting into tears at this stage. I looked into the camera and said, "Only joking", and ripped up the cheque.

'Ansett had been saying to me right up to the last minute, "Look, if you don't sell out, we're going to throw hundreds of millions into this and we're going to drive you out of the market." And then only about three days later, Ansett announced that they were bankrupt.' **Sir Richard Branson**

keeps fares unsustainably low, Virgin America will find it tough to take off.

When I ask Branson about the difference between success and failure in aviation, he is precise: 'Very slim,' he says. 'A percentage above break-even can make you very profitable, a percentage below can lose you money very quickly.' Does the phrase 'Quit while you're ahead' occur often to him? 'No.'

6. STANSTED, OR BUST

Do we occasionally piss people off? Of course we do
Michael O'Leary, chief executive, Ryanair

*He's as tough as nails, a businessman through and through, no
compromise*
Sir Richard Branson

*If I can get a £7 flight to somewhere within two hundred miles of
Venice, well I'll fucking take it. Seven quid, I don't care where I
fucking go!*
Sir Bob Geldof

RYANAIR FLIGHT 203: STANSTED–DUBLIN

'Here you are, folks, a little late but safe and sound in foggy
Dublin.' That is how the Ryanair captain announces our
arrival in the Irish capital. His boss is less circumspect. 'Three
dumb bastards decide they're not going to go to the gate on time.'
It sounds like the start of a joke. But the lean Irishman whose
frown, eyebrows and chin are as well-defined as Cape Clear is not
laughing. I am running an hour behind schedule, and Michael
O'Leary has made it his business to find out why.

If you are late for a meeting because your flight is delayed, try
to make sure that your appointment is with the boss of the airline.
But few chief executives are so hands-on that they would greet
you with a tirade against their own tardy customers. A week and
a day after the 11 September attack on America, the chief

executive of Europe's leading no-frills airline is fuming at a trio of dawdling passengers. 'With all the extra security we're checking in two hundred bags a flight and it takes us twice as long to get their bags out of the hold.' O'Leary is taking it personally. 'They should be strung up.'

Lynching passengers is not part of the business plan at Ryanair, but O'Leary leaves few expletives undeleted as he talks about his success and others' failures. As I walk into his office, he is on the telephone, discussing the prospects for Irish tourism. If whoever is at the other end of the phone is hoping for a polite assessment, they asked the wrong man to provide it. O'Leary succinctly predicts 'tourism in this country next year is fucked'. I judge that he is not speaking to a radio station, because in live broadcasts he tempers his language to the ideal balance between being hard hitting, controversial and consequently listened to, and being so outrageous that he is never invited back. But in circumstances that can be regarded as private, even an event such as a meeting with stock-market analysts, the air is often peppered with expletives.

'It's interesting that Michael O'Leary has this image as a rough-and-tumble profane Irish farm boy,' says Barbara Cassani, founder of Go. 'He's a trained accountant who went to one of the finest universities in Ireland.' Cassani is correct. The reason O'Leary was hired by the Ryan family to evaluate their small, independent and loss-making airline late in 1988 was his razor-sharp intellect and financial acumen. To be fair, O'Leary has respectable agricultural credentials: he lives on his farm an hour west of Dublin. 'I breed horses and cattle,' he used to say until he married. 'It's the closest thing I get to a sex life.' But since taking over as Ryanair's chief executive on New Year's Day 1994, he has been concentrating less on the animals and more on running Europe's fastest-growing and most profitable airline.

O'Leary says the aviation industry has to ask itself, 'What the hell have we been doing for the last fifty years? We've been gouging the consumer, and putting the cost of air travel beyond the means of 80 or 90 per cent of the travelling public.' The chief decoration in his first-floor office is a poster from the *Evening Standard* announcing JUDGE BLASTS BA 'BASTARDS', an episode where even calling one of my newspaper stories as evidence failed to save British Airways from defeat at the hands of Ryanair.

Once our formal interview begins, the language is toned down but the robust sentiments remain. We are talking at a very sensitive time. Eight days earlier, the worst aviation disaster in history had seen two hijacked aircraft flown into the towers of the World Trade Center in New York, a third hitting the Pentagon in Washington DC, and a fourth deliberately crashed by its passengers in Pennsylvania to foil the hijackers' plan. The previous evening in Dublin, Aer Lingus had announced 1,600 job losses – a hundred more than the total number of people then employed by Ryanair. Michael O'Leary, meanwhile, is in a good mood, wayward passengers excepted. His company's shares, like those of every other airline, had sunk in the aftermath of the attacks. But at close of business the previous night, Ryanair was valued by the markets at a higher capitalisation than either British Airways or American Airlines – an astonishing achievement for an airline that, a decade previously, was, to use O'Leary's succinct description from earlier, fucked.

Ten years earlier, says O'Leary, Ryanair 'was hovering on the verge of bankruptcy. In Spring 1991 I thought it would be a miracle if we were still in business three months later.' Ten years later, Ryanair was more valuable than the biggest airline in the world. Handily for O'Leary, he owns a handy slice of the airline. How has he done it? 'Michael's vision for the airline, and focus on keeping costs down, are in my view absolutely without peer,' says a rival airline boss, Tim Jeans, managing director of Monarch Scheduled. Jeans spent seven years working for O'Leary at Ryanair before leaving to start his own airline, MyTravelLite, then moving on to Monarch. He calls the experience 'a masterclass'. Kell Ryan, brother of Ryanair's founder, echoes the praise: 'I don't think there's anyone on the planet who understands costs like Michael.'

Michael O'Leary spent much of the final three months of 2001 tussling with another airline multi-millionaire, Stelios of easyJet, to see who could get the most airtime. The media developed a sudden interest in no-frills flying. The two men were confused in a report on Radio 4's *PM* programme that required an apology: 'Earlier in the programme, we referred to Michael O'Leary as chief executive of easyJet. He is, in fact, chief executive of Ryanair.' But quickly most listeners and viewers were well aware who was at the top of what was, at the time, Europe's biggest no-frills airline. It was the man who, a decade earlier, had taken a basket-case airline and turned it into a carrier that carries more passengers than British Airways. 'We don't look upon ourselves as an Irish airline any more,' says O'Leary. 'We look upon ourselves as a European airline.'

So why isn't it called O'Learyair, then? Not because Ryanair is much easier for a Lithuanian or an Italian to pronounce, but because the airline was the creation of a Tipperary businessman named Tony Ryan. He had been one of the leading figures in the establishment of Guinness Peat Aviation as a leading aircraft leasing company. (Dr Ryan's family still holds 15 per cent of Ryanair's stock, collectively comprising the largest shareholder; his brother, Kell, works for the airline at Stansted.)

In 1985, when aviation on the main routes between Britain and Ireland was limited to Aer Lingus and British Airways, the market was, literally, a carve-up. The two airlines pooled all their earnings on London–Dublin flights, and divided them according to the number of seats that each had operated. With such a cosy arrangement, there was no incentive to raise standards or cut fares. Ryan saw an opportunity. He started an airline that flew between Waterford (where he is still director of a crystal firm) and London, using a single fifteen-seat Bandeirante aircraft, made in Brazil. The airline would carry the family name, which today O'Leary says is an advantage: 'There's an awful lot of bullshit talked about brands. Ryanair is a pretty good, anodyne brand that works across Europe.' The new airline carried five thousand people in its first year. Today, Ryanair carries that many passengers in an hour.

In January 1986, Ryanair made a big media announcement: it was to start flying 747s. Unfortunately, the press release was one digit out. The airline had actually ordered 748s: a small British-built aircraft holding 45 people, rather than a Boeing jumbo carrying ten times as many. With the propeller plane, Ryanair started flying on the Dublin–Luton route, charging £94.99 for an uncomfortable eighty-minute ride between the Irish and English capitals. That fare compares poorly with the lowest available today, but at the time it undercut the lowest prevailing fare on British Airways and Aer Lingus of £99.

The airline rapidly expanded, with ATR 42 planes and the first BAC 1-11 jets taking it from eighty thousand passengers in 1986 to six hundred thousand in 1989. Soon Ryanair was flying nineteen routes, including Dublin to Paris and Munich. But the airline was losing a fortune: £20m in the first four years. Tony Ryan covered the losses because, like many aviation entrepreneurs before him, he believed there was a profitable role for the airline bearing his name. Unlike most of his predecessors, he was correct – but first he had to change the direction, and the management, of Ryanair.

'In the beginning we were just like any other airline, with a business class and a frequent-flyer programme,' says Kell Ryan. Michael O'Leary, who joined Ryanair six weeks before the end of 1988, takes up the story: 'We were trying to do what many other airlines were trying to do in Europe, which was to be a slightly lower fare "me too" carrier to Aer Lingus and British Airways. But the fares were about 20 per cent cheaper, which meant we just lost more money than they did.'

Michael O'Leary maintains he has 'never found aircraft interesting. I'm not one of these people that gets erections looking at aeroplanes or talking about aeroplanes. I didn't grow up in the countryside of Ireland looking at aeroplanes or wanting to be a pilot when I grew up.' Nevertheless he progressed rapidly in Ryanair, becoming deputy chief executive in 1991. Someone suggested a trip to Texas to pick up a few ideas. Who, exactly, is lost in the mists of Ryanair's corporate history. But a call was placed to Southwest Airlines, and Michael O'Leary flew to Dallas. 'Once we saw what Southwest was doing we thought this could be the way forward: selling at the lowest possible price to the maximum number of people.'

The propeller planes were pensioned off, along with all but five of Ryanair's routes. Initially, the airline began its born-again no-frills status using a fleet of six BAC 1-11 jets. These were noisy and inefficient, and – at the start of the 90s – the prospects for independent success were not encouraging. The Gulf War early in 1991 had diminished the demand for air travel. Pan Am, the closest that America had to a national carrier, went bust. In Britain, Air Europe collapsed trying to provide a with-frills service at low fares during the worst recession aviation had known. In the same year, Ryanair cut fares between London and Dublin to £69 return, flew seven hundred thousand people, and turned its first profit. In 1992, Dan-Air went broke – another UK airline that tried to offer low-cost flying and failed. British Airways, keen to capitalise on the opportunity for a ready-made short-haul operation based at Gatwick, picked up Dan-Air for £1.

Which is what a Ryanair flight may cost you ('*plus taxes, fees and charges', as the small print on the ads reads) in 2006. The airline stands to earn less than the price of a cup of coffee from the relatively small number of passengers who pay such low fares, which is why you'll be encouraged to buy a hot drink aboard. Ryanair cashes in on peckish passengers: in-flight sales account for twenty per cent of revenue.

Thanks partly to expensive snacks, but mostly to aggressive marketing, Ryanair's fortunes started to race ahead of its rivals in 1994. By now it was carrying 1.5 million passengers and charging as little as £49 return between the English and Irish capitals. This was the year when Ryanair began replacing its elderly British-built jets with American Boeing 737s, the aircraft that Southwest relies upon. It bought them from Britannia Airways, then Britain's biggest charter carrier, now Thomsonfly; and Lufthansa, the airline that O'Leary loves to pretend to hate. (At the end of 2005, Ryanair was still flying some of its original Boeing 737-200 fleet, which by then were around 25 years old. Yet Ryanair has one of the youngest fleets in the sky, thanks to a rapidly expanding fleet of fresh-out-of-the-box Boeing 737-800s – some of which are maintained by Lufthansa.)

In the mid-90s, Ryanair used the 'new' aircraft to create a UK–Ireland network based at its headquarters in Dublin. Initially the strongest routes were from Gatwick and Luton to the Irish capital, but quickly a whole network of options was built up, from Cardiff to Teesside. Then, crucially, Ryanair discovered Stansted.

As white elephants go, the Essex airport was outstanding. Prodigious amounts of glass and steel had gone into Sir Norman Foster's beautiful but empty terminal. From opening day on 19 March 1991, the new Stansted was an extravagant embarrass-ment. A perfectly adequate small, regional airport had existed for decades, serving mostly cargo, charters and Air UK's network of domestic and European flights. Then Stansted was nominated as the best placed of London's airports to expand to alleviate the chronic shortage of aviation capacity in south-east England. A huge new terminal was built on the far side of the airfield from the existing low-rise facility. Regular travellers, accustomed to the ease and simplicity of the previous terminal, found it infuriating to have to walk for miles or take a shuttle train to the gate. But they could not complain about overcrowding. Stansted was empty. The airlines, and hence the travelling public, shunned it in favour of Heathrow and Gatwick.

Within a year of its opening, an IRA bomb attack on the City of London had shown the vulnerability to terrorism of large steel and glass structures. Armed troops were detailed to protect Stansted and, on some days, there were more people guarding the terminal than travelling through it. Except for the Air UK network, only a few oddball airlines like Cubana (offering a weekly Ilyushin flight to Havana via Gander) served the airport. The place was ripe for a deal.

O'Leary learned early on the importance of driving down the price for using an airport – one of relatively few costs over which an airline has control – and of playing off one airport against another. Stansted would be a useful counterpoint to Luton and Gatwick. Gradually, Dublin services were moved across from Luton to take advantage of the lower airport charges, and frequencies gradually increased. Not all the flights in the timetable actually flew, mind: 'I'm not going to deny that at one time in Ryanair's history, if fifty were booked on the 12 o'clock from Dublin to Stansted and there were fifty booked on the 1 o'clock, there would be a magical combination of those two flights,' says Tim Jeans, then Ryanair's marketing director. 'Consolidation' or 'amalgamation' of departures in this manner is a useful tactic for airlines with precarious profitability, but aggravating for passengers. Ryanair says it no longer cancels departures for commercial purposes, though in October 2005 it 'amalgamated' around two hundred flights when a strike at Boeing left it temporarily short of aircraft.

In October 1995, Ryanair decided to branch out from Ireland – and take the bold step of opening a new domestic route in Britain, from Stansted to the Ayrshire airport of Prestwick, serving Glasgow. For the first time in post-war Britain, a foreign airline would operate a domestic service within Britain.

This was revolutionary. A century after the first powered flight, nations are still intolerant about who can fly to, from, over and most particularly within their territory. There is barely any history of a nation allowing foreign carriers to operate domestic flights within its territory – the practice of 'cabotage'. Traditionally, this was partly to protect the national carrier, but equally important was the perceived risk if war broke out. Not only did a government want to have a fleet of transport aircraft to call upon, it did not necessarily relish having a potential enemy's planes parked on its runways. By the closing years of the twentieth century, Britain had decided that Ryanair did not pose a threat to national security, and was prepared to permit 'cabotage' – the freedom for a foreign airline to fly within the UK.

Britain is party to one of the most anti-competitive airline treaties anywhere: the Bermuda II agreement that restricts flights between the US and UK. But within Europe, it has been at the forefront of encouraging competition. When the rules were relaxed, there was not exactly a stampede among overseas carriers for slots within the UK. Lufthansa tried flying between Birmingham and Newcastle, but lost money on the route and soon gave up.

Few paid much attention to the start of flights between two of Britain's most underemployed airports, except Stelios – who was preparing to launch easyJet's first route from Luton to Glasgow the following month. British Airways and British Midland (now BMI) did not regard it as competition. They operate from Heathrow to Glasgow's main airport. This is the prime business route between the largest cities in England and Scotland. Anyone using Ryanair to travel from the centre of London to the middle of Glasgow has to cover at least seventy miles of the journey by road or rail. By 2005, though, the Stansted-Prestwick route had ten flights each way, every day, more than BMI from Heathrow to Glasgow (and easyJet from Luton).

When I suggest to Michael O'Leary that easyJet, not Ryanair, brought the no-frills model to the UK, the boss of the Irish airline ripostes robustly: 'Ryanair was the first low-fares/no-frills airline in Europe, and the first low-fares/no-frills route was flying from the UK seven years before easyJet started. Ryanair also began flying (between London and Glasgow) before easyJet even started flying its first route. Whatever else Stelios and easyJet may have done, they certainly weren't the first or the founders – Ryanair was.'

Ryanair has gone easy on cabotage in the UK since then, and easyJet has easily overtaken it as the main domestic no-frills airline; besides the Prestwick link, Ryanair's domestic routes from Stansted are to Blackpool, City of Derry and Newquay. O'Leary's airline has recently been much more interested in starting routes to places you never knew you wanted to go – or places that are not quite where you thought they were.

When you buy a ticket on any other airline to Frankfurt or Barcelona, Stockholm or Oslo, you will arrive at the airport that serves the city. But when Ryanair says 'Frankfurt' it means a former US Air Force base near the Luxembourg frontier, and sixty miles from the German financial hub. Similarly, 'South' in Ryanair's sense of Stockholm (South) and Oslo (South) means sixty miles away. Most ambitious of all is 'Barcelona', which is the airport serving the fine Catalan city of Girona. That, mind you, is an improvement; in the days when Ryanair did not fly to Spain, it suggested Perpignan, in France, as the perfect gateway to Spain's second city. National borders prove no obstruction to airline's assertions; in 2001, Ryanair announced it was flying to the Danish capital, Copenhagen. It had no intention of doing anything of the sort, but it did have a flight to Malmö, in Sweden, from where a bus connection operated to Copenhagen. The costs at Malmö are far lower than at the Danish capital's airports.

Low-cost airlines like low-cost airports, and in Ryanair's case that ideally means nothing more than a shed with a runway attached. And there are plenty more like that waiting to be discovered. 'There's all kinds of places in Scandinavia and down through Germany where NATO had bases during the cold war,' says O'Leary. 'Even in the UK there's dozens of airports.' So how does Ryanair decide where to fly? 'Usually we make a decision based on that airport providing us with a very good package of facilities and they have to be efficient facilities, at low cost. Whichever airport provides us with the best package is the next new route we open.'

'Michael has a view that all you have to do is find an airport that will give a discount or doesn't want to be paid at all,' says Stelios, founder of easyJet. 'He says, "There's a desperate airport – I'm going to take advantage of it." ' Stelios says there is a problem with Ryanair's strategy. 'You end up flying from very small places, which means you end up flying at very low frequency, struggling to fit one flight a day, maybe two. Our strategy says, go to proper places – big catchment areas or big destinations – and blitz them on frequency.'

Small airports have three obvious advantages for the traveller: quicker boarding and disembarkation; with fewer arrivals and departures, there is less chance of air traffic control delays; and quicker taxiing, meaning less time before take-off and after landing. There is a fourth benefit, too, of which the traveller may not be aware: the flight may be subsidised by the airport, or the regional authority.

Airports provide airlines with a service: a runway on which to land its planes, a terminal in which to handle passengers, and the many tasks that go with the business of running a safe airfield. For this, usually, the airline pays a fee based partly on the size of the aircraft and partly on the number of passengers. But at some airports on Ryanair's network, this arrangement is turned on its head: they pay the airline for the privilege of working for it. Why on earth would airports and local authorities do this? Because the arrival of an airline can transform the fortunes of an area, bringing thousands of tourists and enhancing business access. They also know that regional authorities have plenty of cash to dole out. In the right circumstances, they can effectively claim a bounty for each passenger they land. This is usually described as 'marketing support', but since marketing is such a crucial element of a no-frills airline's costs this is not so innocuous a term as it may look. It is a polite phrase for 'subsidy'.

In 1998, Ryanair started flights from Stansted to Rimini, on the Adriatic coast of Italy. The incentives offered by Aeradria, the airport authority, to Ryanair totalled a handy £400,000 – 'for tourist promotion plus other easements on airport costs', according to a local newspaper report at the time. 'Aeradria considers this an investment,' said the president of the authority. 'It will help us to receive new visitors at Rimini.' The airport was expecting around sixty thousand extra passengers. In other words, the region was paying a subsidy of £7 per passenger.

After two years, Rimini's airport management changed and wanted to renegotiate the arrangement; Ryanair refused and pulled out. Michael Cawley, the commercial director, said at the time, 'What they do not understand is that with ten existing airports [in Italy] and in excess of ten further airports seeking our business, Ryanair has more demands for its flights than it can supply for the foreseeable future.' The airline soon started flying to nearby Forli (known as Bologna on Planet Ryanair) under what is believed to be a similar subsidy arrangement.

Ryanair, like other no-frills airlines, is quick to condemn the way that other European airlines are supported by government aid. The airline has called for such subsidies to be outlawed. Yet the carrier is content to take cash from the municipalities it serves. For several years the people of Wallonia – the French-speaking part of Belgium, where Charleroi airport is located – paid part of the fare of passengers using the local airport. But after complaints from rival airlines, including Virgin Express, the European Commission ruled that the deal was anti-competitive. Ryanair stayed, but trimmed back its plans for 'Brussels South', as Charleroi is known. A French court ruled that Ryanair's deal with Strasbourg airport was unfair on Air France, which had abandoned services from Gatwick to Strasbourg after the Irish airline had launched flights from Stansted. Ryanair's response to the court ruling was to move its flights to Baden-Baden, thirty miles across the Rhine in Germany. Air France moved back on to the route, though at fares about twice as high as on Ryanair.

The Irish airline spends a lot of time in court. It has a speciality of finding a destination with a significant population base and a

SCOTLAND'S GHOST OF ELVIS

Passengers benefit directly when they book on a new flight to or from Prestwick – free rail travel between the Ayrshire airport and any station in Scotland, which could mean a saving of up to £80. Prestwick makes the offer for the first six months of any new route. Glasgow's second airport is a classic no-frills destination. It is miles away from the city it is supposed to serve, which already has a perfectly good airport of its own. Prestwick was foisted upon Scotland by the post-war government, which wanted a reliable base for transatlantic flights: the weather on the coast north of Ayr is better than elsewhere in the country, with a much lower incidence of fog. While British Airways (and, before that, BOAC) was firmly under government control, it was easy for the Air Minister to demand a connection to New York. Even after that era ended, the government insisted that anyone who wanted to fly transatlantic to Scotland must land only at Prestwick. As soon as that stipulation was lifted, the airlines vanished to the more profitable pastures of Glasgow airport. For a time, the only presence was the ghost of Elvis, who touched down briefly for a refuelling stop on his way to serve in the US Army in Germany; Prestwick is the only piece of UK territory that Presley ever visited.

'secondary' airport that is eager for trade. After having secured a favourable financial deal with the airport, Ryanair will then dream up a description for the airport that may not be geographically sound.

Thomas Mann once observed, 'A great truth is a truth whose opposite is a great truth.' Perhaps Ryanair had the great writer's ambivalence in mind when, in 1999, it began flying to his home town, Lübeck. The airline described the handsome medieval city as 'Hamburg', which already had a major airport and a flourishing business from London. To make matters worse, Ryanair advertised fares that were not only unbeatable, but also unobtainable. When Ryanair promised 'London to Hamburg £19 return', the destination airport was more than forty miles away from Hamburg, in an entirely different city. And the fare the passenger would pay was not £19 return, because a range of taxes and airport fees were not included that took the total to over £50. The offer was still an excellent deal for anyone who knew they were not going to end up where The Beatles cut their musical teeth, but in the birthplace of Thomas Mann.

This ad was the final straw for the Advertising Standards Authority (ASA). The body that tries to ensure ads are legal, decent, honest and truthful believes passengers' main concerns about a flight are where it goes and how much it costs, neither of which was immediately obvious from some of Ryanair's advertising. The ASA had already demanded that fares should include all pre-payable taxes. As a direct result of the Irish airline's ambitious claims about airports and the cities they purport to serve, the advertising watchdog told airlines that the name of the destination airport must be made clear, and that headline prices must match what the passenger pays.

Ryanair has repeatedly had its knuckles rapped by the ASA; the authority's spokesman, Steve Ballinger, said the Irish carrier was 'the worst offender in the budget airline sector.' The authority has no legal powers, and Ryanair is quick to cite its Irish base as a reason why British rules should not apply. But on more than one occasion, Ryanair has ended up in court to explain its alleged transgressions.

EXPENSIVE BA----DS was how Ryanair chose to announce its six new routes for the summer of 1999. The ad, which appeared in London's *Evening Standard* in February of that year, accused British Airways of greed. It claimed that travellers could save hundreds of pounds flying Ryanair rather than BA. The Irish airline naturally chose the departure days to suit its purpose: travelling out from the UK on a Monday or Tuesday, returning on a Wednesday or Thursday. Those had to be the exact dates; a day earlier or later, and Ryanair's fares went up; if a Saturday intervened, then BA's prices fell sharply.

Ryanair also chose not to mention that its flights departed from Stansted, while BA's left from Gatwick and Heathrow – much more convenient for millions of travellers. BA's fares also included free meals and drinks, while on Ryanair you must pay for anything more substantial than water. Small considerations, you may think, since flying to Turin, for example, will cost you £119 on Ryanair and £462 on BA. The problem was that BA did not fly to Turin. Instead, Ryanair quoted BA's fare to Milan, eighty miles away. The fares chart got stranger still. 'Ancona £129', boasted Ryanair, compared with £562 on British Airways. But BA's only destinations on the Italian Adriatic coast were Venice and Trieste, hundreds of miles away.

You get the idea: 'Biarritz £99', against £534 on BA. No, British Airways did not fly to Biarritz. Ryanair contrasted its fare with BA's to Bordeaux, 140 miles north. Oddest of all was Dinard. Ryanair said BA charged £315, compared with its own fare of £99. BA has not flown to the Brittany resort since the 60s, and the price shown was for a flight to Jersey and a connection there to a small Breton airline.

British Airways was furious. The Advertising Standards Authority upheld a complaint that the headline 'was likely to cause serious or widespread offence'. Ryanair undertook not to repeat it. But BA took the case to the High Court, issuing a writ that claimed trademark infringement and malicious falsehood. The airline's case was that Ryanair had failed to compare like with like.

The chilly courtroom at the Royal Courts of Justice on the Strand in central London was fairly empty when Mr Justice Jacob handed down his judgement. One reason was that no one from British Airways had turned up to listen to his verdict. In the Ryanair corner was Michael O'Leary, assorted photographers and journalists who had been tipped off about the judgement, and a retinue of public relations advisers. The chief executive could scarcely have written a better script for the judgement, which effectively concluded that its mud-slinging was justified. Ryanair, said the judge, had not given the unfair impression that its fares were much lower. 'I suspect the real reason BA do not like it is precisely because it is true,' he said. Mr Justice Jacob rejected British Airways' claim of unfairness, saying, 'The average consumer would know BA was cheaper if one stayed over a Saturday.' He also said that conventional airlines like BA 'exploit the fact that in the case of short, mostly business trips, people want to go out and home for the weekend,' and noted that many travellers resent the so-called 'Saturday night rule'.

The judge paraphrased BA's complaint thus: 'that Ryanair exaggerate in suggesting BA is five times more expensive because BA is only three times more expensive.' He added it was 'immature' for two large companies to be fighting such a dispute in court.

BA's absence left the field clear for O'Leary to milk the judgement for all it was worth. For a trained accountant, he has a way with words. Like Laker and Branson before him, the chief executive has mastered the sound bite that positions him as a David fighting on the traveller's behalf against the Goliath of

British Airways. Outside the court, he accused BA of adopting 'bully-boy' tactics in taking the matter to court: 'Today's a victory for the small guy, it's a victory for Ryanair and it's a victory for the consumer.' He said that his airline might take advertising headlined 'Expensive buggers'. In fact, Ryanair steered clear of profanity, instead taking out ads reading IT'S OFFICIAL – BA ARE EXPENSIVE.

British Airways' response was muted. 'We're disappointed and we'll be studying the judgement to consider whether we appeal,' said a spokeswoman. The airline let the case rest, after paying a legal bill estimated to be at least £250,000. The damage to its image was considerably greater. The newspaper poster proclaiming JUDGE BLASTS BA 'BASTARDS' in O'Leary's office shows the extent of the PR disaster.

Ryanair proceeded to rub BA's corporate nose in the dirt. 'British Airways can never match Ryanair's prices, they can't match our punctuality, they can't match our young aircraft fleet either. It's over,' says O'Leary. As he directed his airline's apparently relentless expansion, he targeted two routes that BA served from Gatwick: Trieste and Salzburg. Within months of Ryanair starting flying, BA had withdrawn from each.

In 2004, it was Ryanair's turn to be pilloried in court – this time for being unfair to disabled travellers. Every airline including Ryanair, carries passengers' wheelchairs for free. But some passengers with limited mobility ask for extra assistance simply to get through the airport, from check-in to the departure gate. The airport – or, more usually, a handling company – charges the airline for each passenger. Ryanair passed the charge on to the traveller, until a court decided this amounted to unfair discrimination. O'Leary responded by announcing a 'wheelchair surcharge', representing the amount per passenger he calculated the ruling would inflate ticket prices. To this day, customers will see a 'whcr schg' of £1.50 applied to their fare.

O'Leary specialises in upsetting travel agents, too. For a long time after Ryanair started reciting the low-fares mantra, it adhered to the convention of selling air travel through agents. The agent tapped the passenger's requirements into a computer reservations system (CRS) and booked the flights. For this the reward was 9 per cent commission, the industry standard for international flights. On a typical £59 return flight from Manchester to Dublin, this earned the agent barely a fiver; meanwhile the hosts of the CRS collected almost as much. But if a family of four was travelling, it was business worth transacting.

Unilaterally, Ryanair decided to drop commission to 7.5 per cent, in line with the rate paid on domestic flights. The agents howled, saying they were being asked to sell tickets at a loss. Ian Smith, then boss of Britain's biggest chain of travel agents, Lunn Poly, announced a boycott: his 800-plus Holiday Shops would no longer sell Ryanair. The Advantage consortium of agents said it would launch its own airline to Ireland to compete with Ryanair. (A decade later, this venture has yet to come to fruition.) Some agents said that they would still book Ryanair flights, but needed to apply a service fee for so doing. Ryanair took them to court to stop them. By 2001, at which point Ryanair was selling the vast majority of seats online, the airline sent out a letter to every agent in the country explaining that, at the end of 'a fairly painful retrenchment of Ryanair amongst its travel agency partners', it would no longer sell through the trade. On the day he saw the letter, Stephen Bath, president of ABTA, took the opportunity to rubbish the airline's prevailing offer of £9.99 flights to anywhere in Europe.

'All this talk of £10 flights is tosh as far as I can see. I got my secretary to check some flights on my favourite route to Dublin, and for me to go there and back tomorrow is £156, and the next day it's £189. I asked her to spend half an hour looking for a £10 ticket, and guess what? She couldn't find one. A lot of it is a figment of Mr O'Leary's imagination.'

O'Leary declined the opportunity to speak at the Association of British Travel Agents annual convention in Cairo in 2002, for reasons he explained in a recorded message to delegates: 'We certainly won't be going to Cairo for the ABTA Convention. I can think of no more useless a convention. It's a bit like holding a meeting of Alcoholics Anonymous in a big pub. We prefer to avoid the talking shops – we're too busy carrying passengers at lower fares.'

One of those passengers is the Croatian film producer, Sanja Ravlic, who lives in London. Even though Ryanair does not (yet) fly either to Croatia or to any of the countries that border it, she uses the Irish airline to go home. 'I'm not going to pay £200 to Croatian Airlines to fly from London to Zagreb,' she says. 'I'll go to New York for that. So I fly to Trieste in Italy on Ryanair and travel through Slovenia to reach Croatia.'

Another satisfied customer is, like O'Leary, a prominent contemporary Irishman. Sir Bob Geldof speaks up for the airline that has supplanted Aer Lingus as Ireland's top airline. 'If I can get a £7 flight to somewhere within two hundred miles of Venice, you know, destination unknown, magical mystical tour, well, I'll fucking take it,' says the former Boomtown Rat. 'Seven quid, I don't care where I fucking go.' An even bigger celebrity passenger was Tony Blair, who took his family on their summer holiday in 2001 aboard Ryanair. This episode was a double triumph for O'Leary's airline, since it got one over on both British Airways and easyJet. In June, a Downing Street spokesman had let it be known that the Prime Minister and his family would be travelling to their holiday chateau in south-west France on a no-frills airline. The *Daily Mirror* picked up the story, saying that the Blairs would be flying on easyJet for their French holiday in August. There was no official rebuttal from Alistair Campbell, so easyJet plastered the roadsides of Britain with posters saying, 'Tony Blair got a bargain this summer – so can you'. Unfortunately for Stelios, there was never any intention at 10 Downing Street that the family would fly to what was then easyJet's only French destination, Nice; it would be like flying to Liverpool for a holiday in Yorkshire. The chateau was much closer to Toulouse, served by British Airways, and Carcassonne, where Ryanair flew. Ryanair got the business because, says O'Leary, 'The savings the Blair family made flying with us compared with flying British Airways to Toulouse were in excess of £2,000. Even for the most well-off people these are huge savings which simply can't be ignored.' BA was incensed that the first family chose to fly someone else's flag – and by O'Leary's comments in 2002 to a business travel seminar: 'Businesses now need to be competitive. They need to stop drinking champagne at six o'clock in the morning on British Airways flights. They need to get there on time. With Ryanair statistically you're more on time. The question's got to be asked: why the hell would anyone fly with British Airways and pay four or five hundred quid just to be late?' Tardiness is a subject on which O'Leary keeps a close watch. If any of the first wave of departures from Stansted is more than five minutes late, he wants to know why.

Besides beating BA on timekeeping, Ryanair now carries more passengers. It is no longer the 'small guy'. Being the biggest is not, I suggest, a comfortable place to be. 'Being in the airline business has never been a comfortable place to be. If you want comfort join the local bank or something. This industry is interesting, it's exciting, and the good guys win out in the end.'

So where to next, Michael? We are standing outside his office, surveying his modest management kingdom, and looking at a map of Europe. 'You're now at the heart of our new route development strategy,' he says. Though the shape of the continent is familiar, the detail is not. It consists not of towns and cities, nor of physical features. 'Those dots are all airports,' says O'Leary. 'When you look at an ordinary map you think there's no more airports, in actual fact the place is absolutely awash with airports.'

They are the components with which O'Leary intends to realise his ambition. 'We'll go to half-a-dozen new destinations each year, two new bases every five years, unless we do something stupid like have a crash or join an alliance. There's a challenge every day in the airline industry not to do something stupid. Airlines are characterised by people who do something stupid.'

As O'Leary develops his theme, there are strong echoes of Herb Kelleher's mantra at Southwest: 'Too many airlines that have gotten it right for a certain amount of time have then suddenly started thinking they can walk on water, so they start buying hotels, or expanding into other businesses, or – if you look at British Airways – trying to serve every market you can from Britain.' Rod Eddington, BA's former chief executive, rejects the last assertion: 'The days are gone when any airline can hope to be a global airline. BA are not a global airline, it's a British airline that trades globally. It's not semantics, there's a genuine difference.' But he concedes that Ryanair has stuck to the Southwest business model assiduously: 'One of the reasons that Ryanair haven't slipped, is that they've been pretty disciplined about following the model.'

Like Southwest, Ryanair reacted to the events of 11 September by keeping all its staff, hiring more people and continuing to grow, when almost every other airline was doing the opposite. And O'Leary was unsparing in accusing rivals of using the attacks on America as a scapegoat for all their ills: 'Somebody in the current market has to talk about expansion. A lot of the problems you see in the airline industry – let's take Aer Lingus as a classic example – are not because of the awful incidents in the US. These had been coming for many months and possibly years. Some of Europe's flag-carrier airlines are still grossly overstaffed. They run at losses, they sell below cost, and they're incredibly inefficient. A massive restructuring of those airlines is twenty years overdue.'

In the aftermath of the attacks, O'Leary saw immediate opportunities to cut costs. Taking advantage of Ryanair's big cash reserves and the dire state of the market for new planes, he ordered a hundred Boeings, with options on fifty more. It was the world's biggest aircraft order of 2001.

O'Leary was one of the first to advance the now widely accepted notion that Europe's carriers will consolidate into three or four groupings of full-service airlines, with British Airways, Air France and Lufthansa in the forefront. He also believes that the European aviation industry cannot sustain the present number of no-frills airlines. He predicts that only Ryanair and easyJet will survive, with the others bought up or closed down: 'easyJet is fundamentally a good operation, except it's not a low-fare operation. But it's still very competitive with British Airways, Air France and Lufthansa, and I think they'll do very well.'

In February 2003, Michael O'Leary surprised the aviation world once again by announcing that Ryanair had bought its rival at Stansted, Buzz. Five days earlier, he had told journalists that he had no intention of acquiring another airline. But at the press conference to announce the purchase, he said that the price was so low that Ryanair could not turn the opportunity down. O'Leary took delight in comparing the £3m Ryanair paid for Buzz – 'petty cash', as he called it – with the £374m easyJet had spent on Go.

Even though the airlines were now nearly neck-and-neck in terms of scale, the 'phoney war' between them continued. They competed directly only on one route, from Stansted to Rome Ciampino. Three years on, the number of airport-to-airport pairs on which they are rivals is in single figures. But between them, the airlines have up to five hundred new aircraft on order. They have to fly somewhere. At present, they are studiously avoiding each other. But as both airlines grow, there are bound to be increased conflicts. And when that happens? 'There will be the most unholy scrap,' said Tim Jeans, while he was Ryanair's marketing director. 'There will be blood of unmerciful proportions spilt everywhere because quite clearly there will be a battle for supremacy on a particular route.' Ryanair's determination to oust competition became evident with its fares war with Go between Dublin and Scotland. Meanwhile, easyJet staged a pilot recruitment day at Dublin airport, clearly aimed at attracting Ryanair flight crew. But O'Leary maintains 'The lowest-cost airline will always win, and that will always be Ryanair.'

Some other prominent aviation figures believe that the Ryanair miracle cannot be sustained – notably Barbara Cassani, former chief executive of Go. 'They glorify making the experience as uncomfortable as possible,' says the woman whose offices used to look across an atrium at Stansted into Ryanair's London HQ. 'It's like a flying pub. Most of the time it's all right, though you invariably feel a bit dishevelled when you get off.' Cassani develops her theme. 'Ryanair's profitable, but they don't have a good relationship with their people and they don't have a good relationship with their customers. They have good operational integrity. I'm sorry – two out of four ain't good enough for me.' She singles out Ryanair's uncompromising customer relations policy: 'If a customer has a problem, they enjoy telling you to piss off. They believe that if customers aren't hurting, their costs aren't low enough.'

'Do we occasionally piss people off?' counters O'Leary. 'Of course we do. Of course we do. But most of the time they're asking for a refund on what everyone knows is a non-refundable ticket.' Ryanair's 'robust' customer care policy means passengers are informed, in O'Leary's words, 'We told you it was non-refundable. Now go away.' Malcolm Ginsberg, a leading aviation consultant, says this attitude is counter-productive: 'We have grown up. Tesco is no longer the dirty little store with boxes of food all over the place. The modern Tesco is a spotless organisation, a pleasure to shop in. People expect a little more and should not be driven like cattle. Likewise the Ryanair bubble will burst. It will take time but it will happen.' Surprisingly, perhaps, O'Leary also uses a Tesco analogy: 'The reason we'll be ruling the roost is much the same reason as Tesco's do. We charge the lowest prices and we give the best service. We have new aircraft, the most on-time flights, giving passengers exactly what they want.'

Sir Richard Branson, whose Brussels-based Virgin Express was in competition with Ryanair at Charleroi, is more charitable than Cassani or Ginsberg. 'The quality of the [Ryanair] product is not quite as good as easyJet, certainly not as good as Virgin Blue [Branson's Australian no-frills airline] but good enough for 95 per cent of people.' And he pays a qualified tribute to O'Leary. 'He's as tough as nails, a businessman through and through, no compromise. Arrogant but can get away with it because he's incredibly successful. He's not loved by his staff, but generally loved by the passengers for delivering fantastically low-cost travel.'

Delivering them safely, too: like other big no-frills airlines, Ryanair has an accident-free record. Following 11 September, some passengers actually switched to the Irish airline on the

FLYING ADVERTISEMENTS

Even by the juvenile standards of no-frills airline design, Ryanair's logo is pretty mediocre. Michael O'Leary doesn't care what I think: 'We have no intention of changing the brand or redesigning the image or the rest of that old nonsense. In my thirteen years at this company, Aer Lingus has changed its branding three times, British Airways has changed it three times, we've changed it not once, and the virtue of what we've done has been proven. People don't fly with Ryanair because of our image or our brand, they fly because we guarantee them the lowest fares, when you get on the aircraft it's clean, it's bright, it's safe and reliable.'

The best-looking Boeings in the fleet are those that use a Southwest trick: treating aircraft as flying advertisements. Kilkenny beer, Jaguar cars and the Sun newspaper have been plastered all over the 737s, in a sponsorship deal that is roughly equivalent to having one more passenger aboard every flight. Because the passengers only briefly look at the aircraft when boarding, there have been few objections – it's everyone else who has to look at the plane.

grounds that it would be less of an appetising target for terrorists than a flag-carrier airline. But in August 2002, a Swedish man of Tunisian descent was arrested at Vasteras airport ('Stockholm West', as it is ambitiously known) for trying to smuggle a gun aboard a Stansted-bound jet. O'Leary even managed to turn this to his PR advantage, by citing this as evidence of highly effective security at secondary airports. Other safety 'scares' have come and gone. There is nothing the aviation industry enjoys more than spreading rumours about the health, financial or otherwise, of rivals. Unsubstantiated assertions have been made about Ryanair's oldest Boeings and about the workload of the airline's pilots, and a libellous e-mail alleging safety lapses did the rounds. But O'Leary, like most chief executives, is obsessive about safety standards.

So far he has enjoyed a charmed career. When I ask O'Leary what he is most proud of having achieved at Ryanair, he becomes positively evangelical. 'Saving European air travellers hundreds of millions of pounds every year over the airfares they would have paid to British Airways, and bringing air travel within the pocket or the budget of most ordinary people in Europe. Low-fare carriers like Ryanair, and to a lesser extent easyJet, have proven that you can carry people and make money at fares that are half those of the high-fare airlines.'

What about the fact that British Airways is now aggressively targeting the European market? 'You're always going to be delayed. You'll get crap food, and a free drink worth £2 and you're going to pay £400 for it. The era of these rip-off airfares and horrible wine that you can't even drink are over.' (In his personal habits, O'Leary does not emulate Herb Kelleher of Southwest, and neither smokes nor drinks heavily.)

O'Leary never misses an opportunity to preach the Ryanair mantra and put down the opposition. To launch each new base, he takes a posse of Ryanair staff, analysts and journalists to the chosen airport, in a Boeing 737 bearing the message 'Auf Wiedersehen, Lufthansa' or 'Arrivederci, Alitalia'. When it touches down, he is surrounded by reporters, photographers and television crews. For them, and the public, it is most unusual to meet the boss of a large airline who claims 'We're stuffing it to Lufty' and predicts the demise of the German national airline. He does not hesitate to call or fax a journalist who he believes has misreported a story. Yet for all the outward flamboyance and high-profile hyperbole, O'Leary is an intensely private person who has none of the trappings that you would imagine for a man who has amassed a fortune in an industry where the usual experience is to lose one. He is, however, clear about his ambitions. In 1991: 'the only objective was to survive, to pay next year's bills. We were on the point of bankruptcy.' By 1996: 'We just wanted to be bigger in terms of traffic than Aer Lingus, and we achieved that.' Now that Ryanair is bigger in terms of traffic than BA, does O'Leary see an end in sight? 'I think when in four or five years time and we are the world's largest airline and there are no other mountains to conquer, then they'll probably sack me and put someone sane and sensible in to run the airline.'

O'Leary's advice to others who have succeeded in running airlines is to quit at the top. 'Aviation is littered with people who stayed in for far too long and lost a fortune.' But even though he has made a fortune and need never work again, he still puts in long, tough days. 'This is not work to me. We're running the biggest, fastest-growing low-fares airline in Europe, revolutionising air travel. You can look at us as a small Irish company stuffing it to British Airways and Lufthansa and Air France. This

is sheer fun at this stage. 'I'm absolutely convinced that nothing
will stop us, unless we screw it up ourselves through self-inflicted
stupidity or arrogance.'

7. EASY: YOU DON'T NEED A TICKET

It was 7 a.m., it was a wet, miserable, lousy day in Luton, and equally cold and miserable in Glasgow. I discovered very quickly that this was not going to be glamorous

Stelios Haji-Ioannou, founder of easyJet

The airline industry never has, and probably never will, produce a genius. Never has an airline devised a unique strategy to succeed. Most of what is needed is money

Franco Mancassola, founder of Debonair

Fly to an airport, not an airfield

easyJet advertisement at Stansted, Ryanair's main base

EASYJET FLIGHT 11: LUTON–GLASGOW, 10 NOVEMBER 1995

The entrance to the average airline's headquarters is an impressive affair, intended to impress visitors. But the HQ of Britain's most successful low-cost airline is far from average. For a while, the modest foyer of easyLand – the huddle of temporary buildings from which one of Europe's leading airlines is run – was adorned by a tent. It was a small, two-person job, strung from the roof. The canvas accessory was one of the more unusual weapons in the war waged by a young Greek Cypriot on Europe's traditional airlines since a 'wet, miserable, lousy day in Luton' in 1995.

Take one shipping millionaire, two Boeing 737s normally used for British Airways flights and several dozen gallons of orange paint, and you have a revolution in the skies. But industry watchers like myself were slow to realise the scale of the upheaval signified by the first flight of easyJet.

When the aircraft had landed in the gloom and the captain had welcomed passengers to Glasgow, says Stelios Haji-Ioannou, 'I took the microphone and made a short speech – the first to my customers,' says Stelios, as he likes to be called. 'I don't remember exactly, but I probably said, "This is a very important day for me, thank you for being on board, bye, have a nice day." And I got a round of applause and I thought, "Hey, they appreciate it! It doesn't matter that I've cut back on frills, on legroom, and the business class – they love it."' Also on the flight was easyJet's sales and marketing director, Tony Anderson: 'I sat quietly at the back of the plane relieved to still be on board after a number of my colleagues had been offloaded at the last minute to make way for a film crew from BBC's *Money Programme*.' Stelios had learned early on that the best publicity was free publicity, even if 'the images of Branson and his rock stars, and everything else that I had associated with the launch of Virgin was just not going to be the case in our company.'

EZY flight 11 provided a good story for the media because it was the first departure of an airline that had taken just five months from conception to first steps, far quicker than the normal gestation for an airline. As with Branson's Virgin Atlantic, the speedy birth did not, as existing carriers may fondly have predicted, lead to an early demise. On the contrary: easyJet has grown to become one of Europe's giant airlines, eclipsing rivals who once rated its survival in days or weeks.

In June 1996, just after Nice was added to the easyJet route network, I was waiting in the departure lounge at the Cote d'Azur airport for the flight to Luton. A man, not in uniform, was chatting to the staff at the desk. He was tall and well-built, with a generous grin and broad shoulders that supported an open shirt and a navy-blue blazer. He had dark and close-cropped hair, olive skin and a demeanour that suggested a wealthy upbringing. You could imagine him lazing away his life on a yacht in the south of France or the Aegean – options that were, indeed, open to him. But he had chosen to make life difficult for himself.

'Stelios had none of the airs and graces you would perhaps assume from someone born with a silver spoon (more like a platinum ladel) in their mouth,' says Anderson, who worked with the entrepreneur to create easyJet. 'How many multimillionaires would give up the opportunity for a playboy lifestyle to work in a tin shack in Luton often into the early hours?'

If you want to start an airline, it helps to have a billionaire Greek shipping magnate for a father. Since his birth in Cyprus on St Valentine's Day 1967, Stelios Haji-Ioannou believes he was groomed to take over his father's shipping line, Troodos. 'I saw myself as a ship owner, and that was what I was trained to do,' says Stelios.

He graduated from the London School of Economics in 1987, and took a Masters' degree at the City of London Business School. He also attended the London office that belonged to his father, Loucas Haji-Ioannou. By the age of 21, Stelios began working for the family firm. But after four years, he decided to set up his own operation. 'At the age of 25, somehow I convinced my father to trust me with a very large sum of money to go and start another shipping company,' he says.

A 'very large sum of money' meant $35m, at the time over £20m: 'enough to buy five or six tankers'. The announcement that Stelios was to resign from his father's company and start his own shipping venture made the front page of the Greek maritime journal: 'It's probably the first time I made the front page of a newspaper.'

Stelios was soon to make headlines for the wrong reasons. In 1991, a Troodos tanker named *Haven* was anchored off the Italian port of Genoa. She exploded; five crew members were killed, and her cargo of crude oil spread along the Italian Riviera. The entrepreneur and his father were twice taken to court in Italy for manslaughter. They were acquitted on both occasions.

Today, Stelmar, as the company is known (no prizes for guessing the derivation of the name), is listed on the New York stock exchange and is comfortably profitable. But within three years, Stelios realised that he was not the person to run it. He entrusted the firm to Peter Goodfellow, 'a safe pair of hands', says Stelios, and 'a much better executive than I am or ever want to be. He is more interested in the details, in the nuts and bolts, in running ships.' In 2002, Stelios stood down as chairman at the Stelmar AGM. 'The cycle has been completed from idea, to profitable big company of six tankers, to listing on the NY stock exchange, to retiring from the board in ten years.

'No Greek ship owner in my father's generation would have admitted that. They've always been very hands-on. So I made my mental shift, saying I'm not going to be running businesses in my life, I'm going to be starting businesses. I'm an entrepreneur.'

'The great thing about Stelios is that despite being a rich man's child, he's one of the few rich men's children who's done it with style and panache,' says another entrepreneur, Sir Richard Branson, who is something of a mentor for the easyJet founder. There are plenty of parallels between the chairmen of easyJet and Virgin – indeed, Sir Richard Branson says, 'I suppose I see a younger version of myself in him.'

At the point where the Greek Cypriot began to take his hands off the Stelmar helm, he had not met Branson. But Stelios spent plenty of time shuttling between his two offices in Athens and London. The choice of airlines comprised British Airways, Olympic Airways and a Greek company called South East European Airlines (SEEA), in the guise of Virgin Atlantic – a franchise operation in the colours of Branson's airline. SEEA wanted to expand, and the airline invited Stelios to invest. 'I was thinking of just putting a million dollars into it, something very small.' (This comment shows the financial realm in which Stelios resides.) 'If nothing else, I was thinking I'll be flying from Athens to London for free, that was my motivation.' After studying the market, and meeting Branson, Stelios decided against the investment. But by then, he says, he had contracted the virus that demands, 'I have to have an airline.'

'I think it had something to do with me trying to prove myself to my father. I was desperately trying to get rid of the "daddy's boy" image basically. And I had to do something away from home, in an industry that my father knew nothing about, in an environment where my surname meant nothing to anybody.'

The next twist took place in June 1994, when a story ran in a Greek newspaper. 'This article was saying, "Stelios, ship owner, son of Loucas, is thinking of starting an airline." The next morning there was a phone call from the Boeing representative in Athens, saying, "Can I come and visit you and tell you what Boeing is all about?" That taught me that expressing your thoughts, going public about your intentions, is never a bad thing.' In August of that year, Stelios arrived at the aircraft manufacturer's 737 factory outside Seattle. (Boeing's arch-rival, Airbus, 'did not even pick up the phone and ask me to lunch until 1997', says the man who soon became a regular visitor to Seattle. Yet now easyJet's fleet expansion is based on Airbus jets.)

It was during the first visit to Seattle that someone mentioned 'You have to try Southwest Airlines. You have to see how it works.' Stelios recalls 'In the year and a half that followed, I kept hearing rumours of how low-cost works in the States but it didn't work in Europe. But why would the Europeans be any different?'

The plan to start a European version of Southwest was beginning to crystallise. But first he needed some cash. He first raised the subject of starting an airline with his father over dinner, in the family summer house south of Athens, in the summer of 1995.

Stelios recollects his opening gambit: 'If I set up a marketing organisation, and I don't buy the aircraft yet, I think I can make it take off with five million pounds. That's all I'm asking for at the moment. If it doesn't work, I'll pull the plug. We don't have to start an airline on the operational side. I have found a way of leasing planes, with pilots and everything else. I'll build a brand.' He had already been in negotiations with GB Airways about leasing aircraft. GB Airways has a long and illustrious history, and is one of British Airways' leading franchisees. That last point reassured Loucas on safety standards, and the magnate took out his cheque book. Stelios shrugs, and almost throws away the rest of the story as: 'The airline started after my father gave me the go-ahead and the five million quid. I decided to call it easyJet.' His father made one stipulation about the venture: it must not be based in Athens. 'Probably the best piece of advice I ever took from my father,' says Stelios. 'It would have been a disaster: a small and seasonal market at the end of Europe.' Although easyJet now flies from Luton and Gatwick to Athens, plans for a separate airline, easyJet Greece, aimed at transforming the overpriced and underserved Greek domestic market, have never materialised.

To choose a location for the airline, Stelios first looked at population and concluded there were four options for starting a new airline: France, Germany, Italy and Britain. He says the final decision was based on language. 'I don't speak French so Paris was out of the question. Or German, or Italian. It would have to be the largest possible market in an English-speaking country, so London was the base.'

When most people talk about 'London airport', they mean Heathrow. It handles more passengers – around seventy million annually – than all the rest of the capital's airports combined. And it is effectively full. The city's second airport has long been Gatwick. But while the Sussex airport had some room for expansion, slots were not available at the times when most business travellers want to fly, at the morning and evening peaks. 'It was a process of elimination,' says Stelios. 'Basically the only two options were Stansted and Luton. I went to both and took the cheapest.'

If, in 1995, anyone had suggested that Luton airport would soon have scheduled flights to three dozen destinations, ranging from Aberdeen to Athens, they would have been politely asked to leave the departure lounge.

The Bedfordshire airport was still suffering from the damage to its image wrought by television advertisements in which a fragrant beauty, standing on the balcony of her hotel, was asked by her admirer, 'Were you wafted here from Paradise?' to which her reply came in a broad Essex accent, 'Nah, mate, Luton airport.' Yet, thanks to easyJet, Luton has become one of the budget traveller's windows on the world.

Luton, like Gatwick, had helped to pioneer charter flights. But Gatwick soon gained the upper hand, not least because the Sussex airport was easier to reach by most people in the capital. Getting to Luton airport from central London involved a half-hour train ride to the town's station followed by a fifteen-minute bus or cab ride. The rail line from London passed close to the airport, but a much-needed airport station took another four years to open after easyJet started flying. Yet Luton had an overriding advantage for a fledgling airline: it was the cheapest airport that served the biggest aviation market in Europe.

At the time, the man in charge of Luton was Richard Gooding. 'He was the first guy that realised there was some potential here,' says Stelios. 'He gave me the time of day, as a "paper airline", and sat down and drafted a contract that lasted for five years.' At the time, says Stelios, the original contract read 'like science fiction'. It contained a clause that, if passenger numbers in a year exceeded two million, use of the airport would effectively be free. Gooding was not in fantasy land – he realised that a throughput of passengers on that scale would transform the airport.

In June 1995 Stelios visited the Civil Aviation Authority (CAA) headquarters on Kingsway in central London. The CAA regulates all British airlines' safety and financial standards. On 7 July he applied for an Air Travel Organiser's Licence (ATOL) that the CAA required him to have in order to protect passengers' payments. In the middle of August, he signed the agreement to hire two GB Airways Boeing 737s, along with the services of the pilots and cabin crew – an arrangement known as a 'wet lease' (a 'dry lease' means the aircraft without the people, and a 'damp lease' is the planes and pilots but no cabin crew).

GB Airways is one of the most venerable and respected airlines in Europe.

It began as GibAir 75 years ago, ferrying passengers between Gibraltar and Tangier. Today, its main business is carrying passengers between London, Manchester and the Mediterranean in the colours of British Airways. In 1995, though, it was offering aircraft for charter in the low season. It agreed to supply planes and crew for an airline that, at the time, was still on the drawing board, but which now carries around ten times as many passengers. Yet if GB Airways had declined the contract, someone else would have stepped in. 'If you're small you've got to take your chances,' says the managing director, John Patterson. He joined GB Airways in 1999, but believes the decision to help Stelios was the right one: 'It was quite profitable, it ensured that jobs were retained, and most people look back on it as a good thing.' Stelios was less than impressed with one unnamed executive at the airline when he outlined his venture. The entrepreneur had said, 'Look, this is my business plan. I'm going to reduce fares. And that's how we will make money.' The executive smiled conspiratorially, says Stelios, and said, 'Surely it must be a tax fiddle?'

That summer was, says Stelios, 'a sea change for me' – not because he was dealing with aircraft rather than ships, but because every Greek ship owner is normally to be found on his yacht in summer. 'No self-respecting Greek does any business in the middle of August, and here I was in the middle of London sweating in an office trying to sign a lease for two 737s.'

The office in question bears no relation to the garish orange shed in a corner of Luton airport where easyJet currently resides. War on Europe's traditional airlines was declared from the Stelmar premises at 35 Curzon Street in Mayfair, where property prices reflect the neighbourhood's position on the Monopoly board.

On the evening that the deal was sealed, Stelios organised a celebration.

He was conscious of the huge risk to which he was now committed – along with his father's cash. 'I said to my friends, "You know I'm starting an airline." And people laughed. It's not the sort of thing you drop into a dinner conversation seriously.' The guests reacted with sympathy, not excitement, as though Stelios had told them he had just been mugged.

Up to this point, Stelios's experience of aviation had been purely as a passenger. He was now chief of a nameless airline. 'Once I became serious about it, I moved out of 35 Curzon Street and went up to Luton.' He chose an office in the executive aviation terminal – a small, prefabricated building set away from the main passenger terminal. It became the headquarters of Britain's newest airline. His first appointment was of a finance director: Nick Manoudakis, another son of a rich Greek magnate. Stelios set up shop with one PC from Dixon's, two desks and three phones. Plus 'a big round waste paper bin, with a note from me saying, "Scan documents, then throw them in the bin. This is a paperless office." '

One of the early recruits recalls that this theory did not work perfectly. 'In the airline's first few months the paperless office was implemented in its purest form. All employees had access to every document held within the airline. This inevitably gave rise to some problems, particularly when it was fairly easy to find out how much everyone was paid. If Stelios found paper on your desk it would be swept into the bin. Nick Manoudakis kept a hidden stash of documents in the ladies' toilets – the only place in the whole airline where they were safe from Stelios's eyes. The fact that his wife had become easyJet's administration manager meant that documents could safely be retrieved when required without questions being asked of Nick's use of the ladies' convenience.'

Besides being paperless, it was also an anonymous office, because easyJet had yet to be christened. 'In the early days we went to an expensive brand consultancy,' says Stelios. 'They put together a contract for consultancy for £100,000 payable in three or four instalments.'

Phase one of the contract required the consultants to deliver a 'Mood Board' for £20,000. One month and £20,000 later, says Stelios, 'they came into the office with some magazine clippings stuck on to pieces of cardboard, saying, "This is what the airline will look like." I said, "These are just magazine clippings!" The consultants said, "That's where you start from, that's how you start a branding exercise." I said, "I don't think we can keep the cost down like this, thank you very much, that's the end of the contract." '

So Stelios was £20,000 down, one month closer to the date when the aircraft would arrive, and still had nothing tangible to sell. The search for a name became increasingly urgent. As with Southwest and Virgin, a paper napkin came to the rescue.

'I was jotting down names in Harry's Bar in Mayfair, and the word "easy" kept coming back again and again. So I decided that that was going to be the name.' The easy brand, like Virgin, now applies to a variety of businesses: everything from Internet cafes to car rental. 'He did model his company on Virgin,' says Sir Richard Branson. 'There aren't a lot of companies in the world that stretch their brand, he's attempting that, and he's got a very good brand name to do that with.'

The key decisions that shaped easyJet happened quickly. As with Southwest, there would be no free meals. But unlike Southwest, easyJet would become the first airline in the world to dispense with the travel agent's services. 'I was only capable of cutting out the travel agents because I knew nothing about the travel business,' Stelios now says. 'I had no allegiances, I had no friends in that industry, I just said this doesn't make sense, we will not do it.'

The tricky part, as Branson found with Virgin, was to sell a new concept to a healthily cynical public. Stelios employed headhunters to find a young, imaginative marketing guru. Tony Anderson was at the time working for the Thomas Cook conglomerate in European project development.

'I was approached by the agency Norman Broadbent,' recalls Anderson. 'They told me that someone was looking to create a European version of Southwest. I was sceptical, but interested. I had worked in the States for BA and Thomas Cook, so I believed it could work here. And it was the opportunity to get involved in something very exciting.' At the interview Stelios, says Anderson, was charismatic, 'but not quite as confident and self-assured as he is today'. Anderson was appointed vice-president of sales and marketing – 'We tried the American titles for six months and it didn't work' – and started to formulate a marketing campaign. The problem: how to sell an entirely new concept in a business like aviation where customers are traditionally dubious of new companies?

'I was trying to answer the question "What's the catch?" One of the biggest decisions we took before launching the airline was to go one hundred per cent direct and sell all our flights direct to our customers.' The new airline was the first in the world to insist that every passenger had to book direct by phone, and pay with a credit card. 'A number of trends were in our favour,' says Anderson. 'The UK had the world's highest penetration of credit cards outside North America, and there was an established culture of buying over the telephone with companies such as First Direct and Direct Line having blazed a trail for us to follow.'

Britain's travel agents found themselves in the uncomfortable position of being frozen out by the new airline – and playing a central role as baddies in easyJet's campaign. 'It gave us a fantastic marketing opportunity to position ourselves as the airline that cut out the middleman, a concept that our customers could readily understand. While travel agents weren't reviled by the great British public they weren't exactly loved. I dreamed up an ad with a cartoon of Stelios putting a stake through a cartoon travel agent's heart under the headline, "at easyJet we know how to deal with bloodsuckers" but I bottled out, not least because I'd spent the three years of my life prior to joining easyJet with Thomas Cook.' The airline still boasts that it is the first airline in the world that has never paid a penny in commission to a travel agent. From day one, the cost of 'distribution' – the industry name for selling seats – was far lower than for other airlines. Reservations staff were paid £1 for each seat they sold. Because easyJet was always a 'point-to-point' airline that had no intention of providing connecting services with other airlines, it did not need an expensive computer system. But to get the phones ringing, it needed a brand.

The brand was designed in a tiny design consultancy in Luton called White Knight ('I'd found them in the *Yellow Pages*,' says Anderson). The company was based on a grim industrial estate a few miles from the airport. 'It was in one of the sessions at White Knight that the telephone number on the side of the aeroplane and our original version of the easyJet cartoon plane was born.'

It was also where easyJet became orange, with Stelios sitting behind the operator of the Apple Mac directing operations. The results, according to one competitor, were 'sub-GCSE graphics'. But Stelios believes the unsophisticated design, based on the shade of orange known as Pantone 021C, works. 'It just happened. And ever since then I've been fighting creative people who want to change it.' The response is always the same: 'No, don't touch it. It has to be orange. Don't try and inject creativity into it, consistency's what builds us.'

Having procured the planes, the premises and the paint, the next problem was choosing some routes. This was the easy part.

'I was trying to minimise risk,' says Stelios. 'All that had been proven to me up to now was that this thing works in a domestic environment.' The biggest domestic air markets from London were both in southern Scotland – so Glasgow and Edinburgh became the first easyJet destinations. With the routes and the start date planned, the press was let in on the secret. The first I knew about the new airline was when a scruffy fax turned up at the Independent office announcing the first flight of a carrier that was promising something different. New airlines that promise something different come and go at an alarming rate (one had gone out of business a few weeks earlier). Many of them never get off the ground at all. This one had a funny name, and a strange premise. It issued no tickets. Neither did it assign seats, nor get involved with complications like frequent-flyer schemes. Enough journalists were interested in the project to provide a decent turnout at the media launch, which was held at Planet Hollywood in Leicester Square, London. Anderson recalls that, 'A litany of travel correspondents turned up to predict our demise.' Stelios says he had to handle a huge amount of scepticism: 'Is it safe? What sort of planes do you fly? Are they the little propeller planes with rubber bands? Where is Luton?'

Luton was where work was continuing feverishly, to get the planes in the air by the appointed date. But the preparations were accompanied by the kind of management upheavals that would have finished off many a start-up. The chief executive, Peter Leishman, left abruptly. 'There was a clash of roles,' says Tony Anderson. 'Stelios wasn't expecting to be so hands-on, but he caught the bug and became de facto chief executive. And Peter was commuting back and forth from his home in Switzerland. I don't think it was ever going to work.' Leishman returned to Switzerland, where he became involved in Swiss World Airlines, which tried without success to operate a low-cost service to New York. Next, the chief operating officer, Dave McCulloch, fell seriously ill and died a few days later. And a month before the launch, easyJet was upstaged as the first no-frills airline between London and Scotland by Ryanair – at least according to Michael O'Leary, boss of the Irish airline: 'easyJet weren't the first low-cost airline between London and Glasgow. We started flying from Stansted to Prestwick in October 1995.'

Stelios disagrees about the nature of the Irish airline's flights. 'In those days Ryanair was just transforming itself into a low-cost carrier. In my mind, it was still essentially an ethnic carrier. They hadn't actually taken the low-cost model to the degree they have now. So it was still a conventional airline with tickets sold through travel agents, and I think you could still get free orange

EASYJET'S FREQUENT-FLYER SCHEME

According to the flight information company, OAG Worldwide, 98 per cent of business travellers collect frequent-flyer
points. 'I've always considered Air Miles to be my biggest
enemy,' says Stelios, the founder of easyJet. He would warn
his staff, 'It's not BA you are fighting, it's Air Miles.'

When he launched his third route, between Aberdeen and
Luton, Stelios believed 'These corporate executives would
not consider flying with us because they were being bribed
by BA.' So with a little inspiration from Southwest Airlines
in the 70s, he invented his own frequent-flyer scheme.
Anyone paying the highest fare, of £69, was entitled to
collect a bottle of Scotch upon check-in at Aberdeen. Stelios
insisted that, if the passenger's flight had been paid for by his
company, the bottle had to be donated to the office
Christmas party.

There was, though, a catch. 'Our low-cost consciousness
got the better of us,' says Tony Anderson. 'It was actually a
half bottle of whisky which didn't go down too well with
some of the passengers queuing up at the sales desk to collect
their bribe.'

juice on board. They hadn't quite taken it to its logical conclusion,
just bought some cheap aircraft from Britannia and that sort of
thing. In my mind there was Southwest out there, no one was
really doing it in Europe, and I had one chance of doing it.'

Ryanair's service to Prestwick, close to the town of Ayr, began
in October. The only less-auspicious time to launch a new airline
flying between an unfamiliar airport north of London and
Scotland is the middle of November, which is when easyJet took
off. 'That's when the aircraft was available,' says Stelios. 'It
wasn't a matter of choice, and we probably paid for it in terms of
losses in the first month, but that's neither here nor there. The
point was to get it off the ground, and aircraft are cheaper in the
winter than they are in the summer.'

Once easyJet was off the ground, Tony Anderson immediately
launched an attack on Ryanair – but with an ad that landed
easyJet in legal trouble. AYR MILES read the headline, explaining
that easyJet flies from Glasgow International, not Prestwick,
saving the 33-mile journey from Ayr. Ryanair did not object, says

Anderson: 'The response came from Air Miles [a subsidiary of British Airways] in the form of a lawyer's letter telling us that our use of the expression "Ayr Miles" was a phonetic infringement of their copyright.'

Anderson says that easyJet's arrival was treated with 'scorn and derision' by British Airways. But the load factors suggested the obituaries were premature: from the first day, easyJet was filling four out of five seats. Five days later, the Luton–Edinburgh run began with similar success. Predictably, the two much bigger rivals soon hit back with a classic squeeze to try to crush the upstart. British Airways and British Midland (now BMI) suddenly started offering return flights between London and Scotland for £58 – which just happened to be easyJet's return fare – with the added attractions of departures from Heathrow and on-board frills. Passengers who had been previously paying much higher fares were delighted, but easyJet's sales were dented. 'We were really hurting,' says Anderson. The strain took its toll on the airline boss, he says: 'Stelios was volatile and short tempered in the first six months when things were looking difficult.'

'I realised very early on that the key to this is filling the plane – occupancy, driving demand and everything else will follow,' says Stelios.

'So I went to Nick Manoudakis [easyJet's finance director] one day and I said, "What's our cash like?" And he said, "Well, about three and a half million." So I said, "Set aside another million for marketing. I'm going to spend a million pounds in the next three months." '

'Stelios opened his cheque book,' recalls Anderson. 'Our advertising budget was thrown out of the window. We bought almost every advertising slot we could find.' He describes 'one memorable meeting with Mike Hellens, the MD of our media buying agency' in which Stelios barked, 'Unless you spend a *million pounds* you're fired.' The world started to turn orange. There were full-page ads in the London Evening Standard and the Scottish press, wall-to-wall radio advertising and even a TV advertising campaign thrown together in a matter of days. Conventional wisdom dictates it takes at least a month to create a television ad, but Stelios had insisted, 'I want to have an ad on television on Friday.'

'It was Tuesday,' recalls Anderson. 'Things like this just do not happen. We came up with someone holding a toy plane. It was truly awful, totally embarrassing. In fact some people told me they thought we'd deliberately made it that way. But the price message, Scotland for £29, was sufficiently strong that it had the desired effect of making the phones ring off the hooks.'

'A man possessed': that is Anderson's description of Stelios during the first half-year of the airline's life. 'We were working seven days a week till late in the evening, our days peppered with crisis meetings. Everything ratcheted up the stress. But it worked, sales rocketed and eventually BA got the message: Stelios had deep pockets and easyJet was here to stay.'

Cheekily, easyJet put up posters at Glasgow airport inviting passengers travelling on BA or British Midland to cash in their full-fare tickets, pay £29 for the easyJet flight and pocket the difference. Not everyone paid £29, though. After the initial launch, the word 'from' crept in to the orange ads. Passengers found that £29 was merely the starting price, available to those who booked early for less-popular flights. Yield management, the technique of squeezing the maximum earnings from each planeload of people, pushed the fare up in £10 increments to £69 – still far less than the full economy fare on British Airways.

While the marketeers were spending a million, Stelios was preparing for his next destination. To choose it, Stelios simply worked down the list. Next was Aberdeen, Scotland's third-largest city. Anderson says there was another important element in the decision: 'At the time Heathrow–Aberdeen was the route with the highest proportion of BA Gold Card holders anywhere on their network.' A few years previously, BA had successfully seen off a challenge from a little-known start-up called Aberdeen–London Express. 'I suspect they were looking forward to dishing out the same treatment to the next airline attempting to encroach on the pot of gold that the Aberdeen route represented,' says Anderson.

By now the public was getting acquainted with the easyJet principle. So to maintain media interest, the airline started dreaming up stunts worthy of Southwest Airlines.

'We managed to secure a number of key advertising sites within the Aberdeen terminal,' says Anderson. 'These sites were strategically positioned around the BA check-in desk and above the luggage carousels where the "Fat Cats" collected their bags.' The airline's booking of the sites was viewed with some trepidation by the people responsible for granting advertising copy clearance; the ads at Glasgow inviting BA and British Midland flyers to switch airlines had already generated controversy. 'We were told in no uncertain terms that our copy would be subjected to close scrutiny prior to approval,' says Anderson. Sensing an opportunity, he drew up the memorable tagline, 'Beware: thieves operate in this airport'. He knew there was no chance that it would gain approval, which was precisely the plan. When the anticipated rejection came in the form of a terse fax, a strategic leak to the media resulted in sensational headlines in the local press. NEW AIRLINE'S ADVERTS BANNED was the headline in the *Aberdeen Press and Journal*.

The first trip I took on an easyJet flight was to Aberdeen, a few days after the route began in January 1996. I actually wanted to go to Edinburgh, but a rugby international was taking place in the Scottish capital that weekend, and yield management meant that the lowest fare being quoted for the one-hour hop from Luton was £59. In contrast, Aberdeen was still on sale at £29. So that was the one I took. My experience was just like that of millions of others since: it was extraordinarily ordinary. The plane was clean and comfortable enough for a one-hour hop. The staff were unusually dressed in a lurid shade of orange, but were polite and professional. I had to pay for coffee and biscuits but, as Stelios says, 'In the same way you don't expect a meal when you get on a commuter train in the morning, why would you expect a meal on a one-hour flight?' I thumbed down the A90 to Edinburgh, and for the first time in a long hitch-hiking career got a lift in a Porsche. I arrived in the Scottish capital earlier and richer than if I had caught the newly privatised train.

The first three easyJet routes demonstrated something that Sir Michael Bishop of British Midland had found when his airline started competing against British Airways on UK domestic routes: when new, low fares become available, the number of passengers increases by more than the extra capacity on the route. In other words, every airline finds it is flying more passengers. The problem for the existing carriers is that those passengers are paying lower average fares than before. By now, Stelios had persuaded British Telecom to allot him the number 0990 29 29 29, to remind people the base fare was £29.

British Airways saw its earnings eroded by the newcomer. But so too did two much smaller, independent airlines that, ironically, had paved the way for greater competition in aviation: Air UK and British Midland. Sir Michael Bishop believes that the part his airline played in opening up aviation has been overlooked by easyJet and Ryanair: 'They didn't have to fight the battles of getting the initial political and legislative freedom to actually run their businesses. That all had to be done, in our case, while we were struggling to survive as an existing business. Compared with the way we had to get into business, they've had a much easier ride.'

As fares between London and Scotland fell, the train companies were soon affected. Virgin Trains and GNER cut their fares to Glasgow and Edinburgh, and ScotRail eventually began selling its premium sleeper seats for as little as £19 each way. One reason the rail companies were able to respond like that was because they receive subsidies from the taxpayer. In contrast, easyJet faced a new tax of up to 18 per cent on air travellers, which came into effect within six months of the first flight.

The tax was Air Passenger Duty (APD), and the man responsible was the last Conservative Chancellor of the twentieth century, Kenneth Clarke: 'I decided that aviation was in an unusual position in that it's the only form of transport where no one was paying any tax on the fuel that it uses. For years and years governments have regarded it as totally normal to impose tax on petrol, diesel fuel and everything used by land and sea. For historic reasons nobody was placing any tax on air fares. For me that was an anomaly, not least because people who use aviation tend to be slightly more prosperous than those who use other forms of transport.' No country had figured out a way to impose a tax on jet kerosene, because of an international understanding that it should be free of duty. The argument used by the airlines against, say, an EU tax on aviation fuel is that planes would end up 'tankering' – ferrying fuel around the world. It would be worth a carrier's while to fill tanks tax-free in, say, Marrakesh or Moscow, in order to fly to London and use the extra to hop across to Amsterdam and back.

Clarke's solution was to impose APD of £5 on each European flight. It added nearly one fifth to the typical easyJet fare of £29. At the time, I called it a 'poll tax with wings', because of the way that it penalised more heavily people who sought cheap flights. Business travellers paying £500 to fly to Athens would barely notice a 1 per cent hike, but it put the airlines in the price-driven low-cost sector at a disadvantage. 'I've always been very, very upset about the way the government has decided to tax the aviation industry,' says Stelios. But APD has plenty of appeal to governments. It is a simple tax, collected by airlines, nigh-impossible to evade and raising over a billion pounds a year.

Shortly before the Tories were voted out of office, the Chancellor announced APD would double. 'That really pissed me off,' says the easyJet chairman. But Clarke is unrepentant: 'I can quite understand why he complains about the tax, but I think his case is made rather weak by the fact that his business has been booming remorselessly. If you look back at what's happened to aviation since the time that I introduced the passenger taxes, it has gone on from strength to strength.'

The incoming Labour Chancellor, Gordon Brown, chose not to cancel Clarke's increase. On a £29 fare, that meant a tax of 35 per cent. Since then, the Chancellor has tweaked APD so that one-way flights within Europe incur a tax of £5, which means that a return domestic trip stays at £10. To pay for this cut, he upped the tax for business- and first-class seats, increasing it to £40 for long-haul flights. But a loophole means that passengers on the new breed of business-class-only aircraft pay just the same tax – £20 – on a flight from London to New York as economy passengers on a hop to Morocco.

Despite the new tax, in April 1996 Stelios took what he now describes as 'the defining moment, the most nerve-wracking moment' in easyJet's history: buying the first aircraft. The acquisition of the Boeing 737 (with 'all my money, and not enough of it') signalled easyJet's admission to the major league. It had to fly somewhere, and Stelios chose Amsterdam, the first time easyJet had flown into one of Europe's key hubs. Links from London Heathrow to Schiphol airport were great moneyspinners for BA, British Midland and the Dutch airline, KLM.

The launch offer from easyJet was to sell all seats on the first day for 39p, which grabbed plenty of headlines. Since then, 'fly free' offers have become commonplace. Tony Anderson devised another twist. He inserted into easyJet's in-flight magazine a coupon addressed to the chairman of KLM, Pieter Bouw, complaining about the price of flights to and from Amsterdam. Loyal (or bored) passengers responded in their thousands. 'We turned up at their offices to personally deliver them to Mr Bouw. Needless to say we weren't granted an audience and only made it as far as the security gatehouse, though a representative did at least have the good grace to come down and collect them.' The event made prime time news on Dutch TV.

The French city of Nice, convenient for Stelios's apartment in Monte Carlo, followed five weeks later, on 5 June 1996. To publicise the new route, he invited the press to fly out with him and watch the Monaco Grand Prix from his apartment. Just as Southwest had demonstrated that the low-cost model could work beyond the boundaries of Texas, so easyJet showed that there was an appetite for no-frills on international routes in Europe. The list of destinations from Luton expanded to include Barcelona, Palma and Madrid – in direct competition with another Luton-based airline, Debonair – plus Geneva and Zurich.

In March 1998, easyJet bought into an ailing Swiss airline, TEA. Stelios moved the base from Basel to Geneva, and rebranded it as easyJet Switzerland. The Swiss have remained aloof from the European Union, and the country does not have the same 'open-skies' approach to airlines wanting to introduce new routes. Swissair opposed easyJet's plans to fly from Geneva to Barcelona. The authorities ruled that Stelios's airline could fly to Spain – but had to obey an obscure rule that its cheap flights must come with accommodation attached. Which explains the tent hanging up at the entrace to easyLand in Luton. The easyJet tent was originally pitched on a site on a rocky hillside close to Spain's border with France, about a hundred miles north of Barcelona. A photograph of it appeared on the website. Anyone who booked a cheap flight from Geneva to the Catalan capital was technically buying a package holiday, and this comprised the accommodation portion.

Eventually the Swiss relented, allowed easyJet to set fares as it wished, and the tent came home to be used as an example of easyJet's passenger-friendly aggressive marketing.

The longest route on the easyJet network – to this day – began on 1 July 1998: Luton to Athens. As with every no-frills launch, Tony Anderson was after some free publicity. The natural target for easyJet's publicity campaign for a new destination is the national airline. But the Greek flag carrier, Olympic Airways, was a complete commercial basket case. 'There was no mileage to be had in picking on such a weak competitor,' says Anderson. Instead, the travel agents were targeted. A series of 'cut out the middleman' advertisements appeared in Greek newspapers, until the travel agents won a court injunction against them.

'We responded by painting the offending expression in ten-foot high letters on the side of one of our aeroplanes and flying it down to Athens,' says Anderson. 'The travel agents rose to the bait in style, launching a high-profile legal battle culminating in a court appearance in Athens by Stelios.'

The easyJet boss had ensured there would be plenty of cameras at the court by promising vouchers for free flights to London for anyone who turned out to support him at the trial. 'On emerging from the courtroom Stelios was greeted by a horde chanting his name, all anxious to get the vouchers,' says Anderson. Some of those claiming the free flights were believed to be travel agents. The Luton–Athens route survives, along with a later easyJet link from Gatwick to the Greek capital. It is in competition with BA and Olympic Airlines – the switch from 'Airlines' to 'Airways' took place during one of the financial overhauls of the Greek airline.

As new routes were added, the easyJet methodology became apparent: Stelios was 'joining the dots'. On a perfect route map, every easyJet city would be linked with every other destination. This has two big benefits. Planes and crews can be worked to the airline's maximum advantage, and marketing spend is much more effective. An ad that promises cheap fares from Amsterdam to one destination is as expensive as one that offers ten alternatives.

By now, easyJet was operating the youngest fleet in the UK, thanks to a dozen new jets from Boeing. Ten days into 1999, a new base was established in Liverpool, with flights to Amsterdam, Barcelona, Geneva and Nice. The same week, *Airline* – the reality TV show – was born.

The ascent of no-frills flying had been paralleled by a television phenomenon, the 'fly-on-the-wall' documentary. It was perhaps inevitable that a low-cost airline and the docusoap should meet. ITV dusted off the name of a documentary series made in the 70s about the daily life of British Airways, *Airline*. There are plenty of casualties of these 'warts and all' programmes in the travel industry. The country's biggest charter airline, Britannia (now Thomsonfly), did not emerge well from its flirtation with the cameras, while depictions of the excesses of some of Unijet's overseas reps reinforced the image of debauchery in Mediterranean resorts. But the number of series of ITV's *Airline*, the everyday story of easyFolk, is approaching double figures.

'I am a risk taker by nature,' says Stelios, when I ask why any commercial organisation should expose its inner workings to prime time TV. 'I like risks, I can manage them. It's very easy to say with the benefit of hindsight, "you're famous anyway, why the hell subject yourself to that tormenting experience?" And the answer is that we weren't that famous back then in '97 when they first approached us. So it was a question of rolling the dice and thinking, "how can we make this company a household name in this country?" And it was the easiest, cheapest way of doing it. We took some risks, but I think people appreciate the openness.'

The airline's officials are permitted to watch the programme before transmission, but final editorial control rests with the production company, LWT. The storylines were already wearing thin by the second series, comprising mainly a sequence of upset and/or abusive passengers who have missed their flights, plus C-list celebrity passengers and over-acting staff. But there seems no limit to the public appetite for irate late arrivals. Every time the programme goes out, there is a visible rise in bookings for easyJet. 'OK, sometimes we're late, and sometimes the check-in desk closes before you arrive, but so what? It happens on every airline. And I think people do appreciate that we're entirely open, and we live with the cameras filming every aspect of our life. At least they remember the name, and they fly with you,' says Stelios. 'To put it bluntly, if that's the worst thing that can happen to you when you fly easyJet, you're probably all right.'

Loyal viewers, of whom there are still several million, have witnessed an airline enjoying constant growth, with a founder who comes across as a genial godfather of no-frills flying – and personally goes to Seattle to kick the tyres of the new Boeings that he orders. The programme shows him working constantly on easyJet flights, talking to every single passenger – 'How did you book with us? What do you think of us?' – which, on the flights I have shared with Stelios, is typical.

The formula was replicated in 2005, when the entrepreneur launched another travel venture: easyCruise. A team of programme makers spent the summer aboard easyCruiseOne, for a Sky TV series called *Cruise with Stelios*. The entrepreneur now appears in the title – and milks every opportunity to cash in on his brand. In 1995, he says, 'basically it was a question of labouring away in Luton trying to make it happen and battling against complete consumer apathy. One thing about the cruise venture is that as soon as I mention the fact that I'm even looking at it we received huge publicity and as we're coming close to the launch it's almost becoming a household name at least in the UK.' Because the name of the cruise docu-soap, unlike *Airline*, gives him a name check, it invites the viewer to make the association with the 'easy' brand. And, thanks to the Internet, it is a short step from there to making a booking on www.easyCruise.com.

When Stelios started easyJet, the Internet was only slowly emerging from its origins in academic life. 'Stelios was himself initially sceptical, setting a limited budget for us to build our first site,' says Tony Anderson. Early in 1998 (about the time filming for *Airline* began), easyJet had a very basic website that did nothing but to tell people to ring the call centre. As is customary in telesales marketing, a unique phone number was assigned so that its reach could be tracked. At a marketing meeting, Stelios discovered that hundreds of callers were dialling the number on the site. 'So that's what convinced me to invest a little bit more money to make the website interactive so it can take bookings.' The airline made its first Internet sale a few months later and has never looked back: almost all easyJet seats are sold via the Internet.

Today, Stelios sees the world-wide web as crucial to his success. 'The Internet has probably had a bigger effect on people's ability to fly than the jet engine. The jet engine was an improvement on the propeller, but what really made [aviation] a mass market for everybody was the ability to fly someone for a pound. The ability to say that "I will rationally and economically speaking let that seat go for £1" – that's quite a revolution. You can only do that with the Internet.' The reason you can do it is because the cost of distribution – selling the seat – falls almost to zero.

Stelios soon realised that the customer needed to be bribed to buy online. 'My contribution to this industry has been the web discount,' says Stelios. 'You incentivise the consumer to behave in a way that saves them money and saves you money, so you've aligned interest.' The airline soon introduced the so-called 'rolling window', restricting telephone bookings only for people flying in the next two months. 'So the people who are keen to get the best prices are forced to go on the Net,' says Stelios. 'That's what pushed easyJet from zero to 90 per cent in two years.' Soon, the booking horizon for technophobes had fallen to a week.

With buoyant sales, and a web of bases at Luton, Liverpool, Amsterdam and Geneva, easyJet was beginning to look a lot like the cherished Southwest Airlines. Which meant that it was time for Stelios to move out of the limelight. 'I'm not interested in running anything – ships or planes. I'm interested in having ideas, implementing them, working very hard on them and handing them over to executives to do the job properly.' The beneficiary was Ray Webster, a New Zealander who had begun working in aviation before Stelios was born. Besides vast amounts of experience, he handily possesses a formidable intellect. He had been appointed as managing director (later chief executive) in February 1996 after an interview of only twenty minutes, as Stelios relates: 'On a phone call from New Zealand, Ray said, "I want the job." And I said, "Are you really interested? Are you keen?" And he said, "Yeah." So I said, "Come over for an interview, but you have to pay for your own ticket from New Zealand." The conversation was on Thursday and he was in Luton on Saturday morning, from New Zealand. It was really a very quick affair.'

I first encountered the former engineer in a car park opposite Guy's Hospital in a particularly unsalubrious part of south-east London. Ray Webster, with 35 years experience in aviation, had accompanied Stelios to the launch of easyRentacar; the chairman seems to have a knack of starting ventures on grey, miserable days. Stelios unveiled his car rental venture, which aimed to strip away the costs of hiring vehicles, and brought along the man who was taking over the easyJet reins. (Later, a passenger whom I met on an easyJet flight to Barcelona told me an interesting story about Stelios. He had met her on a flight, and urged her to book an easyRentacar next time she went to Spain. When she arrived at the Avis desk at Barcelona airport, she found a familiar figure in the queue ahead of her – none other than Stelios.)

Webster was a strategic planner for Air New Zealand who had been given the task of exploring the opportunities for a low-cost airline. 'The company unfortunately took the other option of buying Ansett, and the rest is history,' he said. (History relates that, after massive losses, Air New Zealand closed down Ansett within days of the terrorist attack on America on 11 September 2001.) In 2002, the airline set up a low-cost domestic airline, along the lines that Webster had suggested. But by then, the New Zealander was at his desk, ten thousand miles away in Luton, in a very crowded and very orange easyLand; perhaps a blessing in such an orange environment, Webster is colour-blind.

Unlike all the other airlines' chief executives to whom I talked for this book, Webster had no separate office. 'One of the problems with today's traditional airlines is that they've got used to all these luxurious environments and very comfortable existences for the executives,' he says.

'They're not challenged in their work: "I've got my office, and a secretary to bring me my tea . . . and I've got a driver to take me to lunch."' His desk was located in the middle of an open-plan office (though the precise nature of the plan appears a mystery), close to Toby Nicol, the airline's PR guru. 'We have to make sure that people feel part of the business,' says Webster, 'and that executives are not shut away from the business, but they're all part of it.' Despite half a lifetime of experience in aviation, he soon found that the airline he was piloting was on a journey into the unknown. 'There's no road map to what we're doing, we have to be very quick on our feet, we have to be very quick to seize opportunities.'

The great Gatwick gate grab was an example of that attitude. In the wake of the 11 September attacks, British Airways' initial response was to slice dozens of flights at Gatwick, making thousands of staff redundant. BA was retrenching from the dominant position it had enjoyed at Gatwick for a decade. As soon as the news broke, Webster headed around the M25 from his Luton office to the Sussex airport. The easyJet chief executive snapped up dozens of slots, along with the best gates at the airport: on the South Pier – closest to the main runway, saving valuable taxiing time. Webster has a calm, friendly demeanour. But to see the relaxed smile disappear, you needed only to mention the prospect of head-to-head competition. 'We will certainly not tolerate that. We think the market in Europe is immense: there's absolutely no reason at all why a low-cost airline has to start stamping on the patch of an existing one. There's a big sandpit here and plenty of space.'

That 'zero tolerance' attitude became clear late in 2001, when BA's no-frills venture, Go, announced its plans to fly from Belfast to Edinburgh and Glasgow. 'They will find it very, very difficult to make profits on those routes,' Webster said at the time. 'We have a very good cost base and a very strong brand. As if that wasn't enough, they tried to take on Ryanair by flying into Dublin. These guys are on a suicide mission.'

That might not have been an ideal choice of phrase so soon after the terrorist attack on 11 September. The tragedy in New York, though, had transformed aviation. So-called 'legacy' airlines like British Airways saw their fortunes slump, while by the end of October 2001 easyJet's share price had doubled in a single year. It had flown more than seven million passengers, at an average profit of £5.50 each. But the airline was not growing fast enough. Early in 2002, secret talks began with the owners of Go about a possible takeover. By May, news that the discussions were well advanced had leaked out. While confirming the rumours, Webster also revealed that easyJet was in talks with its arch-enemy, British Airways, about taking over the chronically loss-making German subsidiary, Deutsche BA. At a stroke, easyJet leapfrogged Ryanair to become the largest no-frills airline in Europe – and Stelios announced he would step down as chairman of his creation.

Webster chooses his words carefully when explaining the founder's departure. 'There is a corporate need to make sure that easyJet is seen to be a well-run business in the eyes of shareholders and also in the eyes of the wider community, governments and in the minds of passengers. It is inevitable that you are going to see a less flamboyant company profile, which is an inevitable part of a company growing up.'

Stelios stayed long enough to see through the order for 120 new Airbuses, with options on 120 more. The decision to go for a mixed fleet was controversial, since it goes against Southwest's dogged adherence to the Boeing 737. But Stelios says, 'Economies of scale have diminishing returns: after a certain point, they don't get any cheaper if you're operating the same type. We need about six sets of pilots per aircraft when we had twenty aircraft, we'll need the same when we have 164 aircraft. It doesn't get any better beyond a certain number. The Airbus deal will give us a cost per seat which is 10 per cent lower than the last Boeing deal. Now how often do you get 10 per cent off your cost base by doing one transaction?'

Stelios gave up the helm at easyJet partly to concentrate on his other enterprises: 'I tripped over a few times in the new businesses so I have to get them back on track. I have to clear up some of the mess I made.' While easyJet is a textbook business success, his other ventures have encountered problems. The easyEverything chain of Internet cafes expanded too fast in too many disparate markets; easyRentacar created some off-road rage when customers were charged for damage that they disputed; and easyBus struggled to turn a profit. All three models have been comprehensively overhauled, and the names of the first two have been changed to easyInternetcafe and easyCar. But easyHotel appears a better prospect. The first budget hotel opened in west London in 2005. As an example of the synergies in 'easy' businesses, the basic design of the bedroom is based on the cabins aboard easyCruiseOne. Despite its rooms being classed as Small, Very Small and Tiny, and the absence of windows in most rooms, the prototype has been maintaining close to 100 per cent occupancy. As a franchise business, the exposure to risk is lower than for other enterprises. His cruising business enjoyed a successful summer, and the vessel sailed across the Atlantic to introduce the easyCruise concept to the US market in the Caribbean.

Stelios has proved himself to his father. So as his fortieth birthday approaches, why not give it all up to spend more time with his money? 'I need a job. For me, work is a need, not an optional extra or a subsistence issue. I derive a lot of pleasure from taking on challenges that people say cannot be done.' He also takes pleasure from the difference he has made. 'Appreciation by the people whose lives have changed because of easyJet is what keeps you going in the sense that I was born in a wealthy family so I didn't really have to work to live, I certainly didn't have to endure going through the experience of starting an airline in Luton. I mean I could've stayed in the shipping business, the family business, but ten years later I'm still trying to start businesses and make a difference in people's lives because I really appreciate and take courage from the feedback and the popularity that this business has given me.'

Stelios still believes passionately in his airline creation, and the mantra behind it. 'In this market the lowest cost producer will win. Nothing else matters. Safety's important, and punctuality's important, but once you take those as a given, nothing else matters – not the colour of the plane, not the designer outfits of the cabin crew, not the quality of the sandwiches, not even which airport you fly from.' Over the next five years, he says, 'easyJet will do more of the same, better and better, making a difference in more people's lives.' The airline will be doing that without the involvement of Ray Webster, who stepped down as chief executive ten years and three weeks after that first flight from Luton to Glasgow. He handed over to Andrew Harrison, formerly the boss of RAC – and the antitheses of Webster, in that he has no airline experience. 'They'll probably do a lot better with me out of it, quite honestly,' says Webster. 'We've got a great team of people, very energised, very focused, and this is an opportunity for renewal.' He leaves an airline that has gone from nil to more than 30m passengers a year in a decade – and precipitated the transformation of travel in Europe.

On the morning of 10 November 2005, I flew from Luton to Glasgow, replicating that first flight a decade earlier. But I didn't pay £29 – I paid £11 less. Such is the competition between the biggest cities in England and Scotland that off-peak fares are widely available below £20 each way. I returned overnight on a ScotRail sleeper, which cost exactly the same as the price of that first flight – £29 – but besides four hundred miles of rail travel included a bed for the night and tea and biscuits in the morning. Stelios's no-frills revolution has transformed even a with-frills form of terrestrial transport. 'Travel improves understanding,' he says. 'Greater understanding has to be good.'

Stelios now owns one-sixth of the company, while his brother and sister each own slightly more than 12 per cent. FL Group – the parent company of Icelandair – has a 13 per cent stake in the airline. But for most people, easyJet equals Stelios. The genial entrepreneur is not just popular with travellers; he is also well regarded by most of his counterparts in the industry. 'He's a very pleasant sort of person,' says Sir Richard Branson, who was the surprise guest at the last easyJet meeting chaired by Stelios: 'If there was a vote amongst his staff against Michael O'Leary's staff, he'd win it hands down.' Barbara Cassani, founder of Go, says simply, 'He's a brilliant guy.' One of the few other women prominent in the travel industry, Martha Lane Fox, founder of LastMinute.com, believes 'Stelios is fantastic.' Even Franco Mancassola, boss of Debonair – easyJet's low-cost rival at Luton that failed to survive – summons some faint words of praise: 'Stelios is a brave man. Of course it's easy to be financially brave when you've got plenty of money. Bless him.'

8. GO: FROM START TO FINISH

It's inevitable that once you've had a success people will copy you
Stelios Haji-Ioannou, founder, easyJet

I really love this idea of having your cake and eating it too – finding a way of giving people something that was just that little bit more but still very true to being low cost
Barbara Cassani, founder and chief executive, Go

I'd advise her to shut up, take the money, be very happy that she's one of very few people who've made a lot of money out of aviation; easyJet paid far too much for the company
Michael O'Leary, chief executive, Ryanair

GO FLIGHT 901: STANSTED–ROME

Go's first-ever flight took place one sunny May morning in 1998. Along with the usual crowd of airline top brass, excited travellers and seen-it-all-before journalists, there was something strange about seven of the passengers in the queue. They stood out at check-in at Stansted because all, including a large, Mediterranean-looking gentleman, were wearing orange boiler suits. Stelios of easyJet wanted to make sure that Go's inaugural flight was anything but easy. In the tough environment of the no-frills airlines, heaping scorn upon your rivals is standard practice. But this scenario was different; why had Go aroused so much anger from easyJet?

'The low-cost airline from British Airways,' as Go originally called itself, had a short but very eventful life. Its conception was controversial, its birth was noisy and, as a teenager, it 'flew the nest'. But some critics said it was born with a silver in-flight spoon in its mouth, funded by a rich parent with the express intention of squeezing rivals out of business. Their anger focused on one woman: Barbara Cassani, the stylish and – say friends and foes alike – sexy woman who brought Go into existence. For four years, she was the only female airline chief executive in the world. From BA's original investment of £25m, Cassani created a company that was eventually sold for fifteen times as much, in a deal that erased one of the great marketing success stories of the past decade.

In the almost exclusively male higher echelons of aviation, Barbara Cassani is a striking exception, not least because her background is so different from most airline executives. She is first-generation American, born to an Italian father and Irish mother in Boston in July 1960, in the heady summer days when the city was the hub of the Kennedy campaign for the US presidency. Cassani could have been a diplomat. She graduated from the New England college of Mount Holyoke in 1982 with a degree in International Relations, which she followed up with a Masters' in Public Affairs at Princeton, the Ivy League university in New Jersey. 'Your education either teaches you how to think, how to look at things critically, or it doesn't,' she says. 'I was lucky and those were the skills that I took out of my education.'

Cassani headed for Washington DC. But instead of taking her diplomacy expertise to the State Department, she joined Coopers & Lybrand (now PricewaterhouseCoopers) as a management consultant in its international division. 'That was a very helpful way of training my brain to think of different business problems.' But by 1987, Cassani had had enough of trying to sort out other people's problems. 'I was frustrated with coming up with what I thought were great ideas, and then have these idiots that were called the management implementing them.'

So she joined British Airways. At the time, BA had just been privatised. The airline had, until then, been regarded by some of its staff as a particularly comfortable branch of the civil service. The newly aggressive board was keen to import American expertise to shake the company up. So Cassani joined as an internal business consultant, with the eventual intention – on both sides – that she would move into senior management.

The existing BA management team was overwhelmingly male, middle-aged, conservative – and British. Cassani walked in and started to challenge the status quo. Besides being young and attractive, she had to be tough. According to one senior figure in the airline at the time, 'Cassani came in and was fairly quiet at first, but she suddenly seemed to have a meteoric rise and managed to attach herself to the top people. Wherever Cassani was tended to be on the inside.'

In the decade that she spent with the airline before starting Go, Cassani had seven jobs. She says she was called in to work on a project when her bosses were uncertain about the next move: 'We really don't know what to do here, so we'll ask Cassani to do it.' She shudders when she recalls some of the tasks she was asked to work on: 'I had to investigate why one US tour brochure cost $10,000 to produce yet it only generated ten seats. Aaaahh!'

Cassani impressed Bob Ayling. He had joined BA in November 1985 as its legal director, and nimbly moved up the ladder to become the airline's chief executive. 'She always struck me as someone who stood out from others because she's got courage, personal courage. She doesn't say things because they are the party line, she says them because she believes in them.' One of the things Cassani believed was that a job to which she had been assigned should be abolished.

'I was head of sales in the southern part of the UK – it was massive, I could have been Queen, it was huge.' She did not, though, feel that the structure fitted the way the business was generated. 'So I was part of a team that reorganised the sales force, and I got rid of my job. I was very happy doing that. Some people think it's nuts, like, "Why on earth do you want to get rid of your own job?" But I just didn't want to be doing a job that is useless.'

During her time, things she was asked to do led her to making an appearance in Martyn Gregory's book *Dirty Tricks: BA's secret war against Virgin Atlantic*. The writer asserts that Cassani analysed sales and punctuality statistics from Branson's airline. These had secretly been taken from the BA reservations computer that hosted Virgin's flight information. 'I was a manager in the sales department at the time,' she later said, 'analysing information that I subsequently found out had been obtained through Virgin systems. That became one of the areas of interest in the case. It was a bit part, but it was a very sad time in BA's history. There were things going on within the company I didn't know about. I could vouch for my own behaviour as being proper, but there were question marks around the company.'

What turned out to be Barbara Cassani's last line-management job in BA was in the airline's most crucial battleground, the US. When she arrived at BA's New York headquarters, she was alarmed by the airline's pay agreements. The call-centre staff, for example, earned more than any other telephone salespeople in the US. 'It wasn't because the management were stupid and it wasn't because the unions were evil, or because the people were lazy,' says Cassani. 'It was a series of things that happened over years and years and years. The true objectives of remaining competitive in the market, but not ahead of the market, were lost. Some of the management I worked with were very negative about unions, but my view is that it takes two to tango. The unions didn't put these wages up, the management did. Obviously I did play with the cards I was dealt when I was in that job, but I didn't feel comfortable with it.'

During her time in New York, Cassani met a British investment banker, Guy Davis. They married, and have a daughter and son. A less successful relationship was BA's liaison with US Air (now US Airways). British Airways had originally courted United, then the world's biggest airline, as a strategic partner. That deal fell through, precipitating the 'Black Friday' crash in London and Wall Street of 1989. BA settled instead for a substantial stake in US Air, an ailing second-string carrier. 'It was a very good financial relationship for BA – they got pots of money out of it,' says Cassani. But the alliance fell apart amid considerable acrimony. 'There wasn't enough win-win on both sides. BA was winning and US Air didn't feel on a day-to-day basis that they were. BA quite rightly said, "Hey, we coughed up a couple of hundred million bucks and we kept you in business when nobody wanted to talk to you." But it's amazing that as time goes on, a new chief executive comes in place, US Air said, "What have you done for me today?" '

Even before the tempestuous corporate divorce had been completed, British Airways had set its sights on a more attractive partner. The company drafted in Cassani as part of the negotiating team for the proposed strategic alliance with the giant American Airlines. As it had tried with United and US Air, BA wanted to team up with an American carrier to offer joint services and marketing, a shared frequent-flyer scheme and 'seamless' travel to customers. Cassani spent a year in discussions that foundered in a morass of legal challenges over competition issues. By the end of that stint, Cassani was through with BA. 'I loved the company in the sense that I had received an enormous amount of personal opportunities. I had a wonderful time and worked with really good people, but I really needed to do something different.' She told Bob Ayling, 'The only thing I really want to do is to run my own business.'

Bob Ayling had been studying the low-cost sector for some years: 'We had talks with Ryanair about a possible investment by BA but for various reasons this was not proceeded with,' he says. 'There was then an approach by easyJet to British Airways, which we responded to, but those discussions did not proceed to a conclusion. So if there wasn't to be a vehicle in which we could invest, the third route for BA was to establish a business of its own.' Ayling concluded it would be impossible to create a fully fledged no-frills brand within the BA empire: 'Unless you have something which is wholly outside the existing structure, costs leech across.' Vested interests, he believes, will see to that: 'The functional organisations within a mother company are powerful enough to capture and kill a radical new thing like this.' And that meant he needed a tough new boss to head up a new no-frills operation.

'If a low-cost airline set up by British Airways was going to be successful, it had to be run by somebody who had the stamina to take on the rest of the company.' Just as there would be objections from outside, predicted Ayling, there would be jealousy and opposition within BA. 'You had to have someone who had the personality to cope with that.' Barbara Cassani was the woman. In 1997, she was 'completely taken aback' to be offered the chance to start her own business.

'It's like that expression, "Be careful about what you ask for, you just might get it",' she says. Her family were happily settled in New York; her husband, Guy, had never been to America before they met, but was now ensconced in a good financial job in Manhattan. 'I called him up and he said, "You just have to do it! You do!" So I said "Thank you. Bye." And I scooted off to London and started working on the business plan.' The family remained in America for five months, while Cassani commuted between New York and London. She soon discovered that Ayling's concern about internal pressures was well founded. 'In some ways it was a hindrance being part of the BA group because they were people with very strong views of how they thought things should be done, and we had to fight those off.'

When 'Operation Blue Sky', which led ultimately to Go, was launched in November 1997, Cassani was given a free rein in drafting the business plan – apart from three key stipulations that Ayling laid down. The first was safety: 'It was going to be tagged, for some time, as "the low-cost airline from British Airways",' says Ayling. 'Therefore anything that went wrong at Go was going to come back on BA itself.' Go's safety systems, he says, 'were put in under the very close supervision of the BA safety managers.' That, he says, was an area he would not compromise on. 'Barbara just had to live with that.' The second area was customer service. Even though the no-frills operation was a different approach from 'mainline' BA, Ayling believed, 'If people were really fed up they would equally be fed up with British Airways. So the customer proposition had to be an honest one which we knew could be satisfied.' The third issue comprised the trade unions that had just given BA's chief executive a fair amount of grief. Bob Ayling had experienced a damaging and expensive industrial battle with cabin crew, which culminated in a three-day strike: 'I made it clear to Barbara from the very beginning that this was not going to be a non-union business. That had no future. It had to be a unionised business, but with the relationship between the management and the unions, from day one, set up on a completely different and new basis.'

As a number of US airlines have painfully found with their own low-cost offshoots, trying to squeeze significant savings from the industrial agreements that burden the average 'legacy' airline operation is extremely difficult. Barbara Cassani had discovered this five years earlier.

In 1992, Dan-Air was heading for a corporate crash. The Gatwick-based charter airline had diversified into scheduled flights at an extremely inopportune time. In the financial gloom that followed the Gulf War it was bleeding cash across a range of European flights from Gatwick to destinations such as Vienna, Lisbon and Paris. The debt-laden company was on the brink of collapse when British Airways bought the scheduled part of the failing airline for £1. It gained a ready-made European route network, and a large number of staff whose pay and conditions were different from those at BA. Cassani was brought into the team charged with bringing the two operations together.

British Airways has always struggled to make money at Gatwick. The problem is that BA's costs at the Sussex airport are almost as high as at Heathrow, yet passengers are not prepared to pay as much for flights. The usual rule, on otherwise identical routes, is that revenues are 20 per cent higher from Heathrow than Gatwick. BA's network from Gatwick has always had a touch of the arbitrary about it. When the airline amalgamated its existing network with that of British Caledonian in 1987, it was left with an untidy mix of routes: an unwieldy collection of domestic, European and long-haul flights that collectively served as a good definition for the word 'motley'. They had grown up in an random manner, with no sense of underlying strategy. You could fly in from Jersey and transfer to Genoa or Atlanta, but for anything more ambitious it was usually necessary to travel around the M25 to Heathrow. To succeed, the Sussex airport needed more routes and a lower cost base. That was what the young American and her team were told to construct from the remains of Dan-Air.

BA had rescued the company partly because it hoped it could drive a hard bargain with flight crews. By employing staff on terms more favourable to the airline, BA hoped it could reduce costs in line with the lower yields that could be achieved at Gatwick. But the takeover of Dan-Air ignored the human dimension, says Cassani. Staff who found themselves part of BA were not thrilled to be told, 'You should be really happy you have jobs, because your company was just about to go out of business, and by the way, you'll be wearing BA uniforms and we're going to cut your pay by 20 per cent, and that's just life.'

Shortly after the takeover, I flew from Gatwick to Vienna on a former Dan-Air jet with ex-Dan-Air crew. Unprompted, the lead stewardess spent half the flight telling me how bitter she and her colleagues felt about their treatment by the new owners: 'The attitude was "Work with us or don't work at all".'

Cassani recognised the problem in telling staff, 'You have to deliver the same service, you have to work just as hard as the people at Heathrow, but tough luck. You're down at Gatwick.' Ill feeling prevailed for some time until BA relented on its original plan and raised pay for its short-haul crew based at Gatwick. As Cassani went through her career at BA, she says, there were a number of experiences where she thought, 'If I had the chance to start something, I would never do it this way.' Five years after the Dan-Air episode, she got the chance to do it her way.

'The thing that excited me was the opportunity to start up a low-cost airline – that had really, really, really low costs.' But Barbara Cassani was far from certain she would succeed. She told herself, 'I'm not going to waste my time on a business that isn't worthwhile. If I don't think you can make money on it, I'm not going to set up another basket-case airline that is always going to need to be bailed out.' But two months in to the operation, Cassani was convinced it would work. She had settled on Stansted as the base for the operation, and had begun headhunting. 'I had a very profound sense that I could find the right people to do this well, to be safe and secure, to have operational robustness.' To ensure the latter, she brought in Ed Winter, a former captain with a vast amount of experience, as chief operating officer. The other members of Cassani's senior management team bore little resemblance to a traditional airline. The man who became Go's sales and marketing director – a crucial position for any no-frills airline – was a first-generation Anglo-Italian named David Magliano. He was an advertising executive who had previously been masterminding the Ford advertising account, but was assigned to work on the Go launch campaign. Cassani liked his work so much that she signed him up.

Choosing a name took time. The working title, Blue Sky, had been acquired along with British Caledonian in 1988. For a while, the favourite was The Bus, which has echoes of Sir Freddie Laker's mission to make a transatlantic flight as easy as getting on a train. But Cassani did not wish to be known as 'chief executive of The Bus', and the name did not research as positively as the shortest airline name the world has ever known: Go.

Once the name was selected, Cassani broke with the no-frills tradition, from Southwest to easyJet, of spending as little as possible on design.

Instead of a colour scheme and a logo that looks like a failed first-year graphic art project, Cassani invested heavily in a brand that demonstrated no-frills planes need not look awful. 'I did not want my cabin crew wearing a jacket that said, "I'm an easy crew member". That is anathema to what we're about. Our people are professionals. We wanted to create a brand that was modern and simple and inviting. And a service style that was friendly and not stuffy but professional.' Pointedly, the airline's publicity promised, 'We are a different proposition from the other low-cost airlines. Our cabin staff are trained to the highest standard and our food is better. Customers have to pay for it but instead of being given a can of fizzy pop and a bag of crisps, they can have real coffee from a cafetiere and a selection of excellent pastries.' It was this emphasis that led Tim Jeans, then at Ryanair, to observe that, 'Go is the low-cost airline for the middle classes.' Cassani ripostes: 'In some ways it's a good description of why we appeal to virtually everyone. The only aspect is that in Britain when you describe people as part of a class, some are excluded. In an American definition, everyone from the richest businessman to the poorest describes themselves as middle class.'

The branding was created by the multinational consultant, Wolff Olins. Its head of consultancy is Robert Jones: 'Go is about more than just economy. It's about treating people equally well, whether they're rich or poor, customers or staff.' Besides the bright blobs of colour on plain white planes, and the joky 'go to work' or 'off we go' slogan painted near the nose of each aircraft, the branding included a memorable musical sting. But once the ads started to appear, so too did the brickbats and lawyers.

Leading the barrage of condemnation was Stelios of easyJet. He called Go 'a photocopy of the easyJet business plan'. As Southwest knows, no one can copyright the concept of a no-frills airline. But the easyJet boss was incensed that British Airways, the dominant force in UK aviation, was able to sponsor a subsidiary that could attack the rest of the field. He believed the airline was using the BA connection to get favourable terms on financing aircraft, yet claiming to be independent from the parent company. 'Go has been given permission by BA to lose £29 million,' Stelios asserted, 'and then close in three years having put its rivals out of business.'

The Godfather of low-cost flying, Sir Freddie Laker, had urged legal action in a telephone call. 'The phone rang in our downmarket Luton office,' says Stelios. 'I picked it up. "Hello, my name is Freddie Laker, and I just wanted to tell you, that you're doing a great job and you should sue the bastards." I was chuffed. I arranged to meet him immediately, at a hotel in Victoria.' Encouraged by Sir Freddie, Stelios accused BA of using its commercial muscle to support Go in a bid to drive competitors out of business. In February 1998, his airline served a High Court writ on BA seeking an injunction to stop them cross-subsidising Go.

Bob Ayling calls that argument 'silly', comparing the £25 million investment with other industries. 'Look at any other sector – motor car manufacturing, or software development or new media businesses – there, the seed capital's enormous. Twenty-five million quid is a drop in the ocean.' And Cassani is equally vituperative. 'Did easyJet benefit by being owned by a guy with a shipping company? Yeah, they probably did. So did we benefit from BA backing? Yeah, sure we did. The question that was debated in the various lawsuits from easyJet was that cross-subsidisation was unfair. I have been very happy to defend Go's activities, and therefore BA's, at any time.'

Later, Stelios flew to Brussels to meet European competition officials to argue his case that Go constituted unfair competition aboard a specially prepared easyjet aircraft with STOP BA STOP GO emblazoned on the side. 'None of these complaints made any headway,' says Ayling. 'Presumably if there had been any merit in them they would have done.' But Stelios believed the legal action warned BA as to its future conduct in supporting its low-cost offspring.

Ryanair's view of the new arrival was more benign than easyJet's. 'Go did the industry a favour because it was the love child of BA,' said Tim Jeans, at the time with the Irish airline. Hitherto, he said, 'It was basically the Paddies and the Greeks playing at the low-fares game, before BA turned up and gave it some respectability. So it gave it that stamp of credibility that the industry needed.'

Cassani spent some of BA's £25m investment on focus groups in potential destination countries. Each nationality had its own concerns about low-cost aviation. 'In Germany, them saying "I find the orange thing very disconcerting" meant "I don't want it to fall out of the sky". In Italy, the response to credit card bookings was, "I don't want to give you my credit card because then the man down the street can sell the number".'

During the development of the airline, Cassani was so hands-on that she even wrote the announcements that you hear when boarding a Go flight. 'I don't want any airline language, I don't want any disembarking. When do you disembark in your life? You get off things, you get out of your car, off a train.' She believes that the jargon generated around airlines 'is there to develop a barrier between employees and customers. And employees quite like it, one of the reasons they like uniforms and language is to keep people at a distance. I wanted to get rid of that, I wanted our employees to look at our cabin like their living room, as if inviting guests in. Therefore you want people to hit the call button, you want people to ask you things because that means you've created an environment where people feel comfortable enough to do that.'

The people who would answer the call button were drawn from a wide range of businesses: insurance call centres, shops,

WAS GO A CLONE OF EASYJET?

Yes, says Stelios, though the easyJet founder's version of events is starkly at odds with that of BA's chief executive at the time, Bob Ayling. Stelios says Ayling 'was the first executive to believe in us'. A year after easyJet's maiden flight, he says, the two airline bosses met at an aviation conference in New York. 'I wasn't speaking, I was only attending,' says Stelios. 'Who would invite me to speak in those days?' Ayling was one of the speakers. After the presentation, Stelios approached him, and asked if he had heard of easyJet. 'He said, "Of course I've heard of you! You run a great company. Come over for a cup of coffee." '

Back in Britain, says Stelios, he arranged an appointment at British Airways' headquarters, at the time a grim 60s office block on the edge of Heathrow called Speedbird House. His account is that the meeting lasted an hour. Stelios says, 'His parting shot was, "Do you think BA and your company can do something together?" So like what? "Like invest in it, because we believe it's a separate sector. And I believe that you've cracked it." '

The rest, says Stelios, is history. BA sent people into easyJet to take a look at the operation, as any firm considering a big investment would do. Three months later, Stelios says he received a letter saying that the giant airline was no longer interested. 'And Go was invented.'

Bob Ayling has a radically different recollection of events: 'Yes, I did meet Stelios in New York, fleetingly, and yes I had admiration for what he was doing in the industry, but the idea of an investment was theirs. They approached British Airways. I can't remember if it was direct or through an intermediary. Anyway, one of my colleagues had some very preliminary discussions with them, which we decided not to proceed with. That's the end of the story. It's rather a dull one.'

schools. A significant number had previous experience with long-haul flying, which they had given up after starting families. One of the original applicants for cabin crew was Luke Deals, a thirty-year-old radio journalist, keen to shake off office politics. 'They were interviewing hundreds of people. We were all gathered in Enterprise House on a Sunday afternoon.' The selectors, he says, were looking for people who were 'Outgoing, competent and confident'. He clearly was, because he was called the following day, invited back for a second interview and given the job. 'The pay was dire, but I thought that if it all went tits up I'm sure I could go back to journalism.' (Which he has subsequently done.)

The training course was, he says, 'Intense but fun. It was done by British Airways, so you knew you were going to get a good grounding. We had to drag bodies around in the swimming pool, and we were put on the chutes of the 767 simulator. You have to know about heart disease, pregnancy, how to deal with an irate passenger. But nothing prepares you for the day you're faced with 148 rugby fans going up to Edinburgh.'

Initially, he says, the atmosphere was 'like a big family'. When the first 737 arrived, 'everyone was excited by it'. So were some people over at Luton airport.

The first three destinations chosen for Go by Cassani were Milan, Rome and Copenhagen. All were already served from Heathrow or Gatwick by British Airways. The routes were chosen because they could offer a good mix of business and leisure travel. These markets have different characteristics, and when one is weak the other tends to be strong.

The next routes were also duplicating BA's network, while steering clear of competition from other no-frills airlines: Bologna and Naples served destinations some distance away from Ryanair's airports in Italy, while Go's Venice flights went direct to the city's main Marco Polo airport rather than the more distant Treviso, served by the Irish airline. In addition, Go started flights to Munich and Lyon – business destinations that also served ski resorts.

When the initial trio of routes, and the date of the maiden flight, from Stansted to Rome, were announced, easyJet – Go's most vocal rival – block-booked ten seats on the first departure. Any airline boss cherishes its maiden flight: just ask Branson or Stelios. Some people have likened the first departure to an act of sexual consummation at the end of an intense courtship. Certainly, one executive described the moment the wheels lift from the tarmac as 'orgasmic – no, actually it was better than sex'. It is the sort of moment that needs to be celebrated with people to whom you are close, which is why Barbara Cassani invited her husband, Guy, and her five-year-old daughter, Lauren, on board. She did not invite Stelios and his staff. But he gatecrashed the party anyway. And Cassani was expecting him.

'I'm convinced that if Stelios hadn't such a distinctive name, we would have taken them by surprise,' says Tony Anderson, the easyJet executive who bought the flights. 'I booked the seats in three separate calls. The itinerary for Stelios's booking came back with a handwritten note from Barbara Cassani saying, "looking forward to seeing you on board".' There is no law against buying a seat on a rival's flights, yet some of the easyJet staff were uneasy. 'The day before the first flight,' says Stelios, 'we had a marketing meeting in the office and half the people defected. They said, "No, you're going to be arrested. It's not possible to go on somebody else's inaugural flight." So I said, "If people don't want to come, fine." We ended up with seven people on board and three defections.' When they planned the details of the public relations assault, Stelios made two rules: 'We have to be light hearted and we have to be giving some things away. So we put on the orange boiler suits so we were making a fool of ourselves, and appeared non-threatening, and gave away free tickets, which always works.'

Across at Stansted, Barbara Cassani was anxious. 'We realised there was a group of easyJet people quite early on. I guess it was inevitable. My first consideration was I don't want them to do anything that was unsafe. I was concerned about what they would do. Once I was convinced that was fine, I thought I'd put on a big smile and play with them.' Some of the photographs taken en route suggest a less than cordial journey, especially when the easyJet boss started giving interviews to the journalists whom Go had invited on board. Yet Cassani insists 'I'll be forever grateful for Stelios'. She says 'Ironically we ended up with far more publicity than we would have got otherwise.'

Go's other rivals responded to the first flight with the more conventional weapon of fare cuts. The immediate response from Debonair was to undercut Go's fare to Rome by £1. Richard Branson's Virgin Express sliced a fiver off the lowest fare to the Italian capital, though passengers had to change planes at Brussels. The same pattern emerged at Milan: KLM UK knocked £1 off the Go fare, while Virgin Express again undercut the new airline by £5. To Copenhagen, the Scandinavian airline SAS weighed in with a £99 ticket, including meals and drinks. When the Stansted–Munich route was launched, Lufthansa started its own service from the Essex airport – and undercut Go's fare by

£2, while still offering all the frills. At this point, it was time for Go's lawyers to complain about predatory pricing. When that action failed, Go abandoned the Munich route, though it subsequently returned to the network.

The first casualty of Go's subsequent expansion was KLM UK (formerly Air UK), which for years had been the only substantial airline serving Stansted.

Years of perseverance counted for nothing; once Go started flying from the Essex airport to Glasgow and Edinburgh, the full-service airline retired hurt from all its Anglo-Scottish routes. It then mutated its Stansted operation into the disastrous no-frills experiment known as Buzz, now part of Ryanair. Today its only ghostly presence is an empty executive lounge on one of the piers.

In July 1998, Go began flying from Stansted to Lisbon, a route already flown non-stop from Gatwick by AB Airlines. Within a few months, the competition had gone out of business. And soon after that, Go abandoned the route to its parent British Airways and Air Portugal. Debonair, damaged by the new competition on its flight to Rome, followed AB Airlines into oblivion in 1999 – at which point Stelios said that British Airways had 'blood on its hands'.

By early 2000, Bob Ayling had parted company with BA. The airline's board allowed him the honour of presiding over the opening of the British Airways London Eye (the 'Millennium Wheel'), his lasting legacy for the capital, but removed him the following day.

Ayling's successor as BA's chief executive, Rod Eddington, lost little time in abandoning the plan for Gatwick to be the 'hub without the hubbub'. One of his first decisions was to cut back services from the Sussex airport savagely, to reduce the duplication of routes from Heathrow. The structure that Cassani had painfully put together after the Dan-Air takeover began to unravel.

Go, too, would have to go, said the new BA boss. The airline had lost £20m in each of its first two years, but was moving into profit. So why would British Airways want to put its high-achieving corporate child up for adoption? While Bob Ayling had seen Go as an essential long-term investment to ensure that British Airways was strongly represented in the no-frills sector, his successor thought otherwise. 'If you're a full-service network carrier, setting up your own no-frills carrier to compete with your no-frills competitors is no solution. What you have to do is fix your own business.'

Few tears were shed at Waterside, the palatial headquarters of British Airways northwest of Heathrow. Barbara Cassani had made plenty of enemies within BA. Flight crew were alarmed that her cost-savings would be replicated at the parent airline. Marketing people responsible for selling Europe saw Go nibbling away at their earnings. Eddington relates that 'When I first went to Madrid, our senior sales guy there said the Go reps are telling customers who have been doing business with BA for twenty years to stop doing business with BA and do business with Go.' Plenty of BA staff saw 'cannibalisation' of the parent's passengers as an inevitable consequence of starting a stand-alone low-cost subsidiary: the parent airline would fill fewer seats and earn a lower average fare for each ticket that it did sell. 'We were pouring money into a company that was stealing our customers and reducing our yields,' says one insider. 'It was mad. Go had to be closed down or sold.' To get shareholders a return on their investment in Go, Eddington chose the latter course – even though it would create a competitor.

No one had sold a prospering low-cost airline in Britain before, so valuing the company properly was a tricky business. Initially, the City believed Go would fetch at least £300m, possibly even as much as half a billion. 'Bad PR management by BA,' says Cassani. 'We hadn't even announced our first profit figures. They left that impression.'

There was some speculation that easyJet would take over Go. But after months of negotiations, Go was sold for £110m. The largest share was taken by a venture capital company, 3i, with just over one-fifth taken by the airline's management. The selling price was, as it turned out, enough to save British Airways from incurring a loss in BA's first post-11 September financial results.

'We were able to extricate Go from the BA network with relative ease,' says Cassani, 'as a result of the way we set up the company, which made it very easy to separate.' The ink was barely dry on the deal before the no-frills upstart began biting the hand that had nurtured it, by pouring scorn on BA's latest round of World Offers. Go abruptly stopped advertising its links with BA, then publicly rubbished the value of those deals. Other connections were quickly broken; the free flight privileges Go's staff enjoyed from British Airways were soon cancelled.

A hitherto-unbroken no-frills rule was transgressed, too. In the final few years of the twentieth century, there had been plenty of room for expansion for the large no-frills carriers, Go, easyJet and

Ryanair. Airlines did not need to trespass on each other's turf. Then Go decided to start flying to Nice, one of the most established destinations on the easyJet network. 'We've been flying to Nice for five and a half years,' said Stelios, 'and in that time we've seen a number of competitors come and go. I don't know how long Go will last on that route.'

Cassani shrugged off the disparaging remarks. 'Could easyJet be making more money if we didn't fly to Nice? Maybe. But that's what competition's about. If there's a distinct market between Stansted and Nice, it's my job to fill it. It isn't my job to see if it offends easyJet's sensibilities.' In the slanging match that ensued, Go made much of the extent to which Luton–Nice fares on easyJet could rise. Michael O'Leary of Ryanair watched from the sidelines. 'It's ridiculous – like two Jack Russells fighting over a bone,' he said. 'They're having a row over who had the highest low fares.' His airline claims to be the only one to guarantee to have the lowest fares, though since Ryanair's nearest destination to Nice was Genoa across in Italy, this was immaterial.

'Who charges the highest low fares?' O'Leary asked me, rhetorically. 'Who cares?'

Cassani was working twelve hours a day for one of Europe's fastest-growing airlines, and loving it. 'The reason I like the airline business is because the problems and opportunities are more interesting than anywhere else I can think of. You've got huge assets to manage with your aircraft. You've got huge groups of people to manage, and then finally you've got this wonderful consumer marketing challenge. It's a business everyone can relate to. And I think you either enjoy that, or it wears you down and you exit to selling widgets or something.' She was genuinely evangelical about her company, which she rated as a cut above the competition: 'I really love this idea of having your cake and eating it too – the idea that you could find a way of giving people something that was just that little bit more, but still very true to being low cost and being safe and secure.' In Go terms, that means 'You're not putting your life and your savings at risk by booking or travelling with us. We have our good days and bad days, but I think we achieve that more than most airlines do, and I'm very proud of that. But I think the second we think we're doing it well, and we stop trying – forget it, we'll have lost it.'

Some in the industry thought Cassani had lost it when Go announced flights to Dublin, the home base of its biggest rival,

Ryanair. The new financial backers of Go suddenly found they were caught up in the mother of all no-frills fares wars. Cassani had no intention of competing directly with Ryanair on its seven daily services from Stansted to the Irish capital. Instead, she launched flights to Dublin from Scotland's two biggest airports: Edinburgh and Glasgow. At the time, the only direct competition was from Aer Lingus; Ryanair flew between the Irish capital and Prestwick, a long way south of Glasgow. But Dublin was Ryanair territory. Not only did Michael O'Leary immediately cut fares on the existing Dublin–Prestwick service; he also launched flights from Edinburgh, which previously was off the Ryanair map.

Tim Jeans, sales and marketing director for Ryanair at the time, says he was amazed at Go's move. 'I could lie awake for hours at night and wonder why they did that. Imagine the scenario: you're just newly enfranchised, the umbilical has been cut from your BA parent, you have £100 million of 3i's cash in your wallet, and what's the first thing you do? You go and blow x millions, having a head to head with the biggest, baddest, boldest bully on the block. It beggars belief that they would do that. I think they thought that we would have a fight from a distance in Prestwick and not follow them into Edinburgh. They were wrong.'

For three months in the autumn of 2001, the fare between Dublin and Scotland fell as low as £10 including taxes and charges. All three airlines were losing money on the services. Aer Lingus, which was sinking ever deeper into a financial morass and had seen its monopoly on a couple of once-lucrative routes smashed, was dismayed. Cassani was not. 'There will be some instances where we double up and it doesn't work. But it's very difficult to predict. It's only when you start observing customer behaviour and whether or not your competitors are behaving rationally that you know whether it makes sense.' Rational or not, Ryanair's behaviour forced Go out of Dublin in March 2002, after six months of losses.

The planes that previously flew to the Irish capital had to be moved somewhere. Cassani and her team decided to open a third UK base, at a venue where no-frills competition was absent: East Midlands, the airport serving Nottingham, Derby and Leicester. More precisely, there was no competition when Go announced the move – but within days a brand-new rival emerged. The local travelling public had waited years for a no-frills airline, and then two came along at once. East Midlands (now known as Nottingham) was the home of BMI, formerly British Midland. Like other traditional airlines with short-haul networks, BMI had been financially hit by no-frills flying. Suddenly, its home base – at which it held a near-monopoly of scheduled flying – was to see competition move in with high-frequency, low-cost flights. BMI responded by deploying some of the excess capacity that had lain idle since 11 September to start up a new no-frills airline, Bmibaby. Its route network was remarkably close to Go's, with a sprinkling of Mediterranean destinations and the Czech capital, Prague. Bmibaby said it had been planning the move for a year, and that its announcement so close to that of Go's was purely coincidental. East Midlands residents could hardly believe their luck: not only had no-frills finally arrived in their area, but two airlines were having a scrap that was forcing fares down.

March 2002 was not going entirely to Barbara Cassani's satisfaction. Besides the rivalry with Bmibaby, she had been invited to dinner by the chairman and chief executive of easyJet. Stelios and Ray Webster told Cassani they were planning to take over her airline. Since the events of 11 September, the aviation world had been transformed. Traditional airlines had suffered, while passengers were flocking to the no-frills carriers. Buying Go would lift easyJet above Ryanair to the top of the European low-cost airline league, generate savings on everything from overheads to new aircraft, and remove a significant competitor. Stelios and Webster were prepared to pay way over the price for which Go had been sold less than a year earlier. And Cassani could have a job, but as Webster's deputy. 'Barbara was offered the number two job after Ray,' says Stelios. 'She decided to turn it down.'

When news of the talks leaked out, a statement was issued on behalf of Go's chief executive that contradicts this version of events: 'Barbara Cassani has never been offered a role at easyJet as part of a merged business with Go. She does not want to be part of the combined business in any capacity and at no stage has she stated otherwise. Should the deal with easyJet proceed, it is her intention to leave the business on completion of the deal.'

'I'm sure Barbara has been instrumental in making Go the success it is today,' said Stelios when the deal had gone through. 'But she's not alone.' A number of senior executives from Go were brought in to easyJet (much to the chagrin of the managers they dislodged at easyLand), notably Ed Winter as chief operating officer and David Magliano as marketing director. But the airline's name was left behind at Stansted. 'The decision to keep the easyJet brand was almost a forgone conclusion because of the Internet address,' says Stelios. 'I said a long time before we had even an intention of acquiring Go, that it is crazy in this day and age promoting a brand for online sales if you do not own the precise Internet address. So, it was a no-brainer for us, we had to keep the brand for which we own the Internet address, which is easyJet. Go is go-fly which introduces another level of complexity.'

Four years after the first Go flight, David Magliano found himself several million pounds richer – and about to begin work extinguishing the brand that he had helped to create, and which had become one of Britain's biggest brand success stories.

Flight GO 226 from Nice touched down at Stansted shortly before midnight on 29 March 2003. It was a far more sombre event than the first flight, less than five years earlier. Once it had taxied to the gate, Go had gone.

Robert Jones, head of consultancy for Wolff Olins and the company that dreamt up the brand, said 'We'll be very sad to see it go. It was a classless notion that had years of life left in it.'

'We change the way people live their lives. I joke that I'm waiting for my Nobel Peace Prize for services to humanity,' said Cassani when Go was a going concern. She has years of life left in her, but she has yet to return to aviation. With an estimated £13m from the sale of Go, she has no financial need to do so. And her old adversary, Michael O'Leary, says she should keep it like that. 'I'd advise her to shut up, take the money, be very happy that she's one of very few people who've made a lot of money out of aviation; easyJet paid far too much for the company.'

Barbara Cassani seems happy. She was the surprise choice to lead the London bid team for the Olympics in 2012. A year before the result was announced, she stepped aside and Lord (Sebastian) Coe took over – and took the credit for the successful bid. Two weeks and two days after London was awarded the Games, Cassani celebrated her forty-fifth birthday. Having achieved more than most people can accomplish in a lifetime, she could rest on her laurels. But rumours still circulate that she is planning a return to aviation.

9. LOW COST EQUALS LOW SAFETY?

Five ninety-two needs immediate return to Miami . . . we're on fire, we're on fire
Cockpit voice recorder of Valujet flight 592, Miami-Atlanta

For those of you who haven't been in a car for the past thirty years, this is how to fasten a seat belt
Safety announcement by Northwest flight attendant

We never anticipate a sudden change in air pressure; if we did, I'd get another job
Safety announcement by Southwest flight attendant

I give you the data, you make the decision
Todd Curtis, founder, airsafe.com

'Welcome to the Flight 592 Memorial.' So begins one of the saddest pages on the Internet. 'This Memorial is dedicated to those who lost their lives in the senseless and unnecessary air disaster of May 11, 1996, and to the families and friends who must endure the pain of their loss forever.'

A slogan for the Florida-based no-frills airline, AirTran, promises 'It's something else'. It certainly is, at least in name. At the time that flight 592 departed from Miami, destination Atlanta, on 11 May 1996, the carrier was known as ValuJet. The website contains a gallery of smiling faces. These are the people who saved a few dollars on the flight from Miami to Atlanta, and paid with their lives. One of them was Dana Lyn Nelson-Lane, who had married her husband, Roger, six months earlier. On the website, her father writes, 'Dana was our leader. Who will lead us now? Dana was a giver ... right up until the time our daughter was taken.' Besides the virtual memorial, there is a monument in black and red granite at Woodlawn Park Cemetery in south-west Miami.

The McDonnell-Douglas DC-9 took off on an easterly runway, heading towards the Atlantic. It flew over Miami and turned to head north-west. Almost immediately, a fire broke out in a cargo hold. Within six minutes, smoke and flames had spread to the passenger cabin and the cockpit. Fifteen miles west of Miami airport, the plane plunged almost vertically into the swamps of the Everglades. It was commanded by the first American woman captain to lose her life in an accident. The aircraft was destroyed so comprehensively that investigators were unable to determine if the crash happened because of a mechanical loss of control or because the crew were incapacitated by the fire.

The cargo hold contained a consignment of oxygen generators. These are the aircraft parts that are used to deliver oxygen to passengers and crew if an aircraft is holed and loses pressure. But it was these very safety devices that brought down the plane. They are classified as hazardous cargo, yet were not labelled as such and had not been properly boxed. They were stored in a hold that had neither a smoke detector nor a fire extinguisher.

The aircraft and the lives of all 105 passengers and five crew were destroyed that day. So too was some travellers' confidence in no-frills aviation. 'That was difficult for the whole industry, but especially for the low-fares airlines,' says Greg Wells, who is vice-president for safety and security for the world's biggest low-cost airline, Southwest. The ValuJet crash, he says 'was directly related to a mechanical issue, a failure apparently with the maintenance department'. The National Transportation Safety Board investigation blamed three organisations: ValuJet, for poor maintenance practices; SabreTech, the firm that supplied the generators; and the Federal Aviation Authority, for failing to give proper oversight. ValuJet's licence was revoked, and the airline stopped flying.

The airline was allowed in the air again a year later, offering a Boston–Philadelphia hop for just $42. But from the public point of view, it was not the same entity: its name had changed to AirTran. The airline has not had a crash since, which is what statisticians would expect from an airline that has operated relatively few flights in its new identity. Fatal accident rates in Europe and North America run at one in every million or two departures.

At this point, I must give a health warning about the available data on aviation disasters: fatal aircraft accidents are, thankfully, so rare that it is tricky and potentially misleading to attach words like 'dangerous' or 'safe' to individual planes or airlines. In a typical year, such as 2002, around ten passenger flights end in tragedy, claiming the lives of about one thousand people in total. This compares with more than a million people who die each year in road accidents.

In July 2000, an Air France Concorde crashed a few minutes after take-off from Charles de Gaulle airport in Paris, killing 113 people. With a £9,000 price tag for a transatlantic round-trip – by far the most expensive plane ticket in the world – surely passengers are buying the best safety possible? Some anxious flyers deduced from the fact that Concorde can crash that other, cheaper airlines would be more likely to fall to earth, killing everyone on board and possibly some unfortunate souls on the ground. If no-frills airlines are obsessed with cutting costs, might they cut corners on safety?

A theoretical argument can be made for a rational consumer accepting a higher degree of risk in return for low fares. After all, cost/risk trade-offs are made all the time on the ground. Motorists often know that the brakes really need adjusting, or the tyres need changing, but they postpone the investment; local government engineers may decide not to invest in a segregated cycle lane, but to spend the cash on something else. In both cases, there is (or should be) an awareness that they are assuming a higher risk of a fatal skid or a dead cyclist, possibly both at the same time.

Another concern sometimes raised by people who have spent a long time in the aviation industry is that, by their nature, no-frills airlines are much younger and less experienced than most traditional carriers. Some passengers may infer that they lack the depth of knowledge that 'legacy' airlines may have.

Low-cost airlines agree on hardly anything. But one topic on which they are unanimous is safety. In particular, they refute any suggestion that buying a cheap flight is a risk. 'Some people may draw that conclusion,' concedes Tim Jeans of Monarch Scheduled, but he insists 'there are no cost compromises on safety'. Indeed, avoiding crashes is even more crucial to low-fares operators than to traditional airlines, Jeans contends. He turns the economic argument – that cutting costs somehow implies reducing safety – on its head. Low-cost carriers, he says, should actually be safer than traditional airlines. 'Safety standards have to be as good, or better than, the full-service competition because clearly the downside to an accident for a low-fares carrier would be considerably greater than for a full-service carrier. We're only too well aware of that.'

'Is the aircraft safe?'

Vladimir Raitz says that was one of the first questions he was asked when he introduced charter flights to Corsica in 1950. Then and now, some people assume there is a catch with every cheap flight. When easyJet started up in 1995, it used a cartoon plane in its advertising. The marketing director at the time, Tony Anderson, soon changed that image: 'At a focus group, a number of the participants thought we flew old propeller-driven aircraft.' The airline's founder, Stelios says, 'Up until a couple of years ago, I still had to defend myself against questions like "Are the planes safe?"' He believes that the public is gradually getting the message that no-frills airlines have even younger fleets than their traditional rivals. The arrival of Go to the no-frills market helped perceptions, because people associated safety with British Airways, the company that was very visibly behind Barbara Cassani's airline. And British Airways is closely associated with Qantas, which many people believe to be the safest airline in the world.

Charlie Babbitt (played by Tom Cruise): Ray, all airlines have crashed at one time or another, that doesn't mean they are not safe.

Raymond Babbitt (played by Dustin Hoffman): Qantas. Qantas never crashed.

This piece of dialogue, in Barry Levinson's 1988 film *Rain Man*, helped him win the Oscar for best director and movie, and Hoffman the award for best actor. But it set back the cause of rational discussion of air safety by years. Movie-goers concluded that Qantas was the only airline in the world never to have suffered a crash. In fact, the Australian airline has had plenty of accidents, but thankfully has always managed to crash gently, without loss of life. Cruise's assertion that 'all airlines have crashed at one time or another' was even more damaging. Plenty of carriers, from Emirates to Virgin Atlantic, have never suffered a fatal accident. Many now-defunct operators, including Laker Airways and Go, went through their whole careers without a crash. But misapprehension characterises fear of flying. 'Air travel is such a different form of travel still,' says Greg Wells of Southwest. 'It's very sensational when a 110,000lb aeroplane for some reason falls out of the sky, and sometimes two hundred people can die. That doesn't happen in an automobile, it doesn't happen in a train.'

A train. That is what I need right now. I am at Salinas station in California, just inland from Monterey, hoping to travel north to San Jose.

This is John Steinbeck country, and considerable wrath has been visited on the shabby, flyblown railroad station. I am waiting for the Coast Starlight, the train that is supposed to get me to San Jose in time to connect with a flight to Seattle. It is a dark, starless night. I ask the ticket clerk when the train might get here.

'That depends what else is on the line.'

Things like freight trains, I speculate.

'Uh huh, and animals, and kids, abandoned cars, that sort of thing.' When the miscellany of trackside impediments is finally cleared, I reach San Jose just in time to catch the next-flight-north-but-one to Seattle. The aircraft used for the shuttle between Silicon Valley and the home of Microsoft is an MD-83 belonging to the semi-low-cost Alaska Airlines; on the last day of January 2000, an identical aircraft crashed into the sea off the coast of Los Angeles, with the loss of 88 lives. Upon our safe arrival in Seattle, I learn that Alanis Morissette is performing in turn. Her first hit, *Ironic*, includes a description of a nervous flyer (*Mr Play-it-safe*) dying in a plane crash. Ironically, I am here to meet a man who knows more about air safety than anyone else on the planet: Dr Todd Curtis.

In 1995, Curtis was employed by Boeing as an aviation safety analyst. He realised the public had a profound interest in the subject of which planes crash, who operates them, and how likely passengers are to die. But accessible information on which to make rational decisions was often cloaked in jargon. 'At parties, I never heard people saying, "The hull-loss rate of that aircraft really worries me," or "Gee, the breakdown rate that doesn't lead to fatal injury of this aircraft concerns me." They were worried about events where people ended up dead.' At the time it was difficult even for those in the aviation industry to gather safety information in a form where sensible comparisons and judgements could be made. Curtis crunched the numbers and put together a website to address travellers' concerns.

airsafe.com answers basic questions like 'What's the safety record of this aircraft or airline?' Users can dig deeper to find out the circumstances of the hundreds of aviation disasters that have taken place since the age of the jumbo jet began in 1970. The subtext that accompanies the traveller's clicks is: 'So am I going to be killed or not?'

Curtis directs his attention towards that fundamental human concern. 'I had a very simple rule: if a passenger had got on the aircraft with the intent of going someplace and they died of other than natural causes, that's a fatal event. I didn't look at crew – not because I don't believe their lives are not valuable, but simply because the paying passenger worries about the paying passenger. They don't worry about the crew. As far as they're concerned that's a workplace hazard, not a travel hazard.' Curtis is keen to stress that his site never says an airline or aircraft is either safe or unsafe. 'In my opinion, that is a subjective judgement call that is up to the individual. No matter how expert I am in some issues, I can't say that something is safe or unsafe. That's like saying this is beautiful or this isn't beautiful. I give you the data, you make the decision.'

The basic currency of the site is the Fatal Event Rate, a measure of the number of accidents per million flights. Way ahead of the pack is Cubana. Not only is Cuba's national airline almost totally devoid of frills (but without the usual accompaniment of low fares), it is also a serial crasher. Since 1970, an average of one departure in fifty-five thousand has ended in disaster. In contrast, almost all the no-frills airlines have a perfect record: easyJet, Ryanair, Jet2, Bmibaby, Germanwings, Hapag–Lloyd Express and SkyEurope, to name just a few European contenders; JetBlue, Spirit, Ted and Frontier in the US; and WestJet in Canada. But all are relatively young. The biggest in Europe, Ryanair, has flown more than its rivals, with around a million missions.

In a numbers game where one fatal accident every two million or so flights is a good average, one airline is way ahead of the pack. Southwest has flown twelve million flights without losing an aircraft in a fatal accident. How does the airline stay aloft? Jim Parker, Southwest's former chief executive, makes it sound simple:

'We have the best pilots in the world. They do more take-offs and landings than at any other airline in the world; that's the most critical part of flight. We have very rigorous training standards, very rigorous operational standards in the cockpit. Our pilots are very manual in the way they fly the aeroplane, it's very much a hands-on operation. Beyond that we have excellent mechanics and maintenance programs. We have, I think, the highest standards of maintaining our aeroplanes, and we have a relatively young fleet.'

'I wish I could bottle their secret and pass it around to everyone in the world,' says Curtis. His take on Southwest's success, like Parker's, uses the word 'very' repeatedly. 'From the very beginning they've had a very hard-nosed attitude towards operational safety. In the early days Southwest featured hot pants-wearing flight attendants. But behind all that they have a very solid operation, run by a very straightforward group of people.'

It helps that the airline has only ever flown one kind of aircraft, the Boeing 737. 'They have a very intimate understanding of how to fly that aircraft. Also, for most of their history, they have flown in places that were not overwhelmed with other airlines – so for example they don't fly into Atlanta, they don't fly into JFK.' Some in the industry maintain that this means there is less danger of involvement in a collision caused by an error on the part of another pilot, such as the one that destroyed an SAS aircraft taking off from Milan in October 2001. They argue that big, busy airports with a large number of small carriers are riskier.

Curtis says the nature of the operation enhances Southwest's safety. 'If you do shorter flights there are certain things that you're not going to be exposed to that will happen on longer flights. They don't fly over water. So they do a particular kind of flying, they do it very well, they do it very frequently, and they have a very thorough understanding of the aircraft and how it flies.'

Consequently, Southwest is the one big US airline where the flight attendants can dare to joke their way through the safety demonstration. Duane Redmond embellishes his announcement by saying, 'We never anticipate a sudden change in air pressure; if we did, I'd get another job.' Another favourite of crews is to indulge in theatrical sighs when the plane touches down: 'Phew . . . we made it!' is typical. But the airline is careful never to boast about its safety record.

'It's not something we use in our advertising,' says Greg Wells, the man responsible for safety at Southwest. 'It really goes all the way down from our pilots to our baggage handlers. I can't see that you can be oversafe.'

None of the Boeing 737s flown by Southwest has crashed with loss of life, but more than fifty others have. The loss of an Air Philippines 737 in a crash in April 1999, in which 124 people died, marked a significant moment. The 737 had equalled the number of crashes sustained by the Boeing 727.

Within two months, another accident in India meant that the 737 had suffered more fatal crashes than any other commercial airplane. But the aircraft chosen by almost all the no-frills cheapies is also the most widely flown jet by far; all other things being equal, you would expect it to suffer more crashes than the rest.

The accident rates for Airbus are slightly less favourable, though still extremely good. It make little sense for a passenger to adopt the policy revealed on one of the top-selling items at the Boeing Everett Tour Center near Seattle: a bumper sticker reading, 'If it ain't a Boeing, I'm not going'.

The construction process at Boeing's 737 plant at Redmond, south of Seattle, is monitored fastidiously. Behind the engineers comes a platoon of inspectors, who go to the extent of using dental mirrors to peer into tight corners to check that a bolt has been correctly lacquered. Even before a new Boeing 737 takes off on its maiden flight, it has been through the equivalent of five flights, and undergone stresses that would never be experienced in normal use. To test the pressurisation, for example, each aircraft undergoes a simulation of flying at 91,000 feet, which is 50,000 feet higher than the normal maximum altitude.

Of the six thousand or so 737s that have been made, about one in a hundred has been lost in an accident. But that gives a fatal event rate of one loss every 2.2 million departures, thirty times better than Concorde. After the supersonic aircraft crashed, some observers insisted that Concorde had previously held the best safety record worldwide. They argued that, because it had not suffered a fatal accident after more than twenty years in service, the supersonic jet was safer than anything else in the skies. But the Boeing 717 and 777, and Airbus's A330 and A340, have flown far more missions without a fatal incident; when an Air France A340 crashed at Toronto in 2005, the passengers and crew all got out alive.

Todd Curtis points out that 'the Boeing 737 series has more flight operations in ten days than the Concorde has had over its entire fleet history. No one would dare remark that the 737 has a remarkable safety record because it has not had a fatal crash this month.'

Aviation safety is built upon a series of disasters. Planes started crashing even before the Wright brothers first got off the ground in 1903. From every accident, investigators learn lessons. Steps are implemented to minimise the chances of repetition: to design out unforeseen risks or sloppy practices, to make allowances for human failings, and to develop systems that change convention for the better.

The United States is the location for around half of the world's civil aviation movements, and sustains an extraordinarily good safety record. One reason could be the flight dispatcher – a highly trained, licensed individual who stays on the ground and helps the captain to make the right decisions.

'People think we're the people on the ground with the paddles,' complains Steve Hozdulick, who runs the Dispatch control centre for Southwest. The dispatcher's job was created when it was deemed that the captain needed someone to watch over them. There had been cases where, for example, a pilot decided to take a chance with the weather in order to get home that night, but came unstuck. The dispatcher helps plan, and then follows, every journey. With an extra pair of eyes, the chances of making an imperfect decision are reduced. These days, if a warning light comes on in the flight deck of a Southwest plane at Los Angeles, the captain will talk to his opposite number at Dispatch in Dallas. Between them, they will decide the best course of action.

Accidents still happen, though not to Southwest. And some disasters lead directly to action that affects startup airlines. After the ValuJet crash in 1996, the rules tightened: the FAA began to monitor the infrastructure, management and standards of all new airlines for five years after they enter the market.

A school of thought among some travellers is that 'lightning doesn't strike twice'. The theory runs that the safest time to fly on an airline is immediately after it has suffered a crash. 'In the aftermath of an accident suddenly everyone remembers exactly what it is that they're supposed to do,' says a pilot. But the evidence of the world's most crash-prone airline, Cubana, suggests otherwise. In the final fortnight of 1999, the Cuban national airline suffered two fatal accidents within five days.

The final few months of 2001 made grim reading for prospective passengers. Between 11 September and 21 November, seven commercial flights were lost with all souls. Four of them were hijacked by suicidal terrorists in the US on 11 September; a fifth came down just after take-off from JFK airport in New York; another was shot down accidentally by the Ukranian military over the Black Sea; and the seventh was the SAS aircraft that hit a stray business jet at Milan. To this already scary total, the assiduous Dr Curtis adds three more fatal events: a Crossair crash at Zurich where most of those on board a regional jet died; a Brazilian flight in which an engine exploded and broke two windows, and one passenger was sucked out in the sudden depressurisation; and a tourist charter flight that crashed moments after take-off from Chichen Itza in Mexico, killing all on board.

If ten flights can crash in as many weeks, surely any sane person would be mad to fly?

No: 2001 was an exceptionally bad year. The following year was more typical. In 2002, ten aircraft suffered fatal crashes, with a total loss of around one thousand souls. For comparison, over one million people died in road accidents. And none of them were large aircraft (a hundred seats or more) belonging to North American, European or Australasian airlines. Indeed, there were no such crashes between the American Airlines disaster at JFK in November 2001 until the mysterious Helios Airways crash between Larnaca and Athens in August 2005; the passengers and crew aboard the Boeing 737 died after the pilots apparently became incapacitated.

Despite these 45 accident-free months, many airline passengers in North America, Europe and Australasia magnify the risks hugely. Flying is very safe. Among US airlines, the average is around one crash for every two million departures. European carriers suffer around one per million flights. The numbers get worse elsewhere in the world, with Asia, Latin America and Africa incurring more frequent rates, though there are some airlines in these regions with excellent records. Overall, people who say 'there's a one-in-a-million chance of this plane crashing' are about right (unless the plane belongs to Cubana).

The single most useful step to reduce your exposure to risk is to find an airline that flies non-stop on your chosen route. Most accidents occur during the take-off, climb, descent and landing phases of flight. An intermediate stop doubles the risky parts of the trip. In this sense, the no-frills airlines have helped the cause of aviation safety by cutting down the number of connecting flights. To travel from Birmingham to Prague, for example, once demanded a change of plane in Amsterdam or Frankfurt or Paris; today, there are twenty flights a week on a choice of two carriers between the West Midlands and the Czech capital. Big jets have a better record than propeller planes and small jets, so you may wish to choose them over small commuter aircraft; on one single day in January 2003, two commuter aircraft crashed in separate accidents, in North Carolina and Turkey, with a combined loss of 96 people.

'We ask you for your complete attention for just a few moments, while the cabin crew point out some of the safety features on board this aircraft, a Boeing 737.' The mandatory safety demonstration to every passenger aboard an aircraft does not help calm nerves. It exacerbates anxiety, suggesting flying is prone to danger. Airlines are legally required explicitly to describe responses to events that, statistically, are extremely unlikely.

The briefing on every Ryanair flight continues: 'To inflate your life jacket, pull down sharply on the right toggle. Do not inflate your life jacket inside the cabin as to do so may impede your exit. Your life jacket is equipped with a light to attract attention.' And a lot of use that is going to be in a storm-ravaged North Sea.

Many frequent travellers, and plenty of cabin crew, believe the whole safety demonstration is laughably archaic. They will chuckle at the flight attendant on Northwest Airlines whose briefing begins, 'For those of you who haven't been in a car for the past thirty years, this is how to fasten a seat belt.' But among nervous travellers, who perhaps travel infrequently or have never even flown before, anxiety can escalate.

'A stress reaction is a primitive, mortal fear that something is going to happen to you,' says Dr Steve Ray, a clinical physiologist at Oxford Brookes University. 'If the people that you perceive to be in control keep you waiting, even if it's only for five minutes, that in itself can cause exasperation.' Passengers may turn to drink, and then turn nasty. Their fears about flying may begin to be self-fulfilling, as anxiety and alcohol start to mix. And, for Todd Curtis, that is a problem that is potentially as dangerous as a hijacking, but far more easily preventable: 'Many air-rage events are associated with passengers who came on board intoxicated. It's clear that is one risk that can be taken away.'

On an average day, three or four flights on UK airlines are affected by disruptive passengers. Most are relatively minor infringements, such as arguing with others or complaining vociferously about the service. But every five days, on average, there is a more serious episode. 'Serious' means passengers starting fires in the toilet when smoking illicitly, becoming violent to crew or passengers, or damaging the aircraft. Men are three times more likely to be troublemakers than are women. Two thirds of

THE PARTY QUESTION

Todd Curtis is an aviation safety analyst and the founder of AirSafe.com. When people meet him at a party and discover what he does, what is the question they always ask?

'A primary concern is, "Well, if the airplane crashes, will I die? Is it 100 per cent certain that I'll just be dead?" My answer to that is: let's look at the numbers from around the world. Most accidents will be relatively minor no injuries, no deaths. A very small number involve passenger fatalities. More than half the time where there's a fatal event involving an airline, there are survivors. In fact most accidents kill fewer than ten of the passengers. Some of them are very dramatic, but it's rare that you have one that kills everyone on board.

'Another question that comes up over and over again is, "Where's the safest place to sit on an aeroplane?" I've looked at all kinds of data, asking, "Is there a pattern around the world of people surviving in certain parts of the aircraft if there's a serious accident?" And the answer is, if it's such a serious accident that a good number of people are killed, there is no rhyme or reason about what area of the aeroplane has the most survivors. It depends on the accident, and it depends on the aircraft.

'If you can tell me what kind of airplane you're flying in and what kind of accident you're going to be in, I can tell you the safest seat on the airplane to sit. In fact if you can tell me the second piece of information, I'd tell you not to fly at all. So that's a question that doesn't have an answer: it's impossible to know ahead of time the safest place to be.

'Some people ask about the safest days of the week, whether male or female pilots are better, etc. You can look at the day-of-the-week question and try and figure out if one day is more prone than another. Weekdays are because more flights are happening then, but as far as flights per million take-offs are concerned there's no pattern.

'The male/female pilot question is one that can be answered. But, as with many other questions in aviation safety, there are certain political or social ramifications of even asking the question, that could put one in very dangerous waters. Some years back when I was at Boeing, that question did come up in conversation one day. I went off into a corner, and I thought how would I answer this? I had to figure out how many female pilots are flying. That was the most difficult part. The other part was how many female pilots have been involved in very serious accidents with jet aircraft, and that was actually very easy. And the answer I got was: no pattern there either.'

offenders are in their 20s and 30s. Only one out of four incidents involves someone travelling alone. So you can understand why airlines are concerned when groups of young men get aboard.

The usual triggers for air rage are the three Ss: stress, smoking and spirits – too much stress, not enough nicotine, and an excess of vodka or whisky. Airlines such as Saudia and Kuwait Airways, which ban alcohol, report low levels of air rage. British World Airlines, which used to charter planes on an ad-hoc basis to Ryanair and other no-frills operators, had an even tougher policy when transporting oil workers around Scotland: 'Any passenger suspected of having alcohol in their bloodstream may be breath-alysed.'

Back in the commercial world, where airlines cannot be quite so strict with their passengers, you can look upon the typical flight as a big psychological experiment. The subjects comprise a group of people who have had a stressful few hours between leaving homes or offices and reaching the airport. Some of them are anxious about the prospect of flying; a proportion of passengers is being deprived of the drug on which they depend – nicotine; another group of people is being fuelled with free alcohol; and often those groups intersect. A smoker who is also an anxious flyer may drink heavily to try to alleviate the stress caused by nicotine deprivation and fear. No wonder many of the normal rules of civilised behaviour change, even among frequent flyers.

The writer Jonathan Glancey sums up the pressures on passengers: 'If you put lots of people into a small cylinder and put them thirty thousand feet up in the air, they suffer from claustrophobia, they get bored and frustrated. Also, they're strapped in for much of the time and if you restrain people, they get angry. I get angry when I travel on aeroplanes, secretly and quietly, as I don't like to be restrained and I don't like being told what to do.' Add unlimited free alcohol, as many traditional airlines do, and you have a rather less appetising cocktail than the G&Ts or Bloody Marys that the passenger has been throwing down her or (more likely) his neck. Todd Curtis warns that, 'Unless something very dramatic happens, unless a drunken passenger results in a crashed airplane, you will still have this controllable risk up there in the sky.'

The no-frills airlines report relatively low levels of disruption. Two reasons no-frills airlines are relatively unaffected: they sell, rather than give away alcohol; and they benefit from the fact that a flight of a couple of hours gives less scope for boredom, frustration or nicotine deprivation than a transatlantic crossing. The air-rage triggers are minimised.

You might imagine that the terrorist hijacks in 2001 would dampen the incidence of disruptive passengers. You would be wrong. 'We haven't had any more or any less than before September 11,' says Greg Wells of Southwest. 'Air rage hasn't changed, it's not going to change, people are people.' The difference now is that passengers and crew are much more alert to the dangers of someone interfering with the safety of the aircraft. 'The passengers are coming to our aid quite a bit,' says Wells. Many captains, in their pre-flight announcement, tell the passengers that if they are concerned about the behaviour of any other passenger, they should take steps to tackle the passenger. 'Throw things at him, throw your purse, throw your shoes, and several of you get together and subdue him,' was the instruction from one flight deck about how to deal with a suspected hijacker.

The panic on the flight deck of ValuJet 592 is palpable from the transcript of the cockpit voice recorder. 'Five ninety-two needs immediate return to Miami . . . we're on fire, we're on fire.' The National Transportation Safety Board report describes the consequences tersely as 'in-flight collision with terrain/water'. The final chapter of the accident was written in December 2001. Earlier, murder and manslaughter charges – one of each for every victim – had been laid against the owners of SabreTech, which had supplied the oxygen generators. It was the first time that a commercial company had been so charged after a crash. In return for dropping the 220 charges, the company agreed to pay half a million dollars to charity, which works out at $4,500 (£3,000) for each life lost. Half the money went to the National Air Disaster Alliance and Foundation, which lobbies for increased safety.

The cash will help, says Dr Todd Curtis, but there are limits to how perfect any machine can be. 'There is a variety of complex technologies on the planet – power plants, spaceships, commercial aircraft – where, as sophisticated as they may be, as well trained as the operators may be, accidents still happen, sometimes due to combinations of events that no one could have foretold ahead of time. That problem has not been resolved in any area of high technology.' Curtis is doing his bit to increase safety and understanding of risk, yet he is not a serene flyer. 'I'm just the kind of person who would much rather be in the cockpit flying the aeroplane than in the back seat not knowing what's going on. It's a total control issue. It's not logical at all. It's emotional.'

For nervous flyers, here's something to think about while you're gripping the armrests on your next no-frills trip: why are flights that go direct from A to B called 'non-stop', since they all stop once, when they reach B? Or, at least, you hope they do.

10. WHERE'S THAT PAINT?

Any new airline has an automatic advantage over any old airline
Tony Wheeler, founder of Lonely Planet

Our first year was more difficult than we expected
Tony Camacho, commercial director, Buzz (2002)

We have an unswerving commitment to developing the low-cost market
Floris Van Pallandt, chief executive, Buzz

Buzz was losing £20m a year
Michael O'Leary, chief executive, Ryanair

No carrier anywhere in the world has demonstrated they can run low-cost as well as another airline simultaneously. They're just incompatible
Ray Webster, former chief executive, easyJet

BUZZ FLIGHT 2584: STANSTED–VIENNA

'Three people had an idea,' went the original Buzz slogan. It was intended to convey the idea that a trio of imaginative souls had dreamed up a no-frills airline that would deliver what others did not. But just how good was the idea? There is plenty of time to consider that question while I wait for Buzz flight 2584 from Stansted to Vienna, on what claims to be 'the low-cost airline that gives you more'. With no-frills airlines like Southwest, easyJet and Ryanair showing how successful the concept can be, it is no surprise that airlines around the world have been tempted to set up low-cost subsidiaries, repainting their aircraft and removing free meals. Qantas produced JetStar, Delta gave birth to Song, and United's second attempt at a no-frills operation, Ted, seems to be proving more successful than the parent company. But it doesn't always work.

From the departure gate where I am sitting, on the patch of terminal turf that KLM UK used to call its own, I am one short of enough fingers and toes to count the passengers for this morning's flight. The 21 of us are barely enough to fill one in five of the seats on the BAe 146 that is operating the flight this bright, sunny October morning.

I have paid £40 for a one-way hop to Vienna. Assuming everyone has paid about the same as me, the grand total of revenue doesn't even reach a grand. Of the £840 that, I guess, Buzz is earning for this flight, the Chancellor of the Exchequer immediately trousers £105 in Air Passenger Duty. He doesn't even need to get out of bed at around 4 a.m., which is what the rest of us have had to do to get here in time.

The airport authorities at Vienna will take a similar slice for supplying parking space. There is precious little for much else, such as fuel, air navigation charges and the wage bill for the two pilots and three cabin crew – whose workload for the day involves just this gentle trip from Stansted to Vienna and back.

KLM UK, son of Air UK, son of Air Anglia, son of Norfolk Airways, began flying from Stansted to Scotland decades ago (the airline's latest incarnation is unable to say just how long). It stoically provided a scheduled airline presence at the Essex airport through the years when no one much else apart from Cubana wanted to fly there. The customers, most of them from Essex, East Anglia and the northern and eastern fringes of London, were loyal. By 1997, Air UK had built up a flourishing network of flights from Stansted to all the leading European business centres – Paris, Brussels, Frankfurt, Milan – plus domestic links to Aberdeen, Edinburgh, Glasgow and Inverness.

The Dutch airline, KLM, bought Air UK and superimposed its initials to create KLM UK. The new owner wanted to secure feeder services to its hub in Amsterdam, and was attracted by some impressive earnings from domestic services. So popular were the airline's Anglo-Scottish flights from Stansted that KLM UK began flying to Edinburgh and Glasgow from London City airport as well.

Then some strangers showed up at Stansted and started filling the place with 737s. Ryanair had begun its British low-cost operations in Luton, but the Essex airport provided a better deal. Stansted also had an embarrassing amount of room to expand. KLM UK found itself further squeezed when a new neighbour, Go, arrived at Stansted. Go moved into the suite of offices opposite Ryanair at the airport's Enterprise House and began flying in May 1998. The new company's first tranche of routes seemed aimed at weaker rivals like Debonair and AB Airlines. But once Go started flying domestically, KLM UK was in the firing line, with its lucrative services to Glasgow and Edinburgh under attack. Even Virgin Express briefly took a bite at the customer base.

The Dutch-owned airline was also hit by easyJet's cut-price flights from nearby Luton to Aberdeen and Inverness, which enticed a lot of customers from north London. Soon, not a single service to Scotland remained; KLM UK had thrown in the tartan towel. The services to Paris and Brussels were hit too, though rail, not air, was responsible: increased competition from Eurostar trains depleted passenger numbers. And if that was not bad enough, the KLM alliance with Alitalia went sour after a few angry months of cohabitation. KLM UK had been forced into a corner. As the network diminished, and it became clear the new no-frills competition could not be beaten, the company decided to join them.

Buzz was deemed to be the best hope for the future. The new airline was unveiled a month after Debonair collapsed. Ominously, the defunct airline had operated the same type of aircraft, BAe146s, as Buzz planned to use. Nevertheless, cheap flights were promised to six destinations in Germany, France, Italy and Austria, starting on the third day of the year 2000.

Loyal KLM UK passengers were not impressed. They saw what was happening as a mere rebranding of existing routes like Paris, Milan and Frankfurt as no-frills flights – without the hot breakfasts and frequent-flyer points to which they had become accustomed.

The existing low-cost airlines lined up to offer a barrage of hostile spin to greet the launch of Buzz. Tim Jeans, then at Ryanair, said, 'It sounds like Debonair mark two, flying to the wrong airports with the wrong kind of aircraft.' Even the names of the airline's restricted and flexible products, 'Done Deal' and 'Open Deal' respectively, attracted criticism. 'They're a joke,' said one rival. 'Some punters are going to think "I've been done", and others are going to assume that Open Deal means it's an open ticket they can change without penalty or get a refund, which they can't.'

'We will never suggest that all our seats are available at the very lowest price,' said Comacho when Buzz was launched. 'We will always show both the lowest and highest prices available.' The pledge did not last long. A year on, Buzz had abandoned the 'deals' policy in favour of what has now become the no-frills industry standard: each flight segment is individually priced, with no penalty for buying a one-way flight or for staying a short time at the destination.

Tony Comacho, commercial director of Buzz, has one of the sharper brains in the airline business. But he also found himself with some of the bluntest planes: the British Aerospace 146 is short, fat and slow. 'Is the 146 the right one? No, in the long term.' Comacho didn't order them: they were surplus to requirements from the KLM UK fleet. But he maintained that the aircraft's small size means Buzz can develop routes that would not be feasible for an all-737 operation. His aim: to 'use what we have sensibly'. But working out what that was involved repeated route changes.

Hamburg, Lyon, Helsinki and Vienna were soon ditched, leaving a rump of German business destinations plus a French and Spanish network based mainly around secondary airports. A network that had started by offering flights to key business cities in 2000 had, by summer 2002, become a niche operation serving small airports in France such as Limoges and La Rochelle. There were even two flights a day to the Normandy city of Rouen – soon cut back to just one departure, and later to zero departures.

'On Vienna and Lyon we overestimated the potential for attracting business travel,' said Camacho. To make matters worse, both Ryanair and Go were piling on capacity to Austria and France with new planes and new routes, many of them taking traffic that Buzz might have expected to enjoy. 'The landscape has changed so much since January 2000,' said Comacho, but he maintained 2001 was 'a very good year' and that it put Buzz 'back on expectations'.

'Final call for Buzz flight 2430 to Berlin. Would passenger Clemence proceed immediately to gate 37, where your aircraft is fully boarded and awaiting your arrival.' If the aircraft is fully boarded, that implies Mr or Ms Clemence is already on board. Still no sign of action on the Vienna flight.

About twenty minutes after the departure time, we are invited to board. There is not too much of a crush getting on to the aircraft. It has seen many better days. The decor is a bilious combination of purple, yellow and lime green. The carpet is scuffed and worn, as on the elderly Boeings that Ryanair bought second-hand from Lufthansa and Britannia. Just as with those aircraft, there is a sense of confusion about which airline, exactly, I am about to fly with. The same staff purport to work for two separate companies. One of the cabin crew is wearing a KLM UK lapel badge and has 'Buzz' embroidered on a pocket.

'You cannot form a low-fare airline simply by spray-painting your planes yellow, and keeping everything else the same,' says Tim Jeans. 'Same crew, same pilot agreements, same airports, fundamentally the same cost base. They're just not at the races.' Barbara Cassani, founder of Go, says, 'They created a low-cost airline by creating a new brand name. It may be better than what was there previously. It's not a sustainable business model.' The issue of union agreements is a key one, says Tony Wheeler, founder of Lonely Planet and one of the world's most frequent flyers. 'Any new airline has an automatic advantage over any old airline.'

Buzz's commercial director, Tony Comacho, called it 'a medium-cost airline,' adding – with some understatement – that 'Our first year was more difficult than we expected.'

When I first boarded a Buzz flight to Vienna, two months after the airline began, the BAe146 got only as far as Belgium. The pilots were so worried by a technical problem that the jet turned around and flew back to Stansted.

Eighteen months and several unanswered letters to Buzz's customer relations department later, I paid up again and booked on the same flight. At the time Barbara Cassani was urging others to sign up for the route to Vienna, too: 'It's the biggest public service they [Buzz] are doing, subsidising people to a monopoly airport, flying them there for £40 return when at least half of that is going to the airport.'

This time, the aircraft looks set to go the distance. By the time I tuck into my chicken with pasta and pour the first cup of coffee from a cafetiere, we are already over Germany. The navigation charges, which each country levies for its air traffic control systems, are eating into the revenue for the flight even more quickly than I am devouring the very tasty pasta.

This is an historic moment for Vienna. In an hour's time, the Austrian capital will lose its only no-frills flight. No one at Schwechat airport seems to be remotely concerned. Buzz's daily flight was of little consequence to the airport authorities. They have a handy near-monopoly of aviation in the region – or at least they did, until SkyEurope started flying from Bratislava, across the border in Slovakia, in 2004, and advertised the airport as 'Bratislava–Vienna'. (In the previous edition of this book, I wrote 'Any day now, I expect the airline to announce flights to the Slovak capital, Bratislava, and to name it "Vienna East".' The airline I had had in mind was Ryanair, but SkyEurope picked up the idea.)

Bizarrely, for anyone in search of cheap frills, the real Vienna is a good place to find them: British Airways charges 50 per cent less for a Vienna–London–New York–London–Vienna ticket in club class than it does for a simple London–New York return. (If you are tempted to take up this deal, note that you must first get to Vienna to start the journey.) Aircraft are extremely expensive assets, and if you own or lease some you have to fly them somewhere. Luckily, they are also extremely flexible: if Stansted–Vienna does not work out, how about Bournemouth–Prestwick? That was the big idea for Buzz at the end of 2002. But almost as soon as it announced the link, Ryanair said it would fly exactly the same route. Buzz retreated, and switched the plane to the French resort of La Rochelle. A former executive with the Irish airline, Tim Jeans, questioned the wisdom of Ryanair's move: 'Sticking a 189-seater on that route just because somebody came and trod on their front garden grass is a mistake because that capacity can probably be deployed elsewhere. Why spend time giving a minnow like Buzz a bloody nose?' In fact, the route has proved reasonably successful, and most of the 189 seats each way, each day between Dorset and Ayrshire are filled. Meanwhile, Jeans was busy nurturing a minnow of his own.

'The best way to make sure you arrive on time is to travel on a new airline's first flight,' announced Tim Jeans, as MyTravelLite's maiden departure trundled across the apron at Birmingham airport on 1 October 2002. Four months earlier, Jeans had been poached from Ryanair by Richard Carrick, MyTravel's chief executive for global development, to head a new no-frills venture.

Forty-five minutes after fate was tempted by that announcement, the Airbus aborted its landing at Beauvais in northern

France. One hundred and eighty passengers spent the next half-hour flying around in circles waiting for the fog to clear. 'It was not exactly what you wanted on a first flight,' said Jeans, once the Airbus had touched down. He revealed that the captain was only minutes from declaring a diversion to Paris's main airport, Charles de Gaulle.

Besides the inauspicious first flight, three things made Tim Jeans' enterprise different from other low-cost airlines-within-an-airline. The first was that it was the offspring of a charter carrier, rather than a scheduled airline. The second was that it had an unwieldy name. The third was that the man who had conceived the airline was kicked out within two months of the first flight.

'It's an idea that we brought to market, I think quicker than any other company has done so,' said Carrick as the plane circled over Picardy. 'We started this project in July of this year and here we are in early October on the first departing flight.' At the time, he was chief executive of global development for MyTravel – the new name for the highly successful Airtours company, which had grown from nothing to one of Britain's two biggest tour operators in less than twenty years. The company had seen its growth dented by the rapid rise of no-frills airlines, which had eaten into the 'seat-only' sales that had previously helped fill many charter flights to capacity.

MyTravel's core business was predicated on the traditional package holiday, which assumes a certain level of demand for outbound or inbound charter flights a week or fortnight apart, together with beds at Mediterranean hotels and apartment complexes. This was the model that Vladimir Raitz had developed more than half a century earlier. But the market for packages reached saturation and, in 2002, began to decline. It is not difficult to see why. Each year around half a million holidaymakers leave the market because they die, or their circumstances change, or they simply lose interest in the offering from the inclusive tour producers and come up with an alternative that they arrange themselves: driving over to France, opting for Bridlington or staying at home watching the latest crop of travel programmes on TV.

The industry has the tricky task of persuading a new generation of holidaymakers that the Great British package holiday is the solution to their travel needs. Furthermore, it must convince them that locking into a particular holiday many months in advance is, despite the uncertain world, a good idea. But the average young person prefers to buy online, in their own time. They will not be swayed into traipsing up and down the high street trying to work out the best deal from artificially inflated brochure prices and absurd discounts. The Internet is revealing many of the tricks of the trade. Anyone with a PC and a modem believes themselves capable of constructing a holiday: sourcing the right flights, surfing the beachside hotel websites, and steering through the car-rental contraflow.

In short, we have become travel agents, or at least we fondly imagine we have. And just thinking it could be enough to wound a travel industry that is still largely living in the early 80s, technologically speaking. The 'Viewdata' booking system that most UK travel agents and tour operators use belongs to the same era as Space Invaders. In the twenty-first century, no-frills airlines were invading the space traditionally occupied by the big tour operators. Initially, Britannia, the largest charter airline, and Air 2000, started behaving like no-frills outfits: selling charter flights seats direct to the public, and offering more flexibility than the usual one- or two-week stay. Tim Jeans says this is 'smashing their duration control and flogging off a few seats that they would have otherwise only sold as seat-only'. In contrast, MyTravel decided to confront the low-cost carriers head on.

As the peak summer season got under way, Carrick and half-a-dozen senior MyTravel executives began devising the new airline. But while the in-house airline had flown hundreds of thousands of charter flights, it had no expertise in running a scheduled operation. So Carrick head-hunted the man whose scalp many travel agents would dearly love: Tim Jeans, who had riled the established travel trade during his six years at Ryanair – a time he describes as 'A masterclass. In business, I have never seen, before, during, or since, anything like it. There's not a day goes by when you don't recall some similar experience at Ryanair, which gives you insight into what you're doing.' Soon he had chosen a base at Birmingham, whose then-managing director, Brian Summers, had a year earlier said he could offer no special deals to no-frills airlines.

Jeans says he changed his tune: 'I think Brian and his team would be the first to recognise that the low-fares train was leaving the station and certain airports were going to be on it, and those that weren't on it would effectively see their businesses grow at a substantially lesser rate than those who were on board that train.' Birmingham is now crowded with low-cost operators.

MyTravelLite's original route network was a mix of safe bets like Alicante and Malaga, a domestic short-hop to Belfast, the business-and-ski destination of Geneva, and three flights a day to Beauvais in northern France. Choosing a name was a matter of bolting 'Lite' on the end of the parent company's title, just as Continental had done with its ill-fated no-frills operation. The easy part was to find the aircraft. It would use the same planes as the company's charter fleet, albeit a dedicated and resprayed pair of Airbuses. The crew would be drawn from the parent company, so one day they could be serving free meals on a MyTravel charter from Birmingham to Malaga, the next charging for coffee on a MyTravelLite scheduled flight on the same route. They noticed the difference – as did the passengers, particularly when things went wrong. A passenger in Malaga could be travelling to Birmingham on a MyTravel Airways charter flight or a MyTravel-Lite scheduled service. The difference would become clear if weather or air-traffic control problems were to disrupt operations. The parent company has had a long-established policy of providing meals and hotel rooms in the event of a long delay. But MyTravelLite photocopied Ryanair's hard-line no-compensation policy, meaning its passengers would have to fend for themselves.

The passengers on the first flight seemed happy enough, even with the half-hour delay. I sat next to a student named Stian Reimers, who had booked it at 10.30 p.m. the previous night. 'Got it for £30. I looked on the website, saw that it was the inaugural flight today and tried to think of reasons why I wouldn't want to go to Paris today. I couldn't think of any, so I turned up.'

The standard no-frills pricing model would normally see a fare of £200 or more so close to departure. But very soon, MyTravel had many bigger numbers to worry about. In the second half of 2002, the company made a series of profit warnings. These culminated in the discovery of 'black holes' in the MyTravel accounts, concerning the way in which income from its Going Places travel agencies and Airtours package holiday operation had been counted. The share price slumped amid rumours of the imminent collapse of the company. It stayed afloat, but the chairman, David Crossland, brought in new senior management to appease city investors. Carrick, who had conceived the no-frills airline, was dumped. The MyTravel name was felt to be so tarnished that plans to rebrand Going Places as MyTravel were rapidly reversed. But Tim Jeans had invested a small fortune in building an image for an airline saddled with the name MyTravelLite. Even with a tiny fleet, the new venture was expected to lose £5m in its first year – a small price to pay, the company believed at the time, for admission to the no-frills club. But Alan Stewart, then chief executive of Thomas Cook, said he had no plans to emulate the move: 'The package holiday will be around for many, many years.' Stewart left Thomas Cook early in 2003.

'I'm not sitting here saying I'm a low-cost airline,' says Jim French. He is the affable, and vastly experienced, managing director of an airline that is in its third identity in three years. Jersey European, a regional airline based in Exeter, expanded to become the largest independent regional airline in Europe. Its Channel Islands-specific name was no longer appropriate. So in 1999 it cheekily borrowed the name of one of British Airways' original components, and rebranded itself British European. But by 2002, French felt he had to repackage the airline once more – and came up with the name FlyBE. It faced a range of challenges. It was a big operator at Birmingham (where MyTravelLite had recently landed), Edinburgh and Glasgow, and had substantial operations from airports uncomfortably close to no-frills competition such as Belfast City. But Jim French says 'We brought low fares into Northern Ireland. We were the first ones to produce £19, £29, £39 fares, we abandoned catering in the economy cabin, we charged for drinks, everyone thought we were mad. We did a lot of great things. The low-costs have picked up the mantle and run a bit faster than us.'

The result: FlyBE continued to chase its traditional market, with a business class and a premium economy service, charging correspondingly high fares, while filling the cheap seats with 'discretionary' passengers who are attracted only by low fares. 'We have a good core business which fills about 60 per cent of all our seats, which means we have got forty seats out of a hundred to sell at incremental cost. And therefore, as long as we sell these seats at incremental levels, mindful of dilution, etc., etc., then, yes we can use these to actually help assist us make profits.' The key word there is 'dilution': if some existing passengers switch from higher fares to the cheaper deals, FlyBE will fill more of its seats but earn less cash. French is confident he can pull off the trick: 'The most profitable period in this airline's history is when we've been very aggressive in low fares in Northern Ireland. As an independent airline we can move very quickly.'

*   *   *

Forty miles away, at Nottingham East Midlands airport in Leicestershire, another independent airline showed how quickly it could move. BMI, formerly British Midland, formerly Derby Aviation, had long revelled in the luxury of having its home base to itself, give or take a few charters and freight operations. Under the guidance of Sir Michael Bishop, it had helped to transform aviation in Europe and made healthy profits along the way. So healthy, in fact, that the airline has the most stylish headquarters of any UK carrier: Donington Hall, a seventeenth-century mansion deep in the countryside yet close to the airport. This was where Tony Davis, the airline's head of corporate affairs, spent some time theorising about how BMI could move into no-frills aviation. It was not a wholly academic exercise. As British Midland, the airline had almost single-handedly changed the rules for European aviation. Until the 80s, most national airlines enjoyed a monopoly on key domestic routes and shared a cosy duopoly on international routes: British Airways could fix fares with Aer Lingus to Dublin, with Air France to Paris and Lufthansa to Frankfurt safe in the knowledge that competition was barred.

'It was clear to me there would be a wave of new thinking about aviation,' says Sir Michael. 'Freddie Laker and the package holiday people were probably among the first people to liberalise aviation, but it was very much confined to the non-scheduled market. What I did between 1978 and 1982 was to persuade firstly the Labour government and then the Thatcher [Conservative] government that liberalisation of UK domestic routes would be a good idea. Then as now, there was a concerted effort by BA to prevent liberalisation from taking place. That was a very big battle. We were a very small business at the time; when we started competing with BA we had less than a thousand employees and only fifteen aeroplanes. All the political battles had to be done by us when we were struggling to survive.'

Travellers between London, Scotland and Northern Ireland saw fares fall and standards rise as soon as British Midland started competing with British Airways' shuttle operation. 'British Airways carried more passengers and the total market grew,' says Bishop. The same effect happened once the no-frills airlines started challenging. 'In life,' says Bishop, 'the more things change, the more they stay the same.'

But in 1999, he had concluded that 'there was going to be a new style of airline, but at the hub airports there would not be the space for them to develop.' So BMI would remain at its main

bases at Heathrow and Manchester, and create a low-cost brand
for its other operations. Three years later, this no-frills offshoot
was still on the drawing board at Donington Hall. There were
several obstacles to progress, notably with existing labour agreements. 'Why should anyone accept worse conditions when the
business appears to be profitable?' asks Bishop, rhetorically.

After 11 September, when BMI had to ground several of its
aircraft, the unions were more prepared to negotiate. But talks
with East Midlands airport were not going well. The owners did
not want to see revenue diminished by cutting charges for a
no-frills splinter of BMI. The impasse ended in March 2002,
hours after Barbara Cassani's Go had announced plans to set up
an operation at East Midlands.

'I'll always be grateful to Barbara Cassani for giving me the
fastest promotion in airline history,' says Tony Davis, who was
rapidly elevated to become chief executive of the new, low-cost
airline. Bmibaby started with two aircraft, but within six months
had expanded to eleven. All its existing with-frills routes from
Nottingham East Midlands had 'migrated' to its young offspring.
Davis also opened a new base at Cardiff. Within a few weeks,
British Airways announced it would close down its operation at
the Welsh capital, leaving the airport wide open to Bmibaby (with
a token flight to Dublin on Ryanair). The airline has since
expanded to Birmingham, giving it the West Midlands as well as
the East Midlands.

Ray Webster, outgoing chief executive of easyJet, found himself
competing with Bmibaby after the takeover of Go went through.
At the time he predicted that Sir Michael Bishop would have to
abolish frills across his aviation empire before Bmibaby could
succeed: 'No carrier anywhere in the world has demonstrated they
can run low-cost as well as another airline simultaneously.
They're just incompatible. When he is prepared to say BMI
doesn't exist anymore, we are just low-cost, that's when he will
be serious.' Bishop riposted that the dual operation was working
– and, besides, easyJet is only a success because of the pioneering
work of British Midland: 'In many ways, although the new wave
of airlines came in after us, they have, because of the work I did
in the early 80s, had it easier.' BMI, he said, can continue to run
two distinct businesses, and make money from both: 'As Mark
Twain would say, stories of the demise of premium traffic are
somewhat premature. There will always be a demand for full-
service airlines.'

By August 2005, it appeared that Webster's argument was prevailing. BMI announced that all but a handful of its routes from Heathrow would become no-frills. Passengers who, until 31 July, had enjoyed 'free' hot meals and cold drinks, found that they were now paying for the privilege of choosing snacks. Some key routes – to Belfast, Brussels and Edinburgh – retained a business class, but most BMI flights were one-class-only. The airline started promoting itself as Heathrow's low-cost alternative, with Bmibaby as the brand. The young pretender has stolen the traditional airline's crown.

Suppliers of aircraft paint have enjoyed a prosperous start to the twenty-first century. Following swiftly in the slipstream of My-TravelLite and Bmibaby, Germanwings and Hapag-Lloyd Express started up in the Federal Republic. Germanwings was the low-cost operation of Eurowings, a regional carrier part-owned by the national airline, Lufthansa. It set up in Cologne, with flights to Stansted and a range of other European destinations, and flies as far as cities in Turkey – among the longest no-frills sectors. Within two months, Hapag–Lloyd Express had established a very similar operation based in Cologne, though its London flights served Luton. HLX, as it was soon abbreviated, is the offspring of the giant German tour operator TUI.

Barely was the paint dry on Germanwings' and HLX's aircraft when Air Berlin stepped up its operations, expanding rapidly from Stansted to seven German airports. Air Berlin is a very different beast from the average no-frills airline – not least because it offers frills. Passengers get free in-flight catering. The airline has also been flying for longer than any other low-cost carrier apart from Ryanair. And its chief executive, Joachim Hunold, boasts that 'We are a low-cost carrier with frills. We have the lowest cost base of any airline' – to which Michael O'Leary of Ryanair responds 'If the guy at Air Berlin thinks his costs are lower than us he's got to go and shoot his accountant.'

By rights, aviation should flourish in the world's second-biggest country: Canada has a wealthy population spread across vast distances. But the travelling public has faced years of high fares and unenthusiastic competition. Then, in 1996, an Englishman named Clive Beddoe, and three other entrepreneurs, set up a new airline.

'It became so obvious,' says Beddoe. 'Our industry was deregulated in Canada in 1988, and no one had done anything about it. Suddenly we stumbled across the opportunity. We had two very inefficient airlines in Canada.' They were Air Canada and Canadian Airlines. 'They were obviously dinosaurs that were going to have to change.' They did change, too: Air Canada took over its smaller rival, extinguishing competition on many routes. But Beddoe has the national carrier in his sights, and has rapidly eaten into the market that Air Canada once had to itself.

In a country where caution is a watchword (Canadians are said to be the most heavily insured people in the world), Beddoe's first challenge was to establish some plausibility for WestJet. 'We had to be credible,' he says. 'We actually flew our aeroplanes before we started the airline, and filmed them flying, so people could see we did have aeroplanes and they did fly.' The key investor, he says, was the Ontario Teachers' Pension Fund, which gave WestJet what he calls 'instant credibility'.

The airline was set up in the 'capital of the West', Calgary. Why there? 'Because that's where we lived. And the West was probably going to need the capacity more. We have more impediments to travel here in the West. A four hundred-mile stage length from here to Vancouver is an 11–12 hour drive.' When the airline began operations in 1996 – three months after easyJet launched – it had three aircraft. Now it has close to one hundred, serving almost every significant population centre in Canada, and earning glowing reports. 'What do you offer that differentiates your product from anybody else's? It's customer service, it's reliability. We've only got thirty million people to draw upon. You cannot afford to tick them off.'

To make sure that WestJet does not upset anyone, Beddoe places a high value on the company culture – just like Southwest. The airline's manifesto says that 'At WestJet we keep the spirit alive by . . . creating internal "magic" and external "wow".' One person who did not have a magical time at 'Team WestJet' was Steve Smith, as exuberant as Clive Beddoe is introspective. Smith was heading up Air Ontario, part of Air Canada, when he was hired as chief executive by Beddoe and his partners. A year later, he was very publicly sacked by the same people. By 2002, he had been rehired by Air Canada and invited to set up a low-cost subsidiary: in Calgary, in a hangar directly opposite WestJet's operational base. Beddoe believes the move was intended as a 'slap in the face from Air Canada'.

'They're welcome to him,' says Beddoe. 'He doesn't understand people. He just doesn't get it.'

The new airline that Smith set up was the idea of Air Canada's president and chief executive, Robert Milton, 'to provide employment opportunities for some of our surplus staff'. The idea was simple: routes where Air Canada could not make money were transferred to Zip, which cut out the frills and made the services viable. 'Air Canada gets off a route, we get on,' says Smith. 'You get a ready-made market. It's a nice perk to have. People aren't coming out of the woodwork to fly. They get off, we get on, that's good.' Smith says that costs can be cut by 25–30 per cent, 'When you take the executive class seats out, fill them up, take all the food off, reduce the number of flight attendants, etc.'

Against those savings must be offset the cost of spraying the aircraft orange, pink, green or blue (each 737 gets a different colour). Smith says he was helped by the Air Canada unions, who 'saw what was going on and said "We want to be part of that" '. They also said that Zip would be capped at a certain level; the airline can operate only twenty aircraft.

And the spat with WestJet? Smith is diplomatic. 'The whole concept behind Zip is not to go after WestJet, as much as they'll tell you the opposite. The whole concept of Zip is to replace Air Canada on fundamental feed routes where locally it loses money. Low-fare carriers are here to stay. Full-service carriers may not be here to stay.'

Zip ceased operations in September 2004.

'Buzz: off' read a headline the day after Ryanair announced its takeover of the KLM subsidiary. Three years after launching a no-frills airline, and three months after Floris van Pallandt, the chief executive of Buzz, had said, 'We have an unswerving commitment to developing the low-cost market', KLM threw in the yellow towel. Buzz was sold for a pittance once the Dutch carrier decided to stem the losses that it incurred during Buzz's brief existence.

The man who bought it took great pleasure in explaining why. 'Buzz was losing £20m a year,' said Michael O'Leary. Ryanair's chief executive had a simple message for Buzz's workers: they would have to work harder. 'We won't have any rubbish about biorythm cycles and all that bollocks. Fly four sectors a day. Either you do things our way, or the door's over there.' He said Buzz would continue as a separate entity, but cost-cutting would make it profitable within a year. 'There'll be a lot less people floating around the HQ drinking cappuccino and talking about the unique brand they've created.' O'Leary said that the BAe 146s ('the wrong planes') would have to stay with Buzz for a further year, at which point they would be returned to KLM: 'We'll fly them to Amsterdam, throw the keys through the window and run.'

But by the end of February, the full extent of Buzz's malaise became clear and life took a turn for the worse for two out of three Buzz employees. Ryanair revealed that their airline was in an even worse state than previously thought, filling fewer than half its seats and losing £100,000 per day. Michael O'Leary took the extraordinary step of grounding Buzz for the month of April 2003, and axing much of the route network while making two-thirds of the staff redundant and repainting the planes in Ryanair colours.

Aircraft paint vendors next switched their attention to Coventry – unkindly described as 'The only airport in Britain with a cattle grid in the middle' by the Midlands comedian, Jasper Carrott. Coventry's Baginton airport (or 'Bag'tn', as the road signs on the A45 unhelpfully describe it) is not exactly new. Air-freight companies use it because of the central location: the geographical heart of England, at Meriden, is a few miles away, which makes Coventry a useful place from which to distribute goods. And the former passenger terminal has found a new lease of life as an office block. The south-east flank is taken up with a fully functioning farm, while the west side of the airport has become a refuge for, bizarrely, old Southern Region railway carriages; 50s rolling stock from the Sutton depot is quietly rusting at the end of the line in a field in Warwickshire. Even compared with some of Ryanair's more wayward secondary airports, Coventry looks like a sticky-tape and string operation.

It is possible, indeed preferable, to announce the start-up of an airline before you have any planes or pilots to fly them. You can then start taking bookings for the new venture, which helps sales and cash flow. Yet to make an announcement before you have an airport terminal deal completely sewn up is ambitious; you are committed to the location, which makes you potentially vulnerable to all kinds of misfortune.

In January 2004, the giant German-owned holiday combine, TUI, announced its Britannia Airways subsidiary would have another go at no-frills flying. In the good old days, before easyJet and Ryanair were invented, Britannia had taken the revolutionary step of moving beyond its charter flights. The airline launched a scheduled route between Luton and Belfast. It carried thousands of passengers for about £30 each, at a time when prevailing fares between London and Northern Ireland were much higher. Britannia could have expanded the simple concept of cheap, flexible flights to and from Luton. But it decided the operation was more trouble than it was worth, and gave up – leaving the runway clear for easyJet to take effective control of Luton. With easyJet growing fast at Gatwick, and Stansted the playground for Ryanair, there was little room for anyone else. The Thomson organisation missed out on all the tasty available slots within forty miles of London, the richest aviation market in the world. So Thomsonfly, as it was to be known, is based at an airport that had not seen a scheduled flight for a decade: Coventry.

This new airline was due to start flying by 31 March. When negotiations with the airport owners got tricky, the company simply produced £6.7m to buy the airport outright. But it had reckoned without the close interest of Warwick District Council, on whose territory Coventry airport stands. It was miffed not to be consulted, and concerned about the extra traffic and noise that the airport would generate. As a result, it was in no great hurry to grant planning permission.

Some initial building work had to be torn down. But passengers checked in as normal at a collection of temporary buildings for the first flight to Jersey. Despite the airport and the airline being part of the same company, the maiden voyage was not quite the seamless experience that had been hoped for: it was half an hour late, due to 'over-zealous security'. For the traveller accustomed to conventional airports, it was an unusual experience: the queues for check-in stretched back out of the terminal building, which itself was a collusion of temporary buildings.

Coventry airport soon had a second airline: Hapag–Lloyd Express, with flights to Cologne, which perhaps not coincidentally is also part of the giant TUI organisation. It called the airport 'Coventry/Birmingham', to the annoyance of Birmingham's 'real' airport, just twelve miles away. And Britannia Airways, the UK's leading charter airline for three decades, disappeared.

The whole company became Thomsonfly, in the same way that Bmibaby swallowed its parent company. Customers are able to buy no-frills flights that are either operated by Britannia's Boeing 757s and 767s (the only type that the airline flies) or the no-frills offshoot's 737s. The assumption is that the travelling public does not much care, as long as the price is right. The company may be 'smashing their duration control', in the words of Tim Jeans, but it has at least reclaimed some of the ground lost to no-frills airlines – and introduced the travelling public to new airport experiences. After setting up at Coventry, Thomsonfly was the launch customer at Robin Hood International Airport. You might conclude that is a Nottinghamshire airport; in fact, the new facility is in South Yorkshire, and was formerly known as RAF Finningley. It is now called Doncaster–Sheffield in the schedules, and holds its own between Doha (Qatar) and Donegal (Ireland) in the schedules. And perhaps appropriately, given Ryanair's fondness for 'secondary' airports, the Irish airline flies daily to Dublin and back.

Back aboard MyTravelLite: the no-frills airline that the troubled tour operator had founded lasted even less time than Buzz, managing just 37 months. 'MyTravelLite will cease to operate as a scheduled airline at the end of October', read a terse statement on its website. 'For flights departing from 1st November 2005, seats are sold through Airtours Holidays, and are subject to the terms and conditions of Airtours Holidays.' Which is where, in a sense, the airline had started.

11. LOSS LEADERS

Airlines are very cash-positive. It's difficult to go out of business

Tim Jeans, managing director, Monarch Scheduled

Please be advised that today's flights to Dublin, Edinburgh, Newcastle &
Belfast have been cancelled. EUjet apologise for the inconvenience
caused and will contact passengers directly. Normal operations will
resume shortly

Website of EUjet on the day it went bust, 26 July 2005

My wife said, 'You've got nothing left to mortgage but the dogs'

Franco Mancassola, founder of Debonair

DEBONAIR FLIGHT 092: LUTON–PERUGIA–ROME

May Day 1999: not a happy occasion at Gatwick airport. It is the first day of the summer charter season. At the start of May, the whole package holiday industry lurches from the undemanding schedule of winter into the peak season, in which everyone and everything is worked to the maximum. To add to the confusion this particular year, British Midland has launched a new handling operation on behalf of charter airlines such as Monarch. There are teething problems, and the whole check-in and baggage system appears to be running at quarter-speed. The concourse of the South Terminal is heaving with increasingly fractious children, their weary parents, and implausible mounds of luggage. As the departure time for what is theoretically an early morning flight to Pisa on Monarch wanders towards lunchtime, I reflect on the irony of taking a charter flight to cover a story about a no-frills scheduled airline.

Franco's coming home. One of aviation's more colourful characters, Franco Mancassola, is about to start flying to his home city, Perugia. But I have to get there before he does, so that the city-break story – '48 Hours in Perugia' – can appear in *The Independent* just before Debonair's scheduled flights from Luton begin. From the research I have done so far, the Umbrian capital sounds a marvellous place – three-dimensional in every sense, with art and history concealed within a maze of streets perched high on a hill. Just the sort of destination you'd like to go for a weekend.

Jaded travel editors owe thanks to the no-frills airlines for an endless sequence of new destinations that can refresh the travel pages: Moenchengladbach, Cergy-Pontoise and now the Umbrian capital, Perugia. And those were just the routes started by Franco Mancassola, founder of Debonair.

Perugia airport is among the most beautifully located in the world. It occupies one of the few flat pieces of land in central Italy, straddling a narrow plain midway between the Umbrian capital itself and the hub of the St Francis industry, Assisi. The tall, stern columns at the airport entrance look all the more out of place because of the way they are planted amid languid agricultural land surrounded by craggy hills. But they correlate closely with the fascist architecture favoured by Mussolini. Beyond them, a long, triumphal drive leads to a terminal building that is in the final stages of renovation. Someone is painstakingly attaching a sign above the new car-rental desk. These are exciting times for the airport: it is about to become linked with Europe's biggest city, thanks to a man who left Perugia nearly four decades earlier.

Several years later, I meet Franco Mancassola at Gatwick airport. He is now running an Italian aircraft supply company, Avia Interiors, which makes seats for airlines. With a handsomely sculpted face, dark hair and alert eyes, he is energetic and expressive, just as he was when he appeared in Debonair's ads. But he looks more relaxed now that he is out of the no-frills race.

How had he got caught up in the business of flying people for less? Early in 1995, Mancassola was living happily in Hawaii. To that point he had enjoyed a lively career working for a range of airlines. 'I fell into aviation when I came to England in the early 60s,' he says. 'I found a temporary job at Monarch, and from there I decided that was what I wanted to do.' Given the delays and uncertainties I encountered on the Monarch flight to Pisa, it would have been handy if he had stayed; he was an effective and inspirational manager.

In the late 60s, Mancassola caught the attention of a US-based airline, Continental. 'It was, at the time, a domestic carrier. I told the chairman that, in a global economy, an airline like Continental should at least be exploring the possibility of some international routes. He said "Can you do it?" I said "Sure." Two years later we were flying into Mexico.' Continental has since expanded all across Latin America, and has become the transatlantic airline that serves the widest range of cities in Britain.

Shortly after the expansion began, the airline decided to move from California to Houston, to take advantage of the Sunbelt's low costs and booming economy. It was in Texas's largest city that Continental was to try to suppress Southwest, now the biggest no-frills airline of all. But while California can, in places, replicate the hills of Umbria, Texas cannot. 'I decided I wanted to stay in California,' says Mancassola. 'So I moved to World Airways.'

At the time, World Airways was a with-a-few-frills airline that was a relative minnow in the US. To try to turn around its fortunes, it decided to break into international aviation. As with so many other airlines, from Laker to American, it started transatlantic flights to and from Gatwick using DC-10 aircraft. World Airways soon established a successful link from the Sussex airport to Baltimore-Washington International, with fast connections to the West Coast. Mancassola believes World Airways, not Laker, was the real pioneer of low-cost flights between the US and the UK.

'World Airways was doing it before Freddie Laker. World Airways was the airline that started affordable but comfortable transatlantic flights. They were inexpensive but the passenger had dignity. They had a good seat pitch, 34 inches, and good service. I've never been a believer that cheap must mean shoddy. In a way I carried that little idea, if you will, into Debonair.' World Airways' improving fortunes meant that the stock that Mancassola says he was planning 'to plaster my bathroom with', turned into good money.

At this point, many people might have taken the cash and flown off into the sunset to enjoy it; Mancassola headed west, but not to relax. 'I decided to go to Hawaii and start my own airline, Discovery.'

In theory, the Hawaiian archipelago is ideal territory for a low-cost airline, with strong year-round demand from both leisure and business passengers, and no effective competition from other modes of transport. But Mancassola says he was squeezed by the existing airlines and political interests in the same manner that Sir Freddie Laker suffered in the early 80s. At the point where it seemed all was lost, he says, 'My wife said, "You've got nothing left to mortgage but the dogs." ' Against the odds, the airline was revived and the dogs survived. Discovery found a buyer who was prepared to pay a reasonable price – enough for Mancassola to live on, and to make him want to try again.

'You can take a man out of Luton,' as the saying nearly goes, 'but you can't take Luton out of a man.' Franco Mancassola decided to move to Britain, specifically to the Bedfordshire airport.

'Deregulation was beginning to take hold in Europe,' he explains. 'At the back of my mind I always knew that Europe was ripe for a low-cost airline. So I packed my bag, and I said to my wife, "Right, off we go," and on the door of my house in Hawaii there's still my wife's fingertips when I –' at this point, Mancassola makes a very Italian scraping noise '– when I drag her away. We came over here and we started Debonair.' His philosophy was a model of clarity: 'Think of the passenger. Keep it simple, keep it affordable, keep it safe, keep it reliable. By providing good and friendly service the passenger will realise that cheap does not mean shoddy. If an airline can achieve these objectives, it will win the loyalty of passengers, it will prosper and it will be satisfying a demand which will grow in the years to come.' Anything else? Yes: 'Who knows? It may even be profitable.'

The man from Perugia was not the only southern European who, in 1995, was keen to start a low-cost airline. Stelios Haji-Ioannou was already looking for opportunities, and eventually reached the same conclusion: that Luton was the place to begin. The difference was that easyJet earned all the publicity that comes with being the first mover, launching something demonstrably different.

'Stelios beat us by five months. Of course he had his own money, while I had to go around and raise it.' That proved difficult. 'We put together a business plan, and I began to canvass financial institutions, banks, potential investors.' Mancassola soon found that 'Everyone's got tons of money until it's time to put it on the table. It went on for about a year, and I was getting disheartened.' Eventually he went back to the US, and talked to a merchant bank in Phoenix. 'They liked the plan, and by the time I landed in London the half-million dollars was already wired, so I put in my bit.' I estimate that to have been around $1m. 'We did a second offering, and raised another $6m, and did a third offering, and raised another $4m.' Then he went to Greece, the home of Stelios. 'I walked into a room full of about two hundred investors and said, "Ladies and gentlemen, I'm here for one reason and one reason only. I want your money." We raised another $4m.'

The airline was still less well capitalised than Mancassola had hoped. He blames this on Europe's rules about airline ownership, which limit non-EU holdings in member states' airlines. 'If I could have gone and raised capital in Hong Kong, I could have probably raised $20m and the airline would have been saved. But that law prevented me. It's an absurd law.'

Mancassola feels that legislation sought to confound him at every turn. One of the Civil Aviation Authority tests for new airlines is sufficient cash reserves to survive for three months with no cash coming in. 'It's an absurdity,' says Mancassola. 'No airline can survive for three months with no income. It's the bureaucracy that keeps you on the ground, burning cash, while bureaucrats have ninety days to respond. A horrid, horrid system.'

Despite the obstacles, Debonair took to the air in 1996, within seven months of Mancassola sealing the funding. The airline's first flight was on 16 June. Early summer is a good time to launch an airline, since it should ensure strong earnings during the peak season. But Stelios's easyJet had beaten him; I calculate by seven months, rather than Mancassola's figure of five.

While Stelios had concentrated on Anglo-Scottish routes initially, Debonair was focused on an entirely different market: continental Europe. 'Moenchengladbach in western Germany, also known as Düsseldorf Express airport; Copenhagen in Denmark; and Barcelona in Spain,' recites Mancassola. 'We expanded to Madrid, and Munich, Newcastle, Rome.' It was a brave move to fly to so many destinations so quickly. 'We had to expand very rapidly to keep up with the market. And the problem is when you expand, you put an airplane on a route, from day one that airplane costs you x. Before you fill it up, you maybe have to bleed for two, three, four months.'

It also helps if the plane doesn't keep breaking down. The shortage of capital meant that Mancassola had opted for British

Aerospace 146s rather than the no-frills industry standard Boeing 737. With hindsight, Mancassola would have chosen differently. 'It was a choice dictated by our lack of finance. At the time, they were available, they were parked in the desert. It turned out to be a poor decision on my part, and I take full responsibility for that.'

The aircraft proved to be unreliable, and in worse condition than anticipated. Not only were Debonair's operations disrupted in the all-important summer launch period, but 'we had to spend tons of money to put it right. It was simply a mistaken choice made by yours very truly.'

What there was no mistake about, he says, was the level of service offered. Of all Europe's no-frills airlines, Debonair came closest to matching the Southwest Airlines product. Passengers could book either direct or through travel agents without penalty. A modicum of free refreshment was available on board – coffee and a muffin – with alcohol available for sale. Seat pitch (the distance between the front of one seat and the front of the next) was a comfortable 32 inches, which is better than many long-haul airlines. 'Comfort is not a class privilege, everyone should fly comfortably,' says Mancassola. Connections were allowed, and some flights operated multi-sector: Newcastle suddenly found itself connected with Madrid, via Luton. And there was a simple but effective frequent-flyer programme: after ten return flights you got a free trip. Mancassola also insisted on a straightforward fare structure. 'One of the key elements of a successful price policy is to keep it simple. Passengers for too long have been confronted by a mass of incomprehensible figures and letters when trying to ascertain how much it will cost them to fly between point A and point B.'

With the no-frills industry in its infancy, and low-cost competition only slowly encroaching, Debonair made it through the first year. April 1997 saw the completion of the so-called third package of the liberalisation of the civil aviation market in Europe, and the introduction of total cabotage. In simple terms, any European airline could fly anywhere it wished within the EU. 'We were the very first to start pan-European services,' says Mancassola. 'We flew as a domestic airline in Germany, and that went straight up the nose of Lufthansa.' The German national carrier reacted 'appallingly', he says. 'They tried every trick in the book to ground us. Anyway, two years later we became almost partners, we were doing some flying for them.'

Plenty of other people saw what Stelios, Mancassola and Ryanair's O'Leary were doing, and believed there was cash to be made. Autumn 1997 saw a so-called 'pathfinder' flight from Hurn airport in Bournemouth to Glasgow. A new airline called Euroscot Express blazed a trail between England's south coast and Scotland's largest city. The words 'doomed to failure' reluctantly but, as it turned out, accurately attached themselves to my report at the time. The market may have been there – as Ryanair is demonstrating with its Bournemouth to Prestwick service – but the aircraft (small propeller planes and 1-11s), the marketing and the fare cuts were insufficient to stimulate it.

Back home in Luton, Franco Mancassola's gleaming Alfa Romeo was still receiving admiring glances, but life was becoming tougher. Inside a year, stage whispers were circulating about the financial health of Debonair.

When rumours take root about the fortunes of a carrier – even if they have no basis in reality – they have an unfortunate habit of becoming self-fulfilling. Individual passengers are reluctant to risk cash in the event of an airline failure, while businesses cannot afford the prospect of executives being stranded. Travel agents have no wish to get involved in cancelled flights, refunds and unpaid bills. In other words, if a competitor is thought of as shaky its rivals benefit.

Debonair was still aloft, and soon to celebrate its second birthday, when Go began flying in May 1998. Two of Go's first three routes were to Debonair destinations: Rome and Copenhagen. Mancassola's low-cost monopoly between London and the Italian and Danish capitals had been broken. With a lower cost base and more scope to offer cheap fares, both routes tempted people across to Stansted from Mancassola's base at Luton. Later, Go attacked Mancassola on routes to Munich and Barcelona. Ryanair increased its presence in Italy, which stole market share from Debonair. And in July 1998, AB Airlines started flying from Gatwick to Nice, with a lead-in fare of £109 return (cheap in those days, but now well above the lowest widely available fare of around £60). A route on which Debonair had initially competed only with British Airways and Air France was now carved up between seven airlines: the new players were easyJet, AB Airlines, British Midland (now BMI, flying on behalf of Air France) and Virgin Express from Gatwick, Heathrow and Stansted via Brussels.

To protect its share of the market and to help expand its route network, Debonair established an alliance with the newcomer, AB Airlines, on routes to Barcelona, Berlin and Shannon. AB, based in Gatwick, was a third incarnation of something that had started off as a sensible and profitable entity: Air Bristol. It was a charter-based airline that had a lucrative contract to shuttle between the British Aerospace facility at Filton, north of Bristol, and the main Airbus factory at Toulouse in south-west France. Every day, a BAC 1-11 would fly there and back purely for the staff of Airbus and BAe. Air Bristol saw the opportunity for liberalisation to open a new route from Gatwick to Shannon. Since Air Bristol would be a confusing name for an airline flying between London and the west of Ireland, the name was changed to AB Shannon. Gradually, other routes emerged – from Gatwick to Nice, and Lisbon in Portugal. So it became AB Airlines. But Tim Jeans of Monarch says the carrier was at the wrong place at the wrong time: 'They focused on Gatwick, at a time when Gatwick was being pumped full of British Airways capacity.'

At the same time, Luton was turning increasingly orange, with easyJet imagery obscuring the neatly designed livery of Debonair. Mancassola had to do something. A series of distinctive Debonair advertisements appeared in the press and on the London Underground, featuring the airline chairman. 'Stelios came out with a very clever idea – "as cheap as a pair of jeans". That was very distinctive, and putting his number on his airplane, I take my hat off to him. So we wanted a spokesperson who said, "Hey, I'm in charge, I take responsibility, you can trust me." ' Debonair's advertising agency suggested giving a face to the airline. 'I wasn't very keen, actually, but in the end I said, "If it's a good idea, for the sake of the airline, I'll do it." It put the airline on the map.' So Mancassola joined Laker (and, much later, Stelios) in presenting the advertisements.

The tag line of the ads was, 'My finance director tells me I'm mad,' for charging low fares while giving passengers more. Franco proclaimed the many virtues of Debonair, next to details of cheap flights from Luton to Europe. The ads were prophetic. Traditionally, travel companies in Britain that are in difficulties fail on Fridays in September. So it proved for Mancassola. 'We were faced with mounting debts, but we had the option to get out with style.' On the last day of September, 1999, Debonair stopped flying.

'We were very close,' says Mancassola, 'very, very, very, very close to making it. But it was not to be. We simply ran out of cash.' Tim Jeans is harsher. 'Debonair tried to be all things to all men: business, leisure, primary airports, secondary airports, hubs, point-to-points, transit traffic.' Mancassola again: 'Debonair had very high loads. Our downfall was rapid expansion. We started off with six aircraft, we finished with sixteen.'

Jeans: 'They just didn't frankly have the direction that was required to succeed.'

Mancassola: 'We had 70 per cent load factors. Our fares were right, our quality was right, we were giving more than the others.'

Jeans: 'They basically floundered around until they put themselves out of their own misery.'

Mancassola: 'On 30 September we paid all the employees, we paid everyone. We simply closed the door.'

Anyone who expected a period of calm reflection among the no-frills airlines for the final three months of the millennium was mistaken. In the wake of Debonair's demise, for the first time Ryanair offered the opportunity for flying for only the cost of taxes, fees and charges. At Luton, easyJet announced what it claimed was the lowest widely available air fare in Europe: £26 return on its new route to Liverpool. 'If we can make twenty or thirty pence per head at this time of year we're happy,' said a spokesman.

Shortly afterwards, AB Airlines followed Debonair into aeronautical oblivion. Gary Barone, one of its executives, looks back fondly on the venture. 'It was one of the most exciting things ever.' Once more, Tim Jeans offers an obituary – this time, so full of initials that Sweden's favourite band almost gets a mention: 'AB – poor old AB. BA were throwing capacity, and very low fares by BA standards into Gatwick, and I think AB just couldn't get to the mass that they needed to sustain profitable operations.' Yet he also maintains 'airlines are very cash-positive businesses'. Unlike, say, a steelworks, which has to pay for raw materials and labour ahead of having anything to sell, airlines take the money anything up to a year before they have to fly the passenger. 'It takes a lot to put an airline under. But there are some who just don't get the model right.'

Stelios, founder of easyJet, says that neither AB Airlines nor Debonair was a true low-cost carrier. 'They pursued the strategy of high cost and low fares. The swansong of Franco Mancassola's Debonair was an affordable business class with a chauffeur-driven pickup. That's not low-cost.'

'I refuse to believe that giving a cup of coffee, or not giving a cup of coffee, makes a difference on the profits of an airline,' counters Mancassola. 'Our mistake was the wrong choice of aircraft, they were very costly, not properly financed; and the rapid expansion and entrance of a lot of low-cost airlines. Ryanair and easyJet expanded very rapidly. And Go coming in – Tyson dressed in kids' clothes, with Big Daddy behind, helping him bash up the other ones. The market share that Go took away from us in Rome and Barcelona was a contribution to our shortfall. We were short by $5m when we closed. If we weren't forced to pay fuel in advance, landing fees in advance, we would have made it.'

Mancassola also believes that the European Commission let him down: 'When you start an airline, it isn't just money. The major carrier's got everything, slots, airplanes, established routes. The field has to be level, otherwise there's no way for competition to flourish, and the consumer will be taken for a ride. I am a believer in competition, and I don't believe there should be regulations, but there should be rules. Rules without freedom is tyranny, but freedom without rules is anarchy.' Sir Richard Branson believes that Debonair was not designed for success. 'They just didn't have a great brand. They didn't have a great vision. They didn't stand out from the crowd.' Dozens of young airlines have failed to grow to maturity, leaving a trail of stranded travellers and angry creditors. (Passengers have little protection when a scheduled airline for which they hold a ticket goes bust.) The aviation sector has as low a life expectancy as dot-com companies. Perhaps that is why Debonair attracts some sympathy from Martha Lane Fox, the celebrated co-founder of the high-profile dot-com, Last-Minute.com. She found the reaction to the business closures in the late 90s depressing: 'I've just been very, very surprised at the glee people take when people fail.'

The only certainty about aviation is that someone will come up with what they hope is the next great idea. Tony Camacho, the former commercial director of Buzz, resurfaced with a new airline that was intended to 'Americanise' air travel in the UK. It had a name, Hop, and a plan: domestic routes between as many as twenty UK airports. An airline called Now got slightly further; a team of high-flyers spent months working at Luton airport on a carrier that would be the first 'next generation' low-cost airline, with a flat fare no matter when you booked. Someone buying three months ahead for a Luton–Rome flight on a Tuesday in November would pay exactly the same as a last-minute buyer on the last Friday evening before Christmas. Luckily for the people involved, the paper airlines never took off. Once new airlines start flying, they have the capacity to lose a fortune very quickly.

In 2003, British Airways announced it was to withdraw many of its services from Birmingham. The airline's management team at the Midlands airport announced a buy-out. A new airline called Duo would fly from Birmingham and Edinburgh to a range of Continental and Scandinavian destinations. The airline promised a 'full business-class service on board', with free meals, drinks and newspapers, yet at fares that competed with the likes of easyJet, Ryanair and MyTravelLite. By the spring of 2004, Duo was expanding rapidly, with services like Birmingham to Pisa and Edinburgh to Bordeaux. Sadly, on May Day it went bust.

At the start of September 2004, it was the turn of EUjet to try to prove it had found a gap in the market. The new airline had certainly found a gap on the map: Kent international airport, comfortably away from the competition. Manston, as the airport perched on the island (now connected to the rest of Kent) used to be known, was expected to go from zero to eight hundred thousand scheduled airline passengers in a year – thanks to a new Irish-based operation. When I turned up for the first flight, the overpowering smell was of fresh paint. The airport owners had turned a military airfield into a twenty-first century civil air terminal in five months flat. The staff were well trained, having spent the previous week practising on a few dozen co-operative locals who were prepared to pretend to be passengers on flights to nowhere.

The airline's founder was P. J. McGoldrick, who used to be chief executive at what was then another small Irish airline, Ryanair. For this venture, he saved on brand development by conceiving the name himself: 'I just thought it up. The dot.com [www.EUjet.com] had to be available, and it was.'

Choosing a name for a new airline proved a lot easier than selling seats to and from an airport no one has heard of, even if the destinations – Prague, Dublin, Amsterdam and many more – were enticing. But McGoldrick was confident about the venture. 'We're outside the London air traffic area, and able to get in and out of here without any holding time.' Usually true, no doubt, but in keeping with the tradition that the maiden flight on every no-frills airline is late, the captain of the Fokker 100 said that the air-traffic control computer at Swanwick had temporarily failed. We waited our turn while Sellotape and string were applied to the system that keeps Britain airborne.

The elderly but well-appointed plane had leather seats and generous legroom, and for ten months the people of Kent enjoyed access to cheap and frequent flights. The day before EUjet closed down, the website was selling seats to Manchester the next morning for £25 including taxes, fees and charges. That sort of fare suggests plenty of 'distressed inventory'. Next day, it was the passengers who were distressed. 'Please be advised that today's flights to Dublin, Edinburgh, Newcastle & Belfast have been cancelled,' announced the website. 'EUjet apologise for the inconvenience caused and will contact passengers directly. Normal operations will resume shortly.' They never did. At the time of the failure, there were 12,000 passengers still abroad and 27,000 who had paid but had yet to travel. The failure caused a lot of grief – but those numbers show how badly EUjet had fared. Even at the start of the school summer holidays, it had under forty thousand paying customers.

The causes of the demise of Debonair, Duo and EUjet can be argued about endlessly. None of them used the Boeing 737 which is the industry standard, nor the Airbus A319 or A320 which are also popular with successful low-cost airlines. Their planes were smaller and older. Underfinancing and overexpansion also played a part. Any new route takes time to turn a profit. This might have happened earlier if Debonair had flown bigger, more reliable aircraft. Expansion is always a tempting option for a new airline, but every new route is a loss leader for a while. The three most successful no-frills airlines – Southwest, easyJet and Ryanair – all began slowly, with a strictly limited route network. They waited until this was generating revenue before launching more cash-draining services. Had Mancassola managed to acquire more finance, he could have turned the corner. At least he was in the right sector of the market, which is more than can be said for some other transport undertakings that were hit by the growth of no-frills flying. The losers are many.

Failure in business is typically the result of not identifying and countering a threat early enough. Traditional airlines were not alone in failing to appreciate the way that no-frills carriers would change the travel landscape. Anyone who used Piccadilly station in Manchester in 1998 will have seen a smart new Eurostar catering building being built by the entrance to the station. It was never put into use, because the trains for which it was supposed to cater never appeared. The Channel Tunnel train company promised that year that Eurostar would be running from Manchester to Paris by early summer, with direct trains from Glasgow and Edinburgh to the Continent following a short time later.

Eurostar had originally planned an extensive range of trains from Plymouth to Brussels and Scotland to Paris – indeed, part of the original justification for the Channel Tunnel was the benefits it would bring to regions outside the south-east. But by the time the trains were ready, Ryanair had established itself at Prestwick and easyJet was building up a base at Liverpool. With fares from (somewhere near) Glasgow to (somewhere near) Paris that were typically less than £100 return, and plenty of options for flyers in the north-west of England, Eurostar concluded there was no sustainable market for regional services.

There are other losers in the no-frills war. The hoteliers of Rimini, for example, were furious when Ryanair unceremoniously pulled out of the airport and shifted all the flights down the coast to Ancona in a row about airport charges; their rage was compounded when MyTravelLite promised flights from Birmingham to Rimini in 2003 then cancelled them. But their anger was nothing compared with the rather larger community of UK travel agents.

Prior to 1995, anyone planning a weekend in Barcelona or Berlin would have trudged along to a travel agent and handed over at least £100 return, of which 9 per cent would have gone straight to the agent. When Debonair was still alive, it dealt happily through travel agents. (Rivals say that the extra costs helped contribute to Debonair's demise.) Nowadays, there is nothing in the cost structure of Ryanair or easyJet that allows for a travel agent's edge.

'We chucked Ryanair out when they cut commission,' says Stephen Bath, who heads the Bath Travel chain and is a past president of the Association of British Travel Agents. 'Since then the service has got even worse, such as not ringing people up when the flight is cancelled.' His Bournemouth-based business received hundreds of calls after Ryanair took over Buzz and promptly ditched the plans that Buzz had laid for a base at the Dorset airport.

In addition, easyJet has done its part by slagging off travel agents in its 'Cut out the middle-man' campaign. 'The travel agency community was livid already,' recalls Tony Anderson, easyJet's first marketing director. 'They were faced with reductions in their commission from the larger airlines, so the insults from this upstart must have been difficult to bear. Indeed the Scottish Passenger Agents Association [which represents the country's travel agents] told us we'd never sell a flight in Scotland without them.' Around fifteen million flights to and from Scotland later, 'they're looking pretty stupid now'. Early in 2002, easyJet took the battle to business travel agents, the people who arrange flights for companies. The airline 'named and shamed' big firms whose travel policies, it said, did not include low-cost airlines. The research was not flawless, though; Marconi complained that it had been unfairly singled out, and that its executives did indeed fly on no-frills airlines.

'Buzz was more agent friendly, or at least slightly less antagon-istic,' says Rachel Crampton, managing director of the Norwich-based chain of Travel Centres. She believes the no-frills airlines are unaware of the proportion of bookings that go through agents. She says the travelling public should go through a travel agent so as to make sure they are getting best value for money. 'There's a big perception that they are the cheapest option, but that's very often not the case.' Crampton's company charges customers £10 extra for seats on no-frills flights.

The travel agency boss has a family connection with the independent airline business; her father, Jim Crampton, founded Air Anglia, later Air UK, later KLM UK, later Buzz. 'It started the growth in regional airports, which the no-frills airlines are now capitalising on.' Crampton senior's airline used to fly some interesting routes, such as Norwich–Heathrow in the days before the M11 was built and the road journey could take five hours. The rising value of slots at Heathrow put an end to the route in the 80s, and for many years Norwich airport resounded only to the occasional departure to Amsterdam or the northern part of Britain. But by the summer of 2006, the first low-cost flights had been established at the Norfolk airport – even though Stansted is so near and so successful. Crampton is philosophical about the rise of the sector that has cost her commission: 'They've enlarged the market, and if the travel agents get a proportion of that, that's good for everyone.'

Even the man who acquired the ba.com website for British Airways believes 'Travel agents still have a role'. Martin Lock, who is now a director of Excel Airways, says 'In ten or fifteen years time, the next generation may wonder what we were doing wandering around shopping centres calling in at travel agents, but there's something to be said for going out on a Saturday afternoon – and for expertise.'

Back at Gatwick, the Monarch flight to Pisa finally starts boarding at lunchtime. Monarch is owned by the Swiss-Italian billionaire

Fabio Mantegassa. It was badly hit by the no-frills operators. In the early 90s it developed an impressive network of scheduled flights to popular Mediterranean destinations. These have been put under such pressure that Monarch now uses no-frills-style advertisements with no-frills-style fares. Mantegassa recruited a man with a long track record with low-cost airlines: Tim Jeans, formerly of Ryanair and MyTravelLite.

'People are now remarkably sensitive – in a way I've never known before – about the price of their air ticket,' says Jeans. Ironically, he arrived at Monarch at the same time as one of airlines' biggest costs began to go through the roof. The price of aviation fuel rose from around $300 per metric tonne to as much as $700 – effectively a heavy new tax on travel, with the earnings going to the oil producers. On an Airbus A320 flight from Gatwick to the Canary Islands, the rise in the price of fuel added up to $4,000 to the cost of the trip, which translates to an extra £15 per passenger.

Not everyone was unhappy about the rise in the price of oil. People concerned about the effect of aviation on the environment believe that fuel should be much more expensive. A Boeing 737 flying on Europe's longest no-frills flight, from Luton to Athens, consumes ten tons of kerosene. That corresponds to about twenty gallons per passenger. The emission is pumped into the stratosphere. The newer the aircraft, the more efficient it is, but anyone who believes some airlines' propaganda that they're doing the world a favour by flying off on holiday should think again – it's cleaner to take out your dirty old diesel car for a run down to Cornwall. Aviation fuel has managed to evade tax for a century, but some airlines are worried that international pressure from environmentalists could see the price rise.

Destinations are suffering too – some of them, like Dublin and Prague, because they are too darn busy at weekends. High-yield holidaymakers are being deterred by the prevalence of boozy young people, mostly from Britain, roaming through the city's streets every Friday and Saturday night.

So far, no one has started flying again from London to Perugia airport, which means that thousands are missing out on this beautiful Umbrian city.

But Mancassola has ended up not far from his home town, in charge of the company that he had once bought aircraft seats from: Avio Interiors. 'The chairman invited me to dinner one

MANCASSOLA ON GO

Franco Mancassola's Debonair faced stronger competition from Go than from anyone else. He has little time for Barbara Cassani, who founded the airline.

'If someone wants to start an airline, and is the son of the Sultan of Brunei and has tons of money, but it's his own money, no problem. Stelios did the right thing, and put his money where his mouth is. He had plenty, that's great. But Barbara Cassani didn't create anything. Everything was given to her. She didn't have to risk a dime or scratch her head twice, because the operations manual was British Airways, the pilots were trained by British Airways. She created nothing, and she founded an airline. And she'd throw airplanes as far as they could go to take market share away.

'We, Debonair, were the weakest because we were running on our own money. We had to pay everything cash in advance. But Go was British Airways, so who the heck is going to ask Go for money in advance? So that helps the cash flow.

'If you look at pilot training, aircraft deposits, British Airways admitted that they guaranteed the airplane. That's a huge amount of cash. If we had had that cash we would be flying today happily. Go was a typical example of how the European Commission, on aviation, don't have a clue of what they're doing. Absolutely none. They allowed state carriers to get subsidised. They allow all these big alliances. So either you sell to a major carrier or you go out of business. What kind of competition is this?

'Go was put into the market by British Airways, with none of the market forces that we had to face. Go certainly eroded some market share that we, Debonair, with our limited resources, could not afford to lose.

'Remember their advertising? "Go, the low-cost airline from British Airways". The next moment they deny it all "We've got nothing to do with British Airways." It's a travesty.

'It wasn't a good investment for British Airways. The fact that the shareholders forced them to sell it means that it was a cash drain. We will never know what the figures really were. It was a fiasco. They know it. They may say the opposite until the cows come home, but I don't believe it.'

night in Monte Carlo, I thought, "That's a hell of a way to go for dinner." Anyway, he met me with a proposal. I said I don't know anything about seats. He said, I want you to bring in an airline mentality. After a week, I was completely out of my depth, wondering whether I'd made a sensible decision. One night, about 7 p.m., I was in the huge factory, and there were about three 747 ship sets [consignments of seats]. I sat on one of those seats, and thought, "Jesus, have I done the right thing?" The airline world is very fast moving and challenging. And I looked at all these seats – there must have been about a thousand – and I thought, "You know what, they're all empty, but unlike in the airline industry, they're all paid for." And that cheered me up immensely.'

Yet Mancassola is also considering a return to the industry, to found another airline: 'I would love to start one. In the US, if you fail for whatever reason, a lot of the time it is put down as an experience – "This guy fell from a horse, next time he'll be more careful" – so I've learned who to trust, who not to trust. Would a low-cost airline flourish again? Hard to say, with these mega-alliances now – a fancy word for a cartel.'

As Franco Mancassola prepares to leave, his eyes fix mine. 'Debonair was, I believe even today, a well-planned, well-run airline. We had the cardinal sin of every airline – we were undercapitalised. Debonair never went bankrupt. We paid everybody. We just closed because we didn't have any cash to go forward. The idea was, and I still believe today strongly, to have an airline that has comfort, that has pizzazz, and is affordable. We quit the race on the last quarter of a mile. And that was a great shame.

12. 11 SEPTEMBER 2001

*Since September's horrific events, our industry has witnessed a
continuous stream of cut-backs, lay-offs, aircraft grounding and airline
bankruptcies*

British Airways

*My son and grandson are the most precious things in my life, and I
wouldn't hesitate for a second to place either one of them on a
Southwest Airlines flight*

Colleen Barrett, president, Southwest

If Al-Qaeda don't get you, the Deep Vein Thrombosis probably will

Mick Webb, Ryanair passenger

At Los Angeles International airport in 1997, a man who was
wanted by the FBI for making terrorist threats was apprehended by security staff at a checkpoint. He was trying to carry a
small arsenal of weapons and ammunition on to a domestic flight.
Instead of being arrested, the culprit simply handed over the
deadly consignment to police and continued his journey. Attempting to take a gun on to an aircraft was a felony only if the weapon
happened to be loaded – carrying ammunition separately circumvented federal law. In the same year, Federal Aviation Administration-conducted tests of airport security, in which agents tried
to smuggle imitation firearms through airport checkpoints, proved
dismal. Out of 173 attempts, they were caught in only 56 – worse
than one in three.

In June 2000, I lived for a while at Gate 21 of Las Vegas airport. I wanted to see if I could spend 24 hours in the city that celebrates money like no other, without a cent to my name. I chose to base myself at a departure gate of McCarran International because airports in America have long functioned like community centres. Passengers and staff mingled amiably with meeters and greeters. There was no impediment to solicitors (as people asking for charitable donations are known). No one challenged my curious behaviour on this survival mission. It turned out to be a remarkably comfortable experience. I spent part of the evening collecting baggage carts; each one that is returned to the machines at the passenger entrance earns 25c, which would amass enough to see me through the following day. The rest of the time I was snoozing on a bench by the departure gate. There was plenty of company: people who had been hounded out of hotels because they had gambled away the rent and had nowhere else to go before their flights home. Any of us could switch at will between landside and airside areas. The boundary was by an undemanding metal detector. My bag, full of electronic equipment, slid through the adjacent X-ray machine. The staff on duty chewed gum and looked bored, as well they might: no one had hijacked a plane to Cuba for decades, and terrorism was something that happened only in other countries.

This relaxed, comfortable world ceased to exist on 11 September 2001, along with thousands of innocent people. Nineteen hijackers took advantage of the relaxed attitude to security to smuggle blades on board four aircraft – two belonging to American Airlines, two to United. Being the biggest airlines in the world, they were prime targets. There was also speculation that their names might have attracted the terrorists to target them; the next biggest airlines, Delta, Southwest, Northwest and Continental, do not have such resonant names for people with a grudge against the United States of America. Two of the hijacked aircraft, both Boeing 767s bound from Boston to Los Angeles, were flown into the twin towers of New York's World Trade Center; they were American flight 11 and United flight 175. A third, a Boeing 757 serving as American Airlines flight 77 from Washington to Los Angeles, was deliberately crashed on the Pentagon. The fourth, United flight 73 from Newark to San Francisco, again a 757, was downed in a field in Pennsylvania after the passengers took on the hijackers. Besides the 33 crew, 214 innocent passengers and the nineteen hijackers, over three thousand people died in the attacks – most of them in the World Trade Center.

About two thousand five hundred flights were airborne above the US when the attacks took place, several hundred of them belonging to Southwest. 'Within half an hour of the second aircraft hitting the World Trade Center, the government mandated that all our planes be set down as quickly as possible,' says Greg Wells, vice-president for safety and security for Southwest. The US government feared that other aircraft had been captured to be used as guided missiles. Captains were told to land at the first available airport. For close on an hour, Steve Hozdulick, Southwest's director of flight dispatch, was uncertain whether any of his aircraft had been targeted. 'There was a huge sense of relief when we got them all down.' Remarkably, all but three were able to land at the 58 airports to which Southwest flies, which made the business of getting back into the air easier when commercial flight was once again permitted, four days later.

It is rare that cameras catch an aircraft in the process of crashing. It is unprecedented that a fatal collision should be shown, live, to an audience of tens of millions. But 11 September was a day that shook the Western world – and continues to affect many travellers. 'I don't think that many people in the history of the modern era have ever seen a plane crashing,' says Professor Robert Bor, a psychologist who specialises in travel at the Royal Free Hospital in London. 'They may have seen the aftermath in newspaper reports, on television and so on, but we very seldom see death on the kind of scale that we did on September 11. It's indelibly set in people's minds, airliners crashing into buildings. I think to actually see the point of impact, for many people who may have been able to subjugate their fear of flying, it's become a very real, very primitive fear.'

'Our passengers were able to watch it all on TV,' says Gareth Edmondson-Jones of the US low-cost airline JetBlue. Around a thousand passengers were in the uncomfortable position of seeing the awful events take place, in real time, while they were flying across the US as JetBlue had installed seatback screens which receive live television pictures. 'The feedback was very positive,' says Edmondson-Jones. 'At some base level there was a comfort having all that information in your hands in the seat, you know what's going on.'

When the enormity of the attacks on New York and Washington became apparent, President Bush talked of it as an act of war.

When wars begin, people stop travelling, particularly if they have witnessed people dying as a result of doing something as harmless as boarding a scheduled flight on one of the world's biggest airlines.

Aircraft are peculiarly vulnerable to hostile acts, and passengers' alarm is heightened by the high profile that hijacks and bombings receive. The earliest act of aircraft piracy took place in Peru in 1931, when an American aviator and his aircraft were seized, on the ground, by a group with a political grievance; he and the plane were released, unharmed, several days later. Since then, aircraft have become the target of choice among terrorist groups. 'If striking terror into the hearts of people is a goal, airplane hijackings can be an effective way of getting there,' says Dr Todd Curtis, founder of the website AirSafe.com. Between 1978 and 1994, 307 fatal airline events were reported in the *New York Times*; Curtis has studied the coverage of each of them. 'One of the most widely reported involved a hijacked TWA 727 that spent several days at the media forefront. In the end, only one passenger was killed.' But the public seems singularly adept at identifying with the passengers on a jet that has come under hostile control, and fuelling their misgivings about getting on board an aircraft.

When planes crash, there is usually a temporary pause in operations at the affected airport and on the airline involved. When Concorde was lost at Paris in July 2000, Air France cancelled its departures for the rest of the day, but started them the following morning; other airlines' flights resumed almost immediately. The impact of 11 September was far more profound. For four days, not a single flight was allowed to take off from the US. Tens of thousands of passengers were stranded many miles from home, including people on dozens of transatlantic flights that did not have enough fuel to return to Europe when the order came through that US airspace was out of bounds. Every airline lost fortunes while their planes were grounded, and in the downturn in travel that followed.

One individual was particularly affected, as Sir Richard Branson concisely relates. 'At nine o'clock in the morning on 11 September, JetBlue was going public and the owner, David Neeleman, was going to make a billion dollars out of it. Obviously it got cancelled by what happened at 8.30 a.m.' Gareth Edmondson-Jones recalls 'We were set to file the submission, so a lot of our senior execs were actually in the Wall Street area, staying in hotels. They'd been up all night at the printers printing the last documents, and they were getting some sleep before going in to file it all.' None of them was harmed, but JetBlue found its aircraft grounded for days at places like Wichita in Texas.

Within hours of the first aircraft striking the World Trade Center in New York, conventional wisdom among business and the media had reached firm conclusions about the future of aviation. Flying would be more stressful and much more expensive. Insurance and security costs would rocket. Jobs and routes would be cut. While aviation would not be cast back quite to the dark ages, only the strong were likely to survive the corporate cull. 'Since September's horrific events, our industry has witnessed a continuous stream of cut-backs, lay-offs, aircraft grounding and airline bankruptcies,' said British Airways.

Almost every part of the travel industry was hit. Cruise lines, for example, were caught in the middle of a buying spree. Buoyed up by high earnings in the 90s, where the US market had grown steadily while overseas demand had rocketed, they had ordered billions of dollars' worth of new ships. Suddenly the market dried up, with many Americans fearing even to take the flight to Miami to board what some of them regarded as a floating target. Car-rental companies found that the decline in air travel meant there were fewer people who needed instant mobility at the end of a flight: within two months, Stelios's car-hire operation was hiring out Mercedes for as little as £1 a day. And hotels found it difficult to fill beds at almost any price. Travelling in America late in 2001, I was twice asked to name my own price for hotel rooms, so desperate were proprietors for business. The verdict of most people within the travel industry was that the world had changed forever, and life had become much, much worse.

For the bereaved mourning the loss of their loved ones this was indisputable. But not everyone agreed that aviation, and in particular no-frills flying, would necessarily be grievously wounded. And there was a sense that some airlines were using the events of 11 September to justify painful measures that would have been necessary anyway.

This is a typical example of the news in the latter part of 2001: Midway Airlines announced it was to halve its workforce, cut seventeen aircraft from its fleet and abandon nine destinations, including the key cities of Washington DC and Los Angeles. 'The instant need for this restructuring has been occasioned by the calamitous drop in business traffic experienced by airlines,' said the company boss, Robert Ferguson.

How much of this was due to 11 September? None of it. Midway made the announcement four weeks to the day before the attack on America. The world's airlines, and in particular those in the US, had been feeling the effects of a downturn in business confidence already. But the hijacking of two aircraft from each of the world's two largest airlines precipitated the biggest-ever slide on the stock markets, with airline stock particularly affected. Like the financial markets, successful civil aviation depends on the confidence of the participants. And plenty of people felt scared, both within and outside America, by what they had seen – amplified by further threats, and the anthrax attacks in the US.

Since cheap fares became widespread across the Atlantic, the US has been a favourite destination for British travellers, with around two million holidaymakers heading there each year, as well as one million business visits. With the exception of a few high-profile attacks on individual tourists, the US has been seen as a safe destination. That image had now been shattered. Places like the Windows on the World restaurant at the top of the World Trade Center had been a big draw for visitors, while in Washington DC you could – until 11 September – take a tour of the Pentagon. America's capital city was basically a governmental theme park which attracted millions of US citizens and foreign visitors. No one would look at either city in quite the same way again. Nor would people so readily fly to Florida for the theme-park experience. In December 2001, fares from the UK to Orlando fell from the usual rock-bottom minimum of £200 to as low as £129.

Between them, US airlines shed around a hundred thousand jobs because of the drop in passenger numbers. Among the major carriers there was one exception: Southwest expressed its intention to maintain services and staff at their present levels, and was continuing to hire staff. 'We were the first airline to get back out with a full schedule,' says Greg Wells, the airline's vice-president for safety and security. 'Our aircraft only make money when people are sitting on them in the air.'

On the other side of the Atlantic, the mood in the days following 11 September was grim. For four days, the skies over London were eerily quiet. Not a single aircraft adopted the usual approach to Heathrow, lining up over the centre of the capital for a direct track to touch down at Britain's busiest airport. To the east, not a single aircraft took off from, or landed at, London City airport. Among airlines that were forced to cancel dozens of flights, and pilots obliged to make awkward approaches to

Heathrow, there were murmurings of an overreaction to the terrorist suicide attacks. When Washington allowed flights to and from America to resume, the US airlines were given a 24-hour head start. Passengers desperate to get home from both sides of the Atlantic had their stress prolonged by the delay resulting from the US Transportation Secretary, Norman Mineta, giving permission to foreign airlines to enter American airspace. Privately, some UK airline executives were seething at the implication that British security procedures were somehow inferior. BA's frosty announcement that the Federal Aviation Administration was finally 'satisfied with British Airways' security measures' was significantly terse.

It was remarkable that the FAA had doubted them. When I began my short career in security at Gatwick airport, the world was a very different place. Every passenger search was carried out manually: we used hand-held metal detectors, and all cabin luggage was inspected by hand. Squads of security guards like me were bused around the airport to each gate, so that passengers were frisked at the very last moment before boarding the aircraft. Almost all flights were treated the same way, from departures to Spain with Laker Holidays to British Caledonian flights to Libya. Only travellers to Belfast and Tel Aviv came in for special attention, having all their hold luggage checked minutely and sealed before being loaded into the hold. In my entire career, I'm relieved to say that I only ever discovered one remotely dangerous item: a camping gas cylinder, which I was instructed to take out on to the apron to discharge safely and return the useless canister to the passenger, who showed admirable restraint in not suggesting where I could place it.

The flights that I took in the days immediately following 11 September, to Dublin and Charleroi, were like going back in time, with meticulous individual searches. Soon, though, the security procedures reverted to their previous level, though anyone who was foolish enough to try to carry on board a potentially dangerous weapon such as a knitting needle or a pair of nail scissors would have to wave them goodbye forever. Glass bottles, which have the potential for far greater harm, were still sold just the other side of security control, full of highly flammable liquids.

The attack that wounded America so badly also killed a significant number of British people, but there was not the lasting damage to confidence that many had predicted. Memories proved shorter, and a consensus built quicker among passengers that it probably wasn't going to happen to them. 'If you're an extremist seeking paradise, you're unlikely to try and get there on a no-frills flight,' says Mick Webb, a passenger on Ryanair at Stansted. 'Anyway, if Al-Qaeda don't get you, the Deep Vein Thrombosis will.' A more sensitive soul than Michael O'Leary, chief executive of Ryanair, might have been appalled by such sentiments. But he was already telling Radio 4's *Today* programme that British Airways and other airlines were 'screwing' the government for financial support after 11 September. 'That's a bit harsh, isn't it?' interjected John Humphrys. 'It's a bit true,' said O'Leary. He and Stelios, of easyJet, took the high ground, as well as the media limelight, and were not about to relinquish their grip. 'There's no joy in running empty planes,' said Stelios. 'You can't save souls in empty churches. So very quickly I realised that unless you make a big bang in advertising, and make a big noise, you just die with lack of passengers.'

'It shows how wobbly the big carriers were – they're dinosaurs, most of them,' says Franco Mancassola, former boss of Debonair. 'It will change aviation, but not because people will be afraid. Aviation will bounce back. It's the heart of the economy. We will see airlines come and go, that's the nature of a market. Aviation left on its own, to fight on its own within the rules, will prosper. I hope new people will start airlines. We need new blood, we need new believers. And I hope the majors will not interfere too much. I'd encourage anyone to invest in aviation, because aviation has a great future.'

Sir Richard Branson had been about to speak to the European Parliament when the news came through. The MEPs were offered the chance to leave, in case the parliament itself was a target, but Branson continued with his speech. As soon as it was over, he was catapulted into weeks of anxiety over Virgin Atlantic, which was more exposed than any other airline to a downturn in traffic on the North Atlantic. Even three months after the event, he used graphic language to describe the impact of 11 September: 'The plane was going straight for the ground and we weren't sure if we were going to die or come out of it. But we're just beginning, I think, to show signs of coming back now.' His airline abandoned its routes to Toronto and Chicago; tellingly, when Virgin expanded again, its first new destination was Port Harcourt, the oil capital of Nigeria.

Two weeks after the attack, while newspapers were full of headlines like LLOYD'S FACES ITS BIGGEST-EVER CLAIM, and

AIRLINES FEAR COLLAPSE WITHOUT STATE RESCUE DEAL, easyJet
and Go were taking out ads aimed at what they saw as an
expanded market. 'Get back to business – make your hard-pressed
travel budget go further with Go,' trumpeted Cassani's airline,
while pointing out, 'Over the last couple of weeks, Go passengers
have experienced very little disruption.' Overleaf, easyJet urged
'Get smart – catch the low cost shuttle!' from Luton to Edinburgh,
Glasgow and Belfast.

Across in Calgary, Clive Beddoe of WestJet was 'just numbed,
stunned'. Canadian airspace was shut down at the same time as
the skies over the US 'But we were the first airline in North
America to be fully operational. It was a great testament to our
people, getting us up and operational. Our bookings fell by 50 per
cent. We were wondering what the heck that meant for the future.
But a week later they had recovered by ten points. Another ten
points the week after that and so on, pretty much a straight-line
basis at ten points a week for five weeks, we were back to
normal.'

In America, the rebound was slower – for good reason, says
Gareth Edmondson-Jones of JetBlue: 'There was all that ugliness,
all that cheap marketing, you know, "fly us for a dollar", or "get
America up and flying sale" and it was so ugly, if you're scared
of flying, don't cheapen my feelings by saying "how about for $10
then? That'll make you less scared", or if, God forbid, you knew
someone who was affected by it, or you thought you were going
to lose your job, there were many reasons why people weren't
flying. Our message was "we'll be here when you're ready".'

For the next three months, it was difficult to believe that
no-frills airlines and traditional carriers were in the same line of
business:

12 September: Southwest Airlines stops using the 'Freedom'
tagline in its advertising.

14 September: Ansett, Australia's second-largest airline, stops
flying when its parent company, Air New Zealand, pulls the plug.
The New Zealand prime minister is on a scheduled flight home at
Melbourne airport when the news comes through; protesting
Ansett workers refuse to let the aircraft leave until she is
offloaded.

14 September: Boeing announces 25,000 lay-offs.

14 September: flights resume across the US, but US airlines are
given fifty new safety directives from the Federal Aviation
Administration (FAA).

15 September: in my column in *The Independent*, I write, 'Last Tuesday's tragedy would be amplified still further if it were allowed to crush travellers' spirit of adventure, and the power for good that aviation represents. Airlines bring people together. That is what they are for. And, as grief resonates around the world, unity is what we need more than ever.' Colleen Barrett of Southwest later trumps this – see 1 December.

17 September: Virgin Atlantic is the first UK airline to announce job cuts; 1,200 are to go, together with the new route to Toronto that had begun only three months earlier and the prestigious service to Chicago.

18 September: Ryanair's Michael O'Leary says it is business as usual: 'Bookings have returned to normal levels, and we would expect to recover last week's slippage over the coming days with a number of seat promotions which we have planned. Advance bookings and loads remain strong, and therefore the immediate consequence of last week's events on Ryanair will not be material.'

18 September: Aer Lingus announces 1,600 job losses, a number that exceeds Ryanair's total employees.

18 September: 'Boeing came to see us,' says Stelios of easyJet. We said, "Make us an offer and we'll talk to you." We are looking to expand.' (Subsequently, his company opted for Airbus.)

21 September: British Airways announces at least 5,000 job cuts, and ends a number of routes including the historic link between Heathrow and Belfast.

28 September: 'The industry's got to be restructured,' easyJet's chief executive, Ray Webster, tells me. 'It's in the interests of the consumers, shareholders and staff. Because if staff are employed by companies that go belly up every time there's a recession, is that a company you want to work for?'

1 October: Continental Airlines sets out to 'improve the mix of coats and ties versus backpacks and flip-flops' – in other words, to go for business passengers at the expense of economy travellers.

1 October: just to throw a Railtrack-sized spanner in the works of both the no-frills and traditional airlines, trains on the East Coast Main Line, for the first time in a year (since the Hatfield disaster), are able to travel between Edinburgh and London in under four hours, diminishing the time advantage of the airlines.

2 October: Swissair, which owes around £6bn, grounds its entire fleet when banks refuse to bail it out. Two days later, the government steps in so that the airline can resume a slimmed-down flying programme. The airline announces its intention to

close down in its present form at the end of October. 'Swissair walked away from billions of dollars of debt,' says Sir Michael Bishop, chairman of BMI. 'Ethics like that wouldn't be tolerated in any other business.'

29 October: easyJet turns in pre-tax profits of £20.1m for the year to the end of September, almost double the previous year, and announces it would be seeking more funds with a share issue. The cash will be used to finance the takeover of intra-European slots that traditional airlines were forced to abandon.

30 October: in Australia, Virgin Blue predicts good profits, saying its financial position is 'incredibly strong'.

2 November: at a press conference to launch the Association of British Travel Agents' convention in Lisbon, the representative of Orlando says she is unable to reveal the downturn in visitor numbers to the city, 'because it would confuse you'. A very senior member of the travel industry observes, 'I suspect the real reason you won't tell us is because you'd lose your job if you did.' ABTA says bookings for the following summer are down 50 per cent on this point a year ago. The association's president, Stephen Bath, says, 'It's anybody's guess when confidence will return. We'll be happy if it's only 5 per cent down next summer.'

7 November: after several attempts at re-financing Sabena, which owes £1.4bn, the Belgian government closes down the national airline.

12 November: Ryanair estimates its profits for the full financial year will top £90m.

12 November: Virgin Express apologises for the disruption caused by the bankruptcy of Sabena – 'our ground personnel are putting your bags on the aircraft themselves' – and announces new routes to Geneva, Zurich, Gothenburg and Stockholm.

12 November: at Earl's Court in London, the World Travel Market begins. At 2 p.m., the news comes through that American Airlines flight 587 has crashed on take-off from New York's Kennedy airport, killing all 260 on board the Airbus A300 and five people on the ground.

19 November: Go becomes the latest no-frills airline to announce higher profits, up by 50 per cent in the six months to the end of September.

21 November: 'More than 1,000 airplanes worldwide are being grounded because of overcapacity' – *Boeing News*.

1 December: Southwest's president, Colleen Barrett, pours out her heart to *Spirit* magazine, putting my efforts to shame. 'As a

small girl growing up in Vermont, I looked wistfully at the Christmas advertisements for the great passenger trains in magazines such as *Life*. The ads I remember most are the ones showing happy families travelling home in a brightly lit dining car against the cold, dark, snowy night. My son and grandson think of that brightness as an airplane bringing life, joy and family through a star-spangled December sky. The 32,000 Proud Americans of the Southwest Airlines Family are hard at work to ensure this brightness will prevail, not just during December but throughout the entire year.' She tells staff: 'My son and grandson are the most precious things in my life, and I wouldn't hesitate for a second to place either one of them on a Southwest Airlines flight.'

4 December: 'Congratulations, you're the forty-second passenger on today's flight. We'll make some money on the next flight, not this one' – Southwest Airlines check-in agent, Seattle airport. One week later, Southwest announces it will be adding new routes in the coming year.

5 December: Buzz announces a 15 per cent increase in passenger numbers. Five days later, it launches nine new routes, plus four domestic services in France.

5 December: 'The freedom to go where you want to go, when you want to go, is a precious liberty,' begins a full-page ad in the *Wall Street Journal*, paid for by Boeing. 'The nation's skyways are once again ready to help you make the most of that freedom.'

8 December: at Will Rogers International Airport at Oklahoma City, I meet Tom Barry, who is going to Salt Lake City for the day to collect his grandson. He feels violated. 'I was one of the people they pulled out at random. I've been poked and prodded and examined.'

Knees jerked in all kinds of directions after 11 September. Security in the US is now so strict that many passengers are subject to multiple searches.

As a ticketless traveller on Southwest, you must queue up to get what amounts to a ticket (in fact, a personal boarding card) and endure no fewer than three photo ID checks to make sure that you are who you say you are – or, at least, that the name on your boarding card and in the computer matches the (possibly false) photo ID you are carrying. Everything is slower and less flexible. Everyone behaves much more meekly (if they are passengers) or sternly (if they are staff).

There are still glaring loopholes: passengers whose names are randomly selected for a further search at the gate are often warned about it in advance, for example if they have the dreaded 'quad-s' indication on the boarding pass. This SSSS symbol warns security staff to give the passenger a more comprehensive going over. But it also gives plenty of opportunity for wrongdoers to get rid of a weapon, or to be secure in the knowledge that someone else has been picked out, not them. Overall the experience feels much more uncomfortable and less flexible, and it is also much more stringent than in the UK.

'Immediately after September 11, [passengers] would have put up with anything,' says Greg Wells, vice-president for security for Southwest, about the travelling public. 'There was a three-to-four-week period when we were on a sort of honeymoon – whatever we did, and however we delayed the passengers, they were OK with that.' That soon changed. 'In our society today, patience isn't there. They're at the point now where they want security as stringent as it has been, only quicker and faster.' Southwest is trying to streamline its procedures, but Greg Wells does not believe that things can ever revert to the way they were before. 'We are getting back to the normal airport experience, but it's going to be a while yet. There's a lot of technology out there that we're looking at as an industry and a government. We expect we can have a more efficient, safer and hopefully not much more expensive security experience at the airports, so people can get to their aircraft and get out on time and still have a low fare.'

Across in Europe, a horrible truth dawned upon high-cost airlines after 11 September. It is neatly summed up by easyJet's outgoing chief executive, Ray Webster. 'Airlines have a very, very low marginal cost base, that's the cost of flying a flight. If you have the option of flying a flight or leaving the aircraft on the ground, the difference in flying and leaving the aircraft parked is very little. So they need very little revenue to justify flying if the aeroplane's there and the crew is there. As against if they want to get rid of the asset, and they have to get rid of the crew, the exit costs are very high.' Airlines that wanted to cut back on flying, after a decade of expansion, found it to be an expensive and painful business.

Not everyone, though, was convinced that the low-cost carriers had called it right. I put it to John Wimbleton of the leading tour operator, First Choice, that the no-frills airlines had stolen the high ground in the weeks following 11 September. 'It's like selling pound notes for 99p,' he replied. 'If I could make money sending people from Scotland to Stansted for £10 I would. Nobody makes a single pound. Anyone can get a cheap headline by giving things away. They've got the high ground and they're welcome to it.'

Even before 11 September, Ryanair was bidding for second-hand Boeing 737s to supplement its fleet; in the weeks since 11 September, the cost of these fell by one third or more. A worldwide shortage of flight crew suddenly turned into a surplus. Several pilots who had left Go for Virgin Atlantic returned to Barbara Cassani's airline. The traditional airlines' schedules dropped by around 20 per cent, which meant demand for aviation fuel, and the price, also fell. And airports were suddenly prepared to negotiate on previously non-negotiable charges. Aer Rianta, the leading Irish airport authority, advertised for new airlines saying it would provide free facilities for three years. But the no-frills carriers still had to face the usual autumnal problem of persuading people to get on their planes. In any normal autumn it is tricky to fill more than around 70 per cent of seats at reasonable fares. In late 2001, it was much worse. Anecdotally, there was evidence that prospective passengers started thinking more about why they travelled – a glib 'because I can' was no longer sufficient. But people don't decide to go to Barcelona because they think it will be fun flying on Iberia or British Airways or easyJet – they go to see the Sagrada Familia, or the Picasso Museum, or FC Barcelona, and to visit the tapas bars and pubs. If the price was right, they would get on board.

It is not quite true to say that anyone can fill a plane if the fare is low enough, but certainly the stated aim of easyJet and Ryanair to get people travelling, was achieved. The trouble is, how much were the airlines earning? A look at the fares I paid in the three months following 11 September suggested that no one was going to do well out of me: Dublin and back, and Charleroi and back on Ryanair for £20; Salzburg return for £21; one-way on easyJet to Zurich for £32.50; Vienna for £35 one-way on Buzz; and £66 return to Malaga on Go. Once the taxes had been taken off, each of these airlines would be struggling to get into double figures for their revenue from each passenger. Great for the traveller, dismal for the financial directors. But besides cheapskates like me having the time of their lives, plenty of business travellers were lining up at the no-frills check-in.

Some companies had banned their executives from flying, albeit temporarily, after the attacks. When they returned to the air, with

SILVER LINING?

In the week when he stood down as chairman of easyJet, Stelios spoke frankly about the way his airline had benefited from the terrible attacks on America. 'I don't think I could have predicted in 1995 what would be happening today because there has been almost a discontinuity because of September 11. In some ways we have been lucky in the sense that it all happened in the States, it affected Americans flying to Europe, so our competitors, i.e. BA, suffered a lot more than we did. The Europeans are more familiar with terrorism, and went back to flying much faster. So we could accelerate our growth while BA had to start a retrenchment, because they were relying on Americans flying the Atlantic.

'One side effect of 11 September was a perceived, at least, recession. And whilst consumers are very easy to convince to try something new in order to save money, businesses usually aren't. After 11 September, because the world started fearing economic recession, businesses tightened their belts and started instructing their employees to fly low-cost airlines. I think that has been the second structural change in the airline business. A coincidence, again, arising out of tragic events, but the net effect is, all of a sudden, competitors weakened, businesses started using low-cost airlines. I think low-cost airlines have become the accepted mode of transport within Europe. It's not a novelty anymore; it's accepted, it's mainstream.'

budgets trimmed back, there was a sudden interest in why some airlines charge more than others. At dawn one autumn morning at Stansted, while checking in for the flight to Charleroi, I met a rather grumpy camera crew from BBC1's *Blue Peter* programme, who had been ordered to take the cheap way to Belgium.

'Even people who are part of large corporations are now sensitive to whether they've paid £500 or £100 for a flight to Frankfurt,' says Tim Jeans of Monarch. 'There's a growing awareness that on most routes there's a choice, and if there is any element of direct budget accountability for that trip – so you, me, everyone except civil servants on junkets, basically – they will choose the low-cost option.'

Eric Torbenson, a leading business writer for the *Dallas Morning News*, whose patch includes both American Airlines (the world's largest) and Southwest, says the amount of cash companies are prepared to spend to save a marginal amount of time had fallen drastically: 'The value of time in American business suddenly got a lot cheaper. In 1998/99, the value of time was at its highest ever. With the Internet boom, first movers had to fly somewhere tomorrow and price wasn't a consequence. Price is a consequence now. The problem with the business model is that it assumes you can charge the business traveller an enormous amount, ten times as much as you would a leisure flyer, and he'll pay it. Corporations used to finance all of an airline's profits and subsidise in some ways all the leisure seats. That doesn't work any more. The legacy carriers have been rudely woken up.'

The events of 11 September 2001 had a direct impact on Tim Jeans's personal finances. As a senior airline executive, he had previously enjoyed free travel on British Airways – the very airline that he spends most of his professional life attacking. Once the depth of BA's problems became apparent, the airline withdrew the concession – partially. Henceforth, Jeans pays half fare.

Vladimir Raitz has seen it all before. 'People have to fly and to get around. Although this war against terrorism will last for a long time, after a while people will get used to the situation. And a foreign holiday has become such an intrinsic part of people's lives that it will go on. Civilisation will go to hell if such gloom persists.' At the back of every traveller's mind, though, is the thought articulated by Dr Todd Curtis, head of the AirSafe.com website. 'There is no technology that can peer into a person's heart and decipher their intentions. It is difficult to stop a determined hijacker from causing mayhem on an aircraft if that person is willing to die along with the other passengers.'

13. SO YOU WANT TO START YOUR OWN AIRLINE?

How do you get to be a millionaire? Be a billionaire, and start an airline
Sir Richard Branson

There's always room for someone doing something different
John Fitzgerald, formerly of Debonair

If you're going to lose lots of money, you might as well have some fun while you're doing it

Gary Barone, formerly of AB Airlines

Y ou've read the tangled tales of success and failure in no-frills aviation, of the fortunes to be made and lost. Now it's time to put those lessons into practice, with advice from the people who've been there, done that and have the ulcers to prove it. This chapter contains the insiders' secrets on everything from choosing your planes to selecting the uniforms, and the all-important business of convincing a wary public that you're the best thing since sliced bread – or at least Southwest.

That was the way that this chapter in the first edition of this book began, but in the intervening years identifying gaps in the market has become increasingly hard. Now that you can fly from Nottingham to Wroclaw and from Norwich to Murcia, it is reasonable to conclude that there are few prime routes remaining on which you can hope to make some cash. Still, if you insist . . .

You will need to take some tough decisions to keep costs down and passengers up. The main cost elements comprise what I shall call the five Ps, most expensive first: people, planes, petrol (technically, jet kerosene), places to put them (airports) and promotion. But the place to begin . . . is the place you begin. Until you know where your home is going to be, you can't make the other choices.

SO WHERE SHALL I START?

'There is only one London,' says Stelios of easyJet. The pool of potential passengers within an hour of the capital amounts to over ten million. This is also, conveniently, the richest corner of the European Union, and the place in Britain to which foreigners and Brits alike want to travel to more than any other. This enables you to balance the routes with substantial numbers of passengers originating at either end. 'The south-east is where the biggest demand from UK travellers is concentrated,' confirms David Magliano of easyJet. But the problem is that the London airports are rapidly filling up. Heathrow, Gatwick and Stansted are full at the peaks, and Luton has little room for expansion.

Gatwick, for example has room to increase its current thirty-two million passengers each year to forty million. But the growth will come from filling middle-of-the-day and late-evening spaces on the runway. Finding the take-off and landing slots you will need to attract business travellers, at the start of the day and in late afternoon-early evening, will be very tough. And even if you get some handy 8 a.m. and 6 p.m. rights during the winter, in summer – when the main charter season is running – you may have to change the times or cancel the flights altogether. The reason is what are known in the industry as 'Grandfather rights': airlines that have traditionally flown from Gatwick to, say, Cyprus at 8 a.m. every Friday, arriving back at 6 p.m. are entitled to claim those same slots each summer. So all your loyal customers who have become accustomed through the winter to the flights to, say, Antwerp and back will find that the ideal departure times have disappeared – as has your revenue.

BUT THERE ARE OTHER LONDON AIRPORTS?

Heathrow has a ridiculously long waiting list of airlines wanting the right to fly from Britain's premier airport. Michael O'Leary of Ryanair has some typically robust thoughts on Heathrow: 'Slots is just an excuse by the big guys for overcharging passengers.' He believes the constraints and delays make Heathrow a waste of time, literally. 'We get at least two more flights per day per aircraft than BA by avoiding Heathrow. We wouldn't fly from there if they paid us.' Interestingly, both Ryanair and easyJet are happy to serve Gatwick, and to pay the substantial associated extra costs, even though the Sussex facility is the busiest single-runway airport on the planet and consequently gets heavily congested. Experience shows that people will pay more to fly from a major airport like Gatwick than from Stansted or Luton, which is why Ray Webster of easyJet was so quick to head around the M25 to Gatwick in the wake of 11 September.

Luton has changed out of all recognition since easyJet set up in 1995 – as 'an afterthought, a bargaining chip', according to the airline's first marketing director, Tony Anderson. When he was taken on, he was told to start looking for a house near Stansted. But Luton offered Stelios a good deal, and turned out to be a fortunate choice for easyJet, if not for Debonair. 'Luton has a fantastic catchment area,' says Anderson. But so successful has easyJet been that spare slots are mostly of interest to airlines based in continental Europe who will arrive at about 9 a.m., after the morning rush, and avoid the evening peak. The same applies at Stansted, which for several years was the fastest-growing airport in Europe. Further growth will come from filling the gaps at quiet times of day, but finding slots to leave between 6 a.m. and 8 a.m. is extremely difficult.

WHAT ABOUT THE ONE YOU HAVEN'T MENTIONED: LONDON CITY?

Very handy for town, but three big negatives. You will be constrained with the aircraft you can use: the 100-seater BAe 146 is about the largest that can land there. The passenger charges are the most expensive in Britain because of the limited throughput of the airport and the high costs associated with running a small airport in a big city. And the airport closes down for half the weekend to give the long-suffering residents of Docklands a break from aircraft noise. Try selling a six-day-a-week operation to the passengers, and the investors. The Israeli airline, El Al, suffers mightily from being grounded during the Sabbath.

IS ANYWHERE OUTSIDE LONDON AN OPTION?

There is much more room: none of Britain's provincial airports is full. And some of the new start-ups believe that the south-east has had its day. Jet2 has set up at Leeds/Bradford, and expanded to Manchester, Newcastle and Belfast International. Flyglobe span.com is operating out of Scotland. But there are few airports where you can escape competition: during 2006, even Newquay and Norwich are gaining prime low-cost flights to Spain. With the Scottish airports already well served, and Liverpool eclipsing Manchester as a low-cost gateway, the options are fast diminishing.

In the last edition of this book, I suggested Manston in Kent as one possibility: 'This former RAF base has a decent-sized runway, plenty of parking and a railway line close by. It is also close enough to the coast to minimise air-traffic control delays of the sort that bedevil London's airports. But the catchment area is poor in both numbers and wealth, and the proximity of ferries and the Channel Tunnel means that there are alternatives to flying.' Sadly, the failure of EUjet proved me right. I also recommended Finningley in South Yorkshire – also known as Robin Hood airport and Doncaster Sheffield – and concluded that the obvious place to start is Coventry. Thomsonfly took up both these suggestions, and the presence of Europe's biggest holiday company as the major player at these airports means life is unlikely to be comfortable for an upstart.

If you are determined to start up in Britain, you will need to choose somewhere well away from predatory competitors. It could conceivably be Carlisle, which like Coventry has not enjoyed scheduled flights for a decade. The problem is that the airports at Prestwick, Glasgow, Newcastle, Blackpool and Manchester are all within relatively easy reach of Cumbria's largest city. Even as the 'gateway to the Lakes', Carlisle airport would find itself challenged by Blackpool and Manchester. Two other even more peripheral, but possibly more successful, suggestions: Harlech, in north-west Wales, and Campbeltown in south-west Scotland.

Both airports would need some considerable enhancements before they are able to handle large, modern jets, but given the marginal locations some funding should be forthcoming. Macrahanish, as the airport at Campbeltown is known, already has a mighty runway due to its former status as a key air force base. It needs, though, some more fire cover to meet CAA standards for any aircraft larger than the present small planes operated by British Airways. Harlech is more problematic: before the necessary substantial engineering work was put in, there could well be many objections from the local community.

PLANES NEXT?

No, be patient. First you need to decide where to fly. That has a bearing on the aircraft you choose. 'Underserved and overpriced' is the Southwest mantra to identifying routes where low fares can prosper: where one or two traditional airlines carve up the service between them, charging whatever fares the market will bear to fly on a limited number of departures.

Choosing a winning route is still something akin to alchemy, but there is plenty you can do to maximise your chances. The tangle of laws that govern aviation links means that you cannot simply look at a map and pick out the big cities without no-frills flights from Britain. That is especially true once you venture outside the European Union; two things happen. First, there's a good chance you won't be allowed to fly the route at all. The EU has at least theoretical open skies (though slot constraints mean that this ideal state of affairs will never exist), with any airline based in one of the member countries able to fly anywhere it chooses. As soon as you step into the rest of the world, the interests of flag-carrier airlines intervene, making it difficult for anyone else to get a look in. So stay inside the EU until you have some experience.

Whether you choose the Welsh or Scottish option, start with the obvious: fly to Stansted, where you will be able to find off-peak slots – a departure at around 7 a.m. should get you to the Essex airport around eight, just as the morning rush to get out is ending. Business travellers from north-west Wales or south-west Scotland, used to long, slow journeys, will pay a premium to be able to reach the City of London by nine in the morning. And given the population base of the capital, it should not be too tricky to fill the return leg. Later, you can add an evening departure to Stansted from your home airport at around 7.30 p.m., which means the final flight back touching down at about 10 p.m. With a couple of trips a day to Stansted, the backbone of your airline will be established (or, you will have run out of cash). Let's dismiss the latter. This is, after all, just a paper airline – the lowest-cost option in aviation, and very often the best choice. Next, serve the national capital: Campbeltown to Edinburgh or Harlech to Cardiff. The road journeys between these points take a good four hours, to the dismay of the many civil servants and local authority staff who have to make the slog. In contrast, either flight would spend barely twenty minutes in the air, and even when formalities and transport into the city are included, the journey time can easily be halved.

Still in business? Good. Let's try overseas.

There is a temptation to go for the routes where a lot of immediate interest is guaranteed: Alicante, Palma and Malaga are easy to fill, but face the greatest competition. There is also the problem of finding suitable slots at these airports, particularly in summer. For a city destination, Amsterdam and Paris are the most attractive nearby capitals – but Dublin and Belfast offer the greatest timesaving compared with other forms of transport.

By now, you might be interested in using your Stansted slots to go a bit further. It might seem that anywhere you ever wanted to fly – and many places you never knew existed – are already served from the Essex base. But there are still some gaps which are very poorly served from the UK.

First: Antwerp. Belgium's second city has flights only from London City, attracting a very different market. It is far enough away from Brussels to have its own distinct catchment, which includes large parts of south-west Holland; for anyone south of Rotterdam, it is as easy to reach Antwerp as Amsterdam. The city is potentially a great short-break destination for leisure travellers, and is something of an economic dynamo. And 'the biggest, baddest, bully on the block', i.e. Ryanair, is safely remote in Charleroi. These properties should help you achieve a good mix of business and leisure travel, with strong demand at both ends of the route.

Next, Corfu. This is a major tourist draw, with a large population of UK expatriates, but off-season people have to fly via Athens – a long, awkward and expensive journey. It will also serve the remaining Ionian islands (Paxos now has a seaplane connection from Corfu), and even Albania thanks to a ferry link. Be warned, though, that your biggest competitor at Stansted is watching you.

'If any so-called "low-cost" imitator wants to throw down a challenge to Ryanair on any of our routes, anywhere, anytime, and any price then they may rest assured that we will meet every such challenge,' says Michael O'Leary. As Go found to its considerable cost when it launched the Edinburgh–Dublin route – which Ryanair previously did not operate – if the Irish airline decides to take on a rival it will shovel in capacity and loss-leader fares. That is a battle to be fought at some time in the future, when you have the cash for a long, expensive war of attrition.

CAN WE TALK ABOUT PLANES NOW?

OK. Some no-frills airlines get by with aircraft holding around one hundred people, or at least they did: Buzz, Debonair and EUjet lost cash by using BAe146s and Fokker 100s. In the US, AirTran uses the Boeing 717. Given the very modest catchments in north-west Wales and south-west Scotland, you may opt for JetBlue's policy of trading down from Airbuses to smaller Brazilian-built Embraers to serve smaller markets.

By the way, many people think that jet planes travel at the same speed. In fact, the BAe 146 is about 10 per cent slower than the Boeing 737-300, which itself plods along 10 per cent behind the 737-700. On short flights, like Campbeltown to Stansted (three hundred miles), the difference is tiny. But when easyJet started flying its -700s to Athens instead of -300s, it saved twenty minutes each way. On the thousand-mile link from Stansted to Corfu, speed is significant.

So let's think big. That could mean the Airbus A320 and its derivatives (in this case, 'derivatives' being jargon for making planes longer or shorter). John Patterson, managing director of the with-frills airline GB Airways, is such a big fan of the A320 and its longer sibling, the A321, that he has converted his entire fleet of Boeing 737s to the European plane. 'The A320 is a broader, wider aircraft which goes down very, very well with the customer.' JetBlue of New York started with the same aircraft, as did MyTravelLite. But most airlines are sticking with the jet that Southwest started off with in 1971, and which David Magliano – former marketing director of Go – calls 'the Ford Escort of the skies': the Boeing 737.

The world's most popular plane is about as exciting as a Ford Escort. But it has become the standard for every successful no-frills airline. Its sheer popularity, says Magliano, means 'planes, pilots and parts are widely available'. It is made in Renton, the Seattle suburb where Jimi Hendrix grew up; the guitarist's grave is barely a mile from the Boeing 737 factory, which overlooks Lake Washington. 'We share the shore with Bill Gates,' jokes one employee.

As you will discover when you go and see the folks at Boeing, the first journey for every one of the jets begins in Wichita, Kansas, where the fuselage is made. They are shipped from the Midwest on extraordinary-looking trains that protect the delicate skin of the aircraft embryo from trees. The journey of two thousand miles along the Burlington Northern Santa Fe track ends when the locomotive hauls the fuselage through the factory gates, and it is transferred to a bright yellow 'dolly' for the next stage of the operation. Assembling the thing – bolting on the wings, tailplane, undercarriage and engines, and laying four miles of cable – takes eighteen working days. Only at the later stages does the interior take shape. You, the customer, supply the seats and the lavatories you want; Franco Mancassola of Avia Interiors in Italy will be pleased to negotiate on the seats, and there's a company in Camberley, Surrey, that will probably give you a good deal on the loos. Finally, the jet is tugged out of the enormous hangar on to Renton Field, where final touches are applied over the following week. The new Boeing 737's first flight is a ridiculously small distance – five miles at most – to Boeing Field, where it spends another fortnight in tests. So from departing Wichita to being ready for you to come and pick up (they never deliver), reckon on close on two months.

HOW MUCH WILL THAT COST ME?

Sir Richard Branson says that right now is a very good time to talk to airline manufacturers: 'They are hungry for people to take their planes, so try to strike a deal with them so your cash flow is good.'

First, a couple of things you need to know while you're talking to Boeing. Never call the aircraft the 'seven-three-seven' – 'seven-three' is sufficient (though you might have thought that 'three' is all they would need to differentiate it from the 747, 757, 767, etc.). And the seven-three comes in separate sizes, indicated by a number in the hundreds. For the industry-standard 737-700, which easyJet fits out with 149 seats, list price is about $30m. No one ever pays list price, though. Even as a first-time customer buying only, say, three jets you can expect a bargain. That's because each aircraft manufacturer is desperately keen that any start-up airline uses its equipment. While it is not uncommon for carriers to switch from Airbus to Boeing or vice versa some years down the line, this will be as part of a package where the aircraft maker pays for pilots and engineers to be retrained. So reckon on $25m each for the aircraft, tops (Ryanair is thought to have paid substantially less for its recent order for a hundred jets). You'll need three planes to operate a sensible schedule at a reasonable frequency, and to cover for scheduled maintenance.

If you don't have $75m immediately available, there are several leasing companies that will be pleased to lend you a plane. Their pleasure derives from having bought the aircraft, often speculatively, then renting them to you at around $100,000 per month. That is a lot of cash to concentrate the mind, and is why David Magliano advises, 'If you can afford to own your aircraft outright, it's a given that you will.'

Or buy second-hand; you could just follow Ryanair and place ads in the aviation press seeking cheap, 'previously operated' jets, the polite phrase for 'old'. A Boeing 737-300 could be yours for about $15m if it is in good nick (and, if it isn't, don't buy it). It's basically an earlier version of the -700, and seats the same number of passengers. Jet2's fleet largely comprises 737-300s picked up cheap from Ansett's liquidators after the Australian airline went bust.

At all costs, make sure you use only one type of aircraft. All your flight crew and engineers must be able to work on all your fleet, even though your planes may come in different sizes. The Boeing 737-600, -700 and -800 are the Small, Medium and Large of no-frills aviation, but most airlines believe that one size fits all.

A NAME: BRIANAIR? EASYPLANE? CMIBABY?

No, and if you use any of those you will certainly be sued for trademark infringement. Either employ consultants (as Go did with Wolff-Olins) to come up with the name, or think of one yourself; Jet2 was dreamed up in a pub near Heathrow. Tony Ryan and Sir Freddie Laker didn't spend much time or money dreaming up Ryanair and Laker Airways. Arguably a snappy name like Go or Buzz is more international and memorable, but the fact that neither airline exists anymore suggests the names did not do either much good.

Even with expert help, picking a suitable title can be a minefield. 'Rise', 'Climb' or 'Lift' might sound good, but they would upset air traffic control: there is plenty of scope for confusion if Climb flight one is instructed to descend.

Don't lock yourself into a particular region or ocean, as Southwest and Northwest, Virgin Atlantic and Cathay Pacific all did. You might imagine that when David Neeleman, founder of JetBlue, needed a name in 1999, he merely picked a couple of elements that combined easyJet and Virgin Blue. Not a bit of it; indeed, you could consider a few of the two hundred discarded names that David Neeleman, founder of JetBlue, rejected. There were joke ones like Dairy Air (say it out loud, in a slightly French accent); more serious options including many that use the traditional 'Air' element: Hiway Air, Imagine Air, Scout Air, Air Avenues and Air Hop. Original thinking (now that's a name in itself) began with It, Yes, The Competition, The High Road, Civilization and Idlewild (the name for Kennedy airport before the president was shot). Taxi was a favourite, until someone pointed out that, like Climb, it could lead to all kinds of confusion on the ground.

After paying $100,000 to the design consultants Landor Associates, Neeleman then settled on True Blue. Unfortunately, another company had already snapped it up. Landor halved the fee, and a company insider applied Jet in place of True. A few more suggestions to save you $100,000: Fresh Air (nearly a name nearly used by another 'paper' carrier), Quest, To Boldly Go and Bare Necessities.

AND A LOGO?

Go paid good money for one, and won awards for it. Ryanair and easyJet did neither of the above. Some aviation insiders insist that good design is important for business travellers. 'People don't feel comfortable with the orange brashness of easyJet,' says Barbara Cassani, founder of Go. Invest in your identity to impress your most valued customers.

SO ARE BUSINESS PEOPLE MY TARGET MARKET?

A large part of it. The natural business constituency of a no-frills carrier is the small or medium enterprise, the sort of people who keep a careful eye on costs – and out of whose pocket, ultimately, the fare is going. But set the controls for the hearts and minds of a wide range of travellers. Divide leisure passengers into two groups: those who are purely travelling on holiday, and those who are visiting friends and relations (VFR, in the jargon). The latter will be more reliable, year-round, but the former will pay higher prices at peak times.

Balance is all when flying an aircraft, and when planning a route. You need to attract business travellers who will fill the plane on morning and evening flights during the week, and leisure passengers who will be attracted by cheap fares in the middle of the day. They will also be prepared to pay a premium for travel at weekends. And you will also want to achieve balance at each end of the route. On a route like Bmibaby's Cardiff–Faro service, almost all the passengers originate in Britain. With a more even spread, you are less susceptible to economic cycles in one country or the other.

SHOULD I DO LOTS OF MARKET RESEARCH?

No. You could try looking round the car parks at each airport, checking out the geographical codes on the licence plates to gauge the catchment area. But most low-cost routes establish a market that no one was certain existed. Market research is not a discipline that is much used among airline entrepreneurs like Sir Richard Branson, whose principle market research for getting into the airline business was to find that the reservations number for PEOPLExpress (the low-cost carrier then flying between Gatwick and Newark) was permanently engaged.

But know your enemy. The competition is anyone who can carry a customer on the route they wish to travel, be they low-cost, traditional or charter airlines. Everyone will be doing their utmost to spoil your party. Be prepared for vicious competition from other airlines, train operators and even ferry companies.

SHALL I MAKE THE DEPARTURE BOARD NOW?

Sure, but when you're working out your schedule, remember that there is a big difference between the airborne duration and the 'block time', which is the figures you publish on your website and the departure screen. A flight officially commences at the start of the push-back on departure, and ends when the pilot applies the handbrake at the destination airport. You have to allow for taxiing at each end of the journey; at Campbeltown, five minutes should do fine. You will also need to 'pad' your schedules to build in extra time for delays, though quiet airports will help. The 'block time' to Stansted should be just over an hour. Allow half-an-hour to 'turn' the flight, and the aircraft should be ready to depart for Corfu at 9 a.m. It will get in at 2 p.m., local time, and be back around 4.30 p.m. at Stansted.

Just time for a quick trip to Antwerp and back (45 minutes each way, with half-an-hour on the ground in Belgium) and look, there are the passengers waiting to fly back to Campbeltown. Or was it Harlech? Either way, you'll take off just after 7 p.m., catching the lucrative evening peak, and arrive in time to squeeze in an extra flight to Edinburgh or Cardiff and back. The aircraft would be in the air for over ten hours, which on such relatively short routes is pretty good going. Remember, as the Southwest mantra insists, 'utilisation is the key'.

THE CREW WILL BE KNACKERED FLYING THAT KIND OF SCHEDULE SEVEN DAYS A WEEK, WON'T THEY?

They would if they were allowed to fly that many missions, but quite sensibly they're not. A hard-working captain will be airborne for only eighteen hours in a busy week.

SO HOW MANY PEOPLE WILL I NEED TO FLY THE AIRCRAFT – AND HOW MUCH WILL I HAVE TO PAY THEM?

For each plane, reckon on five crews: that means five captains, five first officers and fifteen cabin crew. The average first officer is probably not going to get out of bed (especially not for that early morning departure) for less than £60,000 per year, and an experienced captain would certainly be looking for £80,000. And that's cheap: Branson says you must 'make it clear to your pilots and crew when they join that you've got to keep fares at a decent price, say "please don't push the costs out of control." If they really want massive salaries they should go elsewhere.'

Cabin crew come a lot cheaper than pilots, not least because their training takes a month rather than several years – and because there is a seemingly never-ending supply of people who still believe that flying is glamorous and exciting. They are prepared to work for £12,000 per year (and that's after their pay has been topped up by an extra fee for every sector flown).

WHO ELSE WILL I NEED TO EMPLOY?

Your chief operating officer needs to have decades of experience working for an airline. In contrast, arguably the less experience of aviation your marketing director has, the better: he or she will not be hidebound by tradition. The right information technology person is crucial; you will be selling almost all your seats on the Internet. Beyond that, you'll need people who keep any airline going: engineers, ground staff, a sales team ... The good news is that you need not take them on as your own employees. At most airports served by low-cost airlines, the check-in staff are all bought in. For the first couple of months of easyJet's operation,

SECRETS OF THE WARDROBE

Tony Anderson, former marketing director for easyJet, relates the strange tale of choosing the cabin-crew uniforms for his infant airline, a saga that began in the chain store, Next, in a town south of Luton airport:

'We bought a stack of jackets, shirts and trousers. We pulled the stuff off the racks, piled into the car and took them back to easyLand for a modelling session by staff.' The cabin crew were relieved to have avoided the ill-fitting polyester worn by other airlines' staff. But it was clear to Anderson and Stelios that the look wasn't sufficiently distinctive.

'Then Anna, our office manager at easyLand, mentioned that she'd seen someone wandering around in a fantastic orange polo shirt with a Benetton logo. I was duly dispatched to the nearest Benetton shop in Milton Keynes where indeed there was a polo shirt and a matching sweatshirt both in garish easyJet orange, matching almost exactly the official colour. I phoned Stelios who was so enthused that he instructed me to come back to easyLand, pick him up and drive back to Milton Keynes. When he saw the shirts Stelios was suitably impressed and duly bought all the orange polo shirts and sweatshirts in the shop – about eight of each in a variety of sizes.'

Feedback from the rest of the team at easyLand was positive, so Anderson was told to talk to Benetton's HQ in Italy and place an order for a hundred and fifty polo shirts and a hundred and fifty sweatshirts. This proved more difficult than it sounds, as manufacturers do not keep central stocks, particularly of gaudy colours that go out of fashion as quickly as they come in. So Anderson made a road trip around London visiting Benetton stores in Islington, Brent Cross, and Oxford Street. 'God knows what the sales staff made of this strange character that came in, took all the orange sweatshirts and polo shirts off the shelves and stuffed them into a large bag. By the end of the day I had accumulated around 150 shirts, which were piled high in a storage room at easyLand. I joked to Stelios that in our recruitment, which we were shortly to begin, we'd need to find twelve large, twenty medium and eighteen small staff to fit the uniforms we'd bought.'

the orange-clad staff were being 'wet leased' along with the planes from GB Airways. But whether you employ direct or outsource, reckon on about ninety workers for each of your aircraft. Any more than a hundred per plane, and you are getting dangerously close to the employment levels of the larger carriers.

Pick people with care, and motivate them, says Sir Richard Branson. 'If you're starting a low-cost carrier, all your staff must feel that their mission is to enable people to fly who can't afford to fly, to help small businesses get up and running, and to help old people visit their relatives more often. It shouldn't just be a mission to worry about the shareholder's return. I think that if you can get that sort of passion into the airline, and all the staff are 100 per cent believing in what they're doing, and feeling really proud of what they're doing, and proud of the company, and proud of the brand, so they can go home and say, "I work for easyJet, I work for Virgin, I work for Laker", that's three-quarters of the battle.'

One good way to generate loyalty is to have an in-flight magazine in which the staff can take pride. With luck, you can get others to pay for it with advertising. Get someone like Rough Guides to put together the editorial for you, to ensure a credibility that is so often lacking in the genre, or get a rival to do the work for you.

OK, SO NOW CAN I START?

There's the small matter of an Aircraft Operating Certificate (AOC), which you will need to obtain from the Civil Aviation Authority. 'It's a driving licence for airlines,' says David Magliano of easyJet. 'It shows that not only do you meet certain standards in every part of the operation, but also that you have processes in place to maintain those standards.' When easyJet began, it flew under an AOC belonging to Air Foyle, a charter company. Being part of a bigger airline, British Airways, meant Go could have sheltered under the corporate umbrella, but Barbara Cassani chose not to do so. Before you start flying, it will be handy to have some passengers well ahead of time, not least because the cash they supply in advance will make your balance sheet more fragrant. And to do that, you will need an identity.

WHERE DO I ADVERTISE?

Anywhere you can: press, the sides of taxis, billboards on your rivals' turf. Be prepared to spend a fortune: on an average flight, the earnings from half-a-dozen seats will be eaten up by promotional costs.

SHOULD I USE TRAVEL AGENTS?

Incentivise them a little, with a few pounds for each booking they make on the Internet. But don't get caught up with paying the 9 per cent commission that is still the norm in much of the aviation industry. In 1999, British Airways was paying more to distribute its seats – mostly through agents – than it was on putting fuel in the planes. In reality, though, the vast majority of your seats will be sold direct to the public, over the Internet. The other no-frills airlines have done the work for you: travellers know how the low-cost concept works, and they also know how to book flights on the Internet.

HOW MUCH AM I GOING TO CHARGE?

On your first few flights, a flat fare of perhaps £19 each way, including all taxes, fees and charges. You'll be losing a fortune, but you'll get your name known. You must then quickly master the black art of yield management – getting the maximum fare from each seat, while leaving as few as possible unoccupied.

To understand the principle, visit the No. 1 Oriental Buffet in Whitworth Street, Manchester. Between noon and 4 p.m., you can eat all you like for £5.50. From 4–6 p.m., and all day on Sunday, it rises by £1; and after 6 p.m., by £2. On Saturday evenings, you can add another £1, almost double the base price. There are various specials offered during the week to attract students. Exactly the same product costs different prices at different times. That principle works for airlines just as it does for Chinese food, with the extra sophistication of rewarding the early booker. The No. 1 Oriental Buffet could probably increase its occupancy still further by lopping a pound or two off for people who are prepared to commit a week in advance. That would boost the restaurant's 'load factor', but it would deplete the average amount that each diner pays – the yield. These are the two key measures in aviation. You want both of these to be as high as possible, though the natural tendency is for them to work in different directions: fares come down, load factors increase; fares go up, load factors decrease.

Yield management explains a widely held first principle of air travel, that the person next to you has always paid less than you have. Start off by assigning a certain number of seats to each price band. On the Monday morning departure from Campbeltown to Stansted, you will want to make very few cheap seats available, because you can look forward to filling the flight with high-revenue business travellers. But that Tuesday morning flight in November to Corfu is always going to be something of a 'dog flight' – nothing to do with passports for pets, but the industry's acknowledgement that a flight is 'non-optimally scheduled', i.e. you're really going to have to bribe people to get on board. So put plenty of seats on sale at low prices, and keep checking – micro-managing – each departure to make sure that you're filling the plane at the best prices you can.

'The blend of £19/£29/£59/£99 fares is the key to your success,' says Tim Jeans of Monarch. 'Provided demand is strong enough at weekends, high days, holidays and the summer, you will average significantly more than £19, while your operating costs remain exactly the same.'

It is a long-held myth that the later a passenger books a flight, the cheaper it becomes – that is partly the way that traditional airlines used standby flights to try to tackle the Laker Skytrain. In practice, people who book the day before are those who will pay the most to guarantee a place on board. So on all your flights, keep a few seats free for the people who are prepared to pay £200 for a one-way flight.

DISCOUNTS FOR YOUNGSTERS?

No. International aviation rules dictate that anyone aged two or over must occupy a seat. On traditional airlines, there is a case for offering some sort of discount to children between two and eleven (the usual limit) because they are less likely to be knocking back one Jack Daniel's after another. On no-frills flights, since costs are effectively the same regardless of age, it makes no economic sense to offer a discount for anyone who has lived for more than 730 days.

DO I HAVE TO FILL UP ALL THE SEATS?

No. If you are Ryanair, then selling barely more than half is enough to break even. Sometimes, though, you may want to fill up more than all the seats.

SURELY YOU DON'T MEAN OVERBOOKING?

I surely do. It's good for you, and for your passengers. Travellers, and airlines, should be in favour of overbooking. The practice of selling 'confirmed' seats to more people than can fit on a plane is an overwhelmingly positive phenomenon. It helps keep fares down and increases the opportunities for travel. Only when an airline fails to cope adequately with the consequences of everyone turning up does it turn into a negative. The European Commission forces airlines to compensate anyone with a confirmed reservation who is denied boarding because of overbooking, but you should take the chance.

Airlines overbook because passengers aren't perfect. On the average no-frills flight, around five per cent of people holding reservations for a particular departure will fail to show up. So it is fair for the airlines to assume that one in twenty passengers will be a 'no-show', and to accept bookings for seven seats more than are fitted to the typical 737. This enables you to fly with a higher load factor (i.e. with more of their seats filled), the per-passenger cost decreases and fares can be lower than they would otherwise be. A second benefit is that more people are able to travel: if airlines stopped accepting bookings once a plane reached 100 per cent capacity, some prospective travellers would be denied the chance of boarding the flight of their choice, even though – most of the time – there is room for them on board.

SO IF THERE'S NOTHING WRONG WITH OVERBOOKING, WHY DO PEOPLE GET SO UPSET ABOUT IT?

Because sometimes an airline's desire for full planes backfires, and more people turn up than there are seats available. That itself is not a problem, unless you handle the consequences ungenerously or ineptly. As travellers, we almost all have our price. Sure, there are a few passengers on most flights who simply have to get to their destination, for personal or professional reasons. But most of us will, if the price is right, agree to defer our journey.

An overbooked flight is a problem that can easily be solved without anyone getting upset. You just need to throw money at it. Since the profit motive brings the situation about, some of your earnings from the many occasions when you guess right must be given out when the bet goes wrong. Americans, who are by far the leading consumers of air travel, are well used to the idea. If a flight is looking dangerously oversold, announcements will be made at the gate asking for people who are prepared to postpone their travel plans. The initial bribe is often low – maybe £100. As the minutes tick away until departure, add other sweeteners, like a free round trip to anywhere the airline flies. Mostly, though, money talks. If boarding has been completed and there are still confirmed passengers waiting at the gate, increase the bribe until space is found. The result of this aeronautical auction is that the people who really need to travel are able to do so. Meanwhile, the passengers who take the bribes feel chuffed.

Over time, passengers become rational participants in this system. Many travellers, me included, build in as much flexibility as possible to flight plans. If an option to offload voluntarily comes up, then there are plenty of willing takers. As a Continental Airlines flight prepared to depart from Seattle to Cleveland, I took part in a race to the front of the plane to claim the $300 (£210) being offered so that two unaccompanied minors could travel to see their father in Ohio. Running an airline is a high-stakes business.

One sophistication that is just emerging that could help your operation stand out: 'callable' flights. The idea is that the traveller is offered the option of surrendering the flight at a certain point, in exchange for his or her money back and a cash payment. Airlines, the theory goes, can use this as a sophisticated form of overbooking. If, for example, a big sporting event is scheduled after many seats have been sold, with an average fare of £25, the airline knows that the same seats could go for, say, £125. The carrier could split the benefit with all the passengers who agreed to have the flight 'called', a certain time before departure. Everyone gains: the passenger who can travel on an apparently full plane, the person who gives up their seat and makes £50 for doing almost nothing, and the airline which sees its average fare rise.

ANYWHERE I CAN MAKE MORE MONEY?

In-flight sales, an opportunity that existing no-frills airlines rarely seize to the maximum. For example, do a deal with the local rail or bus company to sell tickets from the airport in flight. Tickets weigh next to nothing (important at a time of high oil prices) and take up minimal space, yet you can sell them at a profit to passengers who really don't want to be bothered faffing around to find the right change and persuade the ticket machine to work.

The same hassle factor means you should make a handsome profit selling pre-stamped holiday postcards for the destination – ideal for people who are going over for a quick weekend.

Another opportunity: cash in on tardy passengers. If you set the check-in deadline forty minutes before departure, you can be sure that a few people will turn up in the following ten minutes. You can sell them the right to check in late for, say, £25. They are happy and you are happy, which is what a good business relationship is all about.

One final idea: allow passengers to check in for multiple sectors and transfer bags (e.g. Campbeltown–Stansted–Corfu). Purists will say that it complicates matters and adds cost, but it saves paying the government two lots of Air Passenger Duty for each transferring passenger, and Southwest has always allowed – indeed, encouraged – transfer traffic. Charge £15 for the privilege, though.

ANY OTHER BUSINESS?

Yes. Treat the business of getting people on planes as a military exercise, advises Richard Garrett. He is the former army officer who organised Ryanair's airports in Continental Europe. 'It's all about people and equipment coming together to perform a set drill.' But don't neglect the human side. Remember that check-in isn't like a supermarket check-out. Airports are curious places where the staff are familiar and comfortable with the environment and its geography. So, too, are some of the regular travellers. But no-frills airlines also attract a large number of people who have never travelled before. Many passengers are under stress, heading for events like weddings or funerals. The scope for problems is immense. To make sure people get on the planes on time, 'push from the check in, pull from the gate,' urges Garrett. 'There should never be a void. Attract people to the gate. Make them hungry to get on the plane.' And that means not having a seat assignment for each passenger. 'People are far more comfortable,' and hence likely to be late, 'if there's a seat reserved.'

ONCE WE'RE GOING, IT'S ALL DOWNHILL, ISN'T IT?

No, and letting the eye stray from the ball operationally or strategically is what has brought the downfall of many airlines. Minimise your risk. Short term, keep marketing aggressively. 'It's like a shark,' explains Tim Jeans of Monarch. 'When you stop swimming, you sink.' In off-peak travel periods, set up a promotion with a newspaper. You will get lots of publicity, they will attract readers, and if you stipulate the right conditions you should make sure you don't 'cannibalise' the people who would have paid high fares to travel with you.

WHAT IF THINGS GO WRONG?

Not 'if' – 'when'. Deal intelligently with problems. Suppose a plane 'goes technical' – how do you cope? Try to hire one in on the ad-hoc market, but be warned that you could face a five-figure bill. Instead, you may want to be cruel to holidaymakers to be kind to business travellers.

A two-hour delay on a weekday morning domestic flight, or a service to an important foreign business destination, is likely to cause more upset than the same delay on a 'sunshine' destination such as Greece or Spain. For business travellers, a two-hour wait could wreck the whole trip, while for people going on a fortnight's holiday it will be merely a mild irritation. So if you are forced to choose (and you most certainly will be), go for the option that minimises the damage to your credibility. Delay the sunshine flight so that people can get to Edinburgh or London on time. Long term, limit the downside by hedging. You will be earning cash in pounds and euros, but spending in dollars. So use the financial instrument of hedging to limit your exposure to sharp currency fluctuations. Buying fuel ahead is also essential, to minimise the chances that OPEC can put you out of business.

You will also need a crisis-management plan for use if your aircraft is in an accident. Rent space from British Airways at its Compass Centre at Heathrow, which is where you handle all the calls from distraught relatives, and make sure your PR people can handle a crisis as adroitly as a seat sale.

IF A FLIGHT IS LATE AND PEOPLE DECIDE NOT TO TRAVEL, SHOULD I OFFER REFUNDS?

No. Passengers who opt not to travel can be allowed to rebook on another flight, but only by paying a substantial penalty. In the event of cancellation, make the cancellation charge exactly equal to the fare paid. You will make a lot more money out of people who don't fly than those who do, and avoid spending a fortune sending out refunds.

WON'T I END UP ON *WATCHDOG*?

Quite possibly, but some no-frills operators see the BBC1 consumer programme as an opportunity to preach the low-fares mantra. Michael O'Leary of Ryanair is a regular face on the show.

SMOKING?

Don't allow it. A couple of months after Go got going, the airline had a highly publicised incident at Milan where the captain kept passengers grounded until the one who had been smoking owned up – and he himself was arrested by Italian police for imprisoning the passengers. But it brought home the point that Go was flying to Milan.

GIMMICKS SEEM TO WORK WELL

They certainly can. Sir Richard Branson has performed countless stunts for Virgin Atlantic, while camera-friendly Stelios – who, these days, devotes only a small amount of his time to easyJet – is always wheeled out ahead of the brainy backroom boss at the airline. Television is a crucial medium these days, but the cost of reaching a substantial audience with advertising is so high that any publicity you can generate for free is valuable. An airline needs a leader who projects and promotes the company. Branson says he is 'trying to make sure that if someone's picking up the phone to book a flight, then the first one that comes to their mind is Virgin, rather than American or BA. It also helps to do it all with a little bit of panache, and style and fun, and make people smile, and try and do it in such a way that gets on the front page.'

AND WHAT IF I CAN'T MAKE MONEY?

'Accept that one day you may have the embarrassment of failing, and of having a bankrupt company in your hands, but you'll have great fun in the process,' advises Branson. You'll learn a lot, give a lot back and you should never be embarrassed about failure if you've given it your all.' Gary Barron, formerly of the late AB Airlines and an all-round aviation whizz, says he'd advise anyone with cash to spare to try. 'If you're going to lose lots of money, you might as well have some fun while you're doing it.'

14. A LIFE IN THE DAY

There's a challenge every day in the airline industry not to do something stupid

Michael O'Leary, chief executive, Ryanair

We may annoy you at times, but by God we give you good value

Barbara Cassani, former chief executive, Go

Author's note: These events happened between 2001 and 2005; by necessity they did not take place on the same day. Instead, to compile this chapter I spent a day at Athens, a day at Hahn, a day shadowing Barbara Cassani (with her consent) and a great deal of time travelling elsewhere in Europe. I have also spent more of my life than I care to remember at Stansted and Luton. All times are in GMT.

2.45 A.M., ATHENS: EASYJET FLIGHT 453 FROM LUTON TOUCHES DOWN

Europe's longest no-frills route is no problem to fill in summer and at Christmas, but for much of the year the easyJet link between Britain and the Greek capital struggles to make serious money. One reason: easyJet's twice-daily departure is up against a competing airline that hasn't quite got round to making a profit for thirty years. The Athens service, though, marked an important statement by the airline's founder to his contemporaries in Greece. Stelios Haji-Ioannou has taken on the established airlines; he has already outlasted Branson's Virgin Atlantic on the route; and he makes money, unlike strike- and loss-prone Olympic Airlines.

The Greek national carrier was started half a century ago, as Olympic Airways, by another shipping magnate, the billionaire Aristotle Onassis. Soon, though, it was taken over by the Greek government. Olympic last made a profit in 1971. Every time an attempt is made to straighten out the organisation, to rationalise the fleet and network, and to reduce the wastage and overstaffing, one or more groups of the airline's employees threaten to strike, safe in the knowledge that the Greek state will underwrite the pay deals.

Airlines have a peculiar vulnerability to the threat of industrial action; it is the next worst thing to rumours of bankruptcy. As soon as prospective passengers get a whiff of the notion that an airline's flights might be grounded, they book on other carriers. At once, the airline's cash flow is hit. The Greek unions are no fools: from past experience, they know that ultimately the government is going to pick up the tab. So they are not underambitious about demands for more money, fewer hours and extra perks. Seeing the potential for turning around Europe's worst-managed airline, Rigas Doganis – one of the leading transport academics – took the helm for a while, before his plans for rationalising the business put him out of favour. Even British Airways became a suitor a few years ago. BA talked about an alliance, and even put in an executive, Rod Lynch, to run the operation in the hope that Olympic could be made profitable. After a year, Lynch walked out, unable to find a way through the morass. The last time I flew from Heathrow to Athens on Olympic, the airline operated a Boeing 747 in each direction. It was the exact opposite of no frills. The forty or so passengers on board enjoyed an especially comfortable flight, since each of us had ten seats to choose from, and 0.3 of a stewardess to wait upon us. That sums up the competition that easyJet is up against on its longest route.

Post-script: the overnight flight to Athens has not survived at Luton. Even though it made good use of an aircraft that would otherwise be on the ground, it appears that earnings from the flight were not enough to sustain it.

4 A.M.: AIRBUS A6: VICTORIA COACH STATION – STANSTED AIRPORT

You think you have problems with your journey to work? At least you don't have to brave the maddest bus in Britain, the A6 between London and Stansted.

As anyone trying to run a company at the Essex airport knows, the big problem with Stansted is that it is in the middle of nowhere. While London's other airports are surrounded by residential areas, and benefit from the labour pool and good transport links that go with them, the only nearby town of any size to Stansted is Bishop's Stortford with a puny population base for meeting the staffing needs of Europe's fastest-growing major airport.

Plenty of staff have to come in from London. The obvious link is on the Stansted Express train from Liverpool Street station. But Network Rail, which owns the tracks, restricts trains at night so that maintenance can take place. So unless you have a car, the only way to be sure you will make it in time for a 5.30 a.m. start at work, or to check-in as a passenger for a flight any earlier than 6.30 a.m., is on the Airbus.

At 4 a.m., the A6 is the only show in town at Victoria Coach Station. A couple of bleary American visitors have had problems with the terminal name; in US transport vocabulary, 'Coach' means 'Economy Class'. At around ten past four, the bus sets off through the silent streets of London.

On the longest day of the year, when dawn begins around now, the trip must be a delight – a tour of some of London's most popular tourist attractions. It takes in Hyde Park, Marble Arch, Oxford Street and even Lord's Cricket Ground. But for most of the year, all you see is the occasional destination sign that, for anyone familiar with London's geography, is not encouraging. A bus with this trajectory, aiming north-west from central London, is heading not for Stansted airport, but for Birmingham. This uneasy feeling continues to Golders Green tube station. To me, this seems like something of a gratuitous stop, because the Tube does not start running for another hour or so. Unsurprisingly, no one gets on. But the schedule appears to allow for the driver to take a cigarette break – and then, when he is good and ready, a sharp change of heading, around the North Circular in the direction of Southend.

One hour after leaving Victoria, the bus is still orbiting the capital. Finally, it obeys a signpost pointing to Stansted airport. Happily, competition on the roads is growing as businesses see that it is easier to take passengers to airports than actually to fly them. National Express has a non-stop service from Stratford tube station in east London, and a company called Terravision operates plenty of competing coach services – including many non-stop from Victoria to Stansted. Two out of five passengers arrive at the

Essex airport by public transport, more than any other major UK airport.

5.30 A.M.: BUZZ FLIGHT 2580, STANSTED–VIENNA

At around the time the passengers aboard the Airbus A6 get their first sight of the gleaming terminal through the gloom, a stewardess – who deserves to remain anonymous – is already on duty, preparing for the Buzz flight to the Austrian capital. She was one of the KLM UK cabin crew who, at the end of 1999, found themselves suddenly having to change their mindsets. Overnight, from 2 to 3 January 2000, they had to stop giving out first-rate meals, drinks, hot towels and chocolates, and start selling food. The old put-down about stewardesses being tea-ladies of the air seemed about to resurface.

You might imagine that cabin crew on no-frills airlines have the most unfulfilling jobs imaginable. In the classless low-cost society, there is no chance of working your way upwards. So the standard career progression does not apply: on traditional airlines, after serving your time in economy you minister to the premium passengers who are screened from the riff-raff as you work your way up the ladder, and the airline class structure. The eventual aim is to become cabin services director on a jumbo and seeing the world from a series of luxury hotels. But my new acquaintance is enjoying herself. She says she is glad she switched to Buzz, and not just because of the extra variety of flying to a range of obscure French destinations. 'You get much nicer passengers. On KLM UK they don't even say good morning.' And, she is glad to say, 'We get lots of people who've never flown before, pensioners who might not even have been out of the country before.' What Buzz does not get, so far, is A-list celebrities to match Princess Diana, who flew once on KLM UK. The best she can suggest is the racing favourite, Frankie Dettori. He is a regular; after the private aircraft accident that claimed the lives of the flight crew and almost his own, he now flies only on scheduled airlines. The former Dutch soccer star, Ruud Gullit, was on one of the flights; she was concerned that he was being pestered so much for autographs during the flight that she asked the captain to switch on the seat-belt sign early.

I have not flown with her since Buzz was taken over by Ryanair. But Michael O'Leary's remark to unhappy Buzz staff, that 'The door's over there' is unlikely to have boosted morale.

6 A.M. (7 A.M. IN GERMANY): HAHN AIRPORT

At Hahn airport, perched on a plateau above the Moselle, the information counter is open for business. The staff occupy a desk at one end of the big, bright box that comprises the passenger terminal. By common consent it is a vast improvement on the former terminal, which was the Officers' Mess of the old US Air Force base. During the cold war, Hahn was an essential base for the defence of the Western world against the Warsaw Pact countries. The Berlin Wall came down in 1989, but the Americans hung on until 1993. When they finally went home, hundreds of local people lost their livelihoods. Many of them had worked at the base, while others rented property or supplied goods to the military. To try to revive the community after the US pull-out, the regional authority pumped millions of Deutschmarks into the airport.

Today is payback day. Hitherto, Hahn's only scheduled routes have been Ryanair's flights from London Stansted, Glasgow Prestwick, and Shannon in the west of Ireland. Later this morning, a special flight from Dublin is due to arrive with three dozen worthies on board. Within the next few hours, one of Europe's sleepier aviation backwaters is to reveal a new identity as a leading hub with six new links to airports in Italy, France, Norway – and Dorset.

6.50 A.M.: LEEDS–BRADFORD AIRPORT

'We'd better make an announcement.' Philip Meeson is concerned about the fog that has descended upon Schiphol airport in Amsterdam, the destination for his airline's maiden flight. The captain of Jet2 flight 201 has reported an hour's delay because arrivals into Amsterdam are being rationed. The contingent of journalists waiting to board do not appear worried, perhaps because there is still plenty of champagne in the departure lounge.

The airline belongs to the Dart Group, which began life flying flowers 21 years ago; fresh blooms are light and perishable, making them prime candidates for air travel. Having perfected the art of bringing tulips from Amsterdam, the company is now sending tourists to the Dutch capital. At least, it is trying to. Jet2 has planted its flag at Leeds-Bradford, previously an almost no-frills-free zone. In the next two months it will expand the network from the Yorkshire airport to include Alicante, Barcelona, Malaga, Milan, Nice and Palma.

Not everyone booked on the first flight has shown up. Those who have given it a miss included two customers who were the very first to book seats on Jet2. A shame they were no-shows, because the airline had decided to award the couple with a pair of free flights as the first bookers.

7.15 A.M.: EASYJET FLIGHT 12

The flight from Edinburgh has arrived at Luton airport, and has 25 minutes to be transformed into flight 11 back to the Scottish capital. The choreography involved in making sure the plane is able to depart on cue is impressive. The baggage handlers and refuellers are already waiting when the 737 emerges from the gloom to draw up at the stand. Sets of stairs are eased into position at the front and rear doors on the port side, and a member of cabin crew flings open each door. At almost the same time, the forward hold is opened and unloading begins. Baggage handling is usually a breeze. There is no class structure (and consequently no need to prioritise bags belonging to premium passengers), and bags are never transferred from one flight to another. Hiccups happen when a passenger fails to board in time, and his or her luggage has to be found and unloaded before the plane can leave. As the empty baggage carts fill up, the bags for the departing flight trundle up to wait their turn. 'Turn' is the key word; in the lexicon of no-frills airlines, it translates as 'how quickly can we get the plane airborne again?' The pit-stop mentality prevails.

One stage that could, in theory, be omitted is filling up with fuel. The tanks on an easyJet 737-700 hold sufficient fuel to fly from Edinburgh to London and back half-a-dozen times. But no captain would seriously countenance that. Fuel adds weight, which means you consume extra fuel to lift it. It also makes landing more problematic. Every pilot wishes their aircraft to be as light as possible at the point where they have to reacquaint it with the ground, and no captain wants his or her plane to be carrying an excess of inflammable liquid. So the optimum fuel load is a delicate balance: enough for the planned journey; enough in reserve for a prolonged holding pattern followed by a diversion; and a little bit for luck, because running out of fuel is almost the worst thing that can happen to a plane. The pilots are calculating the load, studying the flight plan, and running through a daunting number of checklists. They may also be talking to air traffic control: all manner of planes, from Far Eastern arrivals coming in over Clacton, to military jets limbering up in Lincolnshire, are clamouring for a space in the crowded skies between Bedfordshire and West Lothian.

The cabin crew, meanwhile, are relaxing over a cup of coffee with their feet up. Only joking. On easyJet, professional flight attendants risk the accusation that they are not merely flying tea-ladies, they are flying cleaners. Traditional airlines employ cleaning contractors to remove rubbish from the seat-pocket, wipe the tray-table and, on a bad day, mop up vomit. But they cost money. No frills means no cleaners; the cabin crew must clean up after the passengers during the brief stop on the ground (assisted, in Canada at least, by the boss of the company: 'When I'm on board, I help clean the cabin,' says Clive Beddoe of WestJet).

The cabin crew conduct a security check, inspecting the overhead lockers. They check the takings from the catering trolley, and restock it for the journey north. Unlike Southwest Airlines where, along with the peanuts, you get juice or coffee, easyJet gives nothing away beyond a plastic cup of water. Having departed from the Scottish capital at 6 a.m., the flight crew will have completed two sectors and nearly seven hundred miles of travelling before 9 a.m. The arriving passengers took five minutes to clear the plane; the new consignment will take eight minutes to board.

I watched the people checking in for flight 11, and looked at those arriving on flight 12. Almost all are male, and most are wearing jackets and ties. Increasingly many businesses realise that, for a simple day trip between the Scottish and English capitals, a fare of around £100 is a better business proposition than twice as much on British Airways from Heathrow. Or it could be a matter of time management: easyJet has the first flight south from Edinburgh, and the last one home.

The passengers have one other thing in common: to a man and woman, they look weary. The northbound contingent have one more chore when they get through to the departure lounge; a market researcher working for the Civil Aviation Authority who is politely demanding 'Where have you come from this morning? How did you travel to Luton today? Are you travelling for business or pleasure? How much did you pay? How many times have you flown in the last twelve months? Have you travelled on any of the low-cost airlines in the past year? Where to? How many people live in your household?'

7.30 A.M. (8.30 A.M. in France): GATE 11, STRASBOURG AIRPORT

A waiter named Julian normally starts his working day dispensing coffee and croissants at the airport cafe at Entzheim, near Strasbourg. Today is different. He goes airside to the departure area, dons a bowler hat and starts serving free tea and fruit cake to the passengers waiting to board FR7773, Ryanair's maiden flight from the 'capital of Europe' to Stansted.

A local television crew films proceedings, though the director has a struggle to find French passengers in the queue; most are British expatriates working with the European Parliament or the Council of Europe, and keen to take advantage of the first cheap flight home. There is also a scattering of Germans from across the Rhine. The film crew boards the plane and faces a tough day ahead; after arrival in Stansted, they have to grab interviews, take the Stansted Express to London Liverpool Street, board a bus to City airport and fly to Basel airport, the only way that they can hope to be back with their tapes in time for the evening bulletin.

Post-script: the Ryanair route to Strasbourg did not survive long. A French court upheld a complaint from Air France that subsidies from the local chamber of commerce were unlawful. Ryanair now flies to Baden-Baden across the Rhine in Germany instead, with much the same clientele.

9 A.M.: ENTERPRISE HOUSE, STANSTED AIRPORT

'Passion . . . commitment . . . teamwork' is one of the messages that pops up on the computer screensaver at Go's headquarters. The reception area is decorated with all kinds of notices, including a poster offering the services of a head masseuse. By the end of today, I may need one.

I am here to spend a day shadowing Barbara Cassani, the only woman to run an airline. Her first task of the day – not counting the two-hour commute from her home in Barnes, west London, to the Essex airport – is to cross the footbridge that cuts through the atrium of Enterprise House and walk into a bare, glaringly lit room to chair the weekly Communications meeting.

At the meeting is a mixed bunch of experienced airline staff and outsiders, such as Clive, Go's new tax accountant. He has recently arrived from a firm of funeral directors. A colleague explains: 'He's used to repatriating dead bodies. We told him, "Same kind of thing, only live passengers".'

The average age of the circle of twenty people looks to be around thirty, meaning that many of them had not even been born when Southwest Airlines started up. Of the twenty, I am the only one wearing a tie. (Most people appear to be segregated by clothing: there is a woolly jumper corner over by the window, and a blue-shirted contingent near the door.) I am also the only one who is not directly concerned with running Go, the newly independent no-frills airline. This is the regular Wednesday occasion when every senior manager finds out what is happening across the airline. Less than a month after 11 September, with other airlines shedding workers in their tens of thousands, the mood is upbeat.

First, the details of the past week's performance are picked over: the number of flights on time (which means anything up to fifteen minutes late), the percentage of bookings online – and the proportion of abandoned calls to the reservations centre. 'Yesterday we had only seventeen abandoned calls in one hour. We're overstaffed.' If this comment sounds odd, it is because one of the measures of productivity of a call centre is the proportion of the public who give up. Were it zero, that would suggest that there are underemployed staff sitting around waiting for the phone to ring.

The news from Newcastle is good. The previous week, Go had said it would start flying to Tyneside from Stansted. A team from Go had been sent to Newcastle airport to sort out the logistics for the operation. They report their reception had been 'very warm – it was almost Bristol-ish', a reference to Go's arrival at Bristol airport the previous year. 'Newcastle United want to charter the aircraft.'

The discussion then takes a turn that many other business people would find strange: 'We're going to reward passengers on our routes that are doing well,' says David Magliano, the airline's sales and marketing director. In other words, Go is to cut fares on its successful Mediterranean routes to Malaga, Alicante and Naples. The airline has also celebrated its top place in a Business Traveller survey of no-frills airlines by buying the most high-profile poster site on the approach to Luton airport to advertise the fact. 'It'll be there for a year,' says Magliano. Ray Webster, chief executive of easyJet, will pass it every day on his way to and from work.

Northern Ireland's first minister also made it to the agenda of the Communications meeting at Go. 'Trimble's pulling in his people,' observed the finance director. He predicted the effects on bookings 'if the peace process implodes'. Magliano predicts that, if the Americans extend the bombing of Afghanistan into Iraq, 'we'll see a spike in oil prices'.

9.15 A.M.: VIRGIN EXPRESS HQ, BRUSSELS AIRPORT

The yield managers for continental Europe's leading no-frills airline are getting into their stride, fixing fares by the hour. Every departure on every route that the Belgian airline flies is 'micro-managed' to make sure the maximum earnings are squeezed out of every seat. Half-a-dozen earnest young men are peering at screens. These show how many people have booked, and the fares they have paid, on flights that won't take off for another month. If bookings are strong, the micro-managers will tweak fares upwards; too few people, and the price comes down. These days, finding the best price for a flight to, say, Doncaster is as tricky a matter as choosing the optimum moment to back a horse at, say, Doncaster.

9.30 A.M.: RYANAIR FLIGHT 23, BEAUVAIS–DUBLIN

'See, that's City airport down there.' The plane is directly overhead Heathrow airport. It is a shimmeringly clear day, and London is laid out like a map beneath us. Captain X dips the starboard wing to give me a better view of the metropolis and in particular the Docklands airport.

I know the captain's real name, but this encounter took place just prior to the events of 11 September 2001, after which attitudes to flight-deck visits became very different. I had approached Captain X on the ground at Beauvais airport in northern France, and told him I was a journalist who would like to interview him. He agreed. Once the flight to Dublin reaches its cruise altitude, he asks the lead stewardess to summon me to the cockpit. He proceeds to tell me about his day.

'We started in Dublin this morning, flew to Paris Beauvais, we're on our way back as I speak to you, and then we're going to turn around and go to Brussels Charleroi, and then back to Dublin and home for lunch.'

Nice work if you can get £90,000 a year for it, which is the going rate for Ryanair captains. Their German counterparts earn up to three times as much working for Lufthansa, which is one reason Michael O'Leary and his team see the opportunity to expand low-cost aviation in Germany. I am sitting in the jumpseat of a Boeing 737-200, which is the elderly workhorse of the

Ryanair fleet. We are flying over the busiest international airport in the world. From our vantage point six miles up, we can see other airports; Gatwick just swept past to port, and the captain's momentary manoeuvre allowed me to see London City.

Everything is going according to plan. The flight plan is a computerised print-out that gives the crew all the information they need for the flight. It lists the navigation beacons over which flight 23 will pass. The plan also predicts the fuel required, and allows the crew to compare what's in the tanks with what should be expected during the course of the eighty-minute flight. It also estimates the ground speed, allowing for the wind, and the frequencies for those navigation beacons. Even in the cruise, when you or I might be tempted to do some sightseeing and take in the view, Captain X and his colleague are working. 'We write everything down that we get from air traffic control, our radar heading, or frequency change. We compare the times we estimate overhead the beacons, and the minimum fuel that we must have, with what we actually have. We keep an eye on it to make sure our fuel situation is normal, and our times are normal.' Another document, the voyage report, records where the aircraft has been, and when: 'the flights, the schedule times, the off-blocks times, which is when we started to push back to when we set the parking brake at the end of the flight, the flight times, our fuel – what we uplifted, what we arrived with – the crew, their duty times, which have to be kept very strictly monitored. The number of passengers, cargo, the delays, the reason for delays, and this is all put into the computer and analysed.' Maybe that £90,000 a year is not enough, after all.

I ask Captain X if he has favourite airports. 'I tend to like the smaller airports like Beauvais. I like that family atmosphere. You met me walking around the aircraft having a stroll, and I like that type of operation. It's a lot less congested so when you land, you literally taxi off the runway and you park. Let the passengers get out, go to the terminal building, get on their bus, then new passengers come on board, we turn the aircraft around, and between landing and taking off we can do it in 25 minutes when we're landing in secondary airports. And I like that.'

And least favourite airports?

'It would be airports that are difficult to make an approach, in that they're very short, or high grounds so they tend to be very windy. Dublin winds tend to be very strong. Leeds-Bradford springs to mind, it's not that I dislike it, but it's harder work flying into an airport like that.'

9.40 A.M. (10.40 A.M. DUTCH TIME): SCHIPHOL AIRPORT, AMSTERDAM

Leeds-Bradford wasn't the cause of the delay to the maiden flight of Jet2; it was fog at Amsterdam. Philip Meeson, chief executive of the airline, finishes an interview with a crew from Yorkshire Television, about the twentieth interrogation he has had so far this morning. But he can still summon up a grin when asked to pose by Dutch news photographers. The departure screens show his flight going to Leedsbradfrd; Denise Anderson, chair of Leeds-Bradford airport, is not amused, but she is looking forward to tourists being attracted to the place she calls 'the centre of the Universe'.

10 A.M.: ENTERPRISE HOUSE, STANSTED

'Ken – you're in charge of quality. Do you want to find a solution?'

Barbara Cassani's inner cabinet has congregated for the Decisions meeting, to sort out some of the thornier problems of running an airline. Ken New, quality manager, is under pressure. One afternoon the previous week, all flights between Scotland and Belfast had run four hours late because of an error over maintenance routines. Every aircraft requires a daily check by engineers. A Boeing was erroneously scheduled without a hop back to Stansted for maintenance, so the jet had missed its routine examination. Getting another aircraft to replace it proved difficult. 'That was a huge number of passengers inconvenienced as a result of one mistake,' says Captain Ed Winter, chief operating officer for the airline. He looks like a taller, friendlier version of Denis Healey, but I sense that you would not want to be on the wrong side of him. 'We haven't seen disruption like that since 11 September. There must be a process to make sure that cannot happen again.'

At least the delays did not create any disruptive passengers. The 'self-loading cargo' that we passengers comprise (a widely used industry expression, but not one that I ever heard at Go) present a constant challenge, especially when we drink too much. This was the root cause of a big air-rage incident the previous week in which a passenger broke another's nose ('We had to get the seat covers changed' . . . 'the police let him off with a caution'), and another when a group on a Stansted–Naples flight decided to stage a mass mooning.

10.05 A.M.: GATWICK

Britain's leading police officer specialising in air rage is preparing to board easyJet flight 838 to Amsterdam. Chief inspector Mike Alderson has not had to go far from his office; he is the officer in charge of Gatwick airport. His final destination is The Hague, where a seminar on disruptive passengers is taking place. He is to urge the airlines to root out possible problems on the ground.

10.30 A.M.: APPROACHING CORK AIRPORT

'Jesus Christ, that's not Shannon!' exclaims the passenger in the window seat as the plane from Stansted breaks through the clouds on its final approach and the distinctive sight of Kinsale harbour appears. Almost at once, the captain makes an announcement that Shannon airport is closed because of fog, and that the aircraft will instead land at Cork. The passenger in the middle seat is Jamie Bowden, who has recently left British Airways after twenty years' experience across the airline, and is now engaged in airline consultancy. BA hired him back to mastermind the public relations for the relaunch of Concorde. Now he is off to see the management of Shannon airport about some work. He checked with Aer Lingus, who wanted £350 for a day trip, and settled for £75 return on Ryanair.

Once on the ground, passengers are told, 'We're getting coaches to take you to Shannon.' Bowden asks a member of staff how long that might take. 'Three hours, and it's a grand journey.' He decides the beautiful scenery will not make up for a missed meeting, and opts to fly straight back to Stansted on the same plane.

'You didn't stay long,' says a stewardess who recognises him from the outbound trip. As the plane levels off, Bowden tells the sorry story to this sympathetic ear.

'You probably need a cup of tea, then.' Bowden gratefully accepts. She returns with the brew, and asks for payment. 'But all my money's in my jacket, which you asked me earlier to put in the overhead locker.' The passenger in the next seat pays the stewardess for Bowden's tea. 'I don't believe it,' he says. 'Eight weeks ago I was flying on Concorde, today I'm having to scrounge money off a stranger to get a cup of tea.'

10.50 A.M.: CITY CLUB, OLD BROAD STREET, LONDON

Jamie Bowden's tea, currently costing £1.75, is one reason Michael O'Leary is able to announce record profits once again. In the lean first half of 2005 his passengers spent an average £5.50 on 'ancillaries' from tea to hotel beds (on which the airline takes a 20p cut if customers are directed from the website). Responding to questions about his future, the new father (Matt, his son, is four weeks old at the time) says he will leave the airline in 'four or five years'. Within a few minutes, that has become 'three or four years'. Ryanair's chief executive says that the airline will need to become 'more professional' once it is the largest in Europe, so that it can deal more effectively with 'the gobshites in the European Commission'. O'Leary then launches into a tirade against the charges levied by BAA Stansted, and threatens to set up a check-in at a truckers' car park off the M11 and bus people straight to the plane.

11 A.M.: ENTERPRISE HOUSE, STANSTED

'I want us to be as proud of our toilets as we are of the rest of the airline. And at the moment, I'm not.'

Barbara Cassani has moved on to operational issues, and the 'lavs', as cabin crew around the world call aircraft lavatories, are causing her concern. 'I've been doing a lot of research into toilets,' pipes up Go's cabin-crew manager, Andrew Goodrum. The problem, as Cath Lynn, head of customer service, succinctly puts it, is that 'toilets stink'.

Flight crew have been complaining that there is an unpleasant odour from the forward lavatory. The discussion opens what I hesitate to call a can of worms. 'In all my time at Go, I've never seen a toilet truck at the front of an aircraft,' says Dominic Paul, who has the unwieldy title of director of people services and business development. Ed Winter ripostes that 'they must get attached sometimes'. The rule is that a toilet truck, which empties the tank where waste is collected, should service each inbound international flight. In contrast, domestic flights have the tanks emptied only on request from the crew (do not read this as an interesting commentary on foreign habits – overseas flights are longer than the typical one-hour domestic hop in Britain). The cost to the airline is £7 per visit.

Some fingers are pointing at the insanitary habits of men. Passengers choose between the forward or rear lavatory depending on gender rather than where they are sitting on the plane. Men tend to be exhibitionists, striding blithely to the front of the aircraft. Once in the forward lavatory, they treat it with less respect than do the women. Female passengers, meanwhile, are shy about bodily functions and tend to retreat to the rear. They leave the 'lav' as they would wish to find it. But the habits of cabin crew are coming in for scrutiny at the Decisions meeting, too. 'I'm getting all kinds of debris, cafetieres, ice tongs, coffee grounds,' says Mike Williams, the chief engineer. 'We get through a hell of a lot of toilet motors.' The management vows to get tough on toilet blockages, and tough on the causes of toilet blockages.

'I'm polishing my Exocet,' says Andrew Goodrum, cabin crew manager. 'I'm just not ready to fire it.'

11.20 A.M.: RYANAIR FLIGHT 7751, DUBLIN–HAHN

Don't bother checking on the website for this flight. It has only ever flown once. And while no one on flight 7751 has paid a European cent for the flight, the fact that it is in the air at all is causing inconvenience to fare-paying passengers. This morning, one Ryanair 737 has already 'gone technical' before it had even left Charleroi (the cause was not a toilet-related problem). The airline could use all the Boeings and crews it has to operate the normal schedule. But one has been commandeered by the chief executive, Michael O'Leary, and his senior managers for a day out in Germany that they intend to milk for all the PR value they can muster. The message 'Auf wiedersehen, Lufthansa' has been painted on the fuselage.

A brass band and a coachload of local schoolchildren waving German and Irish flags wait in a torrential downpour on the apron at Hahn airport to welcome O'Leary. Flanked by the region's finance and labour ministers, O'Leary claims his airline will carry 1.5m passengers in the first year on its nine routes from Hahn, and would force the German national carrier, Lufthansa, to cut its fares by €200m (£120m). 'Lufthansa won't know what hit 'em', says O'Leary. He announces fares of €61 (£38) to Bournemouth and Bergamo (an airport in northern Italy that serves Milan). BA's fares from Frankfurt to Southampton, and Lufthansa's prices from Frankfurt to Milan (Linate, the principal airport) are quoted for comparison. O'Leary says Ryanair's fares will be one sixth of those presently prevailing. 'We're looking forward to a winter of vicious low fares. We're going to take the war to Lufthansa.'

11.30 A.M.: ENTERPRISE HOUSE, STANSTED

'The administrators have contacted us and asked if we'd like to buy Ansett,' says Ed Winter, chief operating officer for Go. The Decisions meeting is on to post-11 September matters – and what a management consultant might call threats and opportunities. The perceived increase in risks from terrorism leads to a discussion on whether passengers should be asked for photographic ID on domestic and Irish flights. The consensus is that they should, but before action is implemented a reporter for the *Daily Telegraph* travels on a Go flight from Edinburgh to Stansted under an assumed name. The story is splashed on the front page of the travel section.

More optimistically, the downturn in the aviation business has provided the opportunity to obtain aircraft and crew more easily and cheaply than before. 'The market is changing dramatically,' says Ed Winter. 'You can get two old dogs for the price of one new one. Boeing field is stacked up with white tails' (the term for new aircraft that are built speculatively, without a definite buyer, to keep the production line going). But the government does not appear to be listening to Go's demands about fair treatment for airlines. 'You could make a career out of talking to the government,' says Stephen Horner, the network director. 'I've wasted time waiting to hear from the Treasury. The reply was, "we might get a letter back to you by 11 October, and here's your customer service number." We've made our views known, they haven't given us the courtesy of a reply.'

Andrew Cowen, director of finance and strategic planning, has had no more luck in his dealings with the Secretary of State for Transport: 'I got the most bullshit letter back I've ever seen from Stephen Byers.'

Back at their unoccupied desks, the screen saver is repeating the Go mantra: 'passion, commitment, teamwork'.

11.40 A.M.: GATE 7, STANSTED AIRPORT

'He's definitely here.' A duty officer, clad in a fluorescent jacket, scans the horizon from Gate 7 at Stansted airport. He is looking for the first-ever Air Berlin flight from Paderborn in Germany to Essex. The Boeing was due half-an-hour earlier, and touched down a few minutes ago, after an air-traffic control hold-up, but has since apparently disappeared.

11.45 A.M.: HAHN AIRPORT

After a press conference in which the most testing question was what might tempt the Germans to fly to Bournemouth ('climate, culture and warm beer,' responded O'Leary), the crowd of two hundred is treated to a video about Hahn airport, featuring the information desk staff with a high-kicking routine to the heavily amplified sounds of Van Halen's 'Jump'. The location is a departure lounge, cordoned off from the travelling public who are checking in for the flight to Stansted. The performing schoolchildren have long been dried off and loaded back on to their coaches, while the adults tuck assertively into some of the Moselle's finer wines. Almost all the promotional lighters have been swiped, but most of the Ryanair T-shirts remain unclaimed. The milieu is fascinating: bewildered local bigwigs unused to their national airline being slagged off by an Irish rival, Frankfurt-based business journalists complaining about the long journey to Hahn from continental Europe's financial centre, and the entire senior management team for Ryanair, becoming increasingly boisterous as the party continues.

11.55 A.M.: GATE 7, STANSTED AIRPORT

'All smiles please – all look this way.' Air Berlin's Boeing has now turned up at the gate. Stansted's staff photographer is further delaying its departure by coaxing the flight crew to pose for a photograph, along with Joachim Hunold – chief executive of Germany's leading low-cost airline. He can afford to smile: 165 people are disembarking from the jet. But upstairs in the departure lounge, just twenty passengers are waiting to board. They will have nine seats each on the Boeing 737-800, the first scheduled flight from Stansted of an aircraft with 'go-faster' winglets – upturned wingtips that improve performance. Within three years of this first touchdown, Air Berlin established a hub at Stansted, with domestic flights to Manchester and Glasgow.

12 NOON: ENTERPRISE HOUSE, STANSTED AIRPORT

Enterprise House is abuzz. As Barbara Cassani chairs a meeting on a personnel matter which it would be inappropriate for me to attend, I perch at the reception desk for Go HQ. It beats even easyJet and Ryanair as the most no-frills reception. The desk stands at a crossroads, where the corridor linking each end of the office meets the path between the door to the outside world and the canteen. 'Crew bag – do not offload', reads the tag on one stewardess's case (passenger bags are fair game, then, I conclude). A group of Spanish cabin crew arrives; with a year-round presence in Spain, Go chooses to recruit the country's nationals, and offers cash to British cabin crew prepared to learn foreign languages.

12.30 P.M.: CUSTOMER SERVICE DEPARTMENT, RYANAIR, DUBLIN AIRPORT

Siobhan O'Neill is checking to see how fast her team is working through today's pile of correspondence. 'We have less than one person in every thousand complaining,' she says with pride. For some weary passengers, the very notion of a customer service department at Ryanair may sound like a contradiction in terms, and the task of running it the worst job in the world. But O'Neill – who joined Ryanair in 1989 as a secretary, and now has a staff of four – enjoys her work. 'We get complaints in, we get queries, we get compliments, some people can be very irate but there are some lovely people here, and we all work very well here. We just get on and do the job. The main thing is that we answer the letters as quickly as we can and get an answer to the passenger, because the worst thing that can happen is a passenger can have a problem and get no answer to it.'

Ryanair insists that all correspondence is in writing, and in English. 'We can't take calls because people will stay longer on the phone than they're meant to,' says O'Neill. 'We investigate the problem and respond back to them as quickly as we can, on the same day if possible.'

As with any airline, bags get lost, and it takes time (and a lot of money) to reunite them with the owner. That is the leading cause for complaint. Next are delays, usually caused by poor weather or technical problems. And a number of people ask for their money back. 'Everyone has very genuine circumstances and unforeseen reasons as to why they need a refund,' says O'Neill. 'Obviously we can't provide refunds and we'd explain to them why we can't. For delays, we'd advise the reason for the delay and include a letter for insurance purposes, because they can claim from their insurance.'

That is not strictly true, because most travel insurance policies kick in only if you miss a connection on your outbound journey, or if your delay is twelve hours or longer – a most unusual event on short-haul airlines.

O'Neill's boss, Michael O'Leary, is rather more robust when I talk to him about customer service. 'We don't go in for all the old bullshit that British Airways and the other airlines have gone on with for years. They'll rape you for the airfare of £500 or £700, and then pretend they're giving something they're not. We have a very well-defined product. It doesn't mean we can eliminate all delays, it doesn't mean that we won't cancel less than one-tenth of 1 per cent of flights, and in those cases we will not give you anything and we make no apologies for it. People who arrive at airports with no money in their pockets and expect us to put them up in hotels or feed them simply because there's a delay will not get fed on Ryanair. But they will not be charged the extra £500 every time they fly with us either. What we're trying to do is to wean people off this notion that air travel is some first class, intercontinental, *Titanic*-like experience – it isn't, this is a bus service.'

By 2005, O'Leary and his couterparts were forced by new European legislation to change their tune; delays of two hours oblige the airline to provide snacks, drinks and phone calls, while cancellations that are the carrier's fault are supposed to trigger payments that could be several times the fare paid.

'Every passenger expects when they travel, quite rightly, a high level of service,' says O'Neill. 'At Ryanair we offer very friendly, professional service from our frontline staff to our airline crew to our complaints department turnaround times.' She travels on Ryanair herself, but increasingly on publicly available fares rather than the airline's concessions, which are available only for standby travel. 'When you're only paying £9.99, it makes sense to go confirmed.' She flies as much as she can: 'When I get on a flight, I like to see how people react.' On a recent flight to Italy, the passengers applauded after the landing. 'It's nice to see that side because I only tend to see the very negative side when they complain.' Complaints outnumber compliments by a ratio of fifty to one, but O'Neill sifts them out and posts letters of praise on the Ryanair website. Some people also enlist her to help with their love lives: 'People telling us they met someone on a flight, and they fell in love with them, and they can't get in touch with them, and can they get their contact details? If we can find out who the passenger was – they might have their name – we would look them up on the system, and then we'd ring the other person and say, "Do you want me to send on this letter?" '

Before we part, I need to ask: does Siobhan O'Neill send out many cheques?

'No, I don't send out many cheques.'

1 P.M.

Lunch with Barbara Cassani is a refreshingly informal experience. The trim, blonde airline boss leads me through the building works that constitute Britain's fastest-growing airport and into the terminal at Stansted. Go's chief executive flutters past the check-in desks, pausing to talk to staff and to introduce herself to unfamiliar faces.

We go to the sandwich counter at Boots, but I guess the most powerful woman in British aviation would prefer it to be Prêt à Manger, which she often cites as a model of good customer service. Today she is taking a few minutes for lunch, rather than working straight through: 'I pepper my day with popping into the different parts of the operation, like sitting on the phones [in the call centre] at lunchtime.'

1.30 P.M.: LUTON AIRPORT, EASYJET FLIGHT 451 TO ATHENS

Check on the easyJet website and you will see that fares for flight 451 to the Greek capital on any given day are generally much higher than for flight 453. That's because the daytime departure, 451, is very civilised, departing Luton at lunchtime and arriving in Athens in good time for dinner. In contrast, the night flight sets off at around pub closing time and arrives at an hour when the civilised world is sound asleep. It neatly sums up the pricing structure of no-frills airlines: the passenger can decide whether convenience or cost is the more compelling. The daytime Athens flight ties up one expensive Boeing for around nine hours for just one return hop. But passengers who value their sleep are prepared to pay for the privilege of a civilised departure time. At night, the aircraft would otherwise be parked. So passengers willing to arrive or depart in the early hours are rewarded with fares that reflect the low marginal costs involved in flying to Greece in the middle of the night.

The aircraft pushes back exactly on schedule, much to the relief of the crew. On board is Stelios, the airline's founder, off to Athens to see family and friends – and to inspect the new airport. As soon as the seat-belt light goes off, he starts work, moving through the cabin, speaking to each and every passenger.

2 P.M.: JOB CENTRE, STANSTED

Following 11 September, dozens of airlines laid off thousands of UK employees. Stansted was especially hard hit, with Continental Airlines, Lufthansa and SAS closing down all their operations at the airport. The redundant workers are keenly aware that the no-frills airlines are still expanding, and are queuing up for interviews.

Those who decide to apply for Ryanair need not spend too long perfecting the CV. 'The only restriction to becoming a member of Ryanair's cabin crew is age,' says Sharon Fitzsimons, cabin services manager for Ryanair. 'You must be at least eighteen years of age. Other than that, you need to have an outgoing personality, be willing to work hard, and be good at dealing with people.'

3 P.M.: EASYJET ACADEMY, LUTON

'Heads down. Stay down. Heads down. Stay down.' I am not used to being yelled at by cabin crew, especially the good folk of easyJet. The scariest thing about this mock-evacuation from the simulator at the easyJet Academy is the sudden switch from charming, helpful crew to an aggressive, military demeanour. I have joined a group of easyJet non-flying staff at the first open day of the Academy, a training centre for the 25 new cabin crew who join the airline each week. We have been ordered to adopt the brace position (incidentally, it is an urban myth that holding your head in your hands and pressing against the seat in front is designed to preserve your jaw intact so your identity can be more easily discovered from dental records). After the imaginary crash landing the yelling begins again. 'Get out! Get out! Faster!' We emerge to find a camera crew from the airline documentary team waiting, and I sheepishly realise I have left the aircraft still clutching my bag. If you ever find yourself in a real emergency evacuation, like the Air France jet in Toronto in 2005 from which everyone escaped alive, leave your possessions behind. Oh, and on the emergency slides (which are more fun than they look, except in a real emergency), grip your lapels with your hands. Otherwise, you risk harming your hands by gripping the sides of the slides – and, more significantly, slowing the evacuation.

4.30 P.M.: ENTERPRISE HOUSE

The first blocks of red appearing on the computer screens are causing a certain amount of concern at the hub of Go's activity:

the Operations room. A corner of the building overlooking the apron is filled with screens, telephones and worried-looking people. Today, all are men, though Go has one female operations manager. They are playing a never-ending game of three-dimensional chess. They have to deal with hiccups such as breakdowns on the Stansted Express, snarl-ups on the M11 and oversleeping staff.

The operational hub of each no-frills airline is a sophisticated computer monitoring system that represents each flight as a bar on a screen. At Stansted, planned flights appear in blue, completed ones in grey. Delays are picked up in red. When circumstances conspire to delay many flights, the image can look fairly bloody. Patches of red are showing up this afternoon, most immediately flight 514 from Edinburgh, which is running half an hour late.

'It was a flight holding inbound because of weather here, then we picked up an air traffic delay northbound,' says Nick Chapple, the operations control manager. 'We schedule so tightly that it's very difficult to pick up once you start getting delays – it tends to roll on.'

'We are flying our aircraft between eleven and twelve hours a day,' says Go's chief operating officer, Ed Winter. 'A traditional airline will probably only get seven or eight hours a day out of their aircraft, because they concentrate on the key business travel periods of the day. High utilisation is one of the key ways we can offer such low fares. We do have 100 per cent [on-time] days, and and we celebrate them. We give all the staff on duty a little present that day.' That gives you some idea of how rare they are.

Plenty of unforeseen events can interfere with what should be a routine operation. Luggage goes missing, or the baggage belt breaks down. Passengers dawdle in duty-free. Refuellers or caterers may be held up working on another delayed flight. 'Firebreaks' are built in to the system in the middle of the day: 'Gaps built in deliberately, so you can catch up and move things around,' says Winter. And, unlike other airlines hidebound by arcane working rules, crews' planned destinations can be switched at short notice. Flight crew who might be expecting a day in the sun in Spain could find themselves in Scotland. 'That's the difference between us and the more traditional airlines,' says Winter. 'Traditional airlines have got complex industrial agreements. So if a crew comes in expecting to go to Alicante and you want them to go to Glasgow, that's not always possible. There are often quite difficult arrangements to get round.'

There certainly are. A British Airways pilot who reports for work expecting to fly to Stockholm, may find that the rostered destination has been changed to Rome. To compensate for what is hardly a huge inconvenience, the airline is required to 'draft' them – an industrial agreement which can involve an additional payment of £750 to a pilot, just for doing his or her job of flying a Boeing for two hours to a European destination, and two hours back to Heathrow.

The cause that takes the largest share of the blame for delays is air traffic control. There is some agreement about the worst regions; the area between the south of Germany and Milan, overflying Switzerland, is a notorious bottleneck with too little capacity and too much traffic. Clacton, as previously mentioned, has aircraft coming into the London terminal area from northern Europe, Scandinavia and almost anywhere in Asia passing overhead. The north-west of England, and in particular the Wirral peninsula, is another pinch-point. Faced with an air-traffic delay, airlines can consider alternative routes, and weigh up the cost of a twenty-minute delay against ten minutes' extra flying time, and the fuel consumed. A flight between Stansted and Dublin might fly at a sub-optimal altitude, such as sixteen thousand feet, to avoid some of the congestion at the higher levels. This consumes more fuel and causes a bumpier ride. The airlines pay air traffic control authorities handsomely for the privilege of being told where, and when, to go. Tim Jeans of Monarch says what are known as en route charges are 'a big thorn in our flesh'. He complains: 'It's frankly a lot of money for a service which has very little accountability to its users.' After a series of computer meltdowns in 2002, which cost the no-frills airlines millions, easyJet wrote off its investment in National Air Traffic Services (NATS). Other no-frills airlines are campaigning for NATS to be accountable to airlines when its systems collapse.

4.35 P.M.: EUROCONTROL HQ, BRUSSELS

At his office opposite the NATO building in the Belgian capital, Ian Jones is aggrieved. He feels his organisation is often unfairly blamed for delays. Jones is head of operations for Eurocontrol's flow management division. 'We get blamed for everything. What we're trying to do is get all the aircraft that want to get away by eight o'clock, away at eight o'clock to wherever they're going. As an air traffic controller I can tell you the truth, supported by all the statistics we have, that 80 per cent or more of all flights, every day in Europe, take off with no air traffic delay at all. It's the other 20 per cent that causes the grief. But it's easy for the girl at the check-in desk to say, "Oh it's due to air traffic." First of all it's very difficult for the passenger to challenge that, and secondly we're remote, faceless, hidden behind large steel doors in protected centres and therefore we're easy victims.'

4.50 P.M.: BBC RADIO FIVE LIVE, *DRIVE* PROGRAMME

From a live outside broadcast at the information desk of Hahn airport, the nation hears about Michael O'Leary's plans to 'stuff it to Lufty' with Ryanair's new hub. The German national carrier does not immediately rise to the bait. 'Lufthansa watches its competitors closely,' says Peter Middleton of the German carrier. 'The airline welcomes competition and is in a strong position to meet any challenges.'

5 P.M.: CITY HALL, THE HAGUE

Chief inspector Mike Alderson, the top policeman at Gatwick airport, is talking at the Air Rage seminar. 'Nobody has to be a disruptive passenger, it's not compulsory, it's not written on the ticket. You have a bad journey round a motorway, a bad check-in, your partner's giving you earache – airlines can recognise that those stresses exist during the journey, they can look at check-in, they can look at the way that people go through central search, they can look at the departure gate.' But Alderson is reluctant to subscribe to the theory that air rage is getting worse. 'I'm perhaps a jaundiced policeman, I've been in the police service for over 24 years now. My experience is that people have always been angry.'

Air rage is not a huge problem in the low-cost sector, partly because the flights are so short – and because no-frills airlines don't hand out unlimited free drinks. Ryanair flies thousands of football supporters between Dublin and Liverpool, Manchester and Leeds, and can 'count on the fingers of one hand the number of times things have got out of hand'. The trick, says the airline, is to fly 'a brand new 737 that goes on time'. And when it doesn't, it helps if a passing executive can demonstrate what's happening. While at Ryanair, Tim Jeans found himself at Bristol when the flight to Dublin was cancelled. 'Passengers were crowding around complaining, so I went into the back office and printed out the weather report that showed fog and drizzle had made visibility below the limits for the 737 that was flying.'

Everyone agrees that alcohol is the single biggest contributor to air rage. Since no-frills airlines do not give away free drink, some passengers decide to take their own on board. 'People can be animals, real monsters,' says Luke Deals, a former steward on Go. 'The number of arguments you would have from people bringing their own alcohol on board was amazing. And when you tell them it's not legal, they say, "we've done it before".' Tim Jeans, now with Monarch, is concerned about the commercial impact from self-catering: 'They can bring their own food, but they can't bring their own alcoholic drink. You wouldn't bring your own drink into a pub and say, well, thanks very much for the environment. If we choose to tell people they can't bring their own drink on to our plane then that's our right. It's not infringing on anyone's civil liberties, it's just our bloody right. It's our plane and we'll tell people what they can eat and drink on it.'

5.10 P.M.: EASYJET FLIGHT 451 PULLS UP AT THE GATE IN ATHENS, TWENTY MINUTES EARLY

To many trained eyes, as well as untrained ones, all easyJet's jets look identical. The airline returned its leased Boeing 737-200s – the stubby ones with a couple of puny-looking engines – soon after it began operating. They were replaced by -300 series planes, with bigger, more efficient engines, and larger cabins holding 149 passengers. Then Boeing stopped making the -300s, substituting the -700; same looks, same length, same capacity, but better performance. In particular, the new version goes faster. The higher speed is barely noticeable on most short hops, but on the 1,500-mile flight to Athens, it shaves twenty minutes off the flying time.

Stelios is a little tired and hungry. Tired because he has been talking to every one of the hundred-plus passengers; hungry because, unlike his rivals on the route, easyJet does not serve an elaborate meal on the flight. Some people, me included, have bought on-board snacks or tucked into pre-prepared picnics, not least because eating alleviates the potential for tedium inherent on a three-hour, forty-minute flight. But Stelios is adamant that his policy is the best one, particularly since most of his flights last two hours or less.

'On a short flight it's irrelevant. A four o'clock departure out of Luton lands in Nice at seven – why the hell would you want to eat? Would you eat at five today, and at nine again? No.'

The passengers say goodbye with a mix of admiration for what a young man has achieved, and gratitude – for getting them to Greece for a fair price, and early to boot. Inside the terminal, Stelios is greeted like the celebrity he is in Greece, by a team of easyJet employees, who proceed to whisk him around the new airport. The airport at which the 737 touches down looks strangely unfamiliar to anyone who had the misfortune of using the old Athens airport, where switching terminals necessitated a £5 taxi ride. Fortunately, in the build up to the 2004 Olympics one of the world's least attractive airports has been replaced by a trillion-drachma, state-of-the-architecture construction on a rural site twenty miles east of Athens.

Eleftherios Venizelos airport is both harder to pronounce and reach than the old one, Hellenikon, which was within spitting distance of the Parthenon. The new airport has already been rechristened Spata, after the nearest town. It is spacious and well designed. For non-smokers, the best news of all is that secondary smoking is no longer a compulsory part of the airport experience. But a line of television satellite trucks is parked outside, and inside there is a clutter of cameras, lights and journalists. A big story is happening today. Not a crash, nor a hijack, but agonising teething problems.

Olympic Airways' computer system keeps spitting out boarding passes that quote a gate number for the old airport. This quickly leads to chaos. The baggage handling system has jammed; at least one foreign airline blames misuse by Olympic staff. The Greek Minister of Transport has stepped in to take personal charge of sorting out the problems.

Greece is scattered across dozens of islands, and there are huge Greek communities in places like Toronto, New York and Melbourne. So air travel is crucial to the country. With Athens at the hub of the network, the implications are very serious when things go wrong. While British Airways, easyJet and Virgin Atlantic flights all depart to London on time, Olympic passengers to Heathrow are delayed for five hours and finally arrive at around two o'clock next morning.

5.30 P.M.: STANSTED EXPRESS, STANSTED AIRPORT – TOTTENHAM HALE

'I've got one speech. I got a really expensive speechwriter to write it for me. I just change it. If it's a small group and it's safe I'll speak off the cuff.'

Barbara Cassani is bright, articulate and influential, and therefore in demand at business events across Britain and abroad. Tonight, the Association of MBAs has booked Go's chief executive for a meeting to be held at the British Medical Association (confusingly, BMA) at Tavistock House near Euston. Cassani judges this one will be worthwhile as an opportunity to speak directly to convince around 200 powerful business people to fly with Go. BT, with one of the biggest travel budgets in the UK, is sponsoring the event.

6 P.M.: SOMEWHERE IN SCHLESWIG-HOLSTEIN

The writer Darius Sanai is not having a good day looking for Lübeck airport. 'Try getting there, in a rental car, from Hamburg. The airport isn't even marked on Michelin or Kummerley & Frey maps. At the Lübeck autobahn exit, a taxi driver just shook his head and said we'd never find it. You have to negotiate the whole of the city, some horrendous traffic jams, a couple of back lanes and a country road to get there.' It took him an hour and forty minutes to cover the 40 km from Hamburg to 'Hamburg', as Lübeck airport is described by Ryanair. 'But running into the terminal we saw all our fellow passengers sitting around at the gate. There had been a delay. Great – could we get on? "No" said the man at check-in. We showed our locator number and e-mail confirmation, and pointed out the passengers reading magazines and drinking beer just a few metres away through the metal detector. "No," he said. The flight wasn't full, but we had missed the official check-in time and we weren't getting on.'

The reason for enforcing a strict 'minus 40 closure', according to Richard Garrett, who manages the 'out-stations' for Ryanair, is to encourage the others. 'If a passenger gets away with it in, say, Nîmes, they'll try to get away with it in Stansted.' The former army officer says, 'When you come to an airport, you have to play by the airport's rules. I want everyone to travel on time.'

7 P.M.: VIRGIN EXPRESS HQ, BRUSSELS

At eight in the evening, central European time, Neil Burrows is locking up his office and going home to a handsome town house in one of the finer quarters of the Belgian capital. 'I generally work about eleven hours a day during the week. But then of course I pick up quite a lot of phone calls when I go home. I set aside a portion of the weekend to work in my study. But I think if you have the opportunity to have an influence on a growing, thriving organisation, the line between work, creation, and satisfaction is very, very blurred. It's not work if you can see the results, and changes and improvements of it. When an artist paints, how much of it is work and how much of it is the joy of creation?'

7.30 P.M.: OUTSIDE THE BRITISH MEDICAL ASSOCIATION, TAVISTOCK HOUSE, LONDON

Not everything is going according to plan for the great and good business leaders. The two hundred guests at the MBA meeting at the BMA, plus the star guest, Barbara Cassani, plus assorted fire appliances and their crews, are standing around in Burton Street, London WC1 while a fire alarm is investigated. Eventually we are allowed back in. 'I bring congratulations from the firemen,' says the host. 'They say you are one of the most orderly groups of people they have ever had to evacuate.' I lean against one of the mahogany columns in the assembly room to watch the address, and to listen to the comments of the audience. 'She looks amazingly human,' whispers one woman. Cassani talks with passion about her airline, and why it is 'uniquely positioned to grow even faster' since the events of 11 September. She discusses the details of running the organisation: it costs £200 to kit out a member of Go's staff, compared with £2,000 for a uniform at British Airways. Then she questions the very qualification that unites the audience. 'I think your MBA's a waste of time. Common sense rules the day.'

8 P.M.: HAHN AIRPORT, GERMANY

Nadine, the youngest of the information desk officials at what is now Germany's fastest-growing airport, asks me what sort of pizza I would like.

Being a Ryanair passenger, and therefore unaccustomed to hot food, I am taken aback, but recover quickly enough to ask for a funghi. The pizzas are delivered from the nearest takeaway, eight miles away. Over dinner, Nadine's colleague Christine tells me she lives in the nearest village. Its population is fifty. Pity the passenger who expects to get off a flight at Frankfurt Hahn and find a city right outside.

8.05 P.M.: CHARLEROI AIRPORT, BELGIUM

An obscure but handy rule known as IATA Resolution 735d decrees: 'The receiving carrier agrees to transport the listed

If you're not enjoying your flight, remember it could be worse. This is the standard US government advice, issued to travellers by the State Department, on African aviation:

You may have difficulty securing and retaining reservations and experience long waits at airports for customs and immigration processing. If stranded, you may need proof of a confirmed reservation in order to obtain food and lodging vouchers from some airlines.

Flights are often overbooked, delayed, or cancelled and, when competing for space on a plane, you may be dealing with a surging crowd rather than a line. Traveling [sic] with a packaged tour may insulate you from some of these difficulties.

All problems cannot be avoided, but you can:

Learn the reputation of the airline and the airports you will use to forestall problems and avoid any unpleasant surprises.

Reconfirm your onward or return journey immediately upon arrival.

Ask for confirmation in writing, complete with file number or locator code, when you make or confirm a reservation.

Arrive at the airport earlier than required in order to put yourself at the front of the line – or the crowd, as the case may be.

Travel with funds sufficient for an extra week's subsistence in case you are stranded.

passengers (irrespective of class, service or routing) at no additional charge to the forwarding carrier.' The rule gets a mention on the standard Flight Interruption Manifest (FIM), the document you get if you are Involuntarily Re-Routed (IRR) when your flight goes awry. Many airlines, including Ryanair, have 'mutual aid' agreements to carry each other's passengers when things go wrong. The problem, for the hundred-odd passengers at Charleroi hoping to reach Pisa, is that no other airline uses 'Brussels South' airport.

Massimo Bonechi from Florence is due to be at work in about twelve hours' time. 'It's a low-fare condition,' he says philosophically. 'No hotel, no taxi, but they said they would keep the airport open if we want to sleep on the floor.' One group of passengers had their inbound flight cancelled on the way up, too. But Bonechi has made contact with a group of attractive young women and says he is planning 'a certain amount of mingling' during the night.

9 P.M.: BRITISH MEDICAL ASSOCIATION, LONDON

Barbara Cassani is now speaking off the cuff as she takes fifteen minutes of questions, and showing fresh reserves of energy and defiance: 'We may annoy you at times, but by God we give you good value.'

Her show ends to resounding applause. Cassani steps from the stage and is promptly enveloped by people. Just as doctors are weary from people seeking opinions or offering their views on the medical profession, so an airline executive needs the patience of several apostles to put up with a mix of tirades against aviation. Plenty of people want to tell Cassani about their no-frills experiences: 'I flew on easyJet and they were four hours late – I won't ever use them again,' is one comment. They also quiz her on everything from her future plans to the airline's policy on disabled travellers. From the fringe of the throng surrounding her, it is difficult to make out more than the odd line of her responses. 'I'm sorry we let you down.'

A brief opinion survey shows that Barbara Cassani has converted a good proportion of her blue-chip audience. At the end of another thirteen-hour day, she takes a taxi home to Barnes.

9.15 P.M.: WESTJET HQ, CALGARY, CANADA

The local time is 2.15 p.m., a quarter-hour after my appointment with Clive Beddoe, chief executive of Canada's fast-growing no-frills airline. He is still at lunch with an employee who has bid C$100 (£40) for the privilege of eating with the boss, in one of WestJet's regular charity auctions.

9.55 P.M.: EASYJET FLIGHT 23, LUTON–EDINBURGH

The last two flights of the day to Scotland are timed to leave Luton at the same instant, and arrive in Edinburgh and Glasgow seventy minutes later. Today, the departure to the capital wins the race to the runway. With seven flights a day each way between Luton and Edinburgh, a dedicated Scots executive can spend almost fifteen hours in London – or at least in Luton – and still be home the same day.

10.10 P.M.: RYANAIR FLIGHT 883: CARDIFF–DUBLIN

At the only significant Welsh airport, final preparations are being made for the flight to Dublin. Why should the only link between the capitals of Wales and Ireland take off so late in the evening? Tim Jeans, former marketing director for Ryanair, says 'Scheduling is a black art, manipulated by schedulers to make it seem even blacker than it need be. Why particular planes turn up at particular times at certain airports is a mystery even within the airline.'

11 P.M.: HAHN AIRPORT

'BORN-muth.'

The staff at the information desk at Hahn have been meticulously friendly and hospitable to the alien writer. I have heard how local people come along to the new terminal for a Sunday afternoon treat, to look at a shiny new international airport that has replaced the heavy military presence of a nation that defeated Germany in the Second World War. But as the incoming Ryanair flight is reported to be arriving some time after midnight, weariness has set in. And they are in the mood for some payback. 'How do you say this? Bern-a-MOOT?'

Christine used to work at the air force base, and now works on the information counter. She is having problems with Ryanair's latest destination, Bournemouth. She has mastered Stansted, Prestwick and Shannon, but is looking to me for advice on how to pronounce the name of the next British destination.

'BORN-muth,' I repeat, and then write the phonetic pronunciation on a square of paper that, I am pleased to say, is still Sellotaped to the computer screen from which they make the announcements about delayed flights.

Once the final flight departs, the information desk staff have to secure the airport. Any stray passengers are booked into a local hotel for the night. But the information team have to wait until the courtesy car arrives and takes away the passenger before they can go home. 'We never run out of hotel rooms,' says Christine. From the tales I have heard during the evening, that is just as well. I have been regaled with stories of romances broken because one partner was waiting at Frankfurt Main while the other one arrived at Hahn. Tonight, everyone is going home alone.

Post-script: Hahn is now a flourishing airport, but the link with Bournemouth has been dropped by Ryanair.

15. WHERE NEXT?

AEROLINEAS ARGENTINAS FLIGHT 1131: GATWICK–MADRID

Want a cheap flight to Madrid? Try Aerolineas Argentinas from Heathrow. Rome? You'll need Kenya Airways. Copenhagen? The Brazilian airline, Varig. But don't go direct, book through a bucket shop.' That was the advice I gave in 1996 to people seeking a cheap flight to continental Europe.

The traditional airlines kept fares high, because the only significant competition was aboard short-haul legs of intercontinental flights on obscure airlines. British Airways' profits were flying high, and all seemed well within the cosy world of aviation. Yet since then, our perceptions of travel in Europe have been comprehensively overturned. The murky twentieth century history of civil aviation – which, all too often, proved commercially disastrous while at the same time fleecing passengers for high fares – has been left behind.

For almost a century, powered aviation was viewed as a business that somehow evaded the normal rules of economics, just as many believed flight transcended the laws of physics. As that notion disappears, and venture capitalists start eyeing up the prospects from new no-frills opportunities, our outlook on travel is changing too.

The vast majority of travellers between the UK and Spain now travel on no-frills flights. 'Frank Butcher' eases himself into seat 20A aboard the 737 at Stansted airport, destination Malaga. Mike

Reid, the much-loved actor from *EastEnders*, is a convert to no-frills flying. 'I don't fly from anywhere except Stansted,' he says. Most of the remaining passengers to Malaga recognise him, but do not intrude. A few years ago, many of them would have had the notion that highly paid soap stars must fly in business class, and that to find an *EastEnders* actor on a cheapie implied something scandalous. No more.

In 1998, when Go first announced £100 flat fares on its first three routes – to Rome, Milan and Copenhagen – the London *Evening Standard* splashed the news across the front page. By 2005, cheap flights had become so much an accepted part of life that promotions on airlines such as SkyEurope, selling flights to Eastern Europe for below cost, were barely mentioned. Starting with British passengers – who now benefit from the lowest fares in Europe – we travellers have become blasé about cheap travel, and much more knowing about the airline industry. 'The travelling public has recognised that they have been paying an awful lot for frills,' says Neil Burrows of Virgin Express. Travellers, he believes, are starting to assess what exactly they are paying for: 'They look at the difference between the traditional airline's fare and that of a low-cost carrier, and think, "Well, they have to pay for the same fuel, the same technical and engineering quality because of the CAA, similar landing fees." You then start to think, "Gosh that was a jolly expensive newspaper. And that orange juice when I got on – that cost a few quid as well." '

Travellers also possess a new mental map of Europe. No-frills airlines will take you to all sorts of places that you never wanted to go to. Increasingly, Ryanair's route map resembles a bizarre game of Scrabble. Few travellers could point to Bydgoszcz on a map, let alone spell the name of this Polish city. Three years after Michael O'Leary declared he had no interest in flying to Eastern Europe, his airline has eight destinations in Poland, plus one in each of the Czech Republic, Lithuania, Slovakia and Latvia.

Low-cost travel has revolutionised travel – and changed people's lifestyles. The twenty-first century map of Europe has been redrawn dramatically. What happens next?

HOW MANY NO-FRILLS AIRLINES WILL THERE BE IN TEN YEARS' TIME?

In Europe, it depends who you ask: One, says Michael O'Leary, chief executive of Ryanair. 'The industry in Europe is moving in the direction of three large connecting airlines: the BA family, the Air France family and the Lufthansa family and there will be one large successful low-fares airline and that's Ryanair. In a couple of years' time we will be by any calculation the largest airline in Europe.'

'Two or three' – Stelios, founder of easyJet.

'Who knows?' responds Tim Jeans of Monarch. 'It's a very easy business to get into. So will there be new entrants? Yes. Will there be room for them? Yes. Will there be casualties? Inevitably, because that's what happens in a de-regulated market. It will be interesting to see which of the new entrants stay the course.'

The most aggressive new entrants are from the 'accession' countries of Eastern Europe, which joined the EU in May 2004. SkyEurope and Wizz Air are cashing in on the freedom to fly within the EU with the considerable benefit (from the airline's perspective) of low pay compared with rates prevailing in Western Europe. Wizz Air flies Airbus A320s from bases in Budapest, plus the Polish cities of Katowice, Warsaw and Gdansk. SkyEurope is based in Bratislava (also known as 'Vienna') but has a wide range of services, including Manchester to Salzburg.

With labour costing about half the European average, it is easy for Eastern European airlines to acquire a relative advantage. The downside, of course, is that people in the former Warsaw Pact have much less money than their counterparts in the west.

What everyone agrees is that, in the words of Henry C. Joyner, senior vice-president of planning, American Airlines, 'Europe has the potential for explosive growth.'

WHERE WILL THE NO-FRILLS AIRLINES FLY TO NEXT?

Further south and further east. 'Morocco, the Canaries, and Madeira? I don't think their customers would be prepared to put up with the service they provide for that length of journey,' says John Patterson, managing director of GB Airways, the airline that faces the strongest competition from no-frills carriers on Mediterranean routes. But the fact that holidaymakers put up with minimal legroom on narrow-bodied charter flights as far as the Gambia suggests there could be a demand to places like Istanbul or Cyprus; neither is much further than Athens, served by easyJet from Gatwick and Luton.

Late in 2005, the Scottish airline FlyGlobespan announced a link from Stansted to Tenerife, competing against a new Jet2 route to the island from Leeds-Bradford. Both of these new services land at Tenerife South; rumours abound that Ryanair is to start serving Tenerife North from both Stansted and Nottingham. Conventional wisdom says long distances are not suited to no-frills flying, and Go failed to succeed on long flights from Stansted to Reykjavik and Las Palmas on Gran Canaria. But Jet2 has invested in new, bigger aircraft – the 757 – to operate the four-hour flight from Leeds-Bradford to Tenerife. Michael O'Leary believes he could profitably operate a winter-only service from the UK, when demand is usually lower. And the longer passengers are on a plane, the more they tend to spend.

Morocco looks promising territory, if an airline can get permission to fly there (it is, of course, outside the EU). When you compare fares to Malaga, Faro and Almeria at the south of the Iberian peninsula with prices just a little further, to say Tangier, the cost of getting to Morocco looks disproportionate – typically two or three times higher. Tunisia, newly peaceful Algeria and newly rehabilitated Libya could also benefit.

The Balkans is the big gap on the map of Eastern Europe: Croatia, Serbia and Bulgaria are all ripe for no-frills links, though Albania and Romania do not look so financially enticing. Expect the rump of the former Soviet Union to start removing barriers to foreign airlines; Ukraine, Belarus and Russia are being left behind in the rush for no-frills flying. Scarily, there is a regular bus service from Strasbourg in France to St Petersburg – a two-day journey that could be replaced by a three-hour flight.

The main moves in the next few years, though, will be largely taken up with joining the dots on existing networks, and adding frequency on existing routes. There are good commercial reasons for doing this. The marketing costs at a particular airport are pretty much the same whether an airline has one flight a day to one place, or many flights to several destinations. Operational costs per passenger fall as the number of flights from a location rises, and the opportunities for minimising disruption increase. So expect easyJet to consolidate its position at Gatwick (its most profitable base) with flights to as many existing, but unserved, easyJet destinations as slots will allow. Bmibaby and Jet2 will jostle at Manchester with links to the destinations they serve from other airports. Ryanair will increasingly use its one-new-plane-a-week arriving from Boeing in Seattle to boost frequency on more profitable routes. The Irish airline will also convert a couple of its existing destinations into hubs – Brno in the Czech Republic and

Montpellier or Nîmes in France fill in useful gaps – and introduce another batch of places that you did not know you wanted to go to.

Finally, expect the number of charter options to be reduced. Peter Long of First Choice announced his in-house airline was giving up on seat-only sales: 'The flight-only business now is finished as far as we're concerned. The margins are being shot to pieces.'

WHAT ABOUT FURTHER AFIELD?

Fancy a one-way, two-hour flight from Johannesburg to Cape Town? That will cost you just £41 aboard Kulula (the Swahili word for 'easy'). 'There's no bullshit. There are no hidden costs. What you see is what you get,' says this South African airline. Or how about £26 from Chiang Mai to Kuala Lumpur? A journey that used to take backpackers like Tony Wheeler of Lonely Planet three arduous and uncomfortable days now shrinks to a couple of hours. You can even fly from Bangkok to Hanoi for £30. These Asian opportunities are courtesy of Air Asia, based in Malaysia but rapidly expanding through the Far East from Borneo to Bali and Manila to Macau. The airline's figurehead has frequently been called Asia's answer to Stelios or Branson: Tony Fernandes. He summons up the same deities as his counterparts in Europe – 'consumer needs, dedicated staff, hard work, getting the basics right, cost control and the passion to be the best'. Like the two men he is compared to, Fernandes has a flair for matching the public mood. After the second Bali bombing in October 2005, his airline gave away five thousand free tickets from Kuala Lumpur to the Indonesian island, because of 'our desire to help our friendly and peace loving Balinese to get back on her feet again'. Fernandes can call on the expertise of Conor McCarthy, who was group operations director at Ryanair during the fast-moving years from 1996 to 2000. Irish skills are in demand in Asia, by far the most populous part of the planet. Across India and China, rising disposable income combined with loosening restrictions on flying mean that people are beginning to reconsider their travelling habits. The two-day train journey from Delhi to Mumbai or Beijing to Shanghai is at present an economic necessity for most Indians or Chinese. But high-density aircraft – such as the large number of 'classic' 747s that are being phased out by airlines as new aircraft like the A380 arrive – could bring fares so low that flying becomes the norm.

South America has long had one of the most restrictive aviation environments in the world, with a dozen countries seeking to protect their home-team carriers. But Gol, which pioneered no-frills aviation in Brazil, is spreading into Argentina and Bolivia. At present, fares are not down to European levels – a trip from Buenos Aires via Sao Paulo and Rio to Brasilia will cost £275 – but the evidence from elsewhere in the world is that these will fall. And, on the subject of Argentina: the national carrier is, unbelievably, still selling cheap London–Madrid tickets despite all the competition. If you want a cheap weekend trip, the airline will charge you just £80 return from Gatwick to the Spanish capital. You can book by phone for no penalty, and the airline posts (recorded delivery, at its expense) a real ticket. Just like the olden days, but with lower fares.

WHY NO TRANSATLANTIC NO-FRILLS FLIGHTS?

Because there's (almost) no point. The no-frills airlines get the prime cut of their cost advantages from the high utilisation of aircraft and staff. On a typical transatlantic route from London to most places in the US, the aircraft can operate only one rotation (there-and-back trip) in 24 hours. There is little more that can be squeezed out by a low-cost operator, whose edge is eroded with increasing distance. 'The controllable costs where you can make a difference are swamped by uncontrollable costs like fuel and air traffic control charges,' says easyJet's founder, Stelios.

Next, passengers on long flights are prepared to pay a premium for frills, which is why British Airways' superior service to Australia can command higher fares than, say, Malaysia Airlines. 'Athens is towards the end of the usefulness of our no-frills cabin service,' says Ray Webster, chief executive of easyJet. 'Much beyond that and meals would become an issue, maybe some form of entertainment and perhaps bigger seats and more space.' Transatlantic fares even on BA are extremely low: the airline began 2006 with a London–New York fare of under £250. Strip away the tax, and BA is left with barely £120 – about what Sir Freddie Laker charged for his Skytrain service when it began three decades ago.

But in specific circumstances, there is the possibility of no-frills flying returning to the North Atlantic. In high season, when the benchmark UK–US fare can rise to £500 return or more, there is some scope for a low-cost operation using a cheap, old aircraft like a DC-10 or a 'classic' Boeing 747 with high-density seating.

Problem one: what do you do with the plane and its crew for the rest of the year, outside the June–September and Christmas–New Year peak? Problem two: what do you call it? In what it calls 'a defensive move', easyJet has taken ownership of the name easyAtlantic. Problem three: lots of very skilled aviation buffs have looked at the idea, and concluded it simply will not work. MAXjet, which started business-class only flights from Stansted to New York in 2005, started off as an all-economy product, but the projections simply did not add up.

It is not inconceivable that a new operator could use the new long-range Boeing 737s across the Atlantic. These jets can be '180 ETOPS-certified' to fly long distances over water, with the nearest diversion airport three hours away. While passengers would not want to be scrunched up in a 737 all the way from London to New York, some UK–Canada services look feasible. The distance from Glasgow to St John's, Newfoundland, is two thousand miles. This translates to five hours' flying time outbound and four inbound (because of the effect of the jet stream, which blows from west to east), which could be achieved within a flight crew's duty hours. There is no existing competition on what would be the epitome of a 'long, thin' route, and there would be a fair amount of 'ethnic' traffic in both directions, given the strong ties between the north of Britain and the Maritime Provinces of Canada. But don't put your pension on it. 'I'm not qualified to kind of speculate as to whether it's going to work or not,' says Michael O'Leary. 'All I know is it won't be Ryanair doing it.'

WILL I BE ABLE TO GET AROUND FRANCE, GERMANY AND ITALY MORE CHEAPLY?

Yes. The official line from Brussels is that any European airline can fly anywhere it wishes. Debonair put a toe in the water in Germany in 1996, with domestic flights from Moenchengladbach to Munich. Buzz tried the French market for the first time in summer 2002 but found itself up against Europe's best network of high-speed trains; the flights quickly vanished from the schedules. An attempt to inject some competition into Italy, called National Jet Italia, was closed down in 2001 by its owner, British Airways. In 2005, Ryanair overcame all the hurdles placed by Alitalia to start domestic flights from its Rome Ciampino hub to Alghero in Sardinia, Treviso (near Venice) and Brescia (near Verona), and soon took a large share of the market.

In France, the omens do not look especially promising. Despite the EU's protestations, obstructions remain. Indeed, on the day in April 1997 when the new aviation liberalisation rules came into effect, staff at Air France went on strike in protest at what they regarded as a threat to their livelihoods. Some within no-frills airlines believe that all kinds of forces are at work to make sure the free-market runway is anything but level. When Air Lib, the loss-making French no-frills airline, went bust in 2003, its slots at Paris Orly did not become readily available.

There are widespread complaints that the French government obstructs genuine competition, and allegations that even the air-traffic controllers are on Air France's side. I was aboard a Ryanair flight from Biarritz to Stansted that was ready to leave ten minutes early. Yet we ended up departing late, for reasons which, hinted the captain, could be chauvinism on the part of air-traffic controllers. 'All the Air France aircraft are moving around,' he told passengers, 'but we're not being allowed to go anywhere.'

Stelios believes the playing field may be levelled soon, with the likes of Olympic and Alitalia forced to play fair: 'I have a feeling that we might see drastic developments in the next few years. The European Union is running out of patience, and I think the governments have realised that there's not much goodwill left in these carriers.'

In Germany, competition is intensifying on domestic routes to the point where the national railway, Deutsche Bahn, has 'capped' its one-way fares at €110 (£80) to avoid losing too much business on very long domestic journeys.

WILL RAIL HIT THE BUFFERS?

Definitely not, at least on high-speed links within Europe. When the TGV-Est opens up from Paris via Strasbourg into Germany in 2008, a much needed high-speed link will accelerate all kinds of journeys. As the skies become ever more crowded, reliable surface links increase their appeal. Even in Britain, the acceleration of the West Coast Main Line between London and Manchester led to a dramatic switch away from air to rail.

MORE FLYING WILL SURELY MEAN MORE DAMAGE TO THE ENVIRONMENT?

Correct, in terms of noise, air pollution and congestion. The EU has barely begun to look at the problems caused by the seemingly inexorable increase in no-frills flying in Europe. One solution was proposed by the Norwegian government: penalising airlines that do not fill all their seats. A flat-rate tax could apply on every seat, whether or not it was occupied. The idea is that that this would reduce the number of aircraft flying because airlines would be incentivised to fill every seat. 'I can see a logic in that,' says Stelios of easyJet. 'At the moment having taxation per passenger carried pays to be inefficient. At the risk of being controversial and joining with the enemy – but that is something I have never been afraid to do – if you were to bring a tax it should be a tax per aircraft rather than per passenger. Because the more efficient operators would put more bums on that aircraft.' Sir Richard Branson disagrees: 'I don't think airlines need any encouragement to increase their load factors.' And Kenneth Clarke, the man who invented Air Passenger Duty, says a per-seat tax would not be practical: 'The cost in tax per passenger would vary quite considerably, flight by flight, and somewhat unpredictably service by service.'

Most in the industry believe that tax on aviation fuel is likely soon to become a reality. But Michael O'Leary of Ryanair is, predictably, not one of them: 'I fail to understand why it is that the poor ordinary consumer of cheap air travel is expected to pay taxes to salve the conscience of the rich middle chattering classes whacking on about their environmental taxes. If they are really upset about the environment perhaps they should stop driving their cars, kill their pets, that kind of stuff.'

The European authorities could conceivably cap the number of flights between cities with fast rail links. With Brussels barely two hours from London, served by trains that typically run half empty, does it make sense to have two dozen flights each way, each day, consuming fuel, slots and airspace? One more prospect that is under active consideration in the US is a 'gold card' arrangement that would give airlines that were prepared to pay extra the right automatically to go to the front of the air traffic control queue. The ability to get you to your destination on time is an additional frill that full-service airlines will be able to market.

WHAT ABOUT THE NEXT ECONOMIC DOWNTURN?

While no airline relishes a recession, the no-frills carriers believe that a downturn could actually strengthen their hand. Businesses will focus more rigorously on keeping travel expenditure under control, runs their argument, to the benefit of airlines that themselves keep costs, and fares, low. Dr Keith Mason of Cranfield University, author of *Europe's Low Cost Airlines*, says 'In the short-haul market, the additional benefits aimed at the business traveller are becoming less highly valued.' Stelios agrees: 'A recession would be a very good test, and I think we're going to do very well out of it.'

ANY OTHER THREATS?

Not all airlines relish competition, and many nations design rules to protect their existing carriers. In the quest for low-cost aviation, governments have generally proved, in the memorable phrase of the late satirist John Wells, 'about as useful as a one-legged man at an arse-kicking party'. Franco Mancassola, the founder of now-defunct Debonair, says, 'I never understood why politicians meddle in the airline business. They don't meddle in the shoe business.'

It is over thirty years since Freddie Laker wanted to meet the demand for low-cost flying between London and New York, and spent years in legal battles for that right. The same kind of official obstructions remain in force in many parts of the world. Once out of Europe, the attitude to cheap flying changes dramatically.

For British travellers, the big issue is slots. The most desirable one- and two-runway airports in the world are respectively, Gatwick and Heathrow. There are also some arcane ownership and control laws, some of them almost a century old. They were designed to make aeroplanes available to the government in case of an armed conflict. But many aircraft are leased from companies that prohibit their use in war zones. 'It limits the ability of our industry to prosper and expand because it cannot take advantage of capital that may be available in countries of which the airline is not a citizen,' says Franco Mancassola.

One more threat: the no-frills airlines themselves. 'The bigger you are, the more sclerotic you become,' says Sir Bob Geldof, latterly of the Boomtown Rats and currently on the board of the travel website, deckchair.com. 'I try not to feel proud about anything,' says Clive Beddoe of WestJet, 'because I think pride comes before a fall.'

Safety is the main concern of every no-frills airline. If any one of them were to suffer a crash, the effects would reverberate across the industry in the way that the ValuJet disaster in the Everglades awoke anxieties about low-cost carriers. The level of aviation security worldwide is also significant in people's propensity to travel by air. The 'hassle factor', and the extra cost of heightened security, have persuaded some travellers to switch to rail or road.

One other threat – or possibly an opportunity, depending on which side you're on – is internal to the airlines. If you work for a no-frills airline, you are no doubt keen to benefit personally from the growth of the industry. In other words, you would like higher wages. The question being asked prior to 11 September 2001 was: who would throw the first industrial-relations spanner into the well-oiled machine that delivers no-frills flights? Those crews, Boeings and support teams have been calibrated to work at full throttle. But strikes, or even the threat of a strike, can wound an airline deeply: people simply stop booking and switch to other carriers or means of transport, rather than take the risk of having their travel disrupted.

Every no-frills flight requires a minor miracle of co-ordination to be fulfilled. There must be space at the departure airport: in the terminal for the passenger, and somewhere to park an aircraft that is ambitiously scheduled to shuttle to and from Luton or Stansted half a dozen times a day. The airline has to organise the ground staff and crew the jet, and air traffic control must find a path through the complex and crowded skies over Europe. And, upon arrival, baggage handlers must be on hand to unload the luggage, with airport ground staff on hand to check in passengers for the return flight. When any element of this three-dimensional jigsaw goes awry, even something as trivial as a passenger dawdling in duty-free and causing the plane to miss its slot, the whole system can quickly seize up.

Before 11 September, everyone was watching anxiously to see the consequences of a worldwide shortage of pilots. Their industrial muscle had already pushed annual earnings for captains on some airlines to £200,000. In addition, every other small cog in the big machine, from check-in staff to aircraft refuellers, is conscious of their critical role and their potential for disrupting a complex, fragmented business. One small example: a holiday flight to Athens has to traverse the airspace of a dozen different countries. The repercussions of just one nation's air traffic controllers walking out will be visible on the radar screens across Europe. As with increased security, anything that makes air travel less comfortable leads people to consider other modes of transport, or simply not to travel.

HOW WILL NO-FRILLS AIRLINES SELL THE SEATS?

The Internet, almost exclusively. If ever two concepts were made for each other, they were the World Wide Web and no-frills flying. The airlines are seeking to offload sizeable quantities of a generic yet perishable product to a large number of individual purchasers. The offer, and order-taking, are straightforward and extremely cheap operations. Unlike the books and records sold by, for example, Amazon.com, the great trick is that there is nothing to deliver. People take delivery when they turn up at (they hope) the right airport on the right day at the right time. (Somehow, I have turned up at Luton for an easyJet flight that actually left from Gatwick; and arrived at Heathrow eleven months early for my Bmibaby flight.) If passengers go missing, usually that is the end of the story; there is nothing to replace. The consumer is rewarded for using the Internet with a discount compared with reservations by phone or through an agent. Better still, the traveller can arrange all the other elements of their journey, from hotels to car rental, online.

Not everyone agrees. Sir Bob Geldof, rock star turned high-powered businessman, believes the social experience of shopping will never be lost: 'It's too much fun. I buy records down at the record shop, because the guy wants to talk about what's new, because he knows what I like. "Check this out" – and he'll play it and there'll be someone else that'll say, "Yeah that's OK, but their first one's better." Shopping online is consumer wanking. You're just there by yourself and you think, yeah I like that, then you come when you finally make your purchase.'

Many satisfied customers would not agree with Geldof's graphic analogy, though the sites should start to give more solitary pleasure when they become smarter. Both easyJet and British Airways have excellent sites, which allow you instantly to see where the lowest fares can be found, and the rest are catching up fast.

HOW MUCH WILL FLIGHTS COST?

'We passionately believe that even today, Ryanair's air fares are too high,' says the airline's boss, Michael O'Leary. 'They'll have to go much, much lower in the next ten or twenty years.' On average, much the same as they do at the moment: around £60 for the typical flight, perhaps a few pounds less on Ryanair. Within that average, though, there will be wide variations, from

FREE FLIGHTS AT LAST
You can fly completely free of charge, but there are two
catches: the flights are strictly one-way, from Stansted
airport to Knock, in the west of Ireland. And you have to be
dead. Coffins, and their occupants, making the final home-
coming to County Mayo are the only freight that Ryanair
carries. The short turn-rounds on which the airline relies to
make maximum use of planes and crews do not allow for
the regular carriage of cargo. But the chief executive Michael
O'Leary makes a single exception out of respect for Mayo
families.

the lowest possible fare of around £10 (assuming taxes and other
marginal charges are levied) to a maximum of £200 or more for
desirable flights.

WHAT SORT OF PLANES WILL THEY USE?

Until 2002, almost everything had gone Boeing's way. The Seattle
factory had supplied every no-frills airline except JetBlue, and
conventional wisdom was that the 737 was the natural choice. But
easyJet switched to Airbus A319s, showing that Boeing does not
have a divine right to build planes for Britain's biggest no-frills
airline. 'Sticking to old-fashioned fads like "low-cost airlines only
fly Boeing" does not reduce costs,' says Ray Webster of easyJet.

ANY CHANCE OF A FEW, WELL, FRILLS ON NO-FRILLS AIRLINES?

Ryanair is promising to carry a million passengers a year for
nothing within a few years, and hoping to earn cash from new
interactive screens on each seat back. The idea is that people will
pay to watch programmes such as sports events, and indulge in
inflight gambling and that the earnings from those will more than
offset the marginal cost of carrying discretionary passengers.
People with flexibility – retired or unemployed people, and the
growing number of freelance workers – will increasingly be
tempted on board to soak up the excess supply, and their inflight
spending will help to build those profits.

In America, the no-frills airlines have always had some frills,
with JetBlue offering 24-channel television (free) and all-leather
seats. 'JetBlue, for me, between Florida and New York, is the

calibre of choice,' says Stelios. 'They have brand new planes, their staff are motivated and polite and nice, and they have a little TV set where you can watch CNN or whatever.

WHAT DRIVES THE PEOPLE AT THE TOP?

'We have a mission. We believe we can transform air travel around Europe, but it's going to take us another ten or fifteen years to do it' – Michael O'Leary, chief executive, Ryanair.

'Consumers in airlines are like consumers in anything else. What they're looking for is great value. Do not expect to have a five-star lunch or dinner when you come on board, because you haven't paid for that' – Neil Burrows, managing director, Virgin Express.

'It's a lot better to actually be stopped in the street and for someone to say thank you for what you've done than for someone to stop you and say "you filthy rich capitalist you"' – Stelios Haji-Ioannou, founder of easyJet.

HOW WILL OUR TRAVEL HABITS CHANGE?

We will travel more. Much more. Business travellers can make typically twice as many trips on no-frills airlines than they used to be able to make on traditional carriers. Well-to-do Londoners will swap the country cottage in Wales for an apartment in the south of France or a finca in Majorca: the commuting time and travel costs are much the same, and the climate tends to be more agreeable. Families will become more adventurous, substituting the Mediterranean package with island-hopping around Greece or sightseeing in Italy, once they realise the costs are about the same. Priorities will change, too: we will focus less on the journey, as it becomes more routine rather than a once- or twice-a-year event, and more on the 90 per cent plus of a trip that is not spent in an aircraft. Luxury hotels in Amsterdam and Barcelona already report a boom in business from easyJet passengers, who conclude it is far more important to spend cash on a hotel – where you are likely to spend a fair amount of time – than on a flight lasting around an hour.

Today, you can easily travel from London to Rome for around £100, the same as it was thirty years ago, when £100 was worth nearly £900 at today's prices. You won't get rubber chicken (though go ahead and bring some on board if you wish), because you won't pay for it. Thanks to the pioneers who realised that

CAN THE WITH-FRILLS EMPIRE STRIKE BACK?

'Our system-wide short-haul load factor was 60 per cent,' says Rod Eddington, former chief executive of British Airways. 'We were flying a lot of fresh air around. We're going to fill it.' He concedes that the no-frills airlines have stolen a march on the traditional carriers, but believes that the tide is turning: 'The person who always looks for the cheapest fare is going to fly easyJet, but a lot of people are going to think if it's only £30 more expensive, I'll go BA every time.'

Certainly British Airways relishes its slots at Heathrow, but it could certainly do without the baggage of the past, going back to pre-privatisation days – when, as effectively a branch of government, the airline had bottomless pockets and everyone knew it. A job in a state-owned airline has traditionally been regarded as among the cushiest of postings, with low expectations of productivity and high expectations of earnings and pension rights.

'The traditional carriers will completely reconstruct themselves,' says Ray Webster of easyJet. 'A lot of them will disappear. The days of countries having airlines will disappear. Airlines will exist in the same way banks exist, they'll exist because a market of opportunity exists and they're well-run businesses.'

Perhaps the sharpest edge that the no-frills airlines have on their traditional competition is the absence of a history, and in particular no tradition that airlines are run for the benefit of the staff rather than the passenger. Three leading no-frills figures tell different stories. 'My aunt worked for British European Airways thirty years ago,' says one, 'and she's still entitled to free tickets.' Another recalls that in the pioneering days of commercial aviation, crews who were obliged to stay overnight abroad were put up in luxury hotels, and given generous allowances. They still are. A third asserts that the complex system of extra payments for flight crews means that, on occasion, they have been known deliberately to slow down or take an unnecessarily meandering route in order to qualify for a lunch allowance. An on-time arrival at the stand at 11.55 a.m. might not earn them anything, but turning up six minutes later would trigger bonuses. Such practices could persist while there were regular government-sanctioned fare increases.

'We've got a very sick, unsustainable industry,' says Ray Webster of easyJet. 'The only way to fix the body is to undergo treatment, moving the whole industry into a pro-competitive environment where there's an incentive for efficiency, and to ensure that it's the fittest that survive. That will mean that some of the airlines that are less well placed, and less well run, don't survive. But I think everyone is going to be a lot better off as a result of that. In five or ten years' time, you'll either travel round Europe on high-speed trains or low-cost airlines.'

But Neil Taylor, one of the travel industry's leading figures, says he is 'much more optimistic about the future for the frills carriers, particularly given the role of Heathrow. Its location is far better than Gatwick, Stansted or Luton for anyone in west London or down the M4 and it still offers a much wider range of flights than anywhere else, and now at reasonable prices. Perhaps the best parallel is with eating out. I could walk from my flat to a choice of dinners from £3 in McDonalds to say £100 at the Ritz. I expect they are all doing reasonable business since there is a market for them all.'

aviation was for the masses, the traveller in the first decade of the twenty-first century enjoys a degree of freedom no previous generation has ever known. On the new map of Europe, Madrid and Munich are as easy and cheap to reach from south-east England as Manchester. The travelling public has voted with its credit cards (or debit cards, to avoid those pesky £3 supplements), and will not go back to the bad old days.

The closest analogy I can come up with for the no-frills revolution is the way that punk took the music world by storm – and surprise – in the mid-70s. When the prevailing artists grew old and their music bloated, when Led Zeppelin had released one too many albums and Phil Collins and Yes refused to keep quiet, rock had to be reinvented – it was unsustainable. In the same way, air travel could not carry on as it was, charging crippling fares to sustain viciously high costs.

Southwest, who (some say) started it all, just managed to complete the transformation of aviation within a century of its invention. In October 2001, the airline opened its latest base in Norfolk, Virginia. This is the closest airport to the windswept shore where the Wright brothers spent three hungry years pioneering powered flight. Within a century of the first take-off on 17 December 1903, the ordinary working man or woman of Kitty Hawk, Kill Devil Hills or Dismal Swamp has easy access to low-cost air travel, in the same way that most of Britain's population can benefit from cheap seats.

When people learn foreign languages, the first verb to be taught is to be.

Once the concept of existence has been mastered, the next verb is to go. The no-frills airlines allow more people, more often, to travel. Business people can do more deals, clubbers can do more dancing, travellers can enjoy more sex and shopping in exotic places, and everyone who travels can find more common ground with the people they meet. In a world that needs to be brought closer, that must be a force for good.

APPENDIX: NO-FRILLS FLYING: A USER'S GUIDE

WHERE CAN I GO?

From Britain, almost anywhere within three hours' flying time. This is as comprehensive a list as possible of the state of the market at the start of 2006; some routes will be dropped, and many more are sure to be added over the next few years.

In addition to the services shown here, traditional airlines such as British Airways and BMI offer a wide range of low fares. Note that this does not show all the UK domestic flights offered by FlyBE, Air Southwest and other low-cost carriers using smaller aircraft, nor the many quasi-scheduled services operated by charter companies. For example, I have not included the mainly charter operations of Thomsonfly – only the pure no-frills scheduled services.

Domestic services within the UK are given first, followed by European countries in alphabetical order. To book flights on these airlines, simply prefix the name with www. and end it with .com

Aberdeen

Fly from: Luton (easyJet).
Airport: four miles north-west; frequent buses.
Main attraction: the leafy Old Town, and the strange old fishing community of Footdee.
Also handy for: the Dee Valley, including Balmoral.

Belfast International

Fly from: Bristol, Edinburgh, Gatwick, Glasgow, Liverpool, Luton, Newcastle, Stansted (all easyJet), Birmingham, Cardiff, Manchester, Nottingham (all Bmibaby), Blackpool, Bournemouth, Leeds/Bradford (all Jet2).
Airport: twelve miles west of Belfast; buses every half-hour.
Main attraction: a handsome Victorian city that has reclaimed its former civility.
Also handy for: Counties Antrim, Armagh and Down.

Blackpool

Fly from: Belfast, Bournemouth (Jet2).
Airport: Squire's Gate, one of Britain's most historic airports, just two miles south of the Pleasure Beach.
Main attraction: Blackpool is the main attraction, bringing in more visitors than any other UK resort for fun, thrills, drinks and occasionally some sun.

Bournemouth

Fly from: Prestwick (Ryanair).
Airport: three miles north of the resort; take a taxi.
Main attraction: the superb beach, part of it non-smoking, and a surprisingly lively club scene.
Also handy for: the New Forest.

Bristol

Fly from: Belfast, Edinburgh, Glasgow, Inverness, Newcastle (all easyJet).
Airport: eight miles south; buses every half-hour.
Main attraction: historic maritime city; Clifton Suspension Bridge.
Also handy for: Bath, Weston-super-Mare.

Cardiff

Fly from: Belfast, Edinburgh, Glasgow (Bmibaby).
Airport: twelve miles west; regular buses.
Main attraction: a castle and other accoutrements that a capital city should have.
Also handy for: Swansea and the Gower Peninsula.

City of Derry

Fly from: Liverpool, Stansted (both Ryanair).
Airport: five miles north-west of the City of Derry; hourly buses.
Main attraction: the views from the city walls.
Also handy for: Counties Donegal, Londonderry, Tyrone and Fermanagh.

Durham

Also known as: Teeside airport.
Fly from: Newquay (Bmibaby).
Airport: some way from Durham, on the rail line between Darlington and Middlesbrough. One train a week in each direction.
Main attraction: Durham's cathedral, castle and cobbled streets.
Also handy for: Middlesbrough.

Edinburgh

Fly from: Belfast, Bristol, Gatwick, Luton and Stansted (all easyJet); Birmingham, Cardiff, Nottingham (all Bmibaby).
Airport: six miles west of Edinburgh; frequent buses to and from Waverley station.
Main attraction: the Royal Mile leading to the Castle; the elegant New Town; and the port of Leith.
Also handy for: Stirling, Perth, Dundee.

Glasgow

Fly from: Belfast, Bristol, Luton (all easyJet); Stansted (Air Berlin, easyJet and Flyglobespan); Nottingham (Bmibaby).
Airport: six miles west of Glasgow; frequent buses from city centre.
Main attraction: the Charles Rennie Mackintosh architecture and design.
Also handy for: Stirling, and the beautiful, fragmented region of Strathclyde.

Inverness

Fly from: Belfast, Bristol, Gatwick, Luton (all easyJet).
Airport: seven miles north-east; occasional buses.
Main attraction: the five-mile walk along the river to Loch Ness.
Also handy for: the wild north and north-west of Scotland.

Jersey

Fly from: Cardiff, Durham, Manchester, Nottingham (all Bmibaby), Coventry, Doncaster-Sheffield (Thomsonfly).
Airport: three miles from St Helier, the capital.
Main attraction: a tranquil British island with a superb coastline and a strong French influence.
Also handy for: Guernsey and Alderney.

Liverpool

Fly from: Belfast (easyJet).
Airport: Speke, five miles west of the city centre; frequent buses.
Main attraction: the Albert Dock, including the Beatles Museum, which will be central to the city's role as European Capital of Culture in 2008.
Also handy for: Manchester, the Lake District, North Wales.

Newcastle

Fly from: Belfast, Bristol, Stansted (easyJet).
Airport: ten miles north-east of the city; link by Metro train.
Main attraction: post-industrial city with some dynamic new tourist draws.
Also handy for: Sunderland, Hadrian's Wall, Durham.

Newquay

Fly from: Birmingham, Durham (Bmibaby), Stansted (Ryanair).
Airport: six miles east of the resort; take a taxi.
Main attraction: surfing on Cornwall's wild north coast.
Also handy for: anywhere west of Plymouth.

Nottingham

Also known as: East Midlands (or, by Icelandair, as Nothingham).
Fly from: Belfast. Edinburgh, Glasgow (Bmibaby).
Airport: equidistant from Leicester, Nottingham and Derby.
Main attraction: Industrial Revolution cities now rejuvenated and multi-cultural.
Also handy for: Loughborough, destination for Thomas Cook's first organised tour.

Prestwick

Also known as: Glasgow.
Fly from: Bournemouth, Stansted (Ryanair), Cardiff (Bmibaby).
Airport: two miles north of Ayr; half-hourly trains.
Main attraction: the Robert Burns connections across south-west Scotland.
Also handy for: Dumfries and Galloway, Glasgow (33 miles).

AUSTRIA

Vienna

Fly from: Stansted (NIKI).
Airport: 10 miles east; frequent trains and buses.
Main attraction: ravishing architecture, grand palaces and the echoes of the great composers.
Also handy for: Budapest and Bratislava, linked by direct buses.

Graz

Fly from: Stansted (Ryanair).
Airport: six miles south of city centre; bus 630 and 631 hourly.
Main attraction: the World Heritage Site at the centre of Austria's second city, and the Arnold Schwarzenneger Museum (the governor of California was born in the city).
Also handy for: Slovenia and Croatia, whose frontiers are thirty and sixty miles south respectively.

Klagenfurt

Fly from: Stansted (Ryanair).
Airport: three miles north-east of city centre; frequent buses, or you could walk at a pinch.
Main attraction: the Italianate city centre, and the surrounding castles.
Also handy for: Ljubljana; the Slovenian capital is fifty miles south, with easy train connections.

Linz

Fly from: Stansted (Ryanair).
Airport: three miles north; buses meet flights.
Main attraction: fine main square and shimmering modern art museum on the Danube.
Also handy for: the southern Czech Republic.

Salzburg

Fly from: Birmingham, Southampton (FlyBE), Bournemouth, Coventry (Thomsonfly), Manchester (SkyEurope), Nottingham (Bmibaby), Stansted (Ryanair).
Airport: three miles east of city centre; frequent trolleybuses.
Main attraction: the beautifully preserved home town of the Von Trapp family.
Also handy for: Hitler's tea house at Berchtesgaden, across the border in Germany; and the city of Linz, where the dictator grew up.

BELGIUM

Brussels

Fly from: Nottingham (Bmibaby), London City (Virgin Express).
Airport: National, seven miles north-east of the centre, frequent trains.
Main attraction: the Grand Place, one of the finest city squares in the world. And the food.
Also handy for: Antwerp (direct buses from the airport, taking 45 minutes), Bruges and Ghent (direct trains).

Charleroi

Also known as: Brussels (South).
Fly from: Liverpool (Ryanair).
Airport: four miles north of Charleroi (frequent buses); thirty miles south of Brussels (buses connect with flights, in theory).
Main attraction: the much-overlooked city of Namur, 25 miles east.
Also handy for: the Ardennes and the Waterloo battleground.

CZECH REPUBLIC

Prague

Fly from: Belfast (Jet2), Birmingham, Cardiff, Manchester (all Bmibaby), Bristol, Gatwick, Newcastle, Stansted (all easyJet), Doncaster-Sheffield (Thomsonfly), Nottingham (easyJet and Bmibaby).
Airport: seven miles north-east of city centre; frequent buses.
Main attraction: central Europe's most beautiful city.
Also handy for: the castles of Bohemia, Plzen (the lager capital of the world) and Dresden, across the border in Germany.

Brno

Fly from: Stansted (Ryanair).
Airport: five miles east; frequent cheap buses.
Main attraction: the home town of the composer Janacek – and a tranquil central European city with some impressive twentieth-century architecture.
Also handy for: Austerlitz – the site of the battle is a short way east of town.

DENMARK

Copenhagen

Fly from: Stansted (easyJet).
Airport: eight miles south; frequent trains, taking twelve minutes.
Main attraction: an intensely human city, with free rental bikes to help you explore.
Also handy for: Hamlet's home town of Elsinore, the extraordinary Louisiana modern art museum, and Malmo in Sweden – direct trains across the Oresund Link from the airport.

Aarhus

Fly from: Stansted (Ryanair).
Airport: six miles north-west, occasional buses.
Main attraction: Denmark's lively second city, with a big student population.
Also handy for: Legoland and lightly travelled north Jutland.

Esbjerg

Fly from: Stansted (Ryanair).
Airport: six miles north-east, regular buses.
Main attraction: the unspoilt island of Fan, just offshore from Esbjerg.
Also handy for: Legoland and Odense, home town of Hans Christian Andersen.

ESTONIA

Tallinn

Fly from: Stansted (easyJet).
Airport: two miles south-east, frequent public transport.

Main attraction: this handsome port city has survived the ravages of the centuries, and decades of communism, in good shape.
Also handy for: Helsinki, a fast boat ride away across the Baltic.

FINLAND

Tampere

Fly from: Stansted (Ryanair).
Airport: Pirkkala airport is seven miles south, with bus links to town to coincide with flights.
Main attraction: the Manchester of central Finland; well, if that claim doesn't appeal, try the fascinating Lenin Museum.
Also handy for: Turku, the big port city; buses connect with flights.

FRANCE

Paris

Fly from: Cardiff and Durham (both Bmibaby, to Charles de Gaulle), Belfast, Liverpool, Luton, Newcastle, (all easyJet, to Charles de Gaulle), Bournemouth, Coventry, Doncaster-Sheffield (Thomsonfly, to Orly), Leeds/Bradford (Jet2).
Airport: Charles de Gaulle, fifteen miles north-east of the city centre with frequent fast trains on the RER; Orly, twelve miles south with regular buses, or a complicated Orlyval/RER connection.
Main attraction: the world's most popular tourist destination.
Also handy for: Disneyland Paris (direct trains from Charles de Gaulle, fifteen minutes); Parc Asterix (direct buses from Charles de Gaulle, thirty minutes).

Beauvais

Also known as: Paris.
Fly from: Prestwick (Ryanair).
Airport: three miles east of town centre (take a taxi), fifty miles north of Paris; buses connect with flights.
Main attraction: extraordinary medieval cathedral of which only half remains.
Also handy for: Compiegne, Rouen, Chantilly and the equestrian heartland of France.

Bergerac

Fly from: Belfast, Bristol, Birmingham, Southampton (FlyBE), Liverpool, Nottingham, Stansted (Ryanair).
Airport: two miles west of town; no buses, but a pleasant walk.
Main attraction: la France profonde: a typically pretty and relaxing small town.
Also handy for: the Dordogne.

Biarritz

Also known as: Bordeaux.
Fly from: Stansted (Ryanair).
Airport: three miles south-east of Biarritz, six miles south-west of Bayonne (regular buses to both), but within walking distance of Biarritz railway station.
Main attraction: chic seafront, and Bayonne – capital of the French Basque lands.
Also handy for: western Pyrenees, San Sebastian (Spain).

Bordeaux

Fly from: Southampton (FlyBE).
Airport: six miles west; regular buses.
Main attraction: home to France's finest wines and merchants.
Also handy for: the Atlantic coast of south-west France.

Brest

Fly from: Bristol (FlyBE).
Airport: seven miles north-east; occasional buses.
Main attraction: because the city was comprehensively trashed in World War II, the reason to come here is for access to western Brittany.

Carcassonne

Also known as: Toulouse.
Fly from: Liverpool, Nottingham, Stansted (Ryanair).
Airport: three miles east; regular buses.
Main attraction: sublime walled city, with an extraordinary Cathar history.
Also handy for: the eastern Pyrenees, Andorra.

Chambery

Fly from: Birmingham, Exeter, Norwich, Southampton (FlyBE), Leeds/Bradford, Manchester (both Jet2).
Airport: six miles north-west; a dramatic approach or take off over the lake; buses meet planes, at least in theory.
Main attraction: the resort of Meribel.
Also handy for: the rest of the French Savoy region.

Dinard

Fly from: Luton, Nottingham, Stansted (Ryanair).
Airport: four miles south; occasional buses.
Main attraction: the gently fading grandeur of a leading resort.
Also handy for: St Malo, Rennes.

Grenoble

Fly from: Bristol, Stansted, Luton (easyJet), Stansted (Ryanair).
Airport: 25 miles west – almost halfway to Lyon – at the confusingly named village of St Etienne de St Geoirs. Take a taxi to the nearest sensible station, Rives, ten miles east.
Main attraction: the self-styled capital of the Alps; a spectacular location, with successful music and theatre festivals.
Also handy for: gateway to the Alpine Crescent in the Rhone-Alps region.

La Rochelle

Fly from: Bournemouth and Stansted (Ryanair).
Airport: two miles north; walk or take a bus.
Main attraction: blissful Atlantic port city, with easy access to the Ile de Re.
Also handy for: the oyster beds of the Charentes-Maritimes.

Limoges

Fly from: Liverpool, Nottingham, Stansted (Ryanair).
Airport: four miles north-west; take a taxi.
Main attraction: porcelain and enamel.
Also handy for: the unspoilt terrain of Limousin.

Lyon

Fly from: Bournemouth, Coventry, Doncaster-Sheffield (Thomsonfly), Stansted (easyJet).

Airport: Satolas, fifteen miles east; frequent buses.
Main attraction: gastronomic capital of France, and a superbly three-dimensional city.
Also handy for: French Alps.

Marseille

Fly from: Gatwick (easyJet).
Airport: inconveniently located 20 miles north-west; frequent buses.
Main attraction: one of the great Mediterranean cities, with a strong North African influence.
Also handy for: the Rhone delta.

Montpellier

Fly from: Stansted (Ryanair).
Airport: eight miles south-east of city centre; buses hourly or less.
Main attraction: a handsome, atmospheric city with a large student population.
Also handy for: the Camargue.

Mulhouse

See Basel, Switzerland (the two cities share the same airport).

Nantes

Fly from: Nottingham, Stansted (Ryanair).
Airport: four miles south-west; shuttle bus.
Main attraction: the Loire in full flow, a beautiful medieval core, and the starting point for Jules Verne.
Also handy for: southern Brittany.

Nice

Fly from: Belfast, Bristol, Gatwick, Liverpool, Luton, Newcastle, Stansted (all easyJet), Birmingham (Bmibaby), Leeds-Bradford, Manchester (Jet2).
Airport: six miles west; frequent buses.
Main attraction: walking the Promenade des Anglais, and stuffing your face with seafood.
Also handy for: Monaco, Italian Riviera, ferries to Corsica.

Nîmes

Fly from: Liverpool, Luton, Nottingham, Stansted (Ryanair).
Airport: seven miles south-west; regular buses.
Main attraction: marvellous Roman remnants.
Also handy for: Arles and Avignon.

Pau

Also known as: Tarbes.
Fly from: Stansted (Ryanair).
Airport: four miles north-west; take a taxi to Pau, though infrequent buses run to Tarbes and, in summer, Lourdes.
Main attraction: One of the loveliest stretches of the Pyrenees.
Also handy for: Andorra.

Perpignan

Also known as: Barcelona.
Fly from: Birmingham, Edinburgh, Southampton (FlyBE), Stansted (Ryanair).
Airport: four miles north-east; buses, but not on Sundays.
Main attraction: the sleepy city with a railway station that Salvador Dali nominated as the centre of the Universe.
Also handy for: the eastern Pyrenees, Spain's Costa Brava.

Poitiers

Fly from: Stansted (Ryanair).
Airport: two miles west, buses within walking distance.
Main attraction: Futuroscope, the European theme park of the moving image.
Also handy for: the mysterious land- and waterscapes of the Charente-Maritime.

St Etienne

Also known as: Lyon.
Fly from: Stansted (Ryanair).
Airport: ten miles north-west; regular buses.
Main attraction: a post-industrial city that has been imaginatively rejuvenated, with plenty of art.
Also handy for: the Massif Central.

Toulon

Fly from: Stansted (Ryanair).
Airport: twelve miles east; taxis and trains are the way to reach Toulon.
Main attraction: the hills overlooking the Mediterranean; a cable car will take you there.
Also handy for: some spectacular coastal scenery.

Toulouse

Fly from: Birmingham, Bristol (both FlyBE), Cardiff, Nottingham (both Bmibaby), Gatwick (easyJet).
Airport: four miles north-east; frequent buses.
Main attraction: civilised, well-proportioned city with intriguing odd corners.
Also handy for: the Airbus factory, where you can see planes being built (but not the sort that you arrived on); Lourdes.

Tours

Fly from: Stansted (Ryanair).
Airport: Tours Val de Loire.
Main attraction: a magnificent cathedral city astride France's most remarkable river.
Also handy for: exploring the chateaux of the Loire.

GERMANY

Berlin

Fly from: Belfast, Bristol, Gatwick, Liverpool, Luton, Newcastle (all easyJet to Schonefeld), Nottingham, Stansted (both Ryanair to Schonefeld), Stansted (Air Berlin to Tegel).
Airport: Schonefeld, twenty miles south-east (frequent trains); Tegel, eight miles north-west (frequent bus links to the city or the U-Bahn).
Main attraction: the dazzling new capital of united Germany.
Also handy for: Potsdam, the German response to Versailles.

Altenburg

Also known as: Leipzig.
Fly from: Stansted (Ryanair).

Airport: two miles east; the town's station is within easy walking distance.

Main attraction: sleepy old East German town, apparently untouched by the twentieth century.

Also handy for: Leipzig, an hour north by train.

Baden Baden

Also known as: Karlsruhe.

Fly from: Stansted (Ryanair).

Airport: four miles west of the main station (itself three miles west of the town centre); frequent buses.

Main attraction: the amazing baths that first attracted the Romans here; and the casino.

Also handy for: Strasbourg in France, where Ryanair used to fly until it was drummed out.

Bremen

Fly from: Luton (easyJet).

Airport: four miles south; frequent buses.

Main attraction: Boettcherstrasse, a miraculous Art Nouveau thoroughfare created by the man who invented decaffeinated coffee.

Also handy for: the lovely town of Oldenburg.

Cologne

Fly from: Gatwick, Liverpool, Nottingham (all easyJet), Luton, Manchester (both Hapag-Lloyd Express), Birmingham, Edinburgh, Stansted (all Germanwings).

Airport: ten miles south-west; frequent S-Bahn trains.

Main attraction: the cathedral, a Gothic wonder that survived Second World War bombing.

Also handy for: the former capital, Bonn, and the finest stretch of the Rhine Valley.

Dortmund

Fly from: Luton (easyJet), Stansted (Air Berlin).

Airport: six miles east; frequent buses.

Main attraction: beer. This otherwise dowdy city produces some of the best beer in Germany.

Also handy for: the weird post-industrial landscapes of the Ruhr.

Dusseldorf

Fly from: Stansted (Air Berlin).
Airport: four miles north; frequent trains.
Main attraction: the Old Town, beautifully restored after wartime damage, and dozens of excellent bars.
Also handy for: Neanderthal, the location where the eponymous man was tracked down.

Friedrichshafen

Fly from: Stansted (Ryanair).
Airport: three miles north-east of city centre; hourly trains.
Main attraction: the birthplace of the Zeppelin, with a museum on the airship.
Also handy for: Liechtenstein and the western end of Austria.

Hahn

Also known as: Frankfurt.
Fly from: Prestwick, Stansted (Ryanair).
Airport: eight miles east of Traben-Trarbach; buses to various towns and cities including Frankfurt and Heidelberg.
Main attraction: the beautifully intestinal Moselle Valley, with picturesque towns beneath expansive vineyards.
Also handy for: the Roman city of Trier, and Luxembourg.

Hamburg

Fly from: Bristol (easyJet), Gatwick (Germanwings).
Airport: five miles north; frequent buses.
Main attraction: dramatic architecture, old and new; a fascinating history as Germany's main port; and spectacular nightlife in the city where the Beatles grew up.
Also handy for: Stade, a Swedish town in northern Germany.

Hanover

Fly from: Stansted (Air Berlin).
Airport: seven miles north; frequent trains.
Main attraction: Herrenhausen, the former royal palace to which Britain's Royal Family can trace its roots.
Also handy for: Hamelyn, as in the Pied Piper; and the stunning Harz Mountains.

Leipzig

Fly from: Stansted (Air Berlin).
Airport: thirteen miles north-west; regular buses.
Main attraction: the locations where JS Bach, Mendelssohn and Schumann lived and composed, plus some amazing communist civic decoration.
Also handy for: Halle, whose main attraction is the Beatles Museum.

Lubeck

Also known as: Hamburg.
Fly from: Prestwick, Stansted (Ryanair).
Airport: five miles south of Lubeck (frequent buses), forty miles east of Hamburg (buses connecting with flights).
Main attraction: well-preserved Hanseatic city, hub of the world's marzipan trade.
Also handy for: Scheswig-Holstein, Germany's forgotten corner, plus the cities of Kiel, Schleswig and Rostock.

Munich

Fly from: Cardiff, Nottingham (both Bmibaby), Stansted (easyJet).
Airport: twenty miles north; frequent trains.
Main attraction: whether you want high culture or beer by the litre, the beautiful capital of Bavaria can provide.
Also handy for: the German and Austrian ski resorts.

Munster/Osnabruck

Fly from: Stansted (Air Berlin).
Airport: fifteen miles north of Munster, twenty miles south-west of Osnabruck (midway between the two); occasional buses.
Main attraction: Munster (a pretty and venerable university city).
Also handy for: Osnabruck (an ugly and modern army city).

Niederrhein

Also known as: Dusseldorf Weeze.
Fly from: Prestwick, Stansted (Ryanair).
Airport: It is basically RAF Laarbruch rejuvenated, rebranded as the low-cost airport for the lower Rhine valley of Germany. Buses connect Ryanair flights with Dusseldorf.

Main attraction: bucolic scenery away from the industrial heartland of Germany.
Also handy for: south-east Holland, and in particular Arnhem – an historic Dutch city that featured heavily in the closing stages of the Second World War.

Nuremberg

Fly from: Stansted (Air Berlin).
Airport: four miles north; frequent U-Bahn trains.
Main attraction: the chief city of Franconia (northern Bavaria), dripping in opulent architecture.
Also handy for: Bayreuth, a shrine to Richard Wagner.

Paderborn

Fly from: Bournemouth, Southampton, Stansted (all Air Berlin).
Airport: twelve miles south-west; frequent buses.
Main attraction: medieval architecture combined with cutting-edge technology in a compact and entertaining city.
Also handy for: the big, empty lands of Westphalia, close to the former Iron Curtain.

Stuttgart

Fly from Stansted (Germanwings).
Airport: eight miles south, frequent trains.
Main attraction: the Mercedes-Benz Museum, which you can visit only subject to the strictest security. Plus a grand city that is also a leading centre for German wine (better than you may think).
Also handy for: the eastern Black Forest, and the fine town of Rottweil (origin of the name of the dog).

GIBRALTAR

Fly from: Luton, Manchester (Monarch scheduled)
Airport: the strangest in Europe; a strip of Tarmac that extends into the sea just south of the border with Spain.
Main attraction: the Rock, together with its rather sad and bedraggled monkeys.
Also handy for: the south-west end of the Costa del Sol.

GREECE

Athens

Fly from: Gatwick, Luton (both easyJet).
Airport: twenty miles east; frequent buses and trains.
Main attraction: the miraculous Parthenon, and beneath it the old Turkish quarter of Plaka.
Also handy for: the islands, thanks to the direct bus connection to the port of Rafina.

HOLLAND

Amsterdam

Fly from: Belfast, Bristol, Edinburgh, Gatwick, Liverpool, Luton, Stansted (all easyJet), Bournemouth, Coventry (Thomsonfly), Birmingham, Nottingham (Bmibaby), Leeds/Bradford, Manchester (both Jet2).
Airport: eight miles south-west; frequent trains.
Main attraction: depending on your inclination, either superb seventeenth-century architecture, or legally available sex and drugs.
Also handy for: Leiden, Haarlem, the Hague.

Eindhoven

Fly from: Stansted (Ryanair).
Airport: four miles north-west of city centre; frequent services on bus 11 from the Central Station.
Main attraction: a tranquil Dutch city.
Also handy for: Maastricht, Dusseldorf.

Rotterdam

Fly from: Stansted (Transavia).
Airport: four miles north; frequent buses.
Main attraction: pubs, clubs and modern art – in the wonderful Kunsthal.
Also handy for: The Hague.

HUNGARY

Budapest

Fly from: Manchester (Jet2), Stansted (SkyEurope).
Airport: ten miles north-west; frequent buses.

Main attraction: the castle on the Buda side of the Danube, the grand nineteenth-century archicture on the Pest side.

Also handy for: the beautiful Danube Bend, north of the city.

REPUBLIC OF IRELAND

Dublin

Fly from: Aberdeen, Birmingham, Blackpool, Bournemouth, Bristol, Cardiff, Doncaster-Sheffield, Durham, Edinburgh, Gatwick, Leeds/Bradford, Liverpool, Luton, Manchester, Newcastle, Prestwick, Stansted (all Ryanair), Nottingham (Bmibaby).

Airport: seven miles north of the city centre; frequent buses.

Main attraction: the only capital in the world where the Irish pubs are genuine.

Also handy for: the Wicklow coast and mountains; and, at a pinch, the Mourne mountains of Northern Ireland.

Cork

Fly from: Birmingham, Cardiff, Durham, Manchester, Nottingham (all Bmibaby), Gatwick (easyJet and Ryanair), Liverpool, Stansted (both Ryanair), Newcastle (Jet2).

Airport: seven miles south of the city centre; frequent buses.

Main attraction: unreconstructed cityscapes and great music.

Also handy for: Kinsale, and all of Ireland's largest county.

Kerry

Fly from: Stansted (Ryanair).

Airport: three miles north-east of Killarney; take a taxi.

Main attraction: the mountains, lakes and seashore of Kerry.

Also handy for: the far south-west of Cork.

Knock

Fly from: Birmingham and Manchester (Bmibaby), Gatwick, Luton, Stansted (all Ryanair).

Airport: seven miles south of Charlestown; take a taxi.

Main attraction: the 'Knock special', a toasted sandwich about two inches thick, served at the airport cafe.

Also handy for: the Connemara coast, including Westport.

Shannon

Fly from: Gatwick, Bristol, Nottingham, Prestwick, Stansted (all Ryanair).
Airport: twelve miles south of Ennis and fifteen miles west of Limerick; rare buses.
Main attraction: a bizarrely huge 60s airport, which is still a hub for the Russian airline, Aeroflot.
Also handy for: the Clare coastline, including the Cliffs of Moher, plus the Aran Islands and the city of Galway.

ICELAND

Fly from: Stansted (Iceland Express).
Airport: Keflavik, forty miles south; buses meet flights and drop you at your hotel.
Main attraction: exploring the diminutive parliament in the world's northernmost capital; steaming outdoor public baths; a vibrant cultural life; and amazing scenes of binge drinking.
Also handy for: the amazing geology just about everywhere in Iceland.

ITALY

Rome

Fly from: Belfast, Bristol, Gatwick, Newcastle, Nottingham (all easyJet), Durham, Liverpool, Luton, Nottingham, Prestwick, Stansted (all Ryanair), Leeds/Bradford, Manchester (Jet2).
Airport: Ciampino, twelve miles south; frequent bus to Termini station, awkward bus/underground connection to other parts of the city.
Main attraction: more history than any other city in Europe.
Also handy for: the lakes north of Rome, the Mediterranean coast south of it, the superb scenery and hill towns east of it.

Alghero

Fly from: Stansted (Ryanair).
Airport: eight miles north-west; buses meet Alitalia flights but not Ryanair ones.
Main attraction: the north western corner of the least-discovered (by the British) large Mediterranean island.
Also handy for: the towns, coastline and countryside of this corner of Sardinia.

Ancona

Fly from: Stansted (Ryanair).
Airport: seven miles west, in the town of Falconara.
Main attraction: a lovely crescent-shaped harbour, though dese-
crated by twentieth-century war.
Also handy for: eastern Umbria; and boats across the Adriatic to
Croatia.

Bari

Fly from: Stansted (Ryanair).
Airport: six miles northwest; walk out to the main road for buses.
Main attraction: a part of Italy that is rarely reached by outsiders.
Also handy for: cross-Adriatic ferries.

Bergamo

Also known as: Milan Orio al Serio.
Fly from: Cardiff, Nottingham (both Bmibaby), Liverpool, Luton,
Prestwick, Stansted (all Ryanair), Leeds-Bradford (Jet2).
Airport: two miles east of city centre; buses hourly or less
frequently.
Main attraction: the Citta Alta, the medieval and Renaissance
quarter that dominates the city.
Also handy for: Lakes Como and Iseo.

Bologna

Fly from: Stansted (easyJet).
Airport: four miles north; frequent buses.
Main attraction: intensely atmospheric and artistic city.
Also handy for: Florence (frequent fast trains).

Brescia

Also known as: Verona.
Fly from: Stansted (Ryanair).
Airport: twelve miles east; occasional buses.
Main attraction: the delicate Piazza della Loggia, and the cathe-
dral with the third-highest dome in Italy.
Also handy for: Lake Garda.

Brindisi

Fly from: Stansted (Ryanair).
Airport: three miles north west.
Main attraction: a busy port town with some impressive beaches attached.
Also handy for: Greece; the fastest ferries leave from here.

Cagliari

Fly from: Luton (easyJet).
Airport: Elmas, which recently celebrated its seventieth birthday.
Main attraction: a Sardinian town brimming with life and style.
Also handy for: anywhere in southern Sardinia.

Forli

Also known as: Bologna.
Fly from: Stansted (Ryanair).
Airport: three miles south-east; take a taxi.
Main attraction: a palio (crazy municipal horse race) that is less touristy than that in Siena.
Also handy for: Ravenna (European home of the mosaic), and the resort of Rimini.

Genoa

Fly from: Stansted (Ryanair).
Airport: four miles east; regular buses.
Main attraction: the home of Columbus and pesto.
Also handy for: the Italian Riviera, and in particular the Cinque Terre – five towns squeezed between the mountains and the sea.

Milan

Fly from: Gatwick (to both Linate and Malpensa, all easyJet).
Airport: Linate, four miles east; frequent buses; Malpensa, 25 miles north-west, frequent trains.
Main attraction: a city dripping with style and sprinkled with fine art.
Also handy for: Lakes Como and Maggiore (note that Malpensa airport is a lot handier for these).

Naples

Fly from: Manchester (Monarch), Stansted (easyJet).
Airport: six miles north; frequent buses.
Main attraction: graciously decaying Mediterranean port where the pizzas are close to perfection.
Also handy for: Pompeii, Sorrento, Capri and the Amalfi coast.

Olbia

Fly from: Gatwick (easyJet).
Airport: Costa Smerelda.
Main attraction: Costa Smerelda, the beautiful north-east quadrant of the island.
Also handy for: anywhere in the north-east quadrant.

Palermo

Fly from: Stansted (Ryanair).
Airport: twenty miles west; occasional buses.
Main attraction: a superb Mediterranean city, with a life of its own that has very little to do with the rest of Italy.
Also handy for: anywhere in the west of the island.

Pescara

Fly from: Stansted (Ryanair).
Airport: three miles south-west; regular buses.
Main attraction: lovely ten-mile long sandy beach.
Also handy for: the beautiful Gran Sasso d'Italia range.

Pisa

Also known as: Florence.
Fly from: Bristol (easyJet), Bournemouth, Coventry (Thomsonfly), Leeds/Bradford, Manchester (Jet2), Nottingham (Bmibaby), Liverpool, Prestwick, Stansted (all Ryanair).
Airport: two miles south; frequent buses, regular trains, or walk.
Main attraction: the Leaning Tower, now open for business again.
Also handy for: Lucca, a much more attractive and less touristy city twelve miles north; and Florence, with direct trains from the airport.

Treviso

Also known as: Venice.
Fly from: Liverpool, Luton, Stansted (Ryanair).
Airport: three miles south; occasional buses.
Main attraction: lots of canals, but more like Amsterdam than Venice.
Also handy for: Venice (buses connect with flights), the eastern Italian Alps.

Trieste

Fly from: Stansted (Ryanair).
Airport: 25 miles west; buses connect with flights.
Main attraction: a chunk of Austria-Hungary wedged into a corner of Italy.
Also handy for: Slovenia and the northern Croatian coast.

Turin

Also known as: Milan.
Fly from: Luton (easyJet), Stansted (Ryanair).
Airport: eight miles north; frequent buses.
Main attraction: northern Italian architecture on the grandest of scales.
Also handy for: the Italian Alps.

Venice

Fly from: Bristol, Gatwick, Nottingham (all easyJet), Coventry (Thomsonfly), Leeds/Bradford, Manchester (Jet2).
Airport: six miles north; frequent (and expensive) boats; frequent (and cheap) buses.
Main attraction: the fabulous city, for which you must suspend disbelief.
Also handy for: Treviso.

LATVIA

Riga

Fly from: Stansted (Ryanair).
Airport: four miles from the city, but the road journey takes eight miles; regular buses.
Main attraction: a robust, Germanic Old Town.
Also handy for: Latvia's almost unknown coast.

LITHUANIA

Vilnius

Fly from: Stansted (Ryanair).
Airport: four miles south; frequent buses.
Main attraction: yet another candidate for the New Prague; popular with film-makers for its fine locations and low prices.
Also handy for: Minsk, the most miserable capital city in Europe.

Kaunus

Fly from: Stansted (Ryanair).
Airport: four miles away; buses meet flights.
Main attraction: the backwater feeling in the sixteenth-century town.
Also handy for: Vilnius.

NORWAY

Oslo

Fly from: Stansted (Norwegian.no).
Airport: twenty miles north and a dazzling piece of architecture; fast, frequent and expensive trains.
Main attraction: austere but beautiful city centre.
Also handy for: northern Norway, with direct trains from the airport.

Bergen

Fly from: Stansted (Norwegian.no).
Airport: ten miles south; frequent buses.
Main attraction: a fine city with a superb harbourside setting, backed by robust hills.
Also handy for: the southern terminus of the Hurtigruten, Norway's coastal ferry.

Haugesund

Fly from: Stansted (Ryanair).
Airport: eight miles south; buses meet flights.
Main attraction: the sublime coastline and islands of southern Norway.
Also handy for: Stavanger and Bergen, both a beautiful boat ride away.

Torp

Also known as: Oslo.
Fly from: Stansted (Ryanair).
Airport: close to Sandefjord.
Main attraction: the port of Larvik, ten miles south-west.
Also handy for: Oslo, fifty miles north; connecting buses.

Trondheim

Fly from: Stansted (Norwegian.no).
Airport: eighteen miles north-east; regular buses.
Main attraction: the Nidaros cathedral, the biggest in the northern lands.
Also handy for: the northern stretches of the Hurtigruten, Norway's coastal ferry.

POLAND

Warsaw

Fly from: Edinburgh, Gatwick (both Centralwings), Liverpool (Wizz Air), Luton (easyJet and Wizz Air), Manchester (Sky-Europe).
Airport: Okecie, six miles south; frequent buses.
Main attraction: painstakingly reconstructed city centre after wartime obliteration.
Also handy for: western Belarus.

Bydgoszcz

Fly from: Stansted (Ryanair).
Airport: three miles west; frequent buses.
Main attraction: not much besides the name and a reasonable football team.
Also handy for: Torun, the glorious Renaissance town of Torun, where Copernicus made his discoveries.

Gdansk

Fly from: Luton (Wizz Air), Stansted (Ryanair).
Airport: six miles west, named for the Solidarity hero, Lech Walesa; frequent buses.
Main attraction: fine architecture and intriguing history in the birthplace of Solidarity.

Also handy for: Gdynia and the beaches of the Baltic; the Russian enclave of Kaliningrad.

Katowice

Also known as: Krakow.
Fly from: Liverpool, Luton (Wizz Air).
Airport: eight miles north east; frequent buses.
Main attraction: when Katowice was the coal and steel hub of Poland's communist economic, er, miracle, it became one of the most polluted places on the planet. Now Katowice has been cleaned up with a neatly restored old town.
Also handy for: Krakow, Auschwitz, and skiing in the Beskidy mountains.

Krakow

Fly from: Gatwick (Centralwings), Luton (easyJet), Manchester (SkyEurope), Prestwick (Ryanair), Stansted (Ryanair and Sky-Europe).
Airport: six miles west; frequent buses.
Main attraction: the prime candidate as the New Prague. Fine historic core.
Also handy for: the Tatra mountains.

Lodz

Fly from: Nottingham, Stansted (Ryanair).
Airport: six miles out; frequent buses.
Main attraction: Poland's second city has suffered from industrial decline, but there is plenty of evidence of its former economic might in the mansions dotted around the old town.
Also handy for: Warsaw, if you are travelling from the Nottingham area.

Poznan

Fly from: Luton (Wizz Air), Stansted (Ryanair).
Airport: four miles west; frequent buses.
Main attraction: one end of Europe's last remaining mainline steam railway, to Woltzyn.
Also handy for: Woltzyn.

Rzeszow

Fly from: Stansted (Ryanair).
Airport: five miles outside; occasional buses.
Main attraction: this old spa town has a Renaissance square and the air of a Europe that you may have thought had disappeared at some time in the 50s.
Also handy for: the unspoilt valley of the San river, excellent skiing – and a cheap way into Ukraine.

Szczecin

Fly from: Stansted (Ryanair).
Airport: six miles east; frequent buses.
Main attraction: grand turn-of-the-twentieth-century architecture, an impressive Gothic cathedral and busy streetlife.
Also handy for: the nearby island of Wolin, a refuge for migrating birds.

Wroclaw

Fly from: Nottingham, Stansted (both Ryanair).
Airport: four miles west; frequent buses.
Main attraction: the former German city of Breslau survived the Second World War mostly unscathed and is now a cultural hub for south-west Poland.
Also handy for: the strange and little-visited province of Silesia.

PORTUGAL

Faro

Fly from: Belfast, Bristol, Newcastle, Stansted (all easyJet), Gatwick, Luton (both easyJet and Monarch Scheduled), Birmingham, Exeter, Norwich (FlyBE), Manchester (Monarch Scheduled), Nottingham (easyJet and Bmibaby), Cardiff (Bmibaby), Bournemouth, Coventry, Doncaster-Sheffield (Thomsonfly), Leeds/Bradford (Jet2).
Airport: three miles west; regular buses.
Main attraction: a compact, lively town with strong African influences.
Also handy for: the Algarve coast, Spain's Costa de la Luz.

Lisbon

Fly from: Gatwick (Monarch Scheduled).
Airport: four miles north-east; frequent buses.
Main attraction: gracefully crumbling old quarters collide with cutting-edge new developments.
Also handy for: the resorts of Estoril and Cascais.

Porto

Fly from: Stansted (Ryanair).
Airport: twelve miles north; regular buses.
Main attraction: concentrated and delicious – both the city centre, and the local drink.
Also handy for: the marvellous Duoro Valley.

SPAIN

Alicante

Fly from: Belfast, Bristol, Liverpool, Newcastle, Stansted (all easyJet), Exeter, Norwich, Southampton (FlyBE), Gatwick, Luton (easyJet and Monarch Scheduled), Nottingham (Bmibaby and easyJet), Bournemouth, Coventry, Doncaster-Sheffield (Thomsonfly), Birmingham (FlyBE, Bmibaby and Monarch Scheduled), Manchester (Jet2, Bmibaby and Monarch Scheduled), Cardiff, Durham (both Bmibaby), Leeds/Bradford (Jet2).
Airport: eight miles south-west; regular buses.
Main attraction: Alicante is worth an afternoon, but the city of Valencia – 100 miles north through the mountains – is much more enticing.
Also handy for: the Costa Blanca, including Benidorm.

Almeria

Fly from: Birmingham (FlyBE), Gatwick, Stansted (both easyJet), Manchester (Monarch Scheduled), Nottingham (Bmibaby), Stansted (Ryanair).
Airport: four miles east; take a taxi.
Main attraction: the eastern end of the Sierra Nevada, and the lunar landscapes to the north.
Also handy for: Granada.

Arrecife (Lanzarote)

Fly from: Luton (Monarch Scheduled).
Airport: three miles south of Lanzarote's capital; frequent buses.
Main attraction: a small but appealing historic core, and an excellent offshore fort.
Also handy for: the rest of this rugged, volcanic and often beautiful island.

Asturias

Fly from: Stansted (easyJet).
Airport: in the middle of nowhere, with occasional buses to Oviedo.
Main attraction: Oviedo, one of the lovelier provincial cities.
Also handy for: the empty beaches of Spain's green coast.

Barcelona

Fly from: Bristol, Gatwick, Liverpool, Luton, Newcastle, Stansted (all easyJet), Coventry (Thomsonfly), Leeds/Bradford (Jet2), Manchester (Monarch Scheduled), Nottingham (Bmibaby).
Airport: eight miles south-east; frequent buses, regular trains.
Main attraction: superb location, architecture and nightlife.
Also handy for: the Roman city of Tarragona, plus the Port Aventura theme park.

Bilbao

Fly from: Stansted (easyJet).
Airport: twelve miles north; occasional buses.
Main attraction: the Guggenheim museum, which looks like a collage of the offcuts from the Boeing factory.
Also handy for: San Sebastian, Santander and the Basque region of Spain.

Gerona

Also known as: Barcelona.
Fly from: Bournemouth, Liverpool, Luton, Nottingham, Prestwick, Stansted (all Ryanair).
Airport: six miles south-west; take a taxi.
Main attraction: a dramatically beautiful small city with a fascinating Jewish quarter.

Also handy for: Figueres (for the Dali Museum) and the Costa Brava.

Granada

Fly from: Gatwick (Monarch Scheduled), Liverpool, Stansted (Ryanair).
Airport: twelve miles west; regular buses.
Main attraction: the Alhambra, a magnificent collection of palaces in a superb mountain setting.
Also handy for: Alexei Sayle, who owns a small property south of Granada and is a regular traveller on Monarch.

Ibiza

Fly from: Coventry, Doncaster-Sheffield (both Thomsonfly), Gatwick, Liverpool, Newcastle, Stansted (all easyJet); Leeds/Bradford, Manchester (both Jet2), Nottingham (Bmibaby).
Airport: four miles south; occasional buses, or take a taxi.
Main attraction: the island's small capital is a shimmering white town.
Also handy for: the clubs and beaches dotted around the island; and the ferry to Formentera, unspoilt and beautiful.

Jerez

Fly from: Stansted (Ryanair).
Airport: five miles north-east; regular buses.
Main attraction: the sweet, heavy atmosphere that drapes itself over the home of sherry.
Also handy for: the port of Cadiz, the Costa de la Luz, and the city of Seville.

Las Palmas (Gran Canaria)

Fly from: Luton (Monarch Scheduled).
Airport: on the western side of the island; good bus services.
Main attraction: Maspalomas, a sun/sand/Sangria resort.
Also handy for: the much lovelier island of La Palma, accessible from Las Palmas by plane or ferry.

Madrid

Fly from: Bristol, Gatwick, Liverpool, Luton (all easyJet), Manchester (Monarch Scheduled), Nottingham (Bmibaby).

Airport: eight miles north-east; frequent buses and Metro trains, though the latter involves a couple of changes to reach the centre.
Main attraction: some of Europe's finest art galleries scattered around a city that celebrates life.
Also handy for: the gorgeous cities of Toledo, Avila and Salamanca.

Mahon (Menorca)

Fly from: Birmingham, Luton, Manchester (all Monarch Scheduled), Bristol, Gatwick (both easyJet).
Airport: two miles south-west; walk or take a taxi.
Main attraction: a much gentler island than Mallorca, with a fine town at either end – Mahon to the east, Ciutadella to the west.
Also handy for: island hopping to the other Balearics.

Malaga

Fly from: Belfast, Bristol, Liverpool, Nottingham, Stansted (all easyJet), Birmingham (FlyBE, Bmibaby and Monarch Scheduled), Manchester (Jet2, Bmibaby and Monarch Scheduled), Gatwick, Luton (easyJet and Monarch Scheduled), Cardiff, Durham (all Bmibaby), Exeter, Norwich, Southampton (all FlyBE), Nottingham (Bmibaby and easyJet), Bournemouth, Coventry, Doncaster-Sheffield (Thomsonfly), Leeds-Bradford (Jet2), Newquay (Monarch Scheduled).
Airport: six miles west; frequent trains and buses.
Main attraction: a splendidly preserved Old Town, with the impending added interest of a Picasso Museum to honour the city's most celebrated son.
Also handy for: the Costa del Sol and the inland mountains.

Murcia

Fly from: Belfast, Blackpool, Leeds/Bradford, Newcastle (all Jet2), Exeter, Guernsey, Norwich, Southampton (all FlyBE), Gatwick, Bristol (both easyJet), Birmingham (Bmibaby, FlyBE and Monarch Scheduled), Manchester (Bmibaby and Jet2), Nottingham (Bmibaby and Ryanair), Liverpool, Luton, Prestwick, Stansted (Ryanair).
Airport: twenty miles south; take a taxi.
Main attraction: a Renaissance city built on top of an Islamic city, which itself rested on the foundations of a Roman colony.
Also handy for: the relatively unspoilt Costa Calida.

Palma

Fly from: Belfast, Bristol, Gatwick, Liverpool, Luton, Newcastle (all easyJet), Birmingham (Monarch Scheduled and FlyBE), Luton, Manchester (both Monarch Scheduled), Exeter, Southampton (FlyBE), Stansted (Air Berlin and easyJet), Birmingham, Cardiff, Durham, Manchester, Nottingham (Bmibaby), Cardiff (Bmibaby), Bournemouth, Coventry, Doncaster-Sheffield (Thomsonfly), Blackpool, Leeds/Bradford (Jet2).
Airport: six miles east of Palma de Mallorca; regular buses.
Main attraction: Palma, one of the most under-rated Spanish cities – a more manageable version of Barcelona.
Also handy for: the beaches of Arenal (two miles from the airport), and the remainder of the world's favourite holiday island.

Reus

Also known as: Barcelona.
Fly from: Liverpool, Luton, Stansted (Ryanair).
Airport: three miles north; walk or take a taxi.
Main attraction: Tarragona, the ancient Roman city close by.
Also handy for: the foothills of the Spanish Pyrenees.

Santander

Fly from: Stansted (Ryanair).
Airport: four miles south; occasional buses.
Main attraction: Santillana del Mar, a lovely old town just along the coast, with a superb parador (state-owned historic hotel).
Also handy for: the Rioja region.

Santiago

Fly from: Stansted (Ryanair).
Airport: six miles out; occasional buses.
Main attraction: the magnificent cathedral said to house the bones of St James, which is why it is the end of the most renowned pilgrimage in Europe.
Also handy for: the beautiful region of Galicia.

Seville

Fly from: Stansted (Ryanair).
Airport: six miles north; frequent buses.

Main attraction: possibly Europe's most magical city centre, and the third-biggest cathedral in the world (after St Peter's in Rome and St Paul's in London).
Also handy for: Gibraltar.

Tenerife South

Fly from: Birmingham, Luton, Manchester (all Monarch Scheduled), Leeds/Bradford (Jet2).
Airport: Reina Sofia, six miles north of Playa Las Americas, with good bus links north and south.
Main attraction: Las Americas, Los Cristianos and the volcano of Teide.
Also handy for: the island of La Gomera.

Valencia

Fly from: Bristol, Gatwick, Stansted (all easyJet), Bournemouth, Coventry, Doncaster-Sheffield (Thomsonfly), Stansted (Ryanair), Manchester (Jet2).
Airport: Seven miles west; frequent buses and a train (though the latter involves something of a scramble from the station)
Main attraction: the cathedral, which may or may not contain the holy grail, and a marvellous Mediteranean beach.
Also handy for: the fascinating town of Sagunto, a short way north.

Valladolid

Fly from: Stansted (Ryanair).
Airport: five miles outside, occasional buses.
Main attraction: high-altitude and very pleasant Spanish town.
Also handy for: Madrid; this is as close as Ryanair gets (at present).

Zaragoza

Fly from: Stansted (Ryanair).
Airport: four miles outside.
Main attraction: yet another atmospheric old town.
Also handy for: the south-eastern Pyrenees.

SLOVAKIA
Bratislava

Also known as: Vienna.
Fly from: Luton (easyJet), Stansted (Ryanair and SkyEurope), Manchester (SkyEurope).
Airport: three miles north-east; frequent buses.
Main attraction: a well-preserved Old Town that has far fewer tourists than Prague.
Also handy for: north-west Hungary, just across the Danube.

Poprad

Also known as: Zakopane.
Fly from: Stansted (SkyEurope).
Airport: fifteen miles north.
Main attraction: cheap skiing in winter, good walking in summer.
Also handy for: southern Poland.

SLOVENIA
Ljubljana

Fly from: Stansted (easyJet).
Airport: twenty miles north-west; hourly buses.
Main attraction: a diminutive but very handsome city, dominated by a fine castle.
Also handy for: anywhere else in the pocket-sized state of Slovenia; and Croatia.

SWEDEN
Skavska

Also known as: Stockholm.
Fly from: Stansted (Ryanair).
Airport: seven miles west of Nykopping; buses connect with flights to reach Stockholm.
Main attraction: the nearby city of Norrkoping, a kind of Scandinavian Manchester with well-renovated industrial revolution architecture.
Also handy for: Stockholm (sixty miles north-east), and in particular Gamla Stan – the Old Town – and the other islands across which the Swedish capital is scattered.

Vasteras

Also known as: Stockholm.
Fly from: Stansted (Ryanair).
Airport: four miles south-east of Vasteras; buses connect with flights to reach Stockholm.
Main attraction: the Vallby Friluftsmuseum, an open-air collection of historical wooden houses.
Also handy for: Stockholm (sixty miles east), and central Sweden.

Gothenburg

Fly from: Prestwick, Stansted (Ryanair).
Airport: Save, eight miles east; regular buses.
Main attraction: Gothenburg's maritime museum, the world's largest, and a mighty harbour.
Also handy for: northern Denmark, a couple of hours across the Baltic.

Malmo

Also known as: Copenhagen.
Fly from: Stansted (Ryanair).
Airport: twenty miles south-east; regular buses.
Main attraction: the view of the Oresund Link to Denmark; and the historic university city of Lund, twenty miles north.
Also handy for: Copenhagen (bus connects with Ryanair flights).

SWITZERLAND

Basel

Fly from: Liverpool, Luton, Stansted (all easyJet).
Airport: four miles north, in French territory. Frequent buses along the land corridor to Basel; to France, you have to walk.
Main attraction: the capital city of the Rhine, and a place stuffed with artistic treasures.
Also handy for: Mulhouse in France.

Geneva

Fly from: Belfast, Bournemouth, Bristol, Doncaster-Sheffield, Edinburgh, Gatwick, Glasgow, Liverpool, Luton, Newcastke, Stansted (all easyJet); Birmingham, Exeter, Norwich, Southampton (all FlyBE), Nottingham (Bmibaby and easyJet), Cardiff (Bmibaby), Manchester (Jet2).

Airport: three miles north; frequent trains and buses.
Main attraction: the shimmering lake and a fine old town.
Also handy for: the French Alps.

Zurich

Fly from: Luton (Helvetic).
Airport: eight miles north; frequent trains.
Main attraction: the prettiest financial hub in Europe.
Also handy for: 'Europe's Niagara', the modest falls on the Rhine an hour north.

HOW DO I KNOW THAT I'VE GOT THE BEST DEAL?

It's impossible to be sure that the person in the next seat will not have paid less than you, but you can improve the odds in your favour by shopping around assiduously. Until 1995, whatever your intended journey, there was a pretty good chance that a decent travel agent would find the best-value flight for your destination. These days, you have to do the leg-work – or rather the mouse-work – yourself. Never assume that the traditional airlines will be more expensive, particularly at busy times when no-frills fares are at their highest.

WHAT IS THE OPTIMUM TIME TO BOOK – AND TO TRAVEL?

The mantra all the low-cost airlines chant is 'book early for the best deal'. In practice, though, fares tend to fall on poorly selling flights between eight and two weeks before departure.

The very cheap seats will be restricted to off-peak flights; forget Friday and Sunday evenings. Maximum availability is likely to be on Tuesdays and Wednesdays, outside the school holidays. On a route with more than one daily flight, there is likely to be a very early or very late departure that is 'sub-optimally scheduled', and therefore has to be sold at distressed rates.

WHAT ABOUT THOSE GIVEAWAY DEALS: £9.99, £5 AND EVEN FREE?

Look out for newspaper special offers promoting very low fares, but to get some even better bargains sign up online with the airlines. They will often send out deals that are available only to e-mail subscribers. And bear in mind that 'free' seats are subject to a wide range of non-refundable taxes, fees and other charges.

If you see a headline figure like £5 return, bear in mind that all the taxes and charges will add around £20 to that.

HOW MANY STRINGS ARE ATTACHED?

First, you'll almost always have to book on the Internet, because the only way they can offer prices like that is to cut out reservations staff. Some airlines will insist that you stay away for one or two nights, but you can sometimes get around that by buying two one-way tickets. And if for any reason you can't travel on the days in question, you can kiss your cash goodbye. But flights are so cheap that people are learning to book a whole series of these days out and just decide to go or not depending on the weather or how they're feeling on the day. The no-frills airlines love it, because they get to keep all the tax rather than passing it on to the appropriate governments.

CAN BUSINESS TRAVELLERS BENEFIT FROM THESE CHEAP FARES?

Yes, though people travelling on business often prefer Heathrow to Gatwick, Luton or Stansted. Flights can be changed, but in practice a much higher fare is likely to apply, as well as a change fee.

WHAT ABOUT CHILDREN?

Adulthood begins on the second birthday, say the no-frills airlines. The traveller has to occupy a seat whether aged two, forty or eighty (no senior citizen discounts, either). If you want to do anything difficult like send a child unaccompanied, choose a 'frilly' carrier.

HOW MUCH LUGGAGE CAN I BRING?

The usual 20 kg (44 lb) on most of them, but only 15 kg on Ryanair, which stresses that none of its agents is allowed to vary this condition. As a result, you could end up paying more for excess baggage than you did for the fare. At the other end of the spectrum is easyJet, which allows unlimited weight for hand luggage – so long as it fits the frame at check-in.

WHAT RIGHTS DO YOU HAVE WHEN YOU BUY A NO-FRILLS FLIGHT?

Not many, unless you bought it as part of a package holiday. 'A passenger is in a weak negotiating position compared to the airline when buying a ticket or subsequently making the flight,' says the European Commission about aviation in general. The traveller 'will frequently be unaware of the exact terms and have little alternative to accepting them even if dissatisfied. The customer's position is further weakened by the obligation to pay for the service before actually taking the flight.'

New rules that took effect in 2005 were supposed to ensure that airlines provide meals and accommodation for passengers on seriously delayed flights, and cash compensation for cancelled departures. In practice, this is rarely forthcoming.

When things go wrong, many traditional airlines will offer far more than the terms and conditions demand, such as a taxi home if your flight arrives after public transport has shut down for the night. But don't expect that from the no-frills airlines.

'Whilst we do empathise with some of our customers in difficulty, you will understand that the economics of short-haul low-cost flying can not sustain too many taxi fares of £60,' says Stelios, founder of easyJet. 'We are not responsible for ground transport and passengers should build that cost (with some contingency for delays) into their travel budgets.'

Stelios's approach to customer service 'has always been to under-promise and over-deliver. The idea that airlines are a bottomless pit and if you complain loud enough you get paid off is one of legacies of the flag carriers.' Stelios says he wants to change the public's perception. 'Whimsical demands for "compensation" not only increase the cost of flying for everybody, but also they never leave anybody completely satisfied. That's over-promising and under-delivering.'

ATOL, ABTA, IATA – ARE THEY ANY HELP?

Probably not. The Air Travel Organiser's Licence scheme was set up by the Civil Aviation Authority after one tour operator collapse too many. It covers package holidays that include air travel, so if you have booked a package you will be covered – but few tour operators use no-frills airlines when creating packages. The Association of British Travel Agents has a scheme for what's called 'non-licensable' activities, such as self-drive or coach holidays, and guarantees your money back if you buy through an ABTA member. The International Air Transport Association is the trade body that dreams up these rules and regulations, and naturally tries to endow the airlines with maximum flexibility to do whatever they wish.

AS AN INDEPENDENT TRAVELLER, I FIX UP EVERYTHING MYSELF. WHAT RIGHTS DO I HAVE?

Far fewer. If you pay with cash or a debit card direct to a scheduled airline, and it goes bust, you have no rights at all. Paying with a credit card gives you some protection if the booking is for over £100. Most travellers on no-frills flights arrange their own accommodation, which does not count as a package for the purposes of the rules.

MY TRAIN TO THE AIRPORT BROKE DOWN AND I MISSED THE FLIGHT – AM I ENTITLED TO A SEAT ON A LATER PLANE?

No. The train company will point to its terms and conditions and, if you're lucky, offer you the value of your rail ticket back. No-frills airlines say you should (a) allow plenty of time to reach the airport, and (b) be insured against failure in public transport. In practice they will usually try to get you on the next flight out, with a payment of £25–£50 per person.

WHAT HAPPENS IF I MISS A CONNECTION?

If you have made two separate bookings, on different airlines, as is likely to be the case if one or both is on a no-frills airline, then you are in trouble if the first flight goes awry. Suppose you fly on Ryanair from Prestwick to Stansted, and plan to arrive two hours before an easyJet departure to Bologna. If the first flight is so late that you miss the connection, there is no liability on the part of Ryanair to help you out. Nor is easyJet obliged to rebook you on its next flight. Your only recourse is claiming on travel insurance, and even then the insurer may demand evidence that you were not cutting things too fine by allowing insufficient time between flights.

BUT I'M TRANSFERRING AT LUTON FROM ONE EASYJET FLIGHT TO ANOTHER

Tough. Like all the airlines, easyJet emphasises it is a point-to-point carrier. This means each flight is self-contained; unlike with-frills airlines, you will not see your luggage seamlessly transferred, nor will you get both boarding passes. One of the things you are not paying for is the cost of being looked after. The one exception is Air Berlin's operation at Stansted, where passengers from Manchester and Glasgow who are continuing to Germany are treated as transit passengers.

AVIATION GLOSSARY – HELPING YOU DECIPHER THE JARGON OF AIRLINES

ABTA Association of British Travel Agents, a trade body that gives some protection to customers of member companies.

ad-hoc charter hiring an aircraft to cover a gap in a fleet, usually caused by mechanical problems or while waiting for an aircraft to be delivered. European Aviation and Titan are among the companies that regularly fly for no-frills airlines.

Apex Advance Purchase EXcursion, which used to be the standard cheap ticket on scheduled flights. You had to book a couple of weeks in advance, stay away at least one Saturday night and pay heavily to change reservations. These are still often cited by guide books as a good deal. They are not.

Choose as in 'You'll be able to choose your own seat on board very shortly,' announced by airlines that don't pre-assign seats, loosely translates as 'join the massive scrum at the gate if you want any chance of a window seat.'

damp lease you rent the plane and the pilots, and supply your own cabin crew.

dry lease you rent only the plane, and supply your own pilots and cabin crew.

ETOPS Extended Twin-engine OPerationS over water, which means flying a plane with two engines, such as the Boeing 737, a long way from suitable diversion airports. It means these planes can fly quicker and cheaper courses, and make journeys that would not otherwise be allowed.

fifth-freedom the right, under the 1944 Chicago Convention on international air travel, for an airline to fly between two points, neither of which is in its home country. All airlines from EU member states have fifth-freedom rights within the Union.

HAG Have A Go, a term used by check-in staff for a passenger who arrives after the check-in deadline but is permitted to try to get to the gate in time to catch the plane. This is a very rare on no-frills airlines because they do not want to jeopardise their schedules; they are steadily increasing check-in times, easyJet from 20 to 30 minutes and Ryanair from 30 to 40 (at Stansted). Across aviation in general, HAGs have become less common since 11 September 2001 because of increased security concerns.

hotac hotel accommodation for cabin crew or passengers.

IATA International Air Transport Association, the airlines' cartel. Its main purpose is to set standards and fix fares. Even though some no-frills airlines are members, the fare-fixing aspect is irrelevant.

no-show failing to turn up at the check-in desk before the designated flight closure time. On most no-frills fares, you lose the money paid for the flight. Theoretically you may be entitled to a refund for taxes and charges, but the process is sometimes made so difficult that people rarely bother.

oversold overbooked, i.e. selling more seats for a flight than the plane holds. Common practice in aviation, because of the large number of no-shows, with set penalties for the airline to pay an affected passenger. Most airlines will forestall this by offering incentives for people voluntarily to offload.

published fare a fare that appears in airlines' manuals. Tends to be used to distinguish 'official' fares from those sold more cheaply through discount agents.

reprotect transfer to another airline, usually in the event of a mechanical failure or a scheduling change, without charge.

runner see HAG.

self-loading cargo passengers.

standby a standby ticket used to be the only cheap way to fly around Britain and across the Atlantic. Passengers would hang around at the airport to see if there was room on board for them. Even once on board, it was possible to be tapped on the shoulder just before take off and asked to surrender your seat to a busy full-farepaying executive. Increasingly, the term 'standby' refers only to people – who will have paid a variety of fares – hoping to travel on a flight that is apparently full.

wet lease you rent the plane, the pilots and the cabin crew.

white tails aircraft that have been built without a specific customer.

INDEX

Bold entries refer to pages where the subject is treated in depth.